America in the '60s
Cultural Authorities in Transition

America in the '60s
Cultural Authorities in Transition

Edited with an introduction by
Ronald Lora

John Wiley & Sons, Inc.
New York • London • Sydney • Toronto

Library of Congress Cataloging in Publication Data:

Lora, Ronald, comp.
　America in the sixties.

　　1. United States—Social conditions—1960-
—Addresses, essays, lectures.　I.　Title.
HN65,L65　　　　309.1′73′092　　　　73-22224
ISBN 0-471-54610-0
ISBN 0-471-54611-9 (pbk.)

Printed in the United States of America

10 9 8 7 6 5 4 3 2 1

To my mother and father

Preface

This anthology represents significant aspects of American society during the 1960s—its ideas, its institutions, its politics and economics, and its dissent from powerful cultural orthodoxies. There is a need for such a volume because the 1960s are of special importance to all of us—students, teachers, and citizens—since the recurrent problems surrounding democracy, race, poverty, and war were highlighted during that explosive decade in ways that are vital to the meaning of America and of freedom in the contemporary world. Although all of the decades in twentieth-century America share essential continuities, the particular importance of each one consists of its subtly distinctive vision of historical possibility, of the American dream, and of the role of dissent in achieving the promise of the dream. While a fuller and, I believe, more democratic comprehension of civil rights, education, science, and theology was reached in the 1960s, political and economic institutions changed very slowly and never without a great deal of visible pain. The differential rates of change in these areas, between things dreamed to be possible and things actually accomplished, produced the social tensions that we associate with this decade.

I believe that there are salient issues that students should encounter at a deeper level than is possible in textbooks, and that these issues can provide a solid basis for effective teaching, substantive class discussions, and human enrichment. Therefore, I have chosen essays that contribute toward our self-understanding instead of essays that are congruent with my own views. In the introductory essay and in the headnotes to each selection, I raise unanswered questions, or augment the contributors' arguments and, occasionally, I even take issue with the arguments. Primary and secondary materials are mixed throughout, since both are necessary to illuminate the process of social transformation in the United States. Footnotes are generally omitted for reasons of space, but I hope that the stimulating qualities of the essays will encourage many readers to examine the original sources and the larger body of literature.

My debt to the contributors is obvious, and I extend my gratitude for the use of their material. I also thank Loren Baritz of Empire State College, Walter LaFeber of Cornell University, and Frank Annunziata of Eisenhower College for their wise counsel during the early stages of this project. I especially thank Lorin Lee Cary, Francine Cary, Michael Kay, Charles DeBenedetti, William H. Longton, and Robert Freeman Smith, my gracious and helpful colleagues at the University of Toledo, for criticism and suggestions. The staff members of the Wiley organization have been superb in offering editorial assistance, particularly Carl Beers, who took an early interest in this book, and Wayne Anderson and Elaine J. Miller, who helped to prepare the manuscript and guided it through the many stages of production.

Ronald Lora

Contents

VII. Voices in Protest

VIII. A New Theology

IX. Science and Human Nature

X. Students and Higher Education

XI. Reflections on America

America in the '60s
Cultural Authorities in Transition

Introduction

The 1960s:
Cultural Authorities
in Transition

Reflecting on the past decade, Richard Hofstadter, twice the recipient of a Pulitzer prize in history, remarked: "If I get around to writing a general history of the recent past, I'm going to call the chapter on the Sixties 'The Age of Rubbish.' " Richard Poirier dissented: "Living these years in America is one of the most enlivening experiences I can imagine having, precisely because the times are so vitally if portentously confusing. America is now and history." It may be argued that America is now undergoing the most fundamental kind of cultural transformation, and that an enlargement of democratic ideals and an increased sensitivity to the qualitative possibilities of life mark the significance of the 1960s. It also may be true, however, that historians will characterize the 1960s as one of the decades in which the flaws in the American dream became most visible. Because history is so filled with the endless permutations of life styles, and with ambiguities and competing forces, these views are not necessarily contradictory. At the very least, the difficult questions raised during the 1960s—about democracy, privilege, reform, war, and the minimal expectations of people under conditions of relative affluence—will make it one of the most controversial decades of American history.

The 1960s had two distinct phases. The first, characterized by a quickened and even brash feeling of energy, hope, and idealism, quickly set it apart from the 1950s. The optimism began with the inaugural address of John F. Kennedy who, in stilted, pseudo-Homeric rhetoric, announced that the torch had been passed to a new generation, and that national greatness depended on an activist commitment to ideals. The conviction that new frontiers awaited the courageous and dedicated released a moral energy that expressed itself in the Peace Corps, in Vista, and in the burgeoning civil-rights movement. In retrospect, however, the substantive basis for this optimism is not easily found. Kennedy suffered major legislative defeats on civil rights, tax reform, and Medicare. He was embarrassed by the Bay of Pigs disaster, and he set in motion the Vietnam military buildup that Lyndon Johnson later escalated into a full-scale war.

Two events marked the transition to the second phase. The first was the murder of President Kennedy that revived dormant suspicions of the absurdities and darker undercurrents of American society. The second event, the Watts ghetto riots in Los Angeles in August 1965, convinced the citizens of Middle America that passive civil disobedience had given way to revolution. They feared that the center would not hold as the second half of the decade brought a floodtide of change with major social explosions over race, violence, youth, drugs, differing life styles, and the war in Indochina.

The 1960s were crowded with dangers and accomplishments. It was the first decade of lunar exploration, a decade in which significant advances were made in civil rights, in social democracy, in biochemistry and in the biological sciences. President Kennedy took the nation to the brink of nuclear war during the Cuban missile crisis of 1962, a near-disaster that was resolved only when Soviet Premier Khrushchev agreed to remove missile sites recently installed in Cuba. It was a decade of tough talk as many Americans felt like expatriates in their own country. Benjamin DeMott spoke of an "Age of Overkill," of political, poetic, aphoristic, rhetorical overkill: The United States was "the Fourth Reich" (James Baldwin); "The white race is the cancer of history" (Susan Sontag); "The family is the American fascism" (Paul Goodman); "The universities cannot be reformed. They must be abandoned or closed down. They should be used as bases for actions against society, but never taken seriously. The professors have nothing to teach. . . . We can learn more from any jail than we can from any university." (The Berkeley *Barb*).[1] The style of the 1960s demanded new cultural heroes. In favor were Che Guevara, Malcolm X, Dustin Hoffman, the Beatles, the Kennedy brothers, Bob Dylan, Janis Joplin, Lenny Bruce, and Ralph Nader. Passé were

---

[1] Benjamin DeMott, *Supergrow: Essays and Reports on Imagination in America* (New York: E. P. Dutton & Co., Inc., 1969), p. 74.

Gary Cooper, Clark Gable, Dwight D. Eisenhower, Douglas MacArthur, and Jane Russell.

Making sense of the 1960s is not easy, and therefore an ample degree of caution has much to commend itself. For the active participants in the decade's conflicts and movements, the underlying theme was the pursuit of a fuller democracy through a self-conscious revolt against traditional cultural authorities. "Involvement," "participation," "equalitarianism" and "Power to the People" were hailed as the gateways to liberation. They were conjoined in the popular political slogan, "participatory democracy" that had, as its goals, self-determination, self-legitimation, and self-evaluation. The sophisticated articulation of this ideal rested on the old Roman adage—"Whatever touches us all should be decided by all." In its simplest form it meant the right to live private lives unmoved by legitimate institutional demands. Supporters of this position did not allow for logical distinctions between responsible authority and dogmatic authority, and frequently did not acknowledge that men do not live outside of authorities whether public or private. This apolitical refusal had its poignant side, however, in that it reflected an uneasy awareness that "the establishment" was powerfully entrenched in the institutions of big government, big business, big unions, and big education. Confronted with the immensity of "the organization," dissent often took on the appearance of a continuous revolt against authority instead of a reasoned analysis of authorities in transition, which "participatory democracy" clearly entailed.

The revolt against traditional cultural authorities took many forms. At the most abstract level it produced a new theology in which radical Protestant theologians insisted on the "Death of God," an event announced nearly a century earlier by Friedrich Nietzsche and one that became a general cultural awareness during the 1960s. Although critics countered that it was man who had died, it seemed apparent that the idea of traditional theism had effectively disappeared among the educated middle classes. The idea that man must shoulder full responsibility for history was unique for the 1960s not because it was new but because that awareness impressed itself upon unprecedented numbers of people and because it represented the ultimate form of revolt in a cultural situation where authorities everywhere were undergoing reappraisal.

Because the "death of God" movement had deep historical roots in Western culture and was a logical consequence of radical monotheism, it was hardly as faddish as critics supposed. The world wars and economic depressions of the twentieth century had demonstrated the precariousness of the human condition. In Europe this awareness gave birth to existentialism, a philosophy emphasizing man's freedom and his responsibility for shaping his own nature. A variant of existentialism, articulated by Albert Camus, became popular in the United States. In novels and essays

Camus tried to show why the traditional answer of the Church was inadequate in explaining the human predicament. In his novel, *The Plague,* set in Oran, Algiers, in 1943, rats die horribly, and soon men begin to die—thousands of men. Since the bubonic plague makes no distinction between good and evil men, Camus' point is that man lives in a universe that is thoroughly and coldly indifferent to human existence. The plague symbolized the troubles that had come upon war-torn Europe. Many of Camus' readers agreed that the church's traditional explanation for suffering (sinful humanity deserves to suffer, and God chastizes because he loves) no longer acceptably accounted for the bestiality of modern war and the murder of several million Jews.

While this expression of radical theology has remained controversial, few deny that it made religion more responsive to immediate human needs. As in the days of the Social Gospel movement, clergymen became activists and fought for civil rights in the South, organized rent strikes, tenants' councils and welfare unions, and questioned the value system that permitted the myriad forms of exploitation in society. The Church, they said, must equate its interests with the interests of the poor, the alienated, and the outcasts, even as Jesus did. By their example, clergymen testified that if religion is the way in which we share the crisis of life in accordance with the inherited traditions of our community, the end of traditional belief need not lead to the collapse of religion. Because men need a psychological and cultural instrumentality to share tragedy, religion remained important. The new religious man without God may not be able to speak prophetically at the death of a friend but he could nevertheless *be with* those who mourn. This religious act corresponded closely to the intense personalism found among the hippies and other disaffected individuals concerned with human relatedness. Both radical theologians and hippies opposed institutional authority in order to better fulfill the commandment of love. The figure of Jesus had a compelling fascination for them. Radical theologians such as Thomas J. J. Altizer and William Hamilton tried to show that Jesus is meaningful even if God is dead (see selection 24). The religious interest in Jesus among the young, whether of the "Jesus freaks," as they came to be called, or the passionate fans of the rock opera, *Jesus Christ Superstar,* expressed a similar conviction.

Among religious denominations, the challenge to authority waxed strongest where it was most firmly entrenched—in the Catholic Church. Historically, the Catholic community in the United States has been conservative and accommodationist in foreign and domestic policy. But this changed in the 1960s. Pope John XXIII supported theological radicalism and in his 1963 encyclical, *Pacem in Terris,* accepted coexistence with differing ideological systems, including communism. The two Vatican Councils seriously debated institutional and doctrinal reforms. Across

America, priests and nuns opposed the church's position on celibacy, birth control, and the use of Latin in the celebration of the Mass. For the first time in American history, a reformist element of the Catholic Church challenged the secular establishment in foreign policy; it is noteworthy that the antiwar movement found many of its ablest leaders in Irish Catholic priests, among whom Philip and Daniel Berrigan were prominent. By 1970 the Berrigan brothers were in federal prison for destroying draft files and the federal government was soon to indict Philip Berrigan for conspiring to kidnap government officials.

The emergence of radical theology and the growth of doctrinal independence among Catholics were as surprising as another notable event —the intellectual challenge to science as the standard of truth and the motor force of progress. Largely because of recurring wars, the relationship between science and government had become very close. The government furnished universities with research funds, sometimes without strings attached, but at other times it demanded that research be related to military defense. The ability of the National Liberation Front and the North Vietnamese to prevail against American technology raised questions about the limits of technological solutions and the morality of sustained terror bombing of peasant peoples. Thus the question of who controls science and technology in a democracy became increasingly urgent in the 1960s. Should it be the people who, given their education, are unable to comprehend it? The politicians, who understand it little better, have divided loyalties and, all too often, reflect the interests of the ruling elite? The scientists, who all too often reject social responsibility? No one had the answer and effective controls were not established.

Cultural conservatives since Edmund Burke warned repeatedly that an ungoverned science is deleterious to faith and human sensibility and dangerous to man and his world. During the 1960s, humanist critics on the Left made similar points. The argument of the political Left was not to repudiate science but to guard against the monopolization of its uses by ruling elites. The nonpolitical Left, however, criticized science for undercutting the operation of nonintellective powers. In Theodore Roszak's words: "When we challenge the finality of objective [scientific] consciousness as a basis for culture, what is at issue is the size of man's life. We must insist that a culture which negates or subordinates or degrades visionary experience commits the sin of diminishing our existence."[2]

There is evidence that this view has impressed itself upon young people of high-school age. The journal *Science* carried an article in 1964 that revealed that among the top 1 percent of the total student population the

---

[2] Theodore Roszak, *The Making of a Counter Culture* (Garden City, N. Y.: Doubleday & Co., Inc., 1969) , p. 234. See selection 26.

percentage selecting science decreased from 37.77 percent in 1958 to 28.87 percent in 1963; and more than half of those who chose science changed majors when in college.[3] René Dubos attributed this rejection in good measure to an attitude of hostility produced by the realization that "many modern applications of science have nothing to do with human biological needs and aim only at creating new demands, even though these be inimical to health, to happiness, or to the aspirations of mankind."[4] On its present course, Dubos warned, science itself may be responsible for transforming "the anti-utopian outbursts so characteristic of our time from a literary exercise into an antiscience crusade."[5] In rejecting the argument that science should in no way be governed and instead left free to develop any of its inherent possibilities, and in refusing to believe that science held the single key that could explain the mysteries of human life, ecologists, students, and humanist critics challenged yet another authority in society.

In significant ways the youthful segments of the population carried the heaviest burden of the assault on cultural orthodoxies because they were often hit hardest by developments in American society. The 1954 Supreme Court decision in *Brown* v. *Board of Education,* which helped to spur the civil rights movement, affected school children; subsequently, young people filled the ranks of the freedom riders and other activist movements. They suffered unemployment at a rate at least triple the national unemployment average. Required to fight an odious war in Vietnam, the young helped to push the issue of war and peace beyond the usual calculations of power politics and national self-interest. Upheaval on the campuses, the sexual revolution, the drug scene, experiments in new life styles—all of these were phenomena importantly centered in the high school and college age groups. It is small wonder then that the youth of the country found themselves at the vortex of social change, and that they played an important part in the efforts to democratize American society and culture.

It was primarily middle-class whites of college age who made up the "counterculture." Its primary project, wrote one of its ablest protagonists, was "to proclaim a new heaven and a new earth so vast, so marvelous that the inordinate claims of technical expertise must of necessity withdraw in the presence of such splendor to a subordinate and marginal status in the lives of men."[6] The enemy of this revolutionary cultural uni-

[3] Robert C. Nichols, "Career Decisions of Very Able Students," *Science, 144* (June 12, 1964), 1316, 1318.

[4] René Dubos, "Science and Man's Nature," *Daedalus, 94* (Winter 1965), 229, 240. See selection 25.

[5] Ibid., 224.

[6] Roszak, *Counter Culture,* p. 240.

verse was technocracy—planning, organization, modernization, rationalization, and systems analysis—not capitalism per se. Its solution was a new consciousness and moral sensitivity that said "no" to the war system, rejected nationalism in foreign policy, insisted on equality of sexes and races, and demanded cultural and moral freedom. Unable to realize their vision through politics, since government itself was seen as entrapped by the ideology and machinery of the technocracy, the patrons of the counterculture, unlike the New Left, turned to communitarianism, mysticism, and drugs in an effort to avoid the industrial leviathan and to escape any complicity in the nuclear annihilation that politicians assumed all brave men must be prepared to face.

The influence of the counterculture phenomenon can be overrated. Surely its members were provincial in assuming that they represented a unique cultural development. The *Burschenschaften,* a youth movement in Germany 150 years ago, also rejected contemporary values and wore their hair long and their clothes carelessly. Balzac, the early nineteenth-century French novelist, wrote of the greasy coats, long beards, and dirty fingernails of the Bohemian youth of Paris' Left Bank. The revolutionary students in Russia in the 1870s were described in similar terms. And, in the United States, the 1920s witnessed a powerful counterculture movement that attacked materialist values, Puritanical sex codes, and scientism. The point is not merely that countercultures have been a recurring phenomenon in Western societies but that they ultimately collapsed; hence the most recent counterculture may not represent the quantum jump in the qualitative life that its proponents have averred. Nevertheless the flourishing of the counterculture had a democratizing influence because it challenged social myths and cultural authorities by opening up alternatives to the middle-class style of life.

Radical leader Tom Hayden remarked, in 1967, that significant change occurs when people confer legitimacy upon themselves.[7] In part, the much-discussed generation gap resulted from attempts to activate this attitude. Searching for an explanation of the generational conflict, anthropologist Margaret Mead announced the emergence of a "prefigurative" culture, an open system focusing on the future, in which adults learn the style of the present and of the future from their children. In the "postfigurative" culture, a virtual closed system, change is so slow and imperceptible that the past of the adults becomes the future of each new generation.[8] But today, at the onset of the prefigurative age, "none of the young, neither the most idealistic nor the most cynical, is untouched by

[7] Symposium, "Confrontation: The Old Left and the New," *The American Scholar, 36* (Autumn 1967) , 586.

[8] Margaret Mead, *Culture and Commitment* (Garden City, N.Y.: Doubleday & Co., Inc., 1970) , p. 1.

the sense that there are no adults anywhere in the world from whom they can learn what the next steps should be." From now on, Mead concluded, the young will "lead their elders in the direction of the unknown."[9]

With variations, this became a fashionable interpretation. René Dubos explained that the reasons for the emergence of the prefigurational culture could be found in science, which not only increases the tempo at which man changes his environment, but which alone "provides the mental and physical apparatus for rapid changes in our ways of life and even more perhaps in our conceptual views of creation."[10] As plausible as the interpretations of Mead and Dubos at first appeared, they failed to consider the ambiguities of the youth revolt. The issue was not merely the speed of change or the need to channel it but the quality of life itself and the ways in which the current configuration of power and privilege served a small elite. As such, the basis of the youth revolt was hardly new. Moreover, Mead's point that the young will lead their elders is at least arguable. Gerontological research has revealed the possibility of altering man's internal clocks and slowing down aging. Advances in the "free-radical" and "cross-linkage" theories suggest that increased longevity will be available before this century is out. Thus, if the human life span is extended, and if the population levels off with families of two children becoming the norm, the population curve will skew away from the young to the middle aged and once again the young will find themselves shut out from the centers of power and enjoined to wait until age catches up with them.

Much of the effort to explain, exploit, and cater to the young (an obsession during the 1960s) would have been better spent analyzing the adult world and its value system. The hippies, the New Left, black militants, and other protesters can be understood partly as victims of a social storage process that is destructive of the normal routes of maturation. Bennett Berger has written brilliantly of the "artificial postponement of maturity" that American society demands of its college and university population. Postindustrial society "uses institutions of higher education as warehouses for the temporary storage of a population it knows not what else to do with."[11] This Berger identifies as the root cause of student unrest. Inasmuch as society refuses generally to take students seriously, their prolonged campus tenancy encourages juvenilization (youth may well be extended to 25 or 30 years of age) and, in Erik Erikson's formulations, they are forced to play a lengthy game searching for their identity.

[9] Ibid., pp. 87, 94.
[10] Dubos, "Science and Man's Nature," 224. See selection 25.
[11] Bennett M. Berger, "The New Stage of American Man—Almost Endless Adolescence," *The New York Times Magazine* (November 2, 1969), 131.

In this view, it is not youth but the economic, social, and sexual shape of contemporary adult society that is being served by artificially delaying maturity. Society expects students to be idealistic because they have the time to moralize, brood, and play while normal society goes about its business. Yet when they act on their convictions, society reacts unfavorably. It recalls John Dewey's warning in 1935 that in America "liberty is tolerated as long as it does not seem to menace in any way the *status quo* of society. When it does, every effort is put forth to identify the established order with the public good."[12] It is precisely this that occurred in the 1960s. Parents, politicians, and well-meaning liberals such as George Kennan argued that the universities should remain political-free zones where "sagacious men" can pursue knowledge, and where students may engage in harmless social criticism. They failed to perceive that student life unavoidably became political and sometimes violent by the presence on the campuses of ROTC units, government defense projects, and military recruiters.

Late in the decade, the youth culture, which had as its central quest new patterns of daily living, found an unexpected ally in the Women's Liberation Movement. Emerging from their traditional submission, American women became educated in and restless under the discriminatory powers of a patriarchal social structure. The movement, with a widely divergent leadership ranging from the moderate Betty Friedan (whose book *The Feminine Mystique* was immediately responsible for reviving interest in women's status in society) to the radical Ti-Grace Atkinson (who espoused elimination of marriage and traditional family patterns), brought attention to the fact that the median salary for full-time female employees was nearly less than half that for men. Women constituted only 9 percent of the professors, 7 percent of the physicians, 3 percent of the lawyers, 2 percent of the United States House of Representatives, 1 percent of the United States senators, and 1 percent of the engineers. The feminists organized scores of groups like Betty Friedan's National Organization of Women to protest the more subtle forms of "male chauvinism," sex exploitation, the cultural norms that kept bored women in the home, and even the English language where it reflected male dominance. Women asked for equal pay for equal work, a chance at jobs reserved for men, abortion on demand, state-supported child-care centers, and reforms that would institutionalize meritocracy in the economic system.

One of the chief villains of the movement was Sigmund Freud, whose explanation of women's neurosis seemed to reflect the same resentment of the female species that liberationists saw in contemporary society. Histo-

---

[12] John Dewey, *Liberalism and Social Action* (New York: Capricorn Books, 1963), pp. 65–66.

ry, anthropology, and psychology were employed to prove that what had been considered as biological determinants of women's role in society were only the cultural values of Western bourgeois society. In the words of Germaine Greer, author of *The Female Eunuch,* "Women are contoured by their conditioning." Regardless of what science may yet reveal about sexual differences, the Women's Liberation Movement was on solid ground in emphasizing the role that culturally determined birthright played in society. By reopening an important avenue to the realization of a more just and open social system, the battle for women's rights established the authentic nature of the American cultural revolution. For sexual oppression has everywhere been linked to authoritarianism in other areas: in family life and in relations between races, age groups, and social classes.

The most widely spread movement of dissent in American history since the protest against slavery arose during the 1960s against the war in Vietnam. The early passivity of the American electorate that permitted the steady expansion of the war reflected the broad Cold War consensus on America's world role; but the systematic deception practiced by three administrations helps to explain the tenacity of that consensus. Asked Richard Poirier pointedly, is literature any longer the primary source of fiction, when we have had Rusk, McNamara, and Kissinger, "the mothers of invention," reporting on the war in Vietnam? The publication of the Pentagon Papers, a secret study commissioned by Secretary of Defense Robert S. McNamara shortly before he left the Johnson Administration, confirmed the analysis of the antiwar movement that the United States had not stumbled blindly into the Vietnam war but had steadily pushed to the limit the anti-Communist philosophy that, for a generation, had constituted the chief rationale of American foreign policy. The Pentagon study also confirmed that until 1965 the war was to a large degree clandestine in nature, and that every escalation mounted thereafter was based on a growing fear of defeat and of embarrassment to the executive branch of the government.

By evaluating information from sources other than the American government, veteran observers such as Hans Morgenthau, Walter Lippmann, and George Ball, together with growing numbers of young people, first grew suspicious of the imperial nature of the war as the number of American soldiers sent to Vietnam mounted into the hundreds of thousands, as American B–52s bombed North Vietnam, and as American troops undertook "search and destroy" missions. The protracted nature of the war helped to educate other Americans in the limits of American power and technology, a fact that was decisive for many who, by the time of the 1968 presidential election, were not yet convinced of the war's futility. By the end of the decade a solid majority of American citizens had concluded that the war had been ill-conceived and in several opinion polls voiced their belief that it must be brought to an end quickly. Growing numbers in all age groups recalled an old American principle, most recently enshrined in the judgments of Nuremberg and practiced by Daniel Ellsberg and war resisters, that men have loyalties higher than those due the nation state.

In retrospect, it seems clear that on the peace issue the people longed for positive leadership because they responded enthusiastically to President Nixon's dramatic trip to the People's Republic of China. It is, therefore, necessary to question the political assumption of the late Cold War era that Red-baiting was still a necessary technique for gaining public support. For in traveling to China, the President undercut one major rationale for the war: that American soldiers must fight to restrain a truculent and aggressive Asian ideology. Yet the domino theory to justify American intervention in Southeast Asia remained useful, and Nixon exploited it in order to escalate the bombing of North Vietnam and Cambodia. It proved particularly difficult for political leaders to repudiate long-held assumptions of the Cold War. As late as October 1967, Democratic Vice-President Hubert Humphrey expressed the Cold War ideology this way: "The threat to world peace is militant, aggressive Asian Communism, with its headquarters in Peking, China. . . . The aggression of North Vietnam is but the most current and immediate action of militant Asian Communism."[13]

Vice-President Humphrey's sentiments were voiced hundreds of times on the Senate floor and in the House of Representatives by men who feared that diverse Third World strategies of societal development threatened the interests of the United States. The Indochina war grew in large measure from an attempt to internationalize the Great Society model of liberal-capitalist political and economic development. Its utopianism was a manifestation of the centuries-old belief that the example of America would inspire and uplift the world. The mission to extend ideals and thereby protect the American way of life by internationalizing it accounts more fully for the American entanglement in Vietnam than does the one-dimensional argument of economic interest. The two are closely conjoined, however. The problem of domestic unemployment and the continuing politico-economic necessity for war-defense contracts were often decisive in the formulation of United States policy. In the ABM and SST controversies, and in the decision to bail out Lockheed (which existed almost solely on government defense contracts), the economic arguments advanced by proponents of these programs (maintenance of jobs and

---

[13] Quoted in Arthur M. Schlesinger, Jr., "The Necessary Amorality of Foreign Affairs," *Harper's Magazine, 243* (August 1971), 76.

thus prosperity) documented the close linkage between foreign and domestic policy.

After 1965 the American military escalation in Indochina generated a growing movement of draft resistance that renounced the version of patriotism inherent in the motto, "My country, right or wrong." Spontaneous reactions against the draft appeared first on college campuses where it provided a strong impetus for the growth of the Students for a Democratic Society. Protest meetings, sit-ins, and draft-card burnings were organized to oppose Selective Service examinations, military recruitment on campus, and corporations such as Dow Chemical, which depended on defense contracts and manufactured napalm for the war. J. Edgar Hoover stated that nearly 30,000 persons violated the Selective Service Act in 1967 alone.[14] While the vast majority of young men complied with the Selective Service laws thousands registered their protest against the war and the draft by fleeing to Canada, France, Sweden, and elsewhere.[15] Other uncounted thousands entered college as a more respectable method of draft avoidance until this system of escape was ended by the Nixon administration.

The draft resisters raised a number of crucial questions. How in the vastness of modern technocratic society, can the dissenting individual make his voice heard? When must a law higher than that of the state be obeyed? What constitutes treason? Is conscientious objection less sincere when, in a secular age, it becomes an expression of ethical principles rather than of religious belief? The large number of individuals who wrestled with these questions gave rise in the 1960s to the popularity of Thoreau, who wrote, "If [injustice] is of such a nature that it requires you to be the agent of injustice to others, then, I say, break the law. Let your life be a counter friction to stop the machine. What I have to do is to see, at any rate, that I do not lend myself to the wrong which I condemn."[16]

In response to a Supreme Court ruling, the Military Selective Service Act of 1967 eliminated the strict religious provision but aggravated matters by changing the law so that upon graduation, college seniors would be drafted first, along with graduate students whose deferments had been discontinued. The Selective Service system did not respond to a second type of nonreligious conscientious objection that found support, that of

---

[14] "Hoover Sees Peril in the New Left," *The New York Times* (May 19, 1968), 25.

[15] There are no accurate figures on the number of draft evaders in foreign countries. Estimates for Canada alone have ranged from 200 to 100,000. For a review of the sloppy journalism in this matter, see Russel B. Nye, "All Those Draft Resisters Up There," *The Progressive, 36* (May 1972), 42–43.

[16] Henry David Thoreau, *The Works of Henry David Thoreau*, ed. Henry Seidel Canby (Boston: Houghton Mifflin Co., 1937), pp. 796–97

political or "selective" objection in which the nonpacifist individual might choose, for personal or moral reasons, not to fight in a *particular* war. A lottery plan in which a young person took his chance with the draft for one year instead of seven was passed in 1969. Had it come earlier, protest over American military involvement in Indochina might have been less vocal. For the pressures of the draft, with its seven years of uncertainty, exacerbated the problem of how maturing youths gain entry into society.

II

The multiple efforts to transvalue cultural authorities did not achieve the degree of success its partisans hoped for, primarily because of stiff opposition from entrenched economic and political power. To overlook this is to distort the meaning of the 1960s. The vast majority of economists and politicians accepted the prevailing system of managed capitalism; but many advocated a greater degree of government planning and spending to prevent further depressions. It became the conventional wisdom to exalt the coming of age of Keynesian economics. Deficit financing and the use of tax policies to promote economic prosperity became standard liberal fare during the New and Fair Deals. By 1970, conservatives such as Milton Friedman and Richard Nixon had also accepted these measures (the "new economics") although they substituted the label "full employment budget" for "deficit financing."

Measured simply in terms of the Gross National Product (the total output of goods and services), the "new economics" of the 1960s helped to bring six years of unprecedented economic growth. It was a creditable performance worthy of the praise it received, but analysis should begin, not end, at that point. Had those who celebrated the widespread acceptance of Keynesian economics considered whether our ability to control the economy surpassed what it was in the late 1930s? By the end of the decade when both unemployment and inflation were rising rapidly, the major solution was a wage-price freeze (1971) not unlike the ones imposed during the two world wars. Another perplexing question remained: in view of the technological, scientific, and organizational revolutions, combined with more than 50 years of substantial government intervention, why had so little progress been made in achieving a more equitable distribution of wealth?

The economic injustices that grew out of the vastly maldistributed wealth of a rich society revealed a moral and intellectual failure on the part of responsible leaders both private and public. Since a nation willing to finance expensive wars and the development of the technology necessary to place men on the moon could not convincingly plead scarcity of resources, it appeared to social critics that the very will to right the wrongs was lacking. The ultimate success of the counterculture and of reform movements such as civil rights and women's liberation depended heavily on a reevaluation of the fundamental axioms behind modern economic policies. Because the reevaluation did not take place, economic policies constituted a major barrier to reform in the 1960s.

A primary reason for the reluctance to pursue fundamental economic reforms lay in the political unpopularity of deficit financing for the purpose of funding welfare programs that could have eliminated poverty in our land. To circumvent radical demands for income redistribution, orthodox liberal theorists have argued that the elimination of poverty depends on continued economic growth. The theoretical basis lay in the welfare-economics theorem of Vilfredo Pareto, the Italian economist, who maintained that with sufficient economic expansion some people will become better off while no one becomes worse off. According to this theory, time is necessary, but sacrifice is not. The Kennedy-Johnson tax cuts, based upon this reasoning, helped to reduce unemployment but did not redistribute income and, in fact, were regressive.

Economic progress achieved through the politically painless method of growth was often double-edged. Cities built to enhance the cultural and the economic opportunities of people became seats of poverty and unrelieved congestion. Cars, electric power, detergents, and disposable containers that promised a happier life became the agents of land, water, and air pollution. The powerful chemical DDT, developed to check the spread of disease, had lethal effects on certain animal life—and perhaps on humans also. Nor was the growth syndrome altogether gratifying when measured by its wastefulness and triviality and its seeming irrelevance to human needs. Paul Baran and Paul Sweezy, two economists critical of American monopoly capitalism, drew attention to the irrationality of pouring tens of billions of dollars into the military machine, thus preventing people from solving more pressing problems. They questioned the ethics of creating wants, goods, and services that no one needed. And worse, the entire citizenry was involved somehow in the system, from the farmers supplying food to troops who warred against the Vietnamese to the tool and die makers who designed machines for use in "new" cars.[17]

The continued reliance on the method of economic growth helped to establish the large corporation as the basic planning agent in modern society. By 1970, Americans were living in a planned economy despite ubiquitous fears of "economic planning." Large-scale technology seemed to demand it. Because the costs of product development, tooling, and

---

[17] Paul A. Baran and Paul M. Sweezy, *Monopoly Capital* (New York: Monthly Review Press, 1966), p. 344.

marketing are great, security of return is deemed indispensable to large industrial enterprises. In John Kenneth Galbraith's analysis, the large corporation, in the nonsocialist economy, "can fix minimum prices. It can sufficiently manage consumer wants. And it can extract from revenues the savings it needs for its own growth and expansion."[18] In Galbraithian theory the role of the government is largely defined by the limits of corporate planning. Wherever private corporations can do the job at hand, as in establishing minimum prices and manipulating consumer demand, the state is excluded. Wherever the corporation cannot or will not plan, the state enters the economic arena. In certain instances, however, the state determines economic policy by its political decisions. The desire for ever-improved military technology is an example. In such cases, the state indicates what is necessary and draws the corporation into the military-industrial-political complex. The state not only originates the program but serves as the principle underwriter and customer as well. As such it helps to decide the allocation of monies to a degree that must impress even the more radical advocates of national planning.

It follows that government is not and has not been subversive of large capitalist interests as economic conservatives long have alleged. Whereas in 1950 the 200 largest manufacturing companies controlled 40 percent of the country's manufacturing assets, by 1970 the top 200 controlled 60 percent, a consolidation that Peter Drucker terms "the biggest increase in economic concentration ever recorded in this or any other country."[19] The reliance on Keynesian policies fostered this development, particularly in the 1960s when big businessmen, seeing new possibilities for expansion opening before them, came out in favor of heavy government spending. Tax reductions such as the 7 percent tax credit of 1962, government subsidies to defense industries, the funding of space contractors, and liberalization of depreciation laws added up to government borrowing for the purpose of subsidizing corporate profits. As Leo Huberman and Paul Sweezy indicate, corporate profits far outstripped increases in the GNP and in the real wages of workers. (See selection 9.) President Kennedy's secretary of the treasury, Wall Street financier C. Douglas Dillon, acknowledged that the total effect of tax changes in 1962 and 1964 was equivalent to a reduction in the corporate profits tax from 52 percent to 34 or 29 percent (depending on the method of analysis used; see selection 9). It is understandable then that Democratic administrations became linked more closely with big business than at any other time in the twentieth century.

[18] John Kenneth Galbraith, "Market Planning and the Role of Government," *Atlantic Monthly, 219* (May 1967), 77. See selection 10.

[19] Peter Drucker, "The New Markets and the New Capitalism," in Daniel Bell and Irving Kristol, eds., *Capitalism Today* (New York: Basic Books Inc., 1971), p. 75.

The continuing corporate concentration has strengthened the system of privilege in the United States. C. Wright Mills exaggerated only a little when he wrote:

Not great fortunes, but great corporations are the important units of wealth, to which individuals of prosperity are variously attached. The corporation is the source of and the basis of the continued power and privilege of wealth. All the men and families of great wealth are now identified with large corporations in which their property is seated.[20]

According to the calculations of Robert Lampman, the top 1 percent of adults in America own 26 percent of all personal wealth. More revealing on the nature of ownership are the figures on corporate wealth where the top 1 percent of adults hold two-thirds of all stock.[21] The existence of this grossly disproportionate ownership of America's wealth—which brings entrée for the few into the high councils of government, which allows the wealthy to flaunt laws that the average man must obey, and which furnishes for them a qualitatively different life style—is the meaning of privilege in America.

The foregoing analysis raises questions about the inherent limits of capitalism as an agency of reform. Robert Heilbroner argues that it can achieve considerable change within the boundaries imposed by its market mechanism and peculiar system of privilege but is unusually resistant to efforts that would transform it substantially.[22] This judgment is valid if recent history is the measure. Every administration since the Civil War has used various techniques—the maintenance of high employment, minimum welfare expenditures, wage and price controls, regulatory acts, subsidies to big business, and tax laws—as defensive adaptations to the erosions and occasional explosions brought by technological and social change and to make up for the theoretical deficiencies of capitalism under modern assumptions of human welfare.[23] Measured by the test of stability, the American politico-economic process has been uncommonly successful.

Yet the American system tends to neglect the less visible, the less powerful, and the less organized. John F. Kennedy's statement during the 1960 presidential campaign that 17,000,000 Americans went to bed hun-

---

[20] C. Wright Mills, *The Power Elite* (New York: Oxford University Press, 1956), p. 116.

[21] Robert Lampman, *The Share of Top Wealth-Holders in National Wealth, 1922–56* (Princeton: Princeton University Press, 1962), pp. 24–35.

[22] Robert Heilbroner, *The Limits of American Capitalism* (New York: Harper Torchbooks, 1966), pp. 65–134.

[23] Robert Heilbroner, "Phase II of the Capitalist System," *The New York Times Magazine* (November 28, 1971), 76, 78, 85.

gry each night was generally dismissed as campaign rhetoric. Michael Harrington subsequently argued, however, that the problem of the poor was much greater than Kennedy had realized. He estimated that at least 40,000,000 Americans were poor.[24] Based on calculations that a non-farm family of four needed $3130 annual income to avoid poverty while a farm family of the same size needed $2190, President Johnson's Council of Economic Advisers calculated that there were approximately 34,000,000 poor people in the United States—about 18 percent of the popoulation.[25] Sensitive to the needs of the poor, President Johnson declared a "war" on poverty. But the war, while highly publicized, turned out to be mostly a threat of war. Unskilled youths did learn the skills required to get jobs, and unemployed people found temporary jobs, but the overall results were not dramatic. At decade's end, 24,000,000 persons, or 13 percent of the population, still did not enjoy enough income to meet what the government called "a minimum adequate level of living." And in 1970 the number of Americans below the poverty line again began to rise. 1970 saw a 5 percent increase over 1969 in the number of people living in poverty.

Similar figures lead to the conclusion that the United States is more a "limited welfare state" than a welfare state. The poor, the racial minorities, the small farmers and small businessmen, and the millions of working women do not receive the subsidies and political solicitations that are extended to business and educational groups. Attempts to change these conditions were wrecked by the structural configuration and ideological tenacity of modern American capitalism. At nearly every turn, from the fight against poverty to the movement for black liberation, entrenched economic interests countervailed both radical and liberal movements for social and economic reform.

The inflexibility that characterized economic structures was also apparent in political affairs. With due allowance for the extraordinary activity of the federal government on behalf of Great Society welfare programs, the gap between promise and performance and the tendency of politicians to effect short-run solutions rather than to grapple with the shape of the future marked the 1960s as years of political failure. Underlying the rhetoric of both Democrats and Republicans ran a current of old ideas, outworn programs, and avoidance of the root causes of social and economic problems. Perhaps the central political failure was the conclusion of Democratic and Republican leaders alike that the future of freedom in America depended more on the elimination of communism in

[24] Michael Harrington, *The Other America: Poverty in the United States* (New York: The Macmillan Co., 1963). See selection 6 and the appendix to *The Other America*.
[25] Council of Economic Advisers, *Economic Report of the President* (1966), p. 110–111.

Southeast Asia than on the elimination of poverty at home. The respective budgets clearly underscored the priorities—$20 to $30 billion per year on the Vietnam war but less than $2 billion per year on poverty. Although poverty programs proliferated, few were effective in alleviating the plight of the poor. Bureaucratic inertia, administrative skim-off and, by the latter years of the decade, a weakening of will brought the Great Society antipoverty war to ruin.

No doubt part of the responsibility for the failure of the American political process should be shifted from political leaders to the fact that the velocity of history is itself a cause of political malaise. The convulsive forces of rapid change throughout the environment divides the populace and wrests traditional political loyalties from their moorings. There is good reason for Alvin Toffler to have warned that "future shock"—the reaction of panic and anxiety resulting from an overburdening of men's capacity to adapt to change—may well be the special disease of our time.[26] In addition to this dislocating factor, Americans since the Great Depression have asked much of their government. This is altogether proper since there is no other persuasive reason in democratic theory why government should exist.

Under conditions of maldistributed affluence, however, a growing number of alternatives have entered the realm of the possible, making the political question one of priorities, not feasibility. Politics have become more emotional because the argument of scarcity, once so convenient for avoiding reform, is no longer tenable.

As a result, the traditional party alignments were weakened. They were further undermined by better education, high geographical mobility, and a new postwar generation of voters. Ticket splitting was widespread, particularly after mid-decade. As early as 1960 there were demands for "new" political movements. The central quest of John F. Kennedy's "New Frontier" was the release of idealism and spiritual energy. Measured by the test of performance, style counted for more than substance, which is not to say that the New Frontier was unimportant or unserviceable to the growth of reformist energies. In the second political movement, the Republican party in 1964 nominated its most conservative candidate for president in recent history. Senator Barry Goldwater proclaimed the majesty of an earlier America where, he alleged, law and order, purer morals, and a stern individualism were realities. His campaign offered domestic salvation through state rights and an end to government solicitude for the concerns that ushered in the New Deal. Casting "centrist" politics to the wind led to his defeat by the greatest margin in the history of presidential elections (43 million to 24 million in the popular vote).

[26] Alvin Toffler, *Future Shock* (New York: Random House, 1970).

Although several pundits predicted the demise of the Republican party, it was not a decade for prophecy. By the time of the 1968 presidential campaign, the Vietcong Tet offensive had destroyed for many the illusion of victory in Vietnam. This, coupled with the diminished effectiveness of Great Society programs and Senator Eugene McCarthy's strong showing in the New Hampshire primary, led President Johnson to withdraw from the presidential race. McCarthy's "new politics" campaign caught fire among the young, intellectuals, and antiwar Democrats. Others, who were simply antiestablishment, joined in. He had little to say, however, about poverty, civil rights, pollution control, and tax reform, a connection with the limited achievements of Kennedy's administration that did not escape notice. Perhaps it was this that led Emmet John Hughes, formerly an administrative assistant to President Eisenhower, to write that the "new" political movements of the 1960s were engaged in what he somewhat infelicitously termed the "politics of masturbation." "These political exercises were conducted in a spirit that essentially did not care whether they created or communicated or convinced in any fruitful sense; they simply wanted to be heard or felt. Ultimately, they did not much desire to give birth; they aspired only to give pleasure."[27] This judgment is insensitive to the idealistic antiestablishmentarianism and genuine anguish felt about the Vietnam war by McCarthy's supporters, but it correctly emphasizes the failure of Kennedy, Goldwater, and McCarthy to draw up a clearly conceived social and economic program for the country.

A fourth "new" politics movement, led by Governor George C. Wallace of Alabama, was in some ways more indicative of the political crises of the 1960s than the others. For he headed the largest third-party movement in more than a century and in the 1968 presidential election received nearly 10,000,000 votes or 13.5 percent of the total. A new realignment seemed to be taking place, not dissimilar to those that occurred in 1800, 1828, 1860, 1896, and 1932. As in the 1960s, each realignment had been preceded by the emergence of third parties.

Much of Wallace's support grew out of his steadfast opposition to civil rights. Though he often coded his language on racial matters, especially as he moved into national politics, no one doubted that he was flagrantly anti-Negro. This alone does not adequately account for Wallaceism, however. He drew votes outside of the South from farmers, barbers, cab drivers, and blue-collar laborers. It is noteworthy that Wallaceites did not feel at home with business interests and the wealthier groups of society. Generally, Wallace ran best in areas of less than 10,000 population. Always,

---

[27] Emmet John Hughes, "The Politics of the Sixties—From the New Frontier to the New Revolution," *The New York Times Magazine* (April 1971) , 50.

he ridiculed "pointy-headed intellectuals" and social engineers, lamented student and urban disorders, and denounced the "coddling" of criminals and the court-ordered desegregation of public schools. On a more positive note, he wished to champion the interests of the "little people," as he phrased it, who were controlled by the faraway and unresponsive bureaucracy in Washington.

To some political analysts, the Alabama governor symbolized protest politics on the right. Samuel Lubell termed it "rumpus basement politics,"[28] meaning that sympathizers used Wallace to voice their discontent with the two major parties. Hence, Wallace invariably did better in state primary contests than in the presidential election when voters were less willing to risk casting a futile vote.

The thesis of politics against reform finds support in the fact that Richard Nixon, one of the Cold War era's most resolute counterrevolutionaries, won the presidential election of 1968. No president in recent history, not even Eisenhower, had so often declared himself in favor of older social and moral codes. He was in many ways a modern representative of the Puritan caricatured beyond recognition in twentieth-century America. As for a life of leisure, thought, and enjoyment, he said "nothing could be more pitiful."[29] He frequently reiterated his belief that people should help themselves. Thus it is not surprising that in the face of domestic violence and social upheaval he could remark, "I've always thought this country could run itself domestically without a President."[30]

Having lost the presidential race in 1960 and the California gubernatorial race in 1962, and more bitterly disliked than most national politicians, nothing short of political upheaval could have made possible his presidency. The political earthquake of Vietnam opened the way to Nixon's candidacy; disturbances at home assured his victory. Middle America, including suburbanites, white ethnics, and small businessmen, along with traditional Republicans, who were appalled at campus protests, ghetto riots, rising crime rates, the youthful drug culture, and erosion of the authorities mentioned earlier, threw their support to the self-proclaimed apostle of law and order. The political analysts Richard M. Scammon and Ben J. Wattenberg explained it this way:

The Middle Voter is a forty-seven-year-old housewife from the outskirts of Dayton, Ohio, whose husband is a machinist. She very likely has a somewhat different view of life and politics from

---

[28] Samuel Lubell, *The Hidden Crisis in American Politics* (New York: W. W. Norton & Co., 1971) , pp. 80–84.

[29] Garry Wills, *Nixon Agonistes: The Crisis of the Self-Made Man* (Boston: Houghton Mifflin Co., 1970) , p. 18.

[30] Rowland Evans, Jr. and Robert D. Novak, *Nixon in the White House: The Frustration of Power* (New York: Random House, 1971) , p. 11.

that of a twenty-four-year-old instructor of political science at Yale. Now the young man from Yale may feel that he knows more about politics than the machinist's wife from suburban Dayton, and of course, in one sense he does. But he does not know much about politics or psephology, unless he understands what is bothering that lady in Dayton and unless he understands that her circumstances in large measure dictate her concerns. To know that the lady in Dayton is afraid to walk the streets alone at night, to know that she has a mixed view about blacks and civil rights because before moving to the suburbs she lived in a neighborhood that became all black, to know that her brother-in-law is a policeman, to know that she does not have the money to move if her new neighborhood deteriorates, to know that she is deeply distressed that her son is going to a community junior college where LSD was found on the campus—to know all this is the beginning of contemporary political wisdom.[31]

If a sharply restricted meaning is attached to the word "contemporary," this brief statement goes far to explain why after the promise of John Kennedy and the popular assaults on various social myths and nationalistic pieties, Americans in 1968 turned to Nixon. He understood that political power at that given moment lay somewhat to the right of center. No one had cultivated that position so devotedly as the ex-vice-president. By 1968 the conjunction of social and economic forces, political assassinations, the shortcomings of Kennedy-Johnson liberalism, and domestic disturbances over the war provided fertile soil for Nixonian politics.

III

To an important degree the resistances to reform in the politico-economic sphere contributed to the sharp increase in most forms of violence in the 1960s. Beginning with the Watts riot in which 30 persons were killed and hundreds wounded, urban-bred violence spread to other major cities. The rhetoric of violence punctuated the speeches of members of the Johnson Administration, of blacks such as H. Rap Brown and Stokely Carmichael, and of white radicals such as Jerry Rubin and Abbie Hoffman. Four important leaders—two blacks (Martin Luther King and Malcolm X) and two whites (John and Robert Kennedy)—were assassinated. What an investigative commission termed a "police riot" at the 1968 Democratic convention brought home to the millions watching television the extent that violence had invaded even the political process.

[31] Richard M. Scammon and Ben J. Wattenberg, *The Real Majority* (New York: Coward-McCann, Inc., 1970), pp. 70–71. See selection 17.

Television made the Vietnam war the first in history to be broadcast live —or almost so. A hundred forms of violence could be experienced vicariously.

The rediscovery of the pervasiveness of violence in American history, which, as Richard Hofstadter observed, "will undoubtedly be one of the most important intellectual legacies of the 1960s,"[32] surprised people of all classes. But it should be borne in mind that when Americans discussed violence, they generally had in mind not the perpetuation of injustices by those in power or the violence committed in the Indochinese war (the truly significant expressions of American violence in the 1960s) but the conspicuous acts of dissenting groups against property and people. This was the focus of the inquiry by the National Commission on the Causes and Prevention of Violence, which concluded that Americans must somehow eliminate their "historical amnesia" on the subject. This brought into question the well-nourished myth that Americans are preeminently the people of law in the Western world. Not surprisingly, the young were most receptive to the truth of the past. For them, Harvard psychologist Kenneth Kenniston theorized,

the issue of violence is . . . what the issue of sex was to the Victorian world. . . . *what is most deeply repressed, rejected, feared, controlled and projected onto others by the post-modern generation is no longer their own sexuality. . . . [violence] has assumed new prominence as the prime source of inner and outer terror.*[33]

Recent violence of the conspicuous domestic variety generated a fearful political reaction partly because of the variety of new groups that employed it. Terror and harrassment have usually been directed against minority groups—Negroes, Catholics, ethnic groups, radicals, and labor organizations—for the ostensible reason that WASP America needed protection. "A high proportion of our violent actions," Richard Hofstadter noted, has "come from the top dogs or the middle dogs." But today violence has become

to a degree unprecedented in the United States the outgrowth of forcible acts by dissidents and radicals who are expressing hostility to middle class ways and to established power. Many people see it as newly dangerous because it is politically more purposive than in the past, more intimately related to basic social issues, and because it touches the vulnerable sensibilities of the comfortable middle class.[34]

[32] Richard Hofstadter and Michael Wallace, *American Violence: A Documentary History* (New York: Alfred A. Knopf, 1970) , p. 3.
[33] Kenneth Keniston, "Youth, Change and Violence," *The American Scholar, 37* (Spring 1968) , 242.
[34] Hofstadter and Wallace, *American Violence,* p. 11.

It was this that bothered Middle America and Administration officials in Washington. Yet all of the radical movements for reform in the early 1960s began as protests *against* violence: against the legal violence perpetrated by a white establishment against blacks, against impersonal university systems, and against a war that bore so little relationship to the national interest. The black civil-rights movement, which during the 1950s dedicated itself to the principles of nonviolence, hailed as their spiritual leaders Christ, Gandhi, Tolstoy, and A. J. Muste. But by mid-decade, when nonviolent methods appeared to be unsuccessful and the Great Society too slow in operation, the partisans of more direct action gained strength. The belief that there was not enough time to reform society through liberal channels animated the small extremist wing of the New Left and angry participants in the civil-rights movement to rationalize the need for direct action, although they invariably had little philosophy for it beyond the contention that only acts of force could change a society that sanctioned its soldiers to kill Asians and its police to club demonstrators and kill Black Panthers.

The controversy over domestic violence, while often featured in the columns of political pundits, should not obscure the essential point. Not more than one or two percent of the student protest movement, for example, believed in violence, and fewer practiced it. Even within the somewhat vague category of the New Left, nonviolence was always much valued. The majority demonstrated, volunteered help in political campaigns, worked in support of civil rights, or asked for more student representation on the chief governing bodies of the university. They opposed exploitation (as *Playboy* philosophy, for example, did not) and warfare (as the presidents and Congress, in persisting in a military solution in Vietnam, did not), and they believed that all values lose their efficacy if not practiced (as, for example, the "realistic" theorists of foreign policy and the faltering political compromisers did not). It is *not* that the young generation was more moral than its predecessors, but that the present configuration of society, with its incipient terror and real capacity for self-destruction, seemed to demand an activist strategy that would reveal to all citizens the need for radical social reform. The dissenting youths argued that throwing bricks through windows was not equivalent to hurling B–52s at an impoverished people, that shouting obscenities was less obscene than the pious incantation of traditional Americanisms in the service of war and social paternalism. So they believed, and so the vast majority acted.

The practice of violence is closely related to the American respect for power. Physical violence is partly an overt expression of the will to exert power upon the outside world. But its easily perceived brutality does not necessarily make it more injurious than institutionalized and less-obvious forms of force. American capacities to control the environment—rivers, forests, food, animals, metals, and physical laws—have led to a shift from the conquest of things to the conquest of people as things. In political sociology, the infatuation with power is often expressed through social engineering, a modern equivalent, perhaps, of historical pioneering and commercial profiteering.

The American love affair with various forms of power is obviously too broad a phenomenon to be squeezed into a decade. In the 1960s, however, it became in some ways most visible in the intellectual stratum. There is no general agreement on the proper social role of intellectuals. Certain characteristics identify the authentic intellectual, however: a commitment to ideas and to social criticism, an ample degree of playfulness in the uses and disuses of ideas, and an unavoidable interest in moral judgment. "It is the responsibility of intellectuals to speak the truth and to expose lies," wrote Noam Chomsky in criticism of the value-free technology of scholar-experts.[35] In addition, the intellectual has usually been something of an alienated outcast, a person whose social role entails some degree of suffering, sometimes physical, but, in the United States, more often spiritual in nature.

After World War II American intellectuals moved closer to the centers of power as they engaged in what—with pardonable exaggeration—might be called an orgy of accommodation to society. There were several reasons for this. American capitalism emerged from the war greatly strengthened and seemingly impervious to criticism. A victorious nation that contributed materially to the recovery of allies and defeated nations had strengths worth preserving. At home, it offered growing financial rewards to writers and artists. Other intellectuals joined university faculties and found that, contrary to much opinion in the "village," they could maintain their treasured independence. The intellectual's ideological adaptation to society and culture resulted also from the tolerance built into the American democratic order or, in the words of Irving Howe, democratic socialist editor of *Dissent*, "the remarkable absorptiveness of modern society, its readiness to abandon traditional precepts for a moment of excitement, its growing permissiveness toward social criticism, perhaps out of indifference, or security, or even tolerance."[36] That many intellectuals were impressed with their country's achievements is understandable; their capacity for critical judgment, however, suffered accordingly.

By the 1960s, Howe wrote, "there arose a young generation of intellectuals, ambitious, self-assured, at ease with prosperity while conspicuously alienated, unmarred by the traumas of the totalitarian age, bored with memories of defeat, and attracted to the idea of power."[37] Howe

---

[35] Noam Chomsky, "The Responsibility of Intellectuals," *The New York Review of Books, 8* (February 23, 1967) , 23. See selection 19.
[36] Irving Howe, "The New York Intellectuals," *Commentary, 46* (October 1968) , 41.
[37] Ibid., 44.

was describing literary and nonpolitical intellectuals. But his description (excepting alienation) also applied to young mental technicians who seemed to fit only loosely the characterization offered above. Consider, for example, the "whiz kids" of the State Department and the Department of Defense who wrote speeches, prepared position papers, and analyzed options for the higher ranking middle-aged intellectuals like McGeorge Bundy and Walt Rostow, advisers to Presidents Kennedy and Johnson. These computer-intellectuals staffed the semiautonomous Rand Corporation, the most prestigious war-related think tank in the country. They were impressed with President Kennedy's attempt to sanctify politics and government service as an elevated road to power and well-being. It constituted nothing less, wrote Henry Fairlie, than the raping of the intellectuals:

At all times, and no matter who exercises it, power is ugly and brutalizing: President Kennedy was allowed to make it appear attractive and redeeming. Power is shoddy: President Kennedy was allowed to glamorize it. Power is for the aged: President Kennedy was allowed to cast over it the magic of youth. Power is unintellectual: President Kennedy was allowed to give it intellectual excitement. Power is safe only if it is exercised without enchantment, without claim to reason, and without pretense to virtue: President Kennedy was allowed to endow it with all three. Power is, no doubt, necessary: President Kennedy was allowed to make it seem desirable.[38]

The authority word of the young intellectuals was "rationality," and it cast invidious distinctions on all with which it was contrasted: sentimentalism, utopianism, and intuitive judgments. They uncritically assumed that society was operating rationally—irrational as it was to vote more money for Vietnam while on the same hot July day to cut funds for the summer employment of minority youths.

The bureaucracy-serving intellectuals who conceived their role as serving the men of power lived amidst what they perceived to be the end of the age of ideology, a thesis that was fashionable in the early 1960s and found an adherent in President Kennedy. In a Yale University commencement address in 1962, Kennedy summed up the accommodationist belief that the "old sweeping issues" of the past had "largely disappeared." The important domestic problems of our time, he said,

relate not to basic clashes of philosophy or ideology, but to ways and means of reaching common goals—to research for sophisticated solutions to complex and obstinate issues. . . . What is at stake in our economic decisions today is not some grand warfare of

[38] Henry Fairlie, "Johnson and the Intellectuals," *Commentary*, 40 (October 1965) , 50.

rival ideologies which will sweep the country with passion, but the practical management of a modern economy. What we need are not labels and cliches but more basic discussion of the sophisticated and technical questions involved in keeping a great economic machinery moving ahead. . . .[39]

The technical solutions would come from experts. It is not accidental that in his book, *The Essence of Security,* Kennedy's gifted secretary of defense used in profusion such phrases as: "Vital decision-making . . . must remain at the top"; "a full range of rational options"; "the real threat to democracy comes, not from overmanagement, but from undermanagement."[40] This is the language of elitist managerialism clothed in the protective framework of rationality, efficiency, progress, and statistics—in a word, technocracy.

As the decade wore on and American society fractured itself over the Indochina war, Ronald Steel's appraisal of the relationship between the war and the technician-intellectuals seemed close to the truth:

Vietnam was a liberal's war. Not a general's war. . . . Not the bureaucracy's war. . . . Not entirely Kennedy's war . . . nor LBJ's war. . . . It was a war conceived, promoted, and directed by intellectuals fascinated with power and eager to prove their toughness and resolve.[41]

Their concern with power and their eagerness "to prove their toughness and resolve," expressed a major concern of the decade, and it related them more closely to the practitioners of overt violence than they cared to admit. It is in this context that power and violence in the 1960s can be most effectively understood.

IV

What did cultural analysts and social critics make of the war, the violence, the racism, the rejection of authority, the vulgar language craze, and the hysteria over protest? In the pages of *Esquire* (its relevant articles conveniently brought together in *Smiling Through the Apocalypse: Esquire's History of the Sixties)* and in books such as *Our Violent Society,* by the respected psychiatrist David Abrahamsen, explanations centered on the "flawed American Dream." The dream incorporated such symbols and fantasies as the melting pot, Protestant ethic, Horatio Alger, equal opportunity, the desire for strength, the rebirth of man, and "one nation, indivisible." Together they supported the liberal assumption that

[39] John F. Kennedy, "Yale Commencement Address," *The New York Times* (June 12, 1962) , 20.
[40] Robert S. McNamara, *The Essence of Security* (New York: Harper & Row, 1968) .
[41] Ronald Steel, "The Kennedy Fantasy," *The New York Review of Books, 15* (Nov. 19, 1970) , 8.

society is perfectable through materialism, democracy, and science-technology. *Esquire's* history of the 1960s suggested that a new dream was needed. Abrahamsen concluded that the message conveyed by the dream was illusory. Certainly it made for many great achievements, widespread prosperity being among them. But it also "nurtured our dreams of growing rich quickly, of being immune to failure, and of convincing others that our way of life is the *only* way"—attitudes that have "warped our outlook, made us set goals higher than we ever could achieve, and stimulated in us the search for power."[42] For Abrahamsen, as for so many, the dream had become a nightmare. Still more pessimistic observers such as Andrew Hacker argued that because Americans are no longer willing to sacrifice private concerns for their public obligations, the United States "has embarked on its time of decline."[43]

Others, however, showed that it was possible to arrive at an opposite conclusion from the same body of facts. Middle America never relinquished its intuitive conviction that whatever its shortcomings the United States was still the best and freest place to live, and that the views of national decline reflected more on its prophets than it did on reality. An outsider, the French philosopher-critic Jean-François Revel, has boldly elaborated this interpretation. In his provocative book, *Without Marx or Jesus,* Revel volunteered that a new American Revolution had begun, one that involved a thorough reconstruction of society without sacrificing democracy. The twentieth-century American revolution is "the first revolution in history in which disagreement on values and goals is more pronounced than disagreement on the means of existence."[44] Since the twentieth-century revolution joins culture and economic and technological power as a means of opposing the spirit of nationalism, it "offers the only possible escape for mankind today: the acceptance of technological civilization as a means and not as an end, and—since we cannot be saved either by the destruction of the civilization or by its continuation—the development of the ability to reshape that civilization without annihilating it."[45]

Revel's conclusion is so general that it might win everyone's consent. That is also its greatest weakness, for the burden of proof rests with Revel to show by means other than assertion that a thorough reconstruction of society has begun, that democracy is not being sacrificed on the altars of power and privilege, and that the movements for reform and liberation begun in the 1960s can penetrate and begin to uproot the political and economic power entrenched in American institutions.

---

[42] David Abrahamsen, *Our Violent Society* (New York: Funk & Wagnalls, 1970), pp. 196–197, 208.
[43] Andrew Hacker, *The End of the American Era* (New York: Atheneum, 1970), p. 3.
[44] Jean-François Revel, *Without Marx or Jesus,* Afterword by Mary McCarthy (New York: Doubleday & Co., 1971), p. 149. See selection 29.
[45] Ibid., p. 242.

I. The Democratic Faith: Hopes and Promises

I.   John F. Kennedy

Inaugural Address, January 20, 1961

The 1960s began on a note of hope elegantly enunciated by John F. Kennedy, the first Roman Catholic president and the youngest man ever elected to that office. Although many Democratic liberals had reservations about Kennedy's past, particularly his record on McCarthyism and foreign affairs, he had, by the time of the presidential election of 1960, effectively presented himself as an heir of New Deal philosophy. His inaugural address appealed strongly to the idealism of Americans and gave promise that "a new generation of Americans" would reject the complacent social and economic attitudes of the Eisenhower administration and, spearheaded by an activist president, would directly attack what Kennedy termed "the common enemies of man: tyranny, poverty, disease and war itself."

It was not long, however, before disappointment arose over Kennedy's reluctance to champion effective civil rights legislation and his inability to push a Medicare bill through Congress. There seemed little disposition to seek out the broader boundaries of the New Frontier. Suspicions grew that style counted for more than substance. Would fewer supporters have suffered disappointment had they examined more closely the inaugural speech? A paragraph by paragraph analysis demonstrates that combined with the themes of hope and dedication were clashing counterthemes that suggested essential continuities with the concerns of earlier administrations. What were the implications of such phrases as the following: ". . . we shall pay any price, bear any burden, meet any hardship. . . ," and "oppose aggression and subversion anywhere in the Americas"; we must defend freedom "in its hour of maximum danger?" Finally, ". . . ask not what your country can do for you, ask what you can do for your country."

Whatever the conclusions, Kennedy "managed to touch millions in their private lives," as one authority on the presidency has written. He seemed to lift the tone of public life and to inspire many to reach for their better selves, not inconsequential factors. It is appropriate, therefore, that his inaugural address serve as the first selection in a volume devoted to the 1960s.

We observe today not a victory of party but a celebration of freedom—symbolizing an end as well as a beginning—signifying renewal as well as change. For I have sworn before you and Almighty God the same solemn

From *Public Papers of the Presidents, John F. Kennedy, 1961.*

oath our forebears prescribed nearly a century and three quarters ago. The world is very different now. For man holds in his mortal hands the power to abolish all forms of human poverty and all forms of human life. And yet the same revolutionary beliefs for which our forebears fought are still at issue around the globe—the belief that the rights of man come not from the generosity of the state but from the hand of God.

We dare not forget today that we are the heirs of that first revolution. Let the word go forth from this time and place, to friend and foe alike, that the torch has been passed to a new generation of Americans—born in this century, tempered by war, diciplined by a hard and bitter peace, proud of our ancient heritage—and unwilling to witness or permit the slow undoing of those human rights to which this nation has always been committed, and to which we are committed today at home and around the world.

Let every nation know, whether it wishes us well or ill, that we shall pay any price, bear any burden, meet any hardship, support any friend, oppose any foe to assure the survival and the success of liberty.

This much we pledge—and more.

To those old allies whose cultural and spiritual origins we share, we pledge the loyalty of faithful friends. United, there is little we cannot do in a host of cooperative ventures. Divided, there is little we can do—for we dare not meet a powerful challenge at odds and split asunder.

To those new states whom we welcome to the ranks of the free, we pledge our word that one form of colonial control shall not have passed away merely to be replaced by a far more iron tyranny. We shall not always expect to find them supporting our view. But we shall always hope to find them strongly supporting their own freedom—and to remember that, in the past, those who foolishly sought power by riding the back of the tiger ended up inside.

To those peoples in the huts and villages of half the globe struggling to break the bonds of mass misery, we pledge our best efforts to help them help themselves, for whatever period is required—not because the communists may be doing it, not because we seek their votes, but because it is right. If a free society cannot help the many who are poor, it cannot save the few who are rich.

To our sister republics south of our border, we offer a special pledge —to convert our good words into good deeds—in a new alliance for progress—to assist free men and free governments in casting off the chains of poverty. But this peaceful revolution of hope cannot become the prey of hostile powers. Let all our neighbors know that we shall join with them to oppose aggression or subversion anywhere in the Americas. And let every other power know that this Hemisphere intends to remain the master of its own house.

To that world assembly of sovereign states, the United Nations, our last best hope in an age where the instruments of war have far outpaced the instruments of peace, we renew our pledge of support—to prevent it from becoming merely a forum for invective—to strengthen its shield of the new and the weak—and to enlarge the area in which its writ may run.

Finally, to those nations who would make themselves our adversary, we offer not a pledge but a request: that both sides begin anew the quest for peace, before the dark powers of destruction unleashed by science engulf all humanity in planned or accidental self-destruction.

We dare not tempt them with weakness. For only when our arms are sufficient beyond doubt can we be certain beyond doubt that they will never be employed.

But neither can two great and powerful groups of nations take comfort from our present course—both sides overburdened by the cost of modern weapons, both rightly alarmed by the steady spread of the deadly atom, yet both racing to alter that uncertain balance of terror that stays the hand of mankind's final war.

So let us begin anew—remembering on both sides that civility is not a sign of weakness, and sincerity is always subject to proof. Let us never negotiate out of fear. But let us never fear to negotiate.

Let both sides explore what problems unite us instead of belaboring those problems which divide us.

Let both sides, for the first time, formulate serious and precise proposals for the inspection and control of arms—and bring the absolute power to destroy other nations under the absolute control of all nations.

Let both sides seek to invoke the wonders of science instead of its terrors. Together let us explore the stars, conquer the deserts, eradicate disease, tap the ocean depths and encourage the arts and commerce.

Let both sides unite to heed in all corners of the earth the command of Isaiah—to "undo the heavy burdens . . . (and) let the oppressed go free."

And if a beach-head of cooperation may push back the jungle of suspicion, let both sides join in creating a new endeavor, not a new balance of power, but a new world of law, where the strong are just and the weak secure and the peace preserved.

All this will not be finished in the first one hundred days. Nor will it be finished in the first one thousand days, nor in the life of this Administration, nor even perhaps in our lifetime on this planet. But let us begin.

In your hands, my fellow citizens, more than mine, will rest the final success or failure of our course. Since this country was founded, each generation of Americans has been summoned to give testimony to its national loyalty. The graves of young Americans who answered the call to service surround the globe.

Now the trumpet summons us again—not as a call to bear arms, though arms we need—not as a call to battle, though embattled we are —but a call to bear the burden of a long twilight struggle, year in and year out, "rejoicing in hope, patient in tribulation"—a struggle against the common enemies of man: tyranny, poverty, disease and war itself.

Can we forge against these enemies a grand and global alliance, North and South, East and West, that can assure a more fruitful life for all mankind? Will you join in that historic effort?

In the long history of the world, only a few generations have been granted the role of defending freedom in its hour of maximum danger. I do not shrink from this responsibility—I welcome it. I do not believe that any of us would exchange places with any other people or any other generation. The energy, the faith, the devotion which we bring to this endeavor will light our country and all who serve it—and the glow from that fire can truly light the world.

And so, my fellow Americans: ask not what your country can do for you —ask what you can do for your country.

My fellow citizens of the world: ask not what America will do for you, but what together we can do for the freedom of man.

Finally, whether you are citizens of America or citizens of the world, ask of us here the same high standards of strength and sacrifice which we ask of you. With a good conscience our only sure reward, with history the final judge of our deeds, let us go forth to lead the land we love, asking His blessing and His help, but knowing that here on earth God's work must truly be our own.

2. Rockefeller Brothers Fund
The Democratic Prospect for America in the 1960s

The Special Studies Project of the Rockefeller Brothers Fund was organized in 1956 to do three things: to define the primary problems and opportunities that the United States would face in the 1960s, to clarify national purposes and objectives, and to develop a framework of concepts and principles on which national policies could be soundly based. The project grew out of a belief that the United States, while a majestic democratic success, faced a critical situation in the years immediately ahead, particularly because of the existence of communist systems abroad. More than 100 leaders from many walks of life, working together over a period of four years, produced lengthy reports on U.S. foreign policy, military security, foreign economic policy, domestic social and economic policies, and the American educational system.

"The Power of the Democratic Idea," the sixth and final report, was first published in September 1960. A hopeful statement of the prospects for American democracy, it rests on the belief that the complexities of modern society can be understood and regulated beneficently only by free men, and that only free men can provide themselves with the opportunities for the moral and intellectual growth that the times require. A further recurrent theme is the belief in the individual as the supreme fact of life, his spiritual and material well-being the supreme test of all social policy. It is questionable whether the authors of the several Rockefeller reports would have agreed with President Kennedy's often-quoted appeal that citizens ask not what their country could do for them but what they could do for their country because the special-studies panel concluded that "the role of the state, and of all our institutions, is to serve the individual. The citizen is not their servant: they are his."

The following essay, principally authored by Charles Frankel, professor of philosophy at Columbia University, raises many other questions. In an important paragraph, Frankel writes that a government is responsible only when decision makers are visible and can be held accountable, when they can be asked questions, and when they must answer questions. Upon failing to do so, they can be deprived of their power. To ask the right questions, citizens need accurate and sufficient information and also the ability to evaluate the answers they receive. How effective operationally was the ideal of government by the consent of the governed during the ensuing decade? What has been the status of what Frankel calls the "fundamental ideals that distinguish a democratic moral outlook": committment to an open society, equal membership in the moral community, and respect for individual diversity and privacy? To what degree does Frankel's often-eloquent statement reflect the possibilities rather than realities of the American political and economic system? Does the author's loving espousal of the politics of consensus—fidelity to "the rules of the game"—preclude the entrance of minority and dissenting groups into the circles of power? How can effective individual liberty, based on the power of choice, thrive in the midst of a powerful ideological consensus? Hopefully, the selections in this anthology provide some basis for answering these and similar questions and for assessing the effectiveness of American political and economic institutions in the 1960s.

I. The Ideals of Democracy

Every society gives spontaneous signs of the moral weather in which it normally lives. The attitudes of the men and women who compose it will be revealed in their manners, in their behavior toward their parents, their children, and one another, in the atmosphere of their schools, churches, and public squares, in their games and jokes. What the members of a society expect in life and what they think is right and decent will show itself not only in what they explicitly say but in what they do not bother to say.

This is as true of a democratic society as it is of any other. Because democracy gives so much freedom to the individual and leaves so much to his powers of judgment and self-discipline, it depends more than most other forms of government on an unspoken atmosphere and on the willing allegiance of most of its citizens to certain moral principles. A democratic form of government may exist in a society where this atmosphere and moral outlook are weak or still in the process of development. But in any society where democratic government can be said to be reasonably safe, certain attitudes will be deeply ingrained and certain ideals will be widely shared.

What are the fundamental ideals that distinguish a democratic moral outlook?

Democracy's Commitment to an Open Society
A distinctive conviction marks a democratic society. One part of this conviction is that all human arrangements are fallible. A second part is that men can improve the societies they inhabit if they are given the facts and are free to compare things as they are with their vision of things as they ought to be. It is a defining characteristic of a democratic society, accord-

ingly, that nothing in its political or social life is immune to criticism and that it establishes and protects institutions whose purpose it is to subject the existing order of things to steady examination.

This process of self-examination has certain special features. It is conducted in the open. All members of the community are presumed to be free to engage in it, and all are held to be entitled to true information about the state of their society. Moreover, in a democratic society such public criticism has immediate and practical objectives. Men who are imbued with the democratic attitude are not likely to be content with the promise that the realization of their ideals must be put off to an indefinite future. They will want to see these ideals make a difference here and now.

A commitment to democracy, in short, is a commitment to an "open society." Democracy accepts its own fallibility. But it provides a method by which its mistakes can be corrected. It recognizes that men can be power-hungry and prone to self-delusion, that they can prefer old errors to new truths, that they can act without caring about what they are doing to others. And it believes that these human tendencies can only be held in check if they are exposed to the open air and subjected to other men's continuing judgment. This is the way, in the democratic view, that the goodness and rationality of men can have a chance to grow.

Equal Membership in the Moral Community

This belief in a process of criticism that is open to all brings us to another fundamental principle of a democratic outlook. The man with democratic feelings and convictions looks upon all men as members of the same moral community and as initially endowed with the same fundamental rights and obligations. He does not determine his obligations to others by considering their status in society or their racial or religious backgrounds. The respect and concern that a democratically-minded person shows for other men are shown for them as individuals; this respect and concern do not depend on their membership in any group.

Ideas that have kindled the struggle for democracy in the modern world—the rights of man, the dignity of the individual—have expressed this attitude. In this sense, the history of democracy records the growth in scope of man's sense of moral concern. Moreover, this democratic moral sense generally implies something not only about the goals that men should seek but the spirit in which they should seek them. A man of democratic temper will pursue human welfare, but he will not do so in a context of rigid ranks and hierarchies. For he seeks more than the improvement of men's material condition, he seeks their development as independent individuals and their entrance as full participants into the enterprises of their community. To believe in democracy is to wish to help individuals by giving them the tools to help themselves.

Respect for Individual Diversity and Privacy

This sense that all men have an initially equal right to membership in the same moral community suggests another element in the democratic image of the good society. This is the acceptance of the simple fact that human beings are different. It is one thing to believe that all men have a right to be treated in accordance with the same fundamental rules. It is quite another thing to believe that there is any single style of life that is good for everybody. The democratic view is that the burden of proof rests on those who argue that the individual is not the best judge of the way to run his own life. To care about democracy is to care about human beings, not en masse, but one by one. It is to adopt the working hypothesis that the individual, if given the right conditions, does not need a master or a tutor to take care of him. The devoted believer in democracy will act on this hypothesis until he is proved wrong. And he will act on it again when the next individual comes along. For he believes that the exercise of individual judgment is itself an ultimate good of life.

A considered democratic outlook, therefore, will place a special premium on the value of privacy. It will hold that there are aspects of the individual's life that no government may touch and that no public pressure may be allowed to invade. In the absence of very strong considerations to the contrary, these include the individual's right to bring up his children as he desires, to go where he wishes, to associate with those he chooses, and to live by his own religion and philosophy, staking his destiny on the rightness of his choice.

There is, therefore an extraordinary degree of human discipline involved in allegiance to a democratic ethic. It asks men to exercise their own judgments and to choose their own ultimate beliefs. But it asks them to care just as much about the liberties of others and the right of others to think differently. That such a discipline has actually been developed, and that it thrives at all, is a remarkable achievement. It is testimony to democracy's faith in the power of human intelligence and good will. But the very difficulty of this discipline indicates that the citizens of a democracy can never take the continued success of their social system for granted. There is always the temptation to relax such a discipline or to resent it. The survival of this discipline calls for constant vigilance.

Government by Consent

Obviously, a society that accepts the moral ideals that have been described can never say that its work is done. Nor can such a society have a neat and symmetrical design. It will be a mobile society without fixed class barriers, offering opportunities to individual talents and providing an arena within which diverse individuals can struggle for the achievement of their own purposes. Inevitably, furthermore, it will be a society in which groups clash and contend with one another and in which the determination and implementation of public policy must depend on something other than unanimous agreement.

We come at this point to a distinguishing feature of democracy as a political system. Democratic political arrangements rest on the recognition that shared purposes and cooperative endeavor are only one side of any complex society and that disagreement and conflict of interests are also persisting characteristics of any such social order. The working principle of a democracy is to deal with such conflicts by bringing them out in the open and providing a legal and social framework for them. It is this principle that gives a distinctive meaning to the classic political ideal of democracy—the ideal of government by the consent of the governed—as it is understood in the United States and other democracies, and that sets off the theory and practice of these democracies from totalitarian forms of government that use and abuse democratic language.

In the American tradition, "the consent of the governed" has meant a number of things. It has meant, to begin with, that public policies should be subject to broad public discussion, that political leaders must be chosen in free elections where there is honest competition for votes, and that no one is punished or restrained, legally or extralegally, when he works for the political cause of his choice and remains short of violence and insurrection. But government by consent has also meant some things that are perhaps less obvious. For public discussion, free and honest elections, and the rights to freedom of speech and association are essential to achieving government by consent; but the history of democracy in the last century is marked by the growing recognition that they are not sufficient.

In addition to the legal guarantees that are implied by the ideal of government by consent, certain broad social conditions are also implied. Individuals with grievances, men and women with ideas and visions, are the sources of any society's power to improve itself. Modern democracy is an effort to provide such individuals not only with the freedom to struggle for what they think right but with some of the practical tools of struggle. Government by consent means that such individuals must eventually be able to find groups that will work with them and must be able to make their voices heard in these groups. It means that all important groups in the community should have a chance to try to influence the decisions that are made. And it means that social and economic power should be widely diffused in the community at large, so that no group is insulated from competition and criticism. The maintenance of such conditions is the steady business of a democratic society.

What such a society seeks is responsible government. Moreover, it seeks this ideal in a special way. Judged from its working procedures, a democracy does not define "responsible government" as government by men who are benevolent, intelligent, and unselfishly interested in the general welfare. Naturally, a democracy seeks such men, and it will prosper if it finds them. But in aiming at responsible government, a democracy has its eye mainly on institutions, not persons. No matter how able its leaders, or how morally responsible they are as individuals, it reposes only a careful and limited confidence in them.

From the democratic point of view, a government is a responsible government only when those who make the decisions on which other men's destinies depend can be held effectively accountable for the results of their decisions. This means that they can be asked questions, that they have to give answers which satisfy those who ask them, and that they can be deprived of their power if they fail to do so. It means, moreover, that the decision makers in a society are visible and that it is possible to fix responsibility for a policy on definite individuals or groups. Finally, it means that those who ask the questions must know how to ask the right ones and must have sufficient information and good sense to judge the answers they receive intelligently. To list these criteria of responsible government is to remind ourselves not only of what democracy has achieved but also of how much still remains to be accomplished and of new and urgent problems that have emerged in the present generation.

Thus, the ideal of government by consent involves more than free elections and constitutional government. It calls for the existence of instruments of communication that men can use to get in touch with one another when they wish to join together in a common cause. It demands that these instruments of communication be generally available to the community rather than monopolistically controlled. It requires the existence of independent groups that can give expression to the diverse interests that are bound to prevail in any sophisticated modern society and that can do so openly, legally, and without fear of persecution. It requires that these groups be democratically controlled. Most of all, if government by consent is to work over the long pull, it needs the support of a population in which the average level of education is high. A people that dedicates itself to free government cares about its schools as it will care about little else. Government by consent does not exist once and for all, and a people cannot passively enjoy it. They must steadily create it.

Free government thus depends on men and women who possess a subtle blend of skills and attitudes. The ideal citizen of a democracy has enough spirit to question the decisions of his leaders and enough sense of responsibility to let decisions be made. He has enough pride to refuse to be awed by authority and enough humility to recognize that he, too, is limited in knowledge and in the power to be perfectly disinterested. And while he is good-humored when others win fairly, he is implacable toward those who play unfairly. Such qualities of mind and character are not easily come by, but they are the secret, the inner mystery, of a flourishing democracy.

The Democratic Wager

Democratic ideals, like any other ideals, do not exist in a void. They rest on assumptions and express a faith. There is an ultimate conviction and a supreme act of faith behind the ideals of democracy. The conviction is that the value of all human arrangements must be measured by what they do to enhance the life of the individual—to help him to grow in knowledge, sensitivity, and the mastery of himself and his destiny. The faith is that the individual has the capacity to meet this challenge.

The faith must be stated carefully, for it is complex and subtle. Restraints that democracies place on the men who govern them are based on a tough and realistic conception of the actual character of human beings. Constitutional government is a conscious effort to place checks on the power of all individuals; it foresees no time when men can afford to assume that any among them are free from imperfection. "Sometimes it is said that man cannot be trusted with the government of himself," Jefferson once observed. "Can he, then, be trusted with the government of others? Or have we found angels in the forms of kings to govern him?"

Jefferson's remark catches both sides of the democratic faith. Democracy does not expect men to be angels; but it does not propose to treat them, therefore, as sheep. The great wager on which it stakes its destiny is that the imperfectible individual is improvable. And it believes that the best way to improve him is to let him improve himself, to give him as much responsibility as possible for his own destiny and for the destiny of the community to which he belongs. Democratic governments have been prepared to take positive steps to free the individual from avoidable handicaps so that he can run the race on fair terms with others. They are committed today to providing all individuals with the basic forms of economic security that are essential to a decent life. But their objective is not to produce tame, well-tended men and women who are easy to harness to a master plan. Their objective is to release the powers of individuals and to turn loose the flow of human initiative.

There is, therefore, a kind of inner tension that is perennially present in the democratic way of life. A democracy must balance its faith in the potentialities of the individual against its realistic appraisal of his capacities for judgment and responsible behavior. It cannot simply give him room to live his own life; it must also place restrictions upon him. Each generation must make new decisions on this issue, and there is no easy formula by which the questions it raises can be settled. In large measure, men must deal with them by deciding what they wish human life to be and placing their faith and effort on that side of the scales. Democracy, if it must err, chooses to err by trusting the ordinary individual. If it must choose between what he is and what he can be, it leans in the latter direction and places its long-range bet on what he can be.

This faith and purpose give dynamism to the democratic principles that have been described. A democracy's commitment to the continuing criticism of itself is not due to an inner malaise or lack of confidence. It expresses the belief that nothing deserves a higher loyalty from men than the truth and that the only way in which fallible men can find the truth is to keep the process of inquiry open. Democracy bets that men can bear the rigors of this process and learn to love it. And it bets that it will be a stronger social system as a result. For it is the one form of society that has institutionalized the process of reform.

A democracy, therefore, will measure its success in a distinctive way. In the last analysis it will judge itself by the character of the men and women who make it up and the quality of the lives they lead. A democratic society cannot be indifferent to the condition of its economy, the development of its technology, or the material possessions in the hands of its people. It is dangerous sentimentality to think that such issues are unimportant either practically or morally. But a democratic society that has kept its balance and sense of direction will recognize that they are means, not ends. The end is the individual—his self-awareness, his personal powers, the richness of his life. Democracy aims at the individual who can live responsibly with his fellows while he follows standards he has set for himself.

A Democracy's Need to be on the Move

There are many reasons for believing that this democratic wager has been worth making. In the United States, a continental nation has been governed. Successive waves of immigrants have been absorbed into a common way of life, and their children have found the opportunities for which their parents came. American democracy has gone far in delivering men from poverty, in releasing them from the stifling boxes of caste and class, in opening careers to talent, and in making performance rather than inheritance the key to men's positions in life. And having accomplished its great absorbing work of settling a continent, American democracy has gone on to other tasks and carried them off with equal *élan*.

Within the last generation, it has modernized its economic system and fought, together with its allies, a victorious war against an extraordinary threat to the values of all civilized men. It has turned almost overnight from a long policy of isolation to one of active participation in keeping the peace of the world. It has shown itself capable of original social inventions like the Marshall Plan abroad and the Tennessee Valley Authority at home. It has accomplished all this, furthermore, while preserving individual freedom and extending it at many points. American democracy has shown that it has resilience, flexibility, and the power to meet emergencies. The achievement justifies the democratic faith that free citizens can successfully work out their problems together if they are given the chance to try.

While a democracy can take confidence from its past accomplishments, it cannot live on them. Democracy is a system which aims at the minimum of coercion and the maximum of voluntary co-operation. If it is to excite men's devotion it needs to be on the move, and it needs citizens who are alert to the business they have left unfinished and the new business they must undertake. The citizens of America have an educational system that needs strengthening. The problem of mass media of communication as a source of public information and not only as a form of entertainment, intensified by the coming into existence of television, has only begun to receive the attention it requires. The elimination of racial barriers is another piece of unfinished business, and time is growing short. The American people have only begun to realize the extraordinary perils for them and for all humanity in the contrast between their own wealth and the poverty of most of mankind.

Not least, few have as yet asked themselves, earnestly and steadily, what their prosperity is for and where their real wealth lies. A transition to an economy of comfort has been made, but the development of discriminating standards and the projection of goals that will excite the imagination of the concerned citizens of America has still to come. In the past, Americans have responded well when confronted by immediate emergencies and obvious injustices. The great question is whether a comfortable people can respond to an emergency that is chronic and to problems that require a long effort and a sustained exercise of will and imagination.

Questions Democracy Must Face

The marshaling of democratic energies will have to take account of emerging conditions that obscure the democratic idea at many points and challenge its viability at others. The questions American democracy now faces range from the rebuilding of American cities to the proper organization and encouragement of scientific research, from the co-ordination of our foreign activities to the co-ordination of the activities of our state and federal governments, and from the allocation of our national wealth between public and private purposes to the development of new skills in the use of leisure. But underneath these and the myriad other problems that confront the United States, there are certain long-range conditions with which our country, as a country in the modern world, must deal. First and foremost, it faces the problem of keeping the peace and the related problem of maintaining the climate of freedom, at home and in the world, through a prolonged period of international tension. American democracy confronts a massive challenge—the rise to power of enormous nations charged with a sense of mission and governed by men who have set out to prove that our social order cannot keep up the pace if it is put to the test of serious and sustained competition. America today must obey an ultimate imperative—the imperative to survive and to survive in freedom. It must do so while the world confronts the unprecedented danger of nuclear weapons. It will be a complex and subtle effort for Americans to keep their defenses in order and to steer a sane course between impulsiveness and irresolution while they seek to avoid nuclear war and to find ways of assuring the peace of the world.

The success of America's efforts on the international scene will depend in large part on what Americans do at home. Both at home and aboard, American democracy must wrestle with other fundamental issues. One is the unprecedented speed and the radical impact of technological change. A second is the preservation and nourishing of individual freedom, originality, and responsibility in the world of large organizations that has come into being. A third is the impact at home of what has come to be known as "the revolution of rising expectations." This revolution is stirring millions of people abroad and creating for their governments tremendous tasks in economic growth, education, and communication. It has begun to make a visible difference within the Soviet Union and its satellites. And it is taking place in the United States as well, where there is an extraordinary pressure not only for material goods but for the qualitative enrichment of individual life through education, music, books, and the significant use of leisure.

These are interests that have traditionally been the special prerogative of the few. The expectation that they can be shared by the many is fundamentally democratic. If it is to be satisfied and if the standards and the sense of excellence of a discriminating civilization are to be preserved, a major effort in education and communication is required, and a thoroughly reconsidered one. Democracy thrives on the virtues of patience, good humor, and moderation. It will need all these. But it needs excitement, too. There is more than enough excitement in the problems it faces to keep American democracy occupied for some time.

Is American democracy capable of dealing with these issues? Is democracy too loose, too slow, too inefficient, to move with the speed, concentration, and daring these problems demand? Can it set definite goals, follow long-range plans, and pull its citizens together for a concerted effort to achieve clearly formulated objectives? Is democracy a dangerous luxury or an historical anachronism for which there is no longer any room? To begin to answer these questions we must stand back and see what we have. So it is to an account and appraisal of the fundamental characteristics of the American democratic process that we now turn.

II. Consensus in a Democratic Society

American democracy faces the test of an era in which the pace and scope of change are unprecedented. Everywhere, and not least in the United States, habits of thought and patterns of behavior that represent the inheritance of centuries are rapidly losing or have already lost their force. And in many parts of the world, aggressive ideologies have arisen that exercise a wide appeal. Leaning on democratic ideals at some points and subtly distorting them at others, they also challenge the democratic outlook in fundamental ways. If a democratic society is to sail through such storms and arrive successfully at destinations of its own choosing, it must possess inner forces of stability and cohesion on which it can call.

The first question we must therefore consider is the way in which the many groups and interests that compose a democratic society are held together. When a society concerts its efforts for the sake of common goals and when it does so without recourse to violence or terror, it counts on the existence of certain generally held beliefs, attitudes, and feelings. Let us begin by asking what kind of agreement a democracy may and must enforce.

Allegiance to the Rules of the Game

The answer must begin with the recognition that democratic ideals have their origins in a variety of religious and secular traditions and that there is no single embracing philosophy which all citizens of a democracy can be expected to share. Experience shows that men can be equally loyal to democratic ideals even though they give different ultimate reasons for their loyalty. In the United States, Protestants, Catholics, Jews, and freethinkers have all found it possible to agree about the validity of democratic ideals. The practice of toleration that characterizes free societies is the hard-won product of bitter experience. As the religious wars of the sixteenth and seventeenth centuries and the ideological purges in contemporary totalitarian societies indicate, the effort to impose unity of belief in matters of religion and ultimate philosophy, far from unifying a society, can lead to extraordinary bloodshed and brutality and can breed hostilities which it can take centuries to erase.

Accordingly, there is no official creed—religious, philosophical, or scientific—that a democratic state can impose on its citizens. Each individual is free to try to win his fellows to his own views by every fair means. Truth in matters of religion, philosophy, or science cannot be determined by vote, popular pressure, or governmental fiat. The issues with which these fundamental human enterprises are concerned are too important to be regulated by political expediencies, real or alleged. In a democracy the state is neutral with regard to religion, philosophy, or science, and citizens are free to decide for themselves where they stand in relation to the ultimate questions concerning the nature of the universe and man's place within it. This is one reason why those who are deeply concerned about these matters are likely to prize democracy. Democracy does not ask them to conceal, compromise, or apologize for their views on issues so important that concealment, compromise, and apology are incompatible with honor and conscience. In short, cohesion is achieved in a democratic society, in the first instance, by carefully removing certain questions from the sphere of politics, by separating the things that are Caesar's from the things that are God's.

But if a democracy does not demand that all its citizens accept a common religion or view of the cosmos, what is the nature of the agreement at which it must aim and which successful democracies have largely achieved? It consists in a shared allegiance to the rules by which social decisions are reached.

In a democratic society it is expected that men will hold different aims and ideas and that these aims and ideas will sometimes clash. If common policies are achieved and enforced in such a society and if citizens accept peaceably the defeat of their hopes in the public arena, the reason is that they believe it better in the long run to yield and fight another day rather than sacrifice the rules by which victory in such a struggle is determined. In a democracy the preservation of those rules normally takes priority over the achievement of any other social purpose. This is the heart of the democratic political ethic, and the allegiance of an individual to this ethic is the acid test of his allegiance to democracy.

Allegiance to the rules of the democratic competition is not pure ritualism. Written into the rules governing the democratic process are principles that provide for orderly change in the rules themselves. Moreover, the rules that define fair democratic competition are of at least two kinds. Some, like the electoral process or the right of freedom of assembly, are set forth in explicit laws. If governmental decisions are made in contravention of rules of this sort, they lack authority and do not carry a mandate that must be obeyed. Other rules of the democratic process, however, are matters not of legal procedure but of ethical principle. They cover matters too subtle and intricate to be spelled out in detail, but they are exemplified by such principles as honesty in stating the facts, a separation of a public official's public duties from his private interests, and refusal to impugn the loyalty of one's opponents in legitimate democratic competition. The success of the democratic process depends to a considerable extent on the degree to which citizens adhere to such unwritten rules. For unwritten moral assumptions affect the way that written rules are applied and the respect that men hold for these rules. If men think the rules of the game are mere rituals without an ethical substance behind them, they will look upon the rules as deceptions or as meaningless frivolities. When a democratic consensus is vigorous, therefore, loyalty to the rules of the game is loyalty to the inner spirit as well as the external forms of democracy.

Formation of a Democracy's Working Consensus
A minimal agreement to abide by the rules of the democratic process is not enough, however, to produce effective and resolute government in a democracy. Free discussion will yield no practical results unless men talk directly to each other, unless they address themselves to common problems and share some common assumptions; disagreement and conflicts of interest cannot terminate in agreements that men accept voluntarily unless they find a common ground on which to negotiate. In addition to generally shared allegiance to the rules of the game, democracy also requires a practical working consensus about definite issues.

What is this "working consensus"? In any stable democracy that has the power to get ahead with its business, a body of opinion and principle tends to grow up and to be widely shared. Men are not forced or legislated into such a consensus, and no one in a democracy can be required to accept it. But habit, sentiment, common experience, and the appropriate social conditions all contrive to produce it. And if it does not exist, even common allegiance to the rules of the game is jeopardized.

The working consensus serves to define the issues that must be solved and the effective limits of the political dialogue at any given time. Disagreements, often fundamental ones, arise within it; and citizens who stand outside the prevailing consensus often make precious contributions to democracy precisely because they do so. Nevertheless, when such an informal working agreement exists, it serves to define what is and what is not a significant matter for public debate; and in a successful democracy such a consensus usually does exist. Thus, there may be controversy today about the priority that should be given to slum clearance in comparison with other projects, but there is now no debate about whether the elimination of slums falls within the area of the public interest. In short, the decisions that are made in a democracy, the compromises that are reached, and the actions that are taken are made in an environing moral and intellectual atmosphere.

Role of Compromise. How is this working consensus achieved? To a large extent it is achieved by compromise, which is the workaday instrument of practical democracy. In the best of worlds, men have different interests, and since resources are scarce, no individual, no matter how admirable his purposes, can do everything he pleases. The effort of a democracy is to arrive at arrangements that will convince most men that their interests have been taken at least partly into account. Democracy thus depends on the ability of its citizens to negotiate peacefully with each other, to give as well as receive, and to arrive at understandings to which they will mutually adhere. Such understandings form the point of departure for the next round of the democratic debate.

Far from representing a lapse from principle, compromise thus represents one of democracy's most signal achievements. Compromise is incompatible with an unbending commitment to an abstract ideology; but it does not imply weak wills or fuzzy minds. Groups within a democracy may and do struggle hard for the achievement of their purposes; and if they do not achieve their full program at any given moment, they can continue to struggle until they do. The ethic of compromise does not call for them to abandon the struggle for their ultimate purposes. It calls for them only to carry on their fight at all times within the rules of the democratic process. They will use the courts, the press, peaceful public demonstrations, strikes, and elections; they will not use violence, slander, personal threats, or bribes. A notable example from the past of this sort of resolute struggle was the campaign for legislation against child labor. A current example, remarkable for its courage, restraint, and respect for democratic procedures, is the campaign American Negroes are waging for full citizenship.

II. Crisis in Black and White

3. Martin Luther King, Jr.
Letter from Birmingham Jail

The faith in the politics of consensus expressed in the previous selection met its first major test when the civil-rights question emerged as the foremost domestic issue during the early 1960s. It is ironic that this should have been the case because the 1960s marked the centennial of the Civil War. During the century after Appomattox the segregation of black people in eating places, streetcars, buses, schools, and housing establishments were dominant realities of the American way of life. Voting rights were withheld, economic and social discrimination was practiced at every level of society, and legal justice was denied, although in the case of segregation, court decisions had, for more than 50 years, upheld a "separate but equal" doctrine that fostered separate facilities but failed to make them equal.

Encouraged by the landmark Supreme Court decision in the case of *Brown v. Board of Education* (May 1954), and spurred by the subsequent bitter resistance in most Southern states and only token efforts to integrate public schools, black leaders devised a strategy of nonviolent direct action, a dramatic form of civil disobedience, to combat racial discrimination and to achieve black liberation. In 1956, blacks in Montgomery, Alabama, boycotted the segregated bus transportation companies. The leader of the successful boycott was Dr. Martin Luther King, Jr., a young pastor of a local Baptist church, with a Ph.D. in systematic theology from Boston University. A devout Christian, King believed that only nonviolent tactics should be employed to achieve social change. He inspired millions of whites as well as blacks, and, for his courageous work in promoting brotherhood, was awarded the Nobel Peace Prize in 1964. On April 4, 1968, an assassin murdered Dr. King in Memphis, Tennessee. Never before in the nation's history had a black man been so mourned and so honored in death.

In the letter that follows, King, writing in a Birmingham jail, answers eight Alabama clergymen who had deplored the nonviolent sit-ins and demonstrations against segregation in Birmingham, calling them "unwise and untimely." The turbulent demonstrations occasioned the violence of snarling police dogs, the indiscriminate clubbing of blacks, and the use of powerful fire hoses against schoolchildren. In this most eloquent statement of his philosophy, King expresses disillusionment with white moderates and disappointment with the church, defines the doctrine of the higher moral law, draws attention to the historical reality that privileged groups seldom relinquish their privileges voluntarily, and discusses why black people can no longer wait for justice to come from the hands of a recalcitrant majority. King also makes clear his middle position between complacent elements of the Negro community and the movement for black nationalism.

April 16, 1963

My Dear Fellow Clergymen:

While confined here in the Birmingham city jail, I came across your recent statement calling my present activities "unwise and untimely." Seldom do I pause to answer criticism of my work and ideas. If I sought to answer all the criticisms that cross my desk, my secretaries would have little time for anything other than such correspondence in the course of the day, and I would have no time for constructive work. But since I feel that you are men of genuine good will and that your criticisms are sincerely set forth, I want to try to answer your statement in what I hope will be patient and reasonable terms.

I think I should indicate why I am here in Birmingham, since you have been influenced by the view which argues against "outsiders coming in." I have the honor of serving as president of the Southern Christian Leadership Conference, an organization operating in every southern state, with headquarters in Atlanta, Georgia. We have some eighty-five affiliated organizations across the South, and one of them is the Alabama Christian Movement for Human Rights. Frequently we share staff, educational and financial resources with our affiliates. Several months ago the affiliate here in Birmingham asked us to be on call to engage in a nonviolent direct-action program if such were deemed necessary. We readily consented, and when the hour came we lived up to our promise. So I, along with several members of my staff, am here because I was invited here. I am here because I have organizational ties here.

But more basically, I am in Birmingham because injustice is here. Just as the prophets of the eighth century B.C. left their villages and carried their "thus saith the Lord" far beyond the boundaries of their home towns, and just as the Apostle Paul left his village of Tarsus and carried the gospel of Jesus Christ to the far corners of the Greco-Roman world, so am I compelled to carry the gospel of freedom beyond my own home town. Like Paul, I must constantly respond to the Macedonian call for aid.

Moreover, I am cognizant of the interrelatedness of all communities and states. I cannot sit idly by in Atlanta and not be concerned about what happens in Birmingham. Injustice anywhere is a threat to justice everywhere. We are caught in an inescapable network of mutuality, tied in a single garment of destiny. Whatever affects one directly, affects all indirectly. Never again can we afford to live with the narrow, provincial "outside agitator" idea. Anyone who lives inside the United States can never be considered an outsider anywhere within its bounds.

You deplore the demonstrations taking place in Birmingham. But your statement, I am sorry to say, fails to express a similar concern for the conditions that brought about the demonstrations. I am sure that none of you would want to rest content with the superficial kind of social analysis that deals merely with effects and does not grapple with underlying causes. It is unfortunate that demonstrations are taking place in Birmingham, but is is even more unfortunate that the city's white power structure left the Negro community with no alternative.

In any nonviolent campaign there are four basic steps: collection of the facts to determine whether injustices exist; negotiation; self-purification; and direct action. We have gone through all these steps in Birmingham. There can be no gainsaying the fact that racial injustice engulfs this community. Birmingham is probably the most thoroughly segregated city in the United States. Its ugly record of brutality is widely known. Negroes have experienced grossly unjust treatment in the courts. There have been more unsolved bombings of Negro homes and churches in Birmingham than in any other city in the nation. These are the hard, brutal facts of the case. On the basis of these conditions, Negro leaders sought to negotiate with the city fathers. But the latter consistently refused to engage in good-faith negotiation.

Then, last September, came the opportunity to talk with leaders of Birmingham's economic community. In the course of the negotiations, certain promises were made by the merchants—for example, to remove the stores' humiliating racial signs. On the basis of these promises, the Reverend Fred Shuttlesworth and the leaders of the Alabama Christian Movement for Human Rights agreed to a moratorium on all demonstrations. As the weeks and months went by, we realized that we were the victims of a broken promise. A few signs, briefly removed, returned; the others remained.

As in so many past experiences, our hopes had been blasted, and the shadow of deep disappointment settled upon us. We had no alternative except to prepare for direct action, whereby we would present our very bodies as a means of laying our case before the conscience of the local and the national community. Mindful of the difficulties involved, we decided to undertake a process of self-purification. We began a series of workshops on nonviolence, and we repeatedly asked ourselves: "Are you able to accept blows without retaliating?" "Are you able to endure the ordeal of jail?" We decided to schedule our direct-action program for the

Easter season, realizing that except for Christmas, this is the main shopping period of the year. Knowing that a strong economic-withdrawal program would be the by-product of direct action, we felt that this would be the best time to bring pressure to bear on the merchants for the needed change.

Then it occurred to us that Birmingham's mayoral election was coming up in March, and we speedily decided to postpone action until after election day. When we discovered that the Commissioner of Public Safety, Eugene "Bull" Connor, had piled up enough votes to be in the run-off, we decided again to postpone action until the day after the run-off so that the demonstrations could not be used to cloud the issues. Like many others, we waited to see Mr. Connor defeated, and to this end we endured postponement after postponement. Having aided in this community need, we felt that our direct-action program could be delayed no longer.

You may well ask: "Why direct action? Why sit-ins, marches and so forth? Isn't negotiation a better path?" You are quite right in calling for negotiation. Indeed, this is the very purpose of direct action. Nonviolent direct action seeks to create such a crisis and foster such a tension that a community which has constantly refused to negotiate is forced to confront the issue. It seeks so to dramatize the issue that it can no longer be ignored. My citing the creation of tension as part of the work of the nonviolent-resister may sound rather shocking. But I must confess that I am not afraid of the word "tension." I have earnestly opposed violent tension, but there is a type of constructive, nonviolent tension which is necessary for growth. Just as Socrates felt that it was necessary to create a tension in the mind so that individuals could rise from the bondage of myths and half-truths to the unfettered realm of creative analysis and objective appraisal, so must we see the need for nonviolent gadflies to create the kind of tension in society that will help men rise from the dark depths of prejudice and racism to the majestic heights of understanding and brotherhood.

The purpose of our direct-action program is to create a situation so crisis-packed that it will inevitably open the door to negotiation. I therefore concur with you in your call for negotiation. Too long has our beloved Southland been bogged down in a tragic effort to live in monologue rather than dialogue.

One of the basic points in your statement is that the action that I and my associates have taken in Birmingham is untimely. Some have asked: "Why didn't you give the new city administration time to act?" The only answer that I can give to this query is that the new Birmingham administration must be prodded about as much as the outgoing one, before it will act. We are sadly mistaken if we feel that the election of Albert Boutwell as mayor will bring the millennium to Birmingham. While Mr. Boutwell is a much more gentle person that Mr. Connor, they are both segregationists, dedicated to maintenance of the status quo. I have hope that Mr. Boutwell will be reasonable enough to see the futility of massive resistance to desegregation. But he will not see this without pressure from devotees of civil rights. My friends, I must say to you that we have not made a single gain in civil rights without determined legal and nonviolent pressure. Lamentably, it is an historical fact that privileged groups seldom give up their privileges voluntarily. Individuals may see the moral light and voluntarily give up their unjust posture; but, as Reinhold Niebuhr has reminded us, groups tend to be more immoral than individuals.

We know through painful experience that freedom is never voluntarily given by the oppressor; it must be demanded by the oppressed. Frankly, I have yet to engage in a direct-action campaign that was "well timed" in the view of those who have not suffered unduly from the disease of segregation. For years now I have heard the word "Wait!" It rings in the ear of every Negro with piercing familiarity. This "Wait" has almost always meant "Never." We must come to see, with one of our distinguished jurists, that "justice too long delayed is justice denied."

We have waited for more than 340 years for our constitutional and God-given rights. The nations of Asia and Africa are moving with jetlike speed toward gaining political independence, but we still creep at horse-and-buggy pace toward gaining a cup of coffee at a lunch counter. Perhaps it is easy for those who have never felt the stinging darts of segregation to say, "Wait." But when you have seen vicious mobs lynch your mothers and fathers at will and drown your sisters and brothers at whim; when you have seen hate-filled policemen curse, kick and even kill your black brothers and sisters; when you see the vast majority of your twenty million Negro brothers smothering in an airtight cage of poverty in the midst of an affluent society; when you suddenly find your tongue twisted and your speech stammering as you seek to explain to your six-year-old daughter why she can't go to the public amusement park that has just been advertised on television, and see tears welling up in her eyes when she is told that Funtown is closed to colored children, and see ominous clouds of inferiority beginning to form in her little mental sky, and see her beginning to distort her personality by developing an unconscious bitterness toward white people; when you have to concoct an answer for a five-year-old son who is asking: "Daddy, why do white people treat colored people so mean?"; when you take a cross-country drive and find it necessary to sleep night after night in the uncomfortable corners of your automobile because no motel will accept you; when you are humiliated day in and day out by nagging signs reading "white" and "colored"; when your first name becomes "nigger," your middle name becomes "boy" (however old you are) and your last name becomes "John," and your wife and mother are never given the respected title "Mrs."; when you are harried by day and haunted by night by the fact that you are a Negro, living constantly at tiptoe stance, never quite knowing what to expect next, and are plagued with inner fears and outer resentments; when you are forever fighting a degenerating sense of "nobodiness"—then you will understand why we find it difficult to wait. There comes a time when the cup of endurance runs over, and men are no longer willing to be plunged into the abyss of despair. I hope, sirs, you can understand our legitimate and unavoidable impatience.

You express a great deal of anxiety over our willingness to break laws. This is certainly a legitimate concern. Since we so diligently urge people to obey the Supreme Court's decision of 1954 outlawing segregation in the public schools, at first glance it may seem rather paradoxical for us consciously to break laws. One may well ask: "How can you advocate breaking some laws and obeying others?" The answer lies in the fact that there are two types of laws: just and unjust. I would be the first to advocate obeying just laws. One has not only a legal but a moral responsibility to obey just laws. Conversely, one has a moral responsibility to disobey unjust laws. I would agree with St. Augustine that "an unjust law is no law at all."

Now, what is the difference between the two? How does one determine whether a law is just or unjust? A just law is a man-made code that squares with the moral law or the law of God. An unjust law is a code that is out of harmony with the moral law. To put it in the terms of St. Thomas Aquinas: An unjust law is a human law that is not rooted in eternal law and natural law. Any law that uplifts human personality is just. Any law that degrades human personality is unjust. All segregation statutes are unjust because segregation distorts the soul and damages the personality. It gives the segregator a false sense of superiority and the segregated a false sense of inferiority. Segregation, to use the terminology of the Jewish philosopher Martin Buber, substitutes an "I—it" relationship for an "I—thou" relationship and ends up relegating persons to the status of things. Hence segregation is not only politically, economically and sociologically unsound, it is morally wrong and sinful. Paul Tillich has said that sin is separation. Is not segregation an existential expression of man's tragic separation, his awful estrangement, his terrible sinfulness? Thus it is that I can urge men to obey the 1954 decision of the Supreme Court, for it is morally right; and I can urge them to disobey segregation ordinances, for they are morally wrong.

Let us consider a more concrete example of just and unjust laws. An unjust law is a code that a numerical or power majority group compels a minority group to obey but does not make binding on itself. This is *dif-ference* made legal. By the same token, a just law is a code that a majority compels a minority to follow and that it is willing to follow itself. This is *sameness* made legal.

Let me give another explanation. A law is unjust if it is inflicted on a minority that, as a result of being denied the right to vote, had no part in enacting or devising the law. Who can say that the legislature of Alabama which set up that state's segregation laws was democratically elected? Throughout Alabama all sorts of devious methods are used to prevent Negroes from becoming registered voters, and there are some counties in which, even though Negroes constitute a majority of the population, not a single Negro is registered. Can any law enacted under such circumstances be considered democratically structured?

Sometimes a law is just on its face and unjust in its application. For instance, I have been arrested on a charge of parading without a permit. Now, there is nothing wrong in having an ordinance which requires a permit for a parade. But such an ordinance becomes unjust when it is used to maintain segregation and to deny citizens the First-Amendment privilege of peaceful assembly and protest.

I hope you are able to see the distinction I am trying to point out. In no sense do I advocate evading or defying the law, as would the rabid segregationist. That would lead to anarchy. One who breaks an unjust law must do so openly, lovingly, and with a willingness to accept the penalty. I submit that an individual who breaks a law that conscience tells him is unjust, and who willingly accepts the penalty of imprisonment in order to arouse the conscience of the community over its injustice, is in reality expressing the highest respect for law.

Of course, there is nothing new about this kind of civil disobedience. It was evidenced sublimely in the refusal of Shadrach, Meshach and Abednego to obey the laws of Nebuchadnezzar, on the ground that a higher moral law was at stake. It was practiced superbly by the early Christians, who were willing to face hungry lions and the excruciating pain of chopping blocks rather than submit to certain unjust laws of the Roman Empire. To a degree, academic freedom is a reality today because Socrates practiced civil disobedience. In our own nation, the Boston Tea Party represented a massive act of civil disobedience.

We should never forget that everything Adolf Hitler did in Germany was "legal" and everything the Hungarian freedom fighters did in Hungary was "illegal." It was "illegal" to aid and comfort a Jew in Hitler's Germany. Even so, I am sure that, had I lived in Germany at the time, I would have aided and comforted my Jewish brothers. If today I lived in a Communist country where certain principles dear to the Christian faith are suppressed, I would openly advocate disobeying that country's antireligious laws.

I must make two honest confessions to you, my Christian and Jewish brothers. First, I must confess that over the past few years I have been gravely disappointed with the white moderate. I have almost reached the regrettable conclusion that the Negro's great stumbling block in his stride toward freedom is not the White Citizen's Counciler or the Ku Klux Klanner, but the white moderate, who is more devoted to "order" than to justice; who prefers a negative peace which is the absence of tension to a positive peace which is the presence of justice; who constantly says: "I agree with you in the goal you seek, but I cannot agree with your methods of direct action"; who paternalistically believes he can set the timetable for another man's freedom; who lives by a mythical concept of time and who constantly advises the Negro to wait for a "more convenient season." Shallow understanding from people of good will is more frustrating than absolute misunderstanding from people of ill will. Lukewarm acceptance is much more bewildering than outright rejection.

I had hoped that the white moderate would understand that law and order exist for the purpose of establishing justice and that when they fail in this purpose they become the dangerously structured dams that block the flow of social progress. I had hoped that the white moderate would understand that the present tension in the South is a necessary phase of the transition from an obnoxious negative peace, in which the Negro passively accepted his unjust plight, to a substantive and positive peace, in which all men will respect the dignity and worth of human personality. Actually, we who engage in nonviolent direct action are not the creators of tension. We merely bring to the surface the hidden tension that is already alive. We bring it out in the open, where it can be seen and dealt with. Like a boil that can never be cured so long as it is covered up but must be opened with all its ugliness to the natural medicines of air and light, injustice must be exposed, with all the tension its exposure creates, to the light of human conscience and the air of national opinion before it can be cured.

In your statement you assert that our actions, even though peaceful, must be condemned because they precipitate violence. But is this a logical assertion? Isn't this like condemning a robbed man because his possession of money precipitated the evil act of robbery? Isn't this like condemning Socrates because his unswerving commitment to truth and his philosophical inquiries precipitated the act by the misguided populace in which they made him drink hemlock? Isn't this like condemning Jesus because his unique God-consciousness and never-ceasing devotion to God's will precipitated the evil act of crucifixion? We must come to see that, as the federal courts have consistently affirmed, it is wrong to urge an individual to cease his efforts to gain his basic constitutional rights because the quest may precipitate violence. Society must protect the robbed and punish the robber.

I had also hoped that the white moderate would reject the myth concerning time in relation to the struggle for freedom. I have just received a letter from a white brother in Texas. He writes: "All Christians know that the colored people will receive equal rights eventually, but it is possible that you are in too great a religious hurry. It has taken Christianity almost two thousand years to accomplish what it has. The teachings of Christ take time to come to earth." Such an attitude stems from a tragic misconception of time, from the strangely irrational notion that there is something in the very flow of time that will inevitably cure all ills. Actually, time itself is neutral; it can be used either destructively or constructively. More and more I feel that the people of ill will have used time much more effectively than have the people of good will. We will have to repent in this generation not merely for the hateful words and actions of the bad people but for the appalling silence of the good people. Human progress never rolls in on wheels of inevitability; it comes through the tireless efforts of men willing to be co-workers with God, and without this hard work, time itself becomes an ally of the forces of social stagnation. We must use time creatively, in the knowledge that the time is always ripe to do right. Now is the time to make real the promise of democracy and transform our pending national elegy into a creative psalm of brotherhood. Now is the time to lift our national policy from the quicksand of racial injustice to the solid rock of human dignity.

You speak of our activity in Birmingham as extreme. At first I was rather disappointed that fellow clergymen would see my nonviolent efforts as those of an extremist. I began thinking about the fact that I stand in the middle of two opposing forces in the Negro community. One is a force of complacency, made up in part of Negroes who, as a result of long years of oppression, are so drained of self-respect and a sense of "somebodiness" that they have adjusted to segregation; and in part of a few middle-class Negroes who, because of a degree of academic and economic security and because in some ways they profit by segregation, have become insensitive to the problems of the masses. The other force is one of bitterness and hatred, and it comes perilously close to advocating violence. It is expressed in the various black nationalist groups that are springing up across the nation, the largest and best-known being Elijah Muhammad's Muslim movement. Nourished by the Negro's frustration over the continued existence of racial discrimination, this movement is made up of people who have lost faith in America, who have absolutely repudiated Christianity, and who have concluded that the white man is an incorrigible "devil."

I have tried to stand between these two forces, saying that we need emulate neither the "do-nothingism" of the complacent nor the hatred and despair of the black nationalist. For there is the more excellent way of love and nonviolent protest. I am grateful to God that, through the influence of the Negro church, the way of nonviolence became an integral part of our struggle.

If this philosophy had not emerged, by now many streets of the South would, I am convinced, be flowing with blood. And I am further convinced that if our white brothers dismiss as "rabble-rousers" and "outside agitators" those of us who employ nonviolent direct action, and if they refuse to support our nonviolent efforts, millions of Negroes will, out of frustration and despair, seek solace and security in black-nationalist ideologies—a development that would inevitably lead to a frightening racial nightmare.

Oppressed people cannot remain oppressed forever. The yearning for freedom eventually manifests itself, and that is what has happened to the American Negro. Something within has reminded him of his birthright of freedom, and something without has reminded him that it can be gained. Consciously or unconsciously, he has been caught up by the *Zeitgeist,* and with his black brothers of Africa and his brown and yellow brothers of Asia, South America and the Caribbean, the United States Negro is moving with a sense of great urgency toward the promised land of racial justice. If one recognizes this vital urge that has engulfed the Negro community, one should readily understand why public demonstrations are taking place. The Negro has many pent-up resentments and latent frustrations, and he must release them. So let him march; let him make prayer pilgrimages to the city hall; let him go on freedom rides—and try to understand why he must do so. If his repressed emotions are not released in nonviolent ways, they will seek expression through violence; this is not a threat but a fact of history. So I have not said to my people: "Get rid of your discontent." Rather, I have tried to say that this normal and healthy discontent can be channeled into the creative outlet of nonviolent direct action. And now this approach is being termed extremist.

But though I was initially disappointed at being categorized as an extremist, as I continued to think about the matter I gradually gained a measure of satisfaction from the label. Was not Jesus an extremist for love: "Love your enemies, bless them that curse you, do good to them that hate you, and pray for them which despitefully use you, and persecute you." Was not Amos an extremist for justice: "Let justice roll down like waters and righteousness like an ever-flowing stream." Was not Paul an extremist for the Christian gospel: "I bear in my body the marks of the Lord Jesus." Was not Martin Luther an extremist: "Here I stand; I cannot do otherwise, so help me God." And John Bunyan: "I will stay in jail to the end of my days before I make a butchery of my conscience." And Abraham Lincoln: "This nation cannot survive half slave and half free." And Thomas Jefferson: "We hold these truths to be self-evident, that all men are created equal . . ." So the question is not whether we will be extremists, but what kind of extremists we will be. Will we be extremists for hate or for love? Will we be extremists for the preservation of injustice or for the extension of justice? In that dramatic scene on Calvary's hill three men were crucified. We must never forget that all three were crucified for the same crime—the crime of extremism. Two were extremists for immorality, and thus fell below their environment. The other, Jesus Christ, was an extremist for love, truth and goodness, and thereby rose above his environment. Perhaps the South, the nation and the world are in dire need of creative extremists.

I had hoped that the white moderate would see this need. Perhaps I was too optimistic; perhaps I expected too much. I suppose I should have realized that few members of the oppressor race can understand the deep groans and passionate yearnings of the oppressed race, and still fewer have the vision to see that injustice must be rooted out by strong, persistent and determined action. I am thankful, however, that some of our white brothers in the South have grasped the meaning of this social revolution and committed themselves to it. They are still all too few in quantity, but they are big in quality. Some—such as Ralph McGill, Lillian Smith, Harry Golden, James McBride Dabbs, Ann Braden and Sarah Patton Boyle—have written about our struggle in eloquent and prophetic terms. Others have marched with us down nameless streets of the South. They have languished in filthy, roach-infested jails, suffering the abuse and brutality of policemen who view them as "dirty nigger-lovers." Unlike so many of their moderate brothers and sisters, they have recognized the urgency of the moment and sensed the need for powerful "action" antidotes to combat the disease of segregation.

Let me take note of my other major disappointment. I have been so greatly disappointed with the white church and its leadership. Of course, there are some notable exceptions. I am not unmindful of the fact that each of you has taken some significant stands on this issue. I commend you, Reverend Stallings, for your Christian stand on this past Sunday, in welcoming Negroes to your worship service on a nonsegregated basis. I commend the Catholic leaders of this state for integrating Spring Hill College several years ago.

But despite these notable exceptions, I must honestly reiterate that I have been disappointed with the church. I do not say this as one of those negative critics who can always find something wrong with the church. I say this as a minister of the gospel, who loves the church; who was nurtured in its bosom; who has been sustained by its spiritual blessings and who will remain true to it as long as the cord of life shall lengthen.

When I was suddenly catapulted into the leadership of the bus protest in Montgomery, Alabama, a few years ago, I felt we would be supported by the white church. I felt that the white ministers, priests and rabbis of the South would be among our strongest allies. Instead, some have been outright opponents, refusing to understand the freedom movement and misrepresenting its leaders; all too many others have been more cautious than courageous and have remained silent behind the anesthetizing security of stained-glass windows. . . .

Before closing I feel impelled to mention one other point in your statement that has troubled me profoundly. You warmly commended the Birmingham police force for keeping "order" and "preventing violence." I doubt that you would have so warmly commended the police force if you had seen its dogs sinking their teeth into unarmed, nonviolent Negroes. I doubt that you would so quickly commend the policemen if you were to observe their ugly and inhumane treatment of Negroes here in the city jail; if you were to watch them push and curse old Negro women and young Negro girls; if you were to see them slap and kick old Negro men and young boys; if you were to observe them, as they did on two occasions, refuse to give us food because we wanted to sing our grace together. I cannot join you in your praise of the Birmingham police department.

It is true that the police have exercised a degree of discipline in handling the demonstrators. In this sense they have conducted themselves rather "nonviolently" in public. But for what purpose? To preserve the evil system of segregation. Over the past few years I have consistently preached that nonviolence demands that the means we use must be as pure as the ends we seek. I have tried to make clear that it is wrong to use immoral means to attain moral ends. But now I must affirm that it is just as wrong, or perhaps even more so, to use moral means to preserve immoral ends. Perhaps Mr. Connor and his policemen have been rather nonviolent in public, as was Chief Pritchett in Albany, Georgia, but they have used the moral means of nonviolence to maintain the immoral end of racial injustice. As T. S. Eliot has said: "The last temptation is the greatest treason: To do the right deed for the wrong reason."

I wish you had commended the Negro sit-inners and demonstrators of Birmingham for their sublime courage, their willingness to suffer and their amazing discipline in the midst of great provocation. One day the South will recognize its real heroes. They will be the James Merediths, with the noble sense of purpose that enables them to face jeering and hostile mobs, and with the agonizing loneliness that characterizes the life of the pioneer. They will be old, oppressed, battered Negro women, symbolized in a seventy-two-year-old woman in Montgomery, Alabama, who rose up with a sense of dignity and with her people decided not to ride segregated buses, and who responded with ungrammatical profundity to one who inquired about her weariness: "My feets is tired, but my soul is at rest." They will be the young high school and college students, the young ministers of the gospel and a host of their elders, courageously and nonviolently sitting in at lunch counters and willingly going to jail for conscience' sake. One day the South will know that when these disinherited children of God sat down at lunch counters, they were in reality standing up for what is best in the American dream and for the most sacred values in our Judaeo-Christian heritage, thereby bringing our nation back to those great wells of democracy which were dug deep by the founding fathers in their formulation of the Constitution and the Declaration of Independence.

Never before have I written so long a letter. I'm afraid it is much too long to take your precious time. I can assure you that it would have been much shorter if I had been writing from a comfortable desk, but what else can one do when he is alone in a narrow jail cell, other than write long letters, think long thoughts and pray long prayers?

If I have said anything in this letter that overstates the truth and indicates an unreasonable impatience, I beg you to forgive me. If I have said anything that understates the truth and indicates my having a patience that allows me to settle for anything less than brotherhood, I beg God to forgive me.

I hope this letter finds you strong in the faith. I also hope that circumstances will soon make it possible for me to meet each of you, not as an integrationist or a civil-rights leader but as a fellow clergyman and a Christian brother. Let us all hope that the dark clouds of racial prejudice will soon pass away and the deep fog of misunderstanding will be lifted from our fear-drenched communities, and in some not too distant tomorrow the radiant stars of love and brotherhood will shine over our great nation with all their scintillating beauty.

Yours for the cause of Peace and Brotherhood,
Martin Luther King, Jr.

4. Malcolm X
Message to the Grass Roots

Malcolm X, born Malcolm Little in Omaha, Nebraska in 1926, was at
once the most vigorous opponent of Martin Luther King's moderate
philosophy of reform and the most celebrated apostle of Elijah
Muhammad, leader of the Nation of Islam (Black Muslims) in the United
States. He broke with the Black Muslims in 1964 and founded the
nonreligious Organization of Afro-American Unity. Shortly after returning
to the United States from his second journey to Africa and the
Middle East during 1964, Malcolm X was assassinated in New York on
February 21, 1965.

A man of unique leadership skills, Malcolm X excelled in adapting
revolutionary theory to changing historical circumstances. During the
last years of his short life, he sought to unite black nationalism with
Trotskyite Marxism, a creative synthesis that connected Mississippi with
Africa and Asia. A gifted orator, he could express the most abstract
ideas in language intelligible to all his listeners. Malcolm X was one of
those rare persons who continually grew and learned, as his *Autobiography
of Malcolm X,* widely acknowledged as a classic, makes clear.

"Message to the Grass Roots," delivered at a Northern Negro
Grass Roots Leadership Conference in Detroit, in November 1963, was
one of the last speeches Malcolm gave before leaving the Black Muslims.
To clarify his differences with moderate Negro leaders such as King,
James Farmer, and Roy Wilkins, Malcolm defines revolution, contrasts
a black revolution with a Negro revolution, and calls for a worldwide
union of nonwhites against the powerful and privileged position of
the white man.

We want to have just an off-the-cuff chat between you and me, us. We
want to talk right down to earth in a language that everybody here can
easily understand. We all agree tonight, all of the speakers have agreed,
that America has a very serious problem. Not only does America have a
very serious problem, but our people have a very serious problem. America's problem is us. We're her problem. The only reason she has a problem is she doesn't want us here. And every time you look at yourself, be
you black, brown, red or yellow, a so-called Negro, you represent a person who poses such a serious problem for America because you're not
wanted. Once you face this as a fact, then you can start plotting a course
that will make you appear intelligent, instead of unintelligent.

From *Malcolm X Speaks,* copyright © 1965 by Merit Publishers and Mrs. Betty
Shabazz.

What you and I need to do is learn to forget our differences. When we come together, we don't come together as Baptists or Methodists. You don't catch hell because you're a Baptist, and you don't catch hell because you're a Methodist. You don't catch hell because you're a Methodist or Baptist, you don't catch hell because you're a Democrat or a Republican, you don't catch hell because you're a Mason or an Elk, and you sure don't catch hell because you're an American; because if you were an American, you wouldn't catch hell. You catch hell because you're a black man. You catch hell, all of us catch hell, for the same reason.

So we're all black people, so-called Negroes, second-class citizens, ex-slaves. You're nothing but an ex-slave. You don't like to be told that. But what else are you? You are ex-slaves. You didn't come here on the "Mayflower." You came here on a slave ship. In chains, like a horse, or a cow, or a chicken. And you were brought here by the people who came here on the "Mayflower," you were brought here by the so-called Pilgrims, or Founding Fathers. They were the ones who brought you here.

We have a common enemy. We have this in common: We have a common oppressor, a common exploiter, and a common discriminator. But once we all realize that we have a common enemy, then we unite—on the basis of what we have in common. And what we have foremost in common is that enemy—the white man. He's an enemy to all of us. I know some of you all think that some of them aren't enemies. Time will tell.

In Bandung back in, I think, 1954, was the first unity meeting in centuries of black people. And once you study what happened at the Bandung conference, and the results of the Bandung conference, it actually serves as a model for the same procedure you and I can use to get our problems solved. At Bandung all the nations came together, the dark nations from Africa and Asia. Some of them were Buddhists, some of them were Muslims, some of them were Christians, some were Confucianists, some were atheists. Despite their religious differences, they came together. Some were communists, some were socialists, some were capitalists—despite their economic and political differences, they came together. All of them were black, brown, red or yellow.

The number-one thing that was not allowed to attend the Bandung conference was the white man. He couldn't come. Once they excluded the white man, they found that they could get together. Once they kept him out, everybody else fell right in and fell in line. This is the thing that you and I have to understand. And these people who came together didn't have nuclear weapons, they didn't have jet planes, they didn't have all of the heavy armaments that the white man has. But they had unity.

They were able to submerge their little petty differences and agree on one thing: That there one African came from Kenya and was being colo-

nized by the Englishman, and another African came from the Congo and
was being colonized by the Belgian, and another African came from
Guinea and was being colonized by the French, and another came from
Angola and was being colonized by the Portuguese. When they came to
the Bandung conference, they looked at the Portuguese, and at the
Frenchman, and at the Englishman, and at the Dutchman, and learned or
realized the one thing that all of them had in common—they were all
from Europe, they were all Europeans, blond, blue-eyed and white skins.
They began to recognize who their enemy was. The same man that was
colonizing our people in Kenya was colonizing our people in the Congo.
The same one in the Congo was colonizing our people in South Africa,
and in Southern Rhodesia, and in Burma, and in India, and in Afghani-
stan, and in Pakistan. They realized all over the world where the dark
man was being oppressed, he was being oppressed by the white man;
where the dark man was being exploited, he was being exploited by the
white man. So they got together on this basis—that they had a common
enemy.

And when you and I here in Detroit and in Michigan and in America
who have been awakened today look around us, we too realize here in
America we all have a common enemy, whether he's in Georgia or Michigan, whether he's in California or New York. He's the same man—blue
eyes and blond hair and pale skin—the same man. So what we have to
do is what they did. They agreed to stop quarreling among themselves.
Any little spat that they had, they'd settle it among themselves, go into a
huddle—don't let the enemy know that you've got a disagreement.

Instead of airing our differences in public, we have to realize we're all
the same family. And when you have a family squabble, you don't get out
on the sidewalk. If you do, everybody calls you uncouth, unrefined, unci-
vilized, savage. If you don't make it at home, you settle it at home; you
get in the closet, argue it out behind closed doors, and then when you
come out on the street, you pose a common front, a united front. And
this is what we need to do in the community, and in the city, and in the
state. We need to stop airing our differences in front of the white man,
put the white man out of our meetings, and then sit down and talk shop
with each other. That's what we've got to do.

I would like to make a few comments concerning the difference between the black revolution and the Negro revolution. Are they both the
same? And if they're not, what is the difference? What is the difference
between a black revolution and a Negro revolution? First, what is a revolution? Sometimes I'm inclined to believe that many of our people are using this word "revolution" loosely, without taking careful consideration of
what this word actually means, and what its historic characteristics are.
When you study the historic nature of revolutions, the motive of a revolu-

tion, the objective of a revolution, the result of a revolution, and the methods used in a revolution, you may change words. You may devise another program, you may change your goal and you may change your mind.

Look at the American Revolution in 1776. That revolution was for what? For land. Why did they want land? Independence. How was it carried out? Bloodshed. Number one, it was based on land, the basis of independence. And the only way they could get it was bloodshed. The French Revolution—what was it based on? The landless against the landlord. What was it for? Land. How did they get it? Bloodshed. Was no love lost, was no compromise, was no negotiation. I'm telling you—you don't know what a revolution is. Because when you find out what it is, you'll get back in the alley, you'll get out of the way.

The Russian Revolution—what was it based on? Land; the landless against the landlord. How did they bring it about? Bloodshed. You haven't got a revolution that doesn't involve bloodshed. And you're afraid to bleed. I said, you're afraid to bleed.

As long as the white man sent you to Korea, you bled. He sent you to Germany, you bled. He sent you to the South Pacific to fight the Japanese, you bled. You bleed for white people, but when it comes to seeing your own churches being bombed and little black girls murdered, you haven't got any blood. You bleed when the white man says bleed; you bite when the white man says bite; and you bark when the white man says bark. I hate to say this about us, but it's true. How are you going to be nonviolent in Mississippi, as violent as you were in Korea? How can you justify being nonviolent in Mississippi and Alabama, when your churches are being bombed, and your little girls are being murdered, and at the same time you are going to get violent with Hitler, and Tojo, and somebody else you don't even know?

If violence is wrong in America, violence is wrong abroad. If it is wrong to be violent defending black women and black children and black babies and black men, then it is wrong for America to draft us and make us violent abroad in defense of her. And if it is right for America to draft us, and teach us how to be violent in defense of her, then it is right for you and me to do whatever is necessary to defend our own people right here in this country.

The Chinese Revolution—they wanted land. They threw the British out, along with the Uncle Tom Chinese. Yes, they did. They set a good example. When I was in prison, I read an article—don't be shocked when I say that I was in prison. You're still in prison. That's what America means: prison. When I was in prison, I read an article in *Life* magazine showing a little Chinese girl, nine years old; her father was on his hands and knees and she was pulling the trigger because he was an Uncle Tom

Chinaman. When they had the revolution over there, they took a whole generation of Uncle Toms and just wiped them out. And within ten years that little girl became a full-grown woman. No more Toms in China. And today it's one of the toughest, roughest, most feared countries on this earth—by the white man. Because there are no Uncle Toms over there.

Of all our studies, history is best qualified to reward our research. And when you see that you've got problems, all you have to do is examine the historic method used all over the world by others who have problems similar to yours. Once you see how they got theirs straight, then you know how you can get yours straight. There's been a revolution, a black revolution, going on in Africa. In Kenya, the Mau Mau were revolutionary; they were the ones who brought the word "Uhuru" to the fore. The Mau Mau, they were revolutionary, they believed in scorched earth, they knocked everything aside that got in their way, and their revolution also was based on land, a desire for land. In Algeria, the northern part of Africa, a revolution took place. The Algerians were revolutionists, they wanted land. France offered to let them be integrated into France. They told France, to hell with France, they wanted some land, not some France. And they engaged in a bloody battle.

So I cite these various revolutions, brothers and sisters, to show you that you don't have a peaceful revolution. You don't have a turn-the-other-cheek revolution. There's no such thing as a nonviolent revolution. The only kind of revolution that is nonviolent is the Negro revolution. The only revolution in which the goal is loving your enemy is the Negro revolution. It's the only revolution in which the goal is a desegregated lunch counter, a desegregated theater, a desegregated park, and a desegregated public toilet; you can sit down next to white folks—on the toilet. That's no revolution. Revolution is based on land. Land is the basis for all independence. Land is the basis of freedom, justice, and equality.

The white man knows what a revolution is. He knows that the black revolution is world-wide in scope and in nature. The black revolution is sweeping Asia, is sweeping Africa, is rearing its head in Latin America. The Cuban Revolution—that's a revolution. They overturned the system. Revolution is in Asia, revolution is in Africa, and the white man is screaming because he sees revolution in Latin America. How do you think he'll react to you when you learn what a real revolution is? You don't know what a revolution is. If you did, you wouldn't use that word.

Revolution is bloody, revolution is hostile, revolution knows no compromise, revolution overturns and destroys everything that gets in its way. And you, sitting around here like a knot on the wall, saying, "I'm going to love these folks no matter how much they hate me." No, you need a revolution. Whoever heard of a revolution where they lock arms . . . singing "We Shall Overcome"? You don't do that in a revolution. You don't do any singing, you're too busy swinging. It's based on land. A revolutionary wants land so he can set up his own nation, an independent nation. These Negroes aren't asking for any nation—they're trying to crawl back on the plantation.

When you want a nation, that's called nationalism. When the white man became involved in a revolution in this country against England, what was it for? He wanted this land so he could set up another white nation. That's white nationalism. The American Revolution was white nationalism. The French Revolution was white nationalism. The Russian Revolution too—yes, it was—white nationalism. You don't think so? Why do you think Khrushchev and Mao can't get their heads together? White nationalism. All the revolutions that are going on in Asia and Africa today are based on what?—black nationalism. A revolutionary is a black nationalist. He wants a nation. . . . If you're afraid of black nationalism, you're afraid of revolution. And if you love revolution, you love black nationalism.

To understand this, you have to go back to what the young brother here referred to as the house Negro and the field Negro back during slavery. There were two kinds of slaves, the house Negro and the field Negro. The house Negroes—they lived in the house with the master, they dressed pretty good, they ate good because they ate his food—what he left. They lived in the attic or the basement, but still they lived near the master; and they loved the master more than the master loved himself. They would give their life to save the master's house—quicker than the master would. If the master said, "We got a good house here," the house Negro would say, "Yeah, we got a good house here." Whenever the master said "we," he said "we." That's how you can tell a house Negro.

If the master's house caught on fire, the house Negro would fight harder to put the blaze out than the master would. If the master got sick, the house Negro would say, "What's the matter, boss, *we* sick?" *We* sick! He identified himself with his master, more than his master identified with himself. And if you came to the house Negro and said, "Let's run away, let's escape, let's separate," the house Negro would look at you and say, "Man, you crazy. What you mean, separate? Where is there a better house than this? Where can I wear better clothes than this? Where can I eat better food than this?" That was that house Negro. In those days he was called a "house nigger." And that's what we call them today, because we've still got some house niggers running around here.

This modern house Negro loves his master. He wants to live near him. He'll pay three times as much as the house is worth just to live near his master, and then brag about "I'm the only Negro out here." "I'm the only one on my job." "I'm the only one in this school." You're nothing but a house Negro. And if someone comes to you right now and says,

"Let's separate," you say the same thing that the house Negro said on the plantation. "What you mean, separate? From America, this good white man? Where you going to get a better job than you get here?" I mean, this is what you say. "I ain't left nothing in Africa," that's what you say. Why, you left your mind in Africa.

On that same plantation, there was the field Negro. The field Negroes —those were the masses. There were always more Negroes in the field than there were Negroes in the house. The Negro in the field caught hell. He ate leftovers. In the house they ate high up on the hog. The Negro in the field didn't get anything but what was left of the insides of the hog. They call it "chitt'lings" nowadays. In those days they called them what they were—guts. That's what you were—gut-eaters. And some of you are still gut-eaters.

The field Negro was beaten from morning to night; he lived in a shack, in a hut; he wore old, castoff clothes. He hated his master. I say he hated his master. He was intelligent. That house Negro loved his master, but that field Negro—remember, they were in the majority, and they hated the master. When the house caught on fire, he didn't try to put it out; that field Negro prayed for a wind, for a breeze. When the master got sick, the field Negro prayed that he'd die. If someone came to the field Negro and said, "Let's separate, let's run," he didn't say "Where we going?" He'd say, "Any place is better than here." You've got field Negroes in America today. I'm a field Negro. The masses are the field Negroes. When they see this man's house on fire, you don't hear the little Negroes talking about *"our* government is in trouble." They say, *"The* government is in trouble." Imagine a Negro: *"Our* government"! I even heard one say *"our* astronauts." They won't even let him near the plant—and *"our* astronauts"! *"Our* Navy"—that's a Negro that is out of his mind, a Negro that is out of his mind.

Just as the slavemaster of that day used Tom, the house Negro, to keep the field Negroes in check, the same old slavemaster today has Negroes who are nothing but modern Uncle Toms, twentieth-century Uncle Toms, to keep you and me in check, to keep us under control, keep us passive and peaceful and nonviolent. That's Tom making you nonviolent. It's like when you go to the dentist, and the man's going to take your tooth. You're going to fight him when he starts pulling. So he squirts some stuff in your jaw called novocaine, to make you think they're not going to do anything to you. So you sit there and because you've got all of that novocaine in your jaw, you suffer—peacefully. Blood running all down your jaw, and you don't know what's happening. Because someone has taught you to suffer—peacefully.

The white man does the same thing to you in the street, when he wants to put knots on your head and take advantage of you and not have to be afraid of your fighting back. To keep you from fighting back, he gets these old religious Uncle Toms to teach you and me, just like novocaine, to suffer peacefully. Don't stop suffering—just suffer peacefully. As Rev. Cleage pointed out, they say you should let your blood flow in the streets. This is a shame. You know he's a Christian preacher. If it's a shame to him, you know what it is to me.

There is nothing in our book, the Koran, that teaches us to suffer peacefully. Our religion teaches us to be intelligent. Be peaceful, be courteous, obey the law, respect everyone; but if someone puts his hand on you, send him to the cemetery. That's a good religion. In fact, that's that old-time religion. That's the one that Ma and Pa used to talk about: an eye for an eye, and a tooth for a tooth, and a head for a head, and a life for a life. That's a good religion. And nobody resents that kind of religion being taught but a wolf, who intends to make you his meal.

This is the way it is with the white man in America. He's a wolf—and you're sheep. Any time a shepherd, a pastor, teaches you and me not to run from the white man and, at the same time, teaches us not to fight the white man, he's a traitor to you and me. Don't lay down a life all by itself. No, preserve your life, it's the best thing you've got. And if you've got to give it up, let it be even-steven.

The slavemaster took Tom and dressed him well, fed him well and even gave him a little education—a *little* education; gave him a long coat and a top hat and made all the other slaves look up to him. Then he used Tom to control them. The same strategy that was used in those days is used today, by the same white man. He takes a Negro, a so-called Negro, and makes him prominent, builds him up, publicizes him, makes him a celebrity. And then he becomes a spokesman for Negroes—and a Negro leader.

I would like to mention just one other thing quickly, and that is the method that the white man uses, how the white man uses the "big guns," or Negro leaders, against the Negro revolution. They are not a part of the Negro revolution. They are used against the Negro revolution.

When Martin Luther King failed to desegregate Albany, Georgia, the civil-rights struggle in America reached its low point. King became bankrupt almost, as a leader. The Southern Christian Leadership Conference was in financial trouble; and it was in trouble, period, with the people when they failed to desegregate Albany, Georgia. Other Negro civil-rights leaders of so-called national stature became fallen idols. As they became fallen idols, began to lose their prestige and influence, local Negro leaders began to stir up the masses. In Cambridge, Maryland, Gloria Richardson; in Danville, Virginia, and other parts of the country, local leaders began to stir up our people at the grass-roots level. This was never done by these Negroes of national stature. They control you, but they have never incited you or excited you. They control you, they contain you, they have kept you on the plantation.

As soon as King failed in Birmingham, Negroes took to the streets. King went out to California to a big rally and raised I don't know how many thousands of dollars. He came to Detroit and had a march and raised some more thousands of dollars. And recall, right after that Roy Wilkins attacked King. He accused King and CORE [Congress of Racial Equality] of starting trouble everywhere and then making the NAACP [National Association for the Advancement of Colored People] get them out of jail and spend a lot of money; they accused King and CORE of raising all the money and not paying it back. This happened; I've got it in documented evidence in the newspaper. Roy started attacking King, and King started attacking Roy, and Farmer started attacking both of them. And as these Negroes of national stature began to attack each other, they began to lose their control of the Negro masses.

The Negroes were out there in the streets. They were talking about how they were going to march on Washington. Right at that time Birmingham had exploded, and the Negroes in Birmingham—remember, they also exploded. They began to stab the crackers in the back and bust them up 'side their head—yes, they did. That's when Kennedy sent in the troops, down in Birmingham. After that, Kennedy got on the television and said "this is a moral issue." That's when he said he was going to put out a civil-rights bill. And when he mentioned civil-rights bill and the Southern crackers started talking about how they were going to boycott or filibuster it, then the Negroes started talking—about what? That they were going to march on Washington, march on the Senate, march on the White House, march on the Congress, and tie it up, bring it to a halt, not let the government proceed. They even said they were going out to the airport and lay down on the runway and not let any airplanes land. I'm telling you what they said. That was revolution. That was revolution. That was the black revolution.

It was the grass roots out there in the street. It scared the white man to death, scared the white power structure in Washington, D.C., to death; I was there. When they found out that this black steamroller was going to come down on the capital, they called in Wilkins, they called in Randolph, they called in these national Negro leaders that you respect and told them, "Call it off." Kennedy said, "Look, you all are letting this thing go too far." And Old Tom said, "Boss, I can't stop it, because I didn't start it." I'm telling you what they said. They said, "I'm not even in it, much less at the head of it." They said, "These Negroes are doing things on their own. They're running ahead of us." And that old shrewd fox, he said, "If you all aren't in it, I'll put you in it. I'll put you at the head of it. I'll endorse it. I'll welcome it. I'll help it. I'll join it."

A matter of hours went by. They had a meeting at the Carlyle Hotel in New York City. The Carlyle Hotel is owned by the Kennedy family; that's the hotel Kennedy spent the night at, two nights ago; it belongs to his family. A philanthropic society headed by a white man named Stephen Currier called all the top civil-rights leaders together at the Carlyle Hotel. And he told them, "By you all fighting each other, you are destroying the civil-rights movement. And since you're fighting over money from white liberals, let us set up what is known as the Council for United Civil Rights Leadership. Let's form this council, and all the civil-rights organizations will belong to it, and we'll use it for fund-raising purposes." Let me show you how tricky the white man is. As soon as they got it formed, they elected Whitney Young as its chairman, and who do you think became the co-chairman? Stephen Currier, the white man, a millionaire. Powell was talking about it down at Cobo Hall today. This is what he was talking about. Powell knows it happened. Randolph knows it happened. Wilkins knows it happened. King knows it happened. Every one of that Big Six—they know it happened.

Once they formed it, with the white man over it, he promised them and gave them $800,000 to split up among the Big Six; and told them that after the march was over they'd give them $700,000 more. A million and a half dollars—split up between leaders that you have been following, going to jail for, crying crocodile tears for. And they're nothing but Frank James and Jesse James and the what-do-you-call-'em brothers.

As soon as they got the setup organized, the white man made available to them top public-relations experts; opened the news media across the country at their disposal, which then began to project these Big Six as the leaders of the march. Originally they weren't even in the march. You were talking this march talk on Hastings Street, you were talking march talk on Lenox Avenue, and on Fillmore Street, and on Central Avenue, and 32nd Street and 63rd Street. That's where the march talk was being talked. But the white man put the Big Six at the head of it; made them the march. They became the march. They took it over. And the first move they made after they took it over, they invited Walter Reuther, a white man; they invited a priest, a rabbi, and an old white preacher, yes, an old white preacher. The same white element that put Kennedy into power—labor, the Catholics, the Jews, and liberal Protestants; the same clique that put Kennedy in power, joined the march on Washington.

It's just like when you've got some coffee that's too black, which means it's too strong. What do you do? You integrate it with cream, you make it weak. But if you pour too much cream in it, you won't even know you ever had coffee. It used to be hot, it becomes cool. It used to be strong, it becomes weak. It used to wake you up, now it puts you to sleep. This is what they did with the march on Washington. They joined it. They didn't integrate it, they infiltrated it. They joined it, became a part of it, took it over. And as they took it over, it lost its militancy. It ceased to be angry, it ceased to be hot, it ceased to be uncompromising. Why, it even ceased to be a march. It became a picnic, a circus. Nothing but a circus, with clowns and all. You had one right here in Detroit—I saw it on television—with clowns leading it, white clowns and black clowns. I know you don't like what I'm saying, but I'm going to tell you anyway. Because I can prove what I'm saying. If you think I'm telling you wrong, you bring me Martin Luther King and A. Philip Randolph and James Farmer and those other three, and see if they'll deny it over a microphone.

No, it was a sellout. It was a takeover. When James Baldwin came in from Paris, they wouldn't let him talk, because they couldn't make him go by the script. Burt Lancaster read the speech that Baldwin was supposed to make; they wouldn't let Baldwin get up there, because they know Baldwin is liable to say anything. They controlled it so tight, they told those Negroes what time to hit town, how to come, where to stop, what signs to carry, what song to sing, what speech they could make, and what speech they couldn't make; and then told them to get out of town by sundown. And every one of those Toms was out of town by sundown. Now I know you don't like my saying this. But I can back it up. It was a circus, a performance that beat anything Hollywood could ever do, the performance of the year. Reuther and those other three devils should get an Academy Award for the best actors because they acted like they really loved Negroes and fooled a whole lot of Negroes. And the six Negro leaders should get an award too, for the best supporting cast.

5. Norman Podhoretz
My Negro Problem—And Ours

Norman Podhoretz, editor of *Commentary*, was born in the racially mixed
and deteriorating Brownsville section of Brooklyn, New York, in 1930.
It was there that Podhoretz, the son of Jewish European immigrants,
suffered through the experiences he describes in his controversial
essay "My Negro Problem—And Ours." Published first in *Commentary*
in February 1963, it was an immediate sensation, and occasioned
hundreds of letters to *Commentary* and editorials throughout the country.
Alternately damned for "racism" and praised for "honesty," Podhoretz
perhaps differed from many others mainly in that he published his
reflections on the painful consciousness he had of the Negro. He has
written in his confessional autobiography, *Making It* (1966), that the
essay grew out of his "irritation with all the sentimental nonsense
that was being talked about integration by whites who knew nothing about
Negroes, and by Negroes who thought that all their problems could be
solved by living next-door to whites." The problem went deeper
than integrationists imagined, however: "there was something almost
psychotic in the relation of whites to Negroes in America." This
selection records the difficulty one prominent liberal had in his attempt
to come to terms with racial conflict in America.

---

*If we—and . . . I mean the relatively conscious whites and the
relatively conscious blacks, who must, like lovers, insist on, or create,
the consciousness of the others—do not falter in our duty now,
we may be able, handful that we are, to end the racial nightmare,
and achieve our country, and change the history of the world.*
                                                          —James Baldwin

Two ideas puzzled me deeply as a child growing up in Brooklyn during
the 1930's in what today would be called an integrated neighborhood.
One of them was that all Jews were rich; the other was that all Negroes
were persecuted. These ideas had appeared in print; therefore they must
be true. My own experience and the evidence of my senses told they were
not true, but that only confirmed what a day-dreaming boy in the provinces—for the lower-class neighborhoods of New York belong as surely
to the provinces as any rural town in North Dakota—discovers very early: *his* experience is unreal and the evidence of his senses is not to be

trusted. Yet even a boy with a head full of fantasies incongruously synthesized out of Hollywood movies and English novels cannot altogether deny the reality of his own experience—especially when there is so much deprivation in that experience. Nor can he altogether gainsay the evidence of his own senses—especially such evidence of the senses as comes from being repeatedly beaten up, robbed, and in general hated, terrorized, and humiliated.

And so for a long time I was puzzled to think that Jews were supposed to be rich when the only Jews I knew were poor, and that Negroes were supposed to be persecuted when it was the Negroes who were doing the only persecuting I knew about—and doing it, moreover, to *me.* During the early years of the war, when my older sister joined a left-wing youth organization, I remember my astonishment at hearing her passionately denounce my father for thinking that Jews were worse off than Negroes. To me, at the age of twelve, it seemed very clear that Negroes were better off than Jews—indeed, than *all* whites. A city boy's world is contained within three or four square blocks, and in my world it was the whites, the Italians and Jews, who feared the Negroes, not the other way around. The Negroes were tougher than we were, more ruthless, and on the whole they were better athletes. What could it mean, then, to say that they were badly off and that we were more fortunate? Yet my sister's opinions, like print, were sacred, and when she told me about exploitation and economic forces I believed her. I believed her, but I was still afraid of Negroes. And I still hated them with all my heart.

It had not always been so—that much I can recall from early childhood. When did it start, this fear and this hatred? There was a kindergarten in the local public school, and given the character of the neighborhood, at least half the children in my class must have been Negroes. Yet I have no memory of being aware of color differences at that age, and I know from observing my own children that they attribute no significance to such differences even when they begin noticing them. I think there was a day—first grade? second grade?—when my best friend Carl hit me on the way home from school and announced that he wouldn't play with me any more because I had killed Jesus. When I ran home to my mother crying for an explanation, she told me not to pay any attention to such foolishness, and then in Yiddish she cursed the *goyim* and the *schwartzes,* the *schwartzes* and the *goyim.* Carl, it turned out, was a *schwartze,* and so was added a third to the categories into which people were mysteriously divided.

Sometimes I wonder whether this is a true memory at all. It is blazingly vivid, but perhaps it never happened: can anyone really remember back to the age of six? There is no uncertainty in my mind, however, about the years that followed. Carl and I hardly ever spoke, though we met in school every day up through the eighth or ninth grade. There would be embarrassed moments of catching his eye or of his catching mine—for whatever it was that had attracted us to one another as very small children remained alive in spite of the fantastic barrier of hostility that had grown up between us, suddenly and out of nowhere. Nevertheless, friendship would have been impossible, and even if it had been possible, it would have been unthinkable. About that, there was nothing anyone could do by the time we were eight years old.

Item: The orphanage across the street is torn down, a city housing project begins to rise in its place, and on the marvelous vacant lot next to the old orphanage they are building a playground. Much excitement and anticipation as Opening Day draws near. Mayor LaGuardia himself comes to dedicate this great gesture of public benevolence. He speaks of neighborliness and borrowing cups of sugar, and of the playground he says that children of all races, colors, and creeds will learn to live together in harmony. A week later, some of us are swatting flies on the playground's inadequate little ball field. A gang of Negro kids, pretty much our own age, enter from the other side and order us out of the park. We refuse, proudly and indignantly, with superb masculine fervor. There is a fight, they win, and we retreat, half whimpering, half with bravado. My first nauseating experience of cowardice. And my first appalled realization that there are people in the world who do not seem to be afraid of anything, who act as though they have nothing to lose. Thereafter the playground becomes a battleground, sometimes quiet, sometimes the scene of athletic competition between Them and Us. But rocks are thrown as often as baseballs. Gradually we abandon the place and use the streets instead. The streets are safer, though we do not admit this to ourselves. We are not, after all, sissies—that most dreaded epithet of an American boyhood.

Item: I am standing alone in front of the building in which I live. It is late afternoon and getting dark. That day in school the teacher had asked a surly Negro boy named Quentin a question he was unable to answer. As usual I had waved my arm eagerly ("Be a good boy, get good marks, be smart, go to college, become a doctor") and, the right answer bursting from my lips, I was held up lovingly by the teacher as an example to the class. I had seen Quentin's face—a very dark, very cruel, very Oriental-looking face—harden, and there had been enough threat in his eyes to make me run all the way home for fear that he might catch me outside.

Now, standing idly in front of my own house, I see him approaching from the project accompanied by his little brother who is carrying a baseball bat and wearing a grin of malicious anticipation. As in a nightmare, I am trapped. The surroundings are secure and familiar, but terror is suddenly present and there is no one around to help. I am locked to the spot. I will not cry out or run away like a sissy, and I stand there, my heart wild, my throat clogged. He walks up, hurls the familiar epithet ("Hey, mo'f——r"), and to my surprise only pushes me. It is a violent push, but not a punch. Maybe I can still back out without entirely losing my dignity. Maybe I can still say, "Hey, c'mon Quentin, whaddya wanna do *that* for? I dint do nothin' to *you*," and walk away, not too rapidly. Instead, before I can stop myself, I push him back—a token gesture—and I say, "Cut that out, I don't wanna fight, I ain't got nothin' to fight about." As I turn to walk back into the building, the corner of my eye catches the motion of the bat his little brother has handed him. I try to duck, but the bat crashes colored lights into my head.

The next thing I know, my mother and sister are standing over me, both of them hysterical. My sister—she who was later to join the "progressive" youth organization—is shouting for the police and screaming imprecations at those dirty little black bastards. They take me upstairs, the doctor comes, the police come. I tell them that the boy who did it was a stranger, that he had been trying to get money from me. They do not believe me, but I am too scared to give them Quentin's name. When I return to school a few days later, Quentin avoids my eyes. He knows that I have not squealed, and he is ashamed. I try to feel proud, but in my heart I know that it was fear of what his friends might to do to me that had kept me silent, and not the code of the street.

Item: There is an athletic meet in which the whole of our junior high school is participating. I am in one of the seventh-grade rapid-advance classes, and "segregation" has now set in with a vengeance. In the last three or four years of the elementary school from which we have just graduated, each grade had been divided into three classes, according to "intelligence." (In the earlier grades the divisions had either been arbitrary or else unrecognized by us as having anything to do with brains.) These divisions by IQ, or however it was arranged, had resulted in a preponderance of Jews in the "1" classes and a corresponding preponderance of Negroes in the "3's," with the Italians split unevenly along the spectrum. At least a few Negroes had always made the "1's," just as there had always been a few Jewish kids among the "3's" and more among the "2's" (where Italians dominated). But the junior high's rapid-advance class of which I am now a member is overwhelmingly Jewish and entirely white—except for a shy lonely Negro girl with light skin and reddish hair.

The athletic meet takes place in a city-owned stadium far from the school. It is an important event to which a whole day is given over. The winners are to get those precious little medallions stamped with the New York City emblem that can be screwed into a belt and that prove the wearer to be a distinguisted personage. I am a fast runner, and so I am assigned the position of anchor man on my class's team in the relay race. There are three other seventh-grade teams in the race, two of them all Negro, as ours is all white. One of the all-Negro teams is very tall—their anchor man waiting silently next to me on the line looks years older than I am, and I do not recognize him. He is the first to get the baton and crosses the finishing line in a walk. Our team comes in second, but a few minutes later we are declared the winners, for it has been discovered that the anchor man on the first-place team is not a member of the class. We are awarded the medallions, and the following day our home-room teacher makes a speech about how proud she is of us for being superior athletes as well as superior students. We want to believe that we deserve the praise, but we know that we could not have won even if the other class had not cheated.

That afternoon, walking home, I am waylaid and surrounded by five Negroes, among whom is the anchor man of the disqualified team. "Gimme my medal, mo'f——r," he grunts. I do not have it with me and I tell him so. "Anyway, it ain't yours," I say foolishly. He calls me a liar on both counts and pushes me up against the wall on which we sometimes play handball. "Gimme my mo'f——n' medal," he says again. I repeat that I have left it home. "Le's search the li'l mo'f——r," one of them suggests, "he prolly got it *hid* in his mo'f——n' *pants.*" My panic is now unmanageable. (How many times had I been surrounded like this and asked in soft tones, "Len' me a nickel, boy." How many times had I been called a liar for pleading poverty and pushed around, or searched, or beaten up, unless there happened to be someone in the marauding gang like Carl who liked me across that enormous divide of hatred and who would therefore say, "Aaah, c'mon, le's git someone else, *this* boy ain't got no money on 'im.") I scream at them through tears of rage and self-contempt, "Keep your f——n' filthy lousy black hands offa me! I swear I'll get the cops." This is all they need to hear, and the five of them set upon me. They bang me around, mostly in the stomach and on the arms and shoulders, and when several adults loitering near the candy store down the block notice what is going on and begin to shout, they run off and away.

I do not tell my parents about the incident. My team-mates, who have also been waylaid, each by a gang led by his opposite number from the disqualified team, have had their medallions taken from them, and they never squeal either. For days, I walk home in terror, expecting to be caught again, but nothing happens. The medallion is put away into a drawer, never to be worn by anyone.

Obviously experiences like these have always been a common feature of childhood life in working-class and immigrant neighborhoods, and Negroes do not necessarily figure in them. Wherever, and in whatever combination, they have lived together in the cities, kids of different groups have been at war, beating up and being beaten up: micks against kikes against wops against spicks against polacks. And even relatively homogeneous areas have not been spared the warring of the young: one block against another, one gang (called in my day, in a pathetic effort at gentility, an "S.A.C.," or social-athletic club) against another. But the Negro-white conflict had—and no doubt still has—a special intensity and was conducted with a ferocity unmatched by intramural white battling.

In my own neighborhood, a good deal of animosity existed between the Italian kids (most of whose parents were immigrants from Sicily) and the Jewish kids (who came largely from East European immigrant families). Yet everyone had friends, sometimes close friends, in the other "camp," and we often visited one another's strange-smelling houses, if not for meals, then for glasses of milk, and occasionally for some special event like a wedding or a wake. If it happened that we divided into warring factions and did battle, it would invariably be half-hearted and soon patched up. Our parents, to be sure, had nothing to do with one another and were mutually suspicious and hostile. But we, the kids, who all spoke Yiddish or Italian at home, were Americans, or New Yorkers, or Brooklyn boys: we shared a culture, the culture of the street, and at least for a while this culture proved to be more powerful than the opposing cultures of the home.

Why, *why* should it have been so different as between the Negroes and us? How was it borne in upon us so early, white and black alike, that we were enemies beyond any possibility of reconciliation? Why did we hate one another so?

I suppose if I tried, I could answer those questions more or less adequately from the perspective of what I have since learned. I could draw upon James Baldwin—what better witness is there?—to describe the sense of entrapment that poisons the soul of the Negro with hatred for the white man whom he knows to be his jailer. On the other side, if I wanted to understand how the white man comes to hate the Negro, I could call upon the psychologists who have spoken of the guilt that white Americans feel toward Negroes and that turns into hatred for lack of acknowledging itself as guilt. These are plausible answers and certainly there is truth in them. Yet when I think back upon my own experience of the Negro and his of me, I find myself troubled and puzzled, much as I was as a child when I heard that all Jews were rich and all Negroes persecuted. How could the Negroes in my neighborhood have regarded the whites across the street and around the corner as jailers? On the whole, the whites were not so poor as the Negroes, but they were quite poor enough, and the years were years of Depression. As for white hatred of the Negro, how could guilt have had anything to do with it? What share had these Italian and Jewish immigrants in the enslavement of the Negro? What share had they—downtrodden people themselves breaking their own necks to eke out a living—in the exploitation of the Negro?

No, I cannot believe that we hated each other back there in Brooklyn because they thought of us as jailers and we felt guilty toward them. But does it matter, given the fact that we all went through an unrepresentative confrontation? I think it matters profoundly, for if we managed the job of hating each other so well without benefit of the aids to hatred that are supposedly at the root of this madness everywhere else, it must mean that the madness is not yet properly understood. I am far from pretending that I understand it, but I would insist that no view of the problem will begin to approach the truth unless it can account for a case like the one I have been trying to describe. Are the elements of any such view available to us?

At least two, I would say, are. One of them is a point we frequently come upon in the work of James Baldwin, and the other is a related point always stressed by psychologists who have studied the mechanisms of prejudice. Baldwin tells us that one of the reasons Negroes hate the white man is that the white man refuses to *look* at him: the Negro knows that in white eyes all Negroes are alike; they are faceless and therefore not altogether human. The psychologists, in their turn, tell us that the white man hates the Negro because he tends to project those wild impulses that he fears in himself onto an alien group which he then punishes with his contempt. What Baldwin does *not* tell us, however, is that the principle of facelessness is a two-way street and can operate in both directions with no difficulty at all. Thus, in my neighborhood in Brooklyn, *I* was as faceless to the Negroes as they were to me, and if they hated me because I never looked at them, I must also have hated them for never looking at *me*. To the Negroes, my white skin was enough to define me as the enemy, and in a war it is only the uniform that counts and not the person.

So with the mechanism of projection that the psychologists talk about: it too works in both directions at once. There is no question that the psychologists are right about what the Negro represents symbolically to the white man. For me as a child the life lived on the other side of the playground and down the block on Ralph Avenue seemed the very embodiment of the values of the street—free, independent, reckless, brave, masculine, erotic. I put the word "erotic" last, though it is usually stressed above all others, because in fact it came last, in consciousness as in importance. What mainly counted for me about Negro kids of my own age was that they were "bad boys." There were plenty of bad boys among the whites—this was, after all, a neighborhood with a long tradition of crime as a career open to aspiring talents—but the Negroes were *really* bad, bad in a way that beckoned to one, and made one feel inadequate. *We* all went home every day for a lunch of spinach-and-potatoes; *they* roamed around during lunch hour, munching on candy bars. In winter *we* had to wear itchy woolen hats and mittens and cumbersome galoshes; *they* were bareheaded and loose as they pleased. *We* rarely played hookey, or got into serious trouble in school, for all our street-corner bravado; *they* were defiant, forever staying out (to do what delicious things?), forever making disturbances in class and in the halls, forever being sent to the principal and returning uncowed. But most important of all, they were *tough*; beautifully, enviably tough, not giving a damn for anyone or anything. To hell with the teacher, the truant officer, the cop; to hell with the whole of the adult world that held *us* in its grip and that we never had the courage to rebel against except sporadically and in petty ways.

This is what I saw and envied and feared in the Negro: this is what finally made him faceless to me, though some of it, of course, was actually there. (The psychologists also tell us that the alien group which becomes the object of a projection will tend to respond by trying to live up to what is expected of them.) But what, on his side, did the Negro see in me that made me faceless to *him*? Did he envy me my lunches of spinach-and-potatoes and my itchy woolen caps and my prudent behavior in the face of authority, as I envied him his noon-time candy bars and his bare head in winter and his magnificent rebelliousness? Did those lunches and caps spell for him the prospect of power and riches in the future? Did they mean that there were possibilities open to me that were denied to him? Very likely they did. But if so, one also supposes that he feared the impulses within himself toward submission to authority no less powerfully than I feared the impulses in myself toward defiance. If I represented the jailer to him, it was not because I was oppressing him or keeping him down: it was because I symbolized for him the dangerous and probably pointless temptation toward greater repression, just as he symbolized for me the equally perilous tug toward greater freedom. I personally was to be rewarded for this repression with a new and better life in the future, but how many of my friends paid an even higher price and were given only gall in return.

We have it on the authority of James Baldwin that all Negroes hate whites. I am trying to suggest that on their side all whites—all American whites, that is—are sick in their feelings about Negroes. There are Negroes, no doubt, who would say that Baldwin is wrong, but I suspect them of being less honest than he is, just as I suspect whites of self-deception who tell me they have no special feeling toward Negroes. Special feelings about color are a contagion to which white Americans seem susceptible even when there is nothing in their background to account for the susceptibility. Thus everywhere we look today in the North we find the curious phenomenon of white middle-class liberals with no previous personal experience of Negroes—people to whom Negroes have always been faceless in virtue rather than faceless in vice—discovering that their abstract commitment to the cause of Negro rights will not stand the test of a direct confrontation. We find such people fleeing in droves to the suburbs as the Negro population in the inner city grows; and when they stay in the city we find them sending their children to private school rather than to the "integrated" public school in the neighborhood. We find them resisting the demand that gerrymandered school districts be rezoned for the purpose of overcoming de facto segregation; we find them judiciously considering whether the Negroes (for their own good, of course) are not perhaps pushing too hard; we find them clucking their tongues over Negro militancy; we find them speculating on the question of whether there may not, after all, be something in the theory that the races are biologically different; we find them saying that it will take a very long time for Negroes to achieve full equality, no matter what anyone does; we find them deploring the rise of black nationalism and expressing the solemn hope that the leaders of the Negro community will discover ways of containing the impatience and incipient violence within the Negro ghettos.

But that is by no means the whole story; there is also the phenomenon of what Kenneth Rexroth once called "crow-jimism." There are the broken-down white boys like Vivaldo Moore in Baldwin's *Another Country* who go to Harlem in search of sex or simply to brush up against something that looks like primitive vitality, and who are so often punished by the Negroes they meet for crimes that they would have been the last ever to commit and of which they themselves have been as sorry victims as any of the Negroes who take it out on them. There are the writers and intellectuals and artists who romanticize Negroes and pander to them, assuming a guilt that is not properly theirs. And there are all the white liberals who permit Negroes to blackmail them into adopting a double standard of moral judgment, and who lend themselves—again assuming the responsibility for crimes they never committed—to cunning and contemptuous exploitation by Negroes they employ or try to befriend.

And what about me? What kind of feelings do I have about Negroes today? What happened to me, from Brooklyn, who grew up fearing and envying and hating Negroes? Now that Brooklyn is behind me, do I fear them and envy them and hate them still? The answer is yes, but not in the same proportions and certainly not in the same way. I now live on the upper west side of Manhattan, where there are many Negroes and many Puerto Ricans, and there are nights when I experience the old apprehensiveness again, and there are streets that I avoid when I am walking in the dark, as there were streets that I avoided when I was a child. I find that I am not afraid of Puerto Ricans, but I cannot restrain my nervousness whenever I pass a group of Negroes standing in front of a bar or sauntering down the street. I know now, as I did not know when I was a child, that power is on my side, that the police are working for me and not for them. And knowing this I feel ashamed and guilty, like the good liberal I have grown up to be. Yet the twinges of fear and the resentment they bring and the self-contempt they arouse are not to be gainsaid.

But envy? Why envy? And hatred? Why hatred? Here again the intensities have lessened and everything has been complicated and qualified by the guilts and the resulting over-compensations that are the heritage of the enlightened middle-class world of which I am now a member. Yet just as in childhood I envied Negroes for what seemed to me their superior masculinity, so I envy them today for what seems to me their superior physical grace and beauty. I have come to value physical grace very highly, and I am now capable of aching with all my being when I watch a Negro couple on the dance floor, or a Negro playing baseball or basketball. They are on the kind of terms with their own bodies that I should like to be on with mine, and for that precious quality they seemed blessed to me.

The hatred I still feel for Negroes is the hardest of all the old feelings to face or admit, and it is the most hidden and the most overlarded by the conscious attitudes into which I have succeeded in willing myself. It no longer has, as for me it once did, any cause or justification (except, perhaps, that I am constantly being denied my right to an honest expression of the things I earned the right as a child to feel). How, then, do I know that this hatred has never entirely disappeared? I know it from the insane rage that can stir in me at the thought of Negro anti-Semitism; I know it from the disgusting prurience that can stir in me at the sight of a mixed couple; and I know it from the violence that can stir in me whenever I encounter that special brand of paranoid touchiness to which many Negroes are prone.

This, then, is where I am; it is not exactly where I think all other white liberals are, but it cannot be so very far away either. And it is because I am convinced that we white Americans are—for whatever reason, it no longer matters—so twisted and sick in our feelings about Negroes that I despair of the present push toward integration. If the pace of progress were not a factor here, there would perhaps be no cause for despair: time and the law and even the international political situation are on the side of the Negroes, and ultimately, therefore, victory—of a sort, anyway— must come. But from everything we have learned from observers who ought to know, pace has become as important to the Negroes as substance. They want equality and they want it *now*, and the white world is yielding to their demand only as much and as fast as it is absolutely being compelled to do. The Negroes know this in the most concrete terms imaginable, and it is thus becoming increasingly difficult to buy them off with rhetoric and promises and pious assurances of support. And so within the Negro community we find more and more people declaring—as Harold R. Isaacs recently put it in an article in *Commentary*—that they want *out:* people who say that integration will never come, or that it will take a hundred or a thousand years to come, or that it will come at too high a price in suffering and struggle for the pallid and sodden life of the American middle class that at the very best it may bring.

The most numerous, influential, and dangerous movement that has grown out of Negro despair with the goal of integration is, of course, the Black Muslims. This movement, whatever else we may say about it, must be credited with one enduring achievement: it inspired James Baldwin to write an essay which deserves to be placed among the classics of our language. Everything Baldwin has ever been trying to tell us is distilled in *The Fire Next Time* into a statement of overwhelming persuasiveness and prophetic magnificence. Baldwin's message is and always has been simple. It is this: "Color is not a human or personal reality; it is a political reality." And Baldwin's demand is correspondingly simple: color must be forgotten, lest we all be smited with a vengeance "that does not really depend on, and cannot really be executed by, any person or organization, and that cannot be prevented by any police force or army: historical vengeance, a cosmic vengeance based on the law that we recognize when we say, 'Whatever goes up must come down.' " The Black Muslims Baldwin portrays as a sign and a warning to the intransigent white world. They come to proclaim how deep is the Negro's disaffection with the white world and all its works, and Baldwin implies that no American Negro can fail to respond somewhere in his being to their message: that the white man is the devil, that Allah has doomed him to destruction, and that the black man is about to inherit the earth. Baldwin of course knows that this nightmare inversion of the racism from which the black man has suffered can neither win or even point to the neighborhood in which victory might be located. For in his view the neighborhood of victory lies in exactly the opposite direction: the transcendence of color through love.

Yet the tragic fact is that love is not the answer to hate—not in the world of politics, at any rate. Color is indeed a political rather than a human or a personal reality and if politics (which is to say power) has made it into a human and personal reality, then only politics (which is to say power) can unmake it once again. But the way of politics is slow and bitter, and as impatience on the one side is matched by a setting of the jaw on the other, we move closer and closer to an explosion and blood may yet run in the streets.

Will this madness in which we are all caught never find a resting-place? Is there never to be an end to it? In thinking about the Jews I have often wondered whether their survival as a distinct group was worth one hair on the head of a single infant. Did the Jews have to survive so that six million innocent people should one day be burned in the ovens of Auschwitz? It is a terrible question and no one, not God himself, could ever answer it to my satisfaction. And when I think about the Negroes in America and about the image of integration as a state in which the Negroes would take their rightful place as another of the protected minorities in a pluralistic society, I wonder whether they really believe in their hearts that such a state can actually be attained, and if so *why* they should wish to survive as a distinct group. I think I know why the Jews once wished to survive (though I am less certain as to why we still do) : they not only believed that God had given them no choice, but they were tied to a memory of past glory and a dream of imminent redemption. What does the American Negro have that might correspond to this? His past is a stigma, his color is a stigma, and his vision of the future is the hope of erasing the stigma by making color irrelevant, by making it disappear as a fact of consciousness.

I share this hope, but I cannot see how it will ever be realized unless color does *in fact* disappear: and that means not integration, it means assimilation, it means—let the brutal word come out—miscegenation. The Black Muslims, like their racist counterparts in the white world, accuse the "so-called Negro leaders" of secretly pursuing miscegenation as a goal. The racists are wrong, but I wish they were right, for I believe that the wholesale merger of the two races is the most desirable alternative for everyone concerned. I am not claiming that this alternative can be pursued programmatically or that it is immediately feasible as a solution; obviously there are even greater barriers to its achievement than to the achievement of integration. What I am saying, however, is that in my opinion the Negro problem can be solved in this country in no other way.

I have told the story of my own twisted feelings about Negroes here, and of how they conflict with the moral convictions I have since developed, in order to assert that such feelings must be acknowledged as honestly as possible so that they can be controlled and ultimately disregarded in favor of the convictions. It is *wrong* for a man to suffer because of the color of his skin. Beside that clichéd proposition of liberal thought, what argument can stand and be respected? If the arguments are the arguments of feeling, they must be made to yield; and one's own soul is not the worst place to begin working a huge social transformation. Not so long ago, it used to be asked of white liberals, "Would you like your sister to marry one?" When I was a boy and my sister was still unmarried I would certainly have said no to that question. But now I am a man, my sister is already married, and I have daughters. If I were to be asked today whether I would like a daughter of mine "to marry one," I would have to answer: "No, I wouldn't *like* it at all. I would rail and rave and rant and tear my hair. And then I hope I would have the courage to curse myself for raving and ranting, and to give her my blessing. How dare I withhold it at the behest of the child I once was against the man I now have a duty to be?"

III. The Rediscovery of Poverty

6. Michael Harrington

The Two Nations

The rediscovery of poverty in the 1960s marked an important milestone
in the evolution of social consciousness in America. The affluent
majority had scoffed in disbelief when John F.
Kennedy, in the midst of
the 1960 presidential campaign, declared that 17,000,000 Americans
went to bed hungry each night. Almost everybody answered that
the New Deal social programs and two decades of prosperity had
eliminated mass poverty in the world's richest nation. But Michael
Harrington's *The Other America*, published in 1962, demonstrated that
within the United States there existed a "second nation" living in
poverty and misery. Associate editor of *The Catholic Worker* from
1951 to 1953, a political organizer, and later chairman of the American
Socialist party, Harrington brought a passionate but disciplined moral
vision to his work that gained him a hearing in the White House
and contributed to shaping the intellectual rationale behind Lyndon
Johnson's "War on Poverty." No book of its kind had a greater impact
during the 1960s.

Harrington writes that the modern poor are invisible—hidden in rural
areas or bypassed by the interstate turnpikes, segregated in intercity
schools, dressed in inexpensive but very presentable clothing, and tucked
away in the rented rooms that house much of America's aged
population. The poor are also politically invisible. Atomized and
unable to speak for themselves, they have no power to draw the mantle
of the welfare state fully around themselves.

"The Two Nations" is the closing chapter of *The Other America*.
In it Harrington states his controversial thesis that poverty is
something more than just economic deprivation; it constitutes a
"culture," a "way of life" characterized by spiritual emptiness, poor
education, low levels of aspiration, and alienation. Therefore the
elimination of deeply entrenched poverty depends not on automatic
economic progress (which, even if effective, would be intolerably slow
from a moral standpoint) but on the execution of a systematic and
comprehensive crusade designed to bring "the other America" into the
Union.

The United States in the sixties contains an affluent society within its borders. Millions and tens of millions enjoy the highest standard of life the
world has ever known. This blessing is mixed. It is built upon a peculiarly

distorted economy, one that often proliferates pseudo-needs rather than satisfying human needs. For some, it has resulted in a sense of spiritual emptiness, of alienation. Yet a man would be a fool to prefer hunger to satiety, and the material gains at least open up the possibility of a rich and full existence.

At the same time, the United States contains an underdeveloped nation, a culture of poverty. Its inhabitants do not suffer the extreme privation of the peasants of Asia or the tribesmen of Africa, yet the mechanism of the misery is similar. They are beyond history, beyond progress, sunk in a paralyzing, maiming routine.

The new nations, however, have one advantage: poverty is so general and so extreme that it is the passion of the entire society to obliterate it. Every resource, every policy, is measured by its effect on the lowest and most impoverished. There is a gigantic mobilization of the spirit of the society: aspiration becomes a national purpose that penetrates to every village and motivates a historic transformation.

But this country seems to be caught in a paradox. Because its poverty is not so deadly, because so many are enjoying a decent standard of life, there are indifference and blindness to the plight of the poor. There are even those who deny that the culture of poverty exists. It is as if Disraeli's famous remark about the two nations of the rich and the poor had come true in a fantastic fashion. At precisely that moment in history where for the first time a people have the material ability to end poverty, they lack the will to do so. They cannot see; they cannot act. The consciences of the well-off are the victims of affluence; the lives of the poor are the victims of a physical and spiritual misery.

The problem, then, is to a great extent one of vision. The nation of the well-off must be able to see through the wall of affluence and recognize the alien citizens on the other side. And there must be vision in the sense of purpose, of aspiration: if the word does not grate upon the ears of a gentile America, there must be a passion to end poverty, for nothing less than that will do.

. . . I hope I can supply at least some of the material for such a vision. Let us try to understand the other America as a whole, to see its perspective for the future if it is left alone, to realize the responsibility and the potential for ending this nation in our midst.

But, when all is said and done, the decisive moment occurs after all the sociology and the description is in. There is really no such thing as "the material for a vision." After one reads the facts, either there are anger and shame, or there are not. And, as usual, the fate of the poor hangs upon the decision of the better-off. If this anger and shame are not forthcoming, someone can write a book about the other America a generation from now and it will be the same, or worse.

I

Perhaps the most important analytic point to have emerged in this description of the other America is the fact that poverty in America forms a culture, a way of life and feeling, that it makes a whole. It is crucial to generalize this idea, for it profoundly affects how one moves to destroy poverty.

The most obvious aspect of this interrelatedness is in the way in which the various subcultures of the other America feed into one another. This is clearest with the aged. There the poverty of the declining years is, for some millions of human beings, a function of the poverty of the earlier years. If there were adequate medical care for everyone in the United States, there would be less misery for old people. It is as simple as that. Or there is the relation between the poor farmers and the unskilled workers. When a man is driven off the land because of the impoverishment worked by technological progress, he leaves one part of the culture of poverty and joins another. If something were done about the low-income farmer, that would immediately tell in the statistics of urban unemployment and the economic underworld. The same is true of the Negroes. Any gain for America's minorities will immediately be translated into an advance for all the unskilled workers. One cannot raise the bottom of a society without benefiting everyone above.

Indeed, there is a curious advantage in the wholeness of poverty. Since the other America forms a distinct system within the United States, effective action at any one decisive point will have a "multiplier" effect; it will ramify through the entire culture of misery and ultimately through the entire society.

Then, poverty is a culture in the sense that the mechanism of impoverishment is fundamentally the same in every part of the system. The vicious circle is a basic pattern. It takes different forms for the unskilled workers, for the aged, for the Negroes, for the agricultural workers, but in each case the principle is the same. There are people in the affluent society who are poor because they are poor; and who stay poor because they are poor.

To realize this is to see that there are some tens of millions of Americans who are beyond the welfare state. Some of them are simply not covered by social legislation: they are omitted from Social Security and from minimum wage. Others are covered, but since they are so poor they do not know how to take advantage of the opportunities, or else their coverage is so inadequate as not to make a difference.

The welfare state was designed during that great burst of social creativity that took place in the 1930's. As previously noted its structure corresponds to the needs of those who played the most important role in building it: the middle third, the organized workers, the forces of urban liberalism, and so on. At the worst, there is "socialism for the rich and free enterprise for the poor," as when the huge corporation farms are the main beneficiaries of the farm program while the poor farmers get practically nothing; or when public funds are directed to aid in the construction of luxury housing while the slums are left to themselves (or become more dense as space is created for the well-off).

So there is the fundamental paradox of the welfare state: that it is not built for the desperate, but for those who are already capable of helping themselves. As long as the illusion persists that the poor are merrily free-loading on the public dole, so long will the other America continue unthreatened. The truth, it must be understood, is the exact opposite. The poor get less out of the welfare state than any group in America.

This is, of course, related to the most distinguishing mark of the other America: its common sense of hopelessness. For even when there are programs designed to help the other Americans, the poor are held back by their own pessimism.

On one level this fact has been described in this book as a matter of "aspiration." Like the Asian peasant, the impoverished American tends to see life as a fate, an endless cycle from which there is no deliverance. Lacking hope (and he is realistic to feel this way in many cases), that famous solution to all problems—let us educate the poor—becomes less and less meaningful. A person has to feel that education will do something for him if he is to gain from it. Placing a magnificent school with a fine faculty in the middle of a slum is, I suppose, better than having a run-down building staffed by incompetents. But it will not really make a difference so long as the environment of the tenement, the family, and the street counsels the children to leave as soon as they can and to disregard schooling.

On another level, the emotions of the other America are even more profoundly disturbed. Here it is not lack of aspiration and of hope; it is a matter of personal chaos. The drunkenness, the unstable marriages, the violence of the other America are not simply facts about individuals. They are the description of an entire group in the society who react this way because of the conditions under which they live.

In short, being poor is not one aspect of a person's life in this country; it is his life. Taken as a whole, poverty is a culture. Taken on the family level, it has the same quality. These are people who lack education and skill, who have bad health, poor housing, low levels of aspiration and high levels of mental distress. They are, in the language of sociology, "multiproblem" families. Each disability is the more intense because it exists within a web of disabilities. And if one problem is solved, and the others are left constant, there is little gain.

One might translate these facts into the moralistic language so dear to those who would condemn the poor for their faults. The other Americans are those who live at a level of life beneath moral choice, who are so submerged in their poverty that one cannot begin to talk about free choice. The point is not to make them wards of the state. Rather, society must help them before they can help themselves.

II

There is another view about the culture of poverty in America: that by the end of the seventies it will have been halved.

It is important to deal in some detail with this theory. To begin with, it is not offered by reactionaries. The real die-hards in the United States do not even know the poor exist. As soon as someone begins to talk on the subject, that stamps him as a humanitarian. And this is indeed the case with those who look to a relatively automatic improvement in the lot of the other America during the next twenty years or so.

The second reason why this view deserves careful consideration is that it rests, to a considerable extent, upon the projection of inevitable and automatic change. Its proponents are for social legislation and for speeding up and deepening this process. But their very arguments could be used to justify a comfortable, complacent inaction.

So, does poverty have a future in the United States?

One of the most reasonable and sincere statements of the theme that poverty is coming to an end in America is made by Robert Lampman in the Joint Committee Study Paper "The Low-Income Population and Economic Growth." Lampman estimates that around 20 per cent of the nation, some 32,000,000 people, are poor. . . . And he writes, "By 1977-87 we would expect about 10 percent of the population to have low income status as compared to about 20 percent now."

The main point in Lampman's relatively optimistic argument is that poverty will decline naturally with a continuing rate of economic growth. As the sixties begin, however, this assumption is not a simple one. In the postwar period, growth increased until about the mid-fifties. Then a falling off occurred. In each of the postwar recessions, the recovery left a larger reservoir of "normal" prosperity unemployment. Also, long-term unemployment became more and more of a factor among the jobless. There were more people out of work, and they stayed out of work longer.

In the first period of the Kennedy Administration, various economists presented figures as to what kind of Government action was necessary so as really to attack the problem of depressed areas and low-income occupations. There were differences, of course, but the significant fact is that the legislation finally proposed was usually only a percentage of the need as described by the Administration itself. There is no point now in becoming an economic prophet. Suffice it to say that serious and responsible economists feel that the response of the society has been inadequate.

This has led to a paradoxical situation, one that became quite obvious when economic recovery from the recession began in the spring of 1961. The business indicators were all pointing upward: production and productivity were on the increase. Yet the human indexes of recession showed a tenacity despite the industrial gain. Unemployment remained at high levels. An extreme form of the "class unemployment" described earlier seemed to be built into the economy.

At any rate, one can say that if this problem is not solved the other America will not only persist; it will grow. Thus, the first point of the optimistic thesis strikes me as somewhat ambiguous, for it too quickly assumes that the society will make the needed response.

But even if one makes the assumption that there will be steady economic growth, that will not necessarily lead to the automatic elimination of poverty in the United States. J. K. Galbraith, it will be remembered, has argued that the "new" poverty demonstrates a certain immunity to progress. In making his projection of the abolition of half of the culture of poverty within the next generation, Lampman deals with this point, and it is important to follow his argument.

Lampman rejects the idea that insular (or depressed-areas) poverty will really drag the poor down in the long run. As an example of this point, he cites the fact that the number of rural farm families with incomes of under $2,000 fell during the 1947-1957 period from 3.3 million to 2.4 million because of a movement off the farm.

This point illustrates the problem of dealing with simple statistics. A movement from the farm to the city, that is, from rural poverty to urban poverty, will show an upward movement in money income. This is true, among other reasons, because the money income of the urban poor is higher than that of the country poor. But this same change does not necessarily mean that a human being has actually improved his status, that he has escaped from the culture of poverty. As was noted in the chapter on the agricultural poor, these people who are literally driven off the land are utterly unprepared for city life. They come to the metropolis in a time of rising skill requirements and relatively high levels of unemployment. They will often enter the economic underworld. Statistically, they can be recorded as a gain, because they have more money. Socially, they have simply transferred from one part of the culture of poverty to another.

At the same time, it should be noted that although there has been this tremendous exodus of the rural poor, the proportion of impoverished farms in America's agriculture has remained roughly the same.

Then Lampman deals with Galbraith's theory of "case poverty," of those who have certain disabilities that keep them down in the culture of poverty. Here it should be noted again that Galbraith himself is somewhat optimistic about case poverty. He tends to regard the bad health of the poor, physical as well as mental, as being facts about them that are individual and personal. If this book is right, particularly in the discussion of the twisted spirit within the culture of poverty, that is not the case. The personal ills of the poor are a social consequence, not a bit of biography about them. They will continue as long as the environment of poverty persists.

But Lampman's optimism goes beyond that of Galbraith. He believes that disabilities of case poverty ("mental deficiency, bad health, inability to adapt to the discipline of modern economic life, excessive procreation, alcohol, insufficient education") are "moderated over time." And he takes as his main case in point education. "For example, average educational attainment levels will rise in future years simply because younger people presently have better education than older people. Hence, as the current generation of old people pass from the scene, the percent of persons with low educational attainment will fall."

This is true, yet is is misleading if it is not placed in the context of the changes in the society as a whole. It is much more possible today to be poor with a couple of years of high school than it was a generation ago. As I have pointed out earlier, the skill level of the economy has been changing, and educational deficiency, if anything, becomes an even greater burden as a result. In this case, saying that people will have more education is not saying that they will escape the culture of poverty. It could have a much more ironic meaning: that America will have the most literate poor the world has ever known.

Lampman himself concedes that the aged are "immune" to economic growth. If this is the case, and in the absence of ranging and comprehensive social programs, the increase in the number and percentage of the poor within the next generation will actually increase the size of the other America. Lampman also concedes that families with female heads are immune to a general prosperity, and this is another point of resistance for the culture of poverty.

Finally, Lampman is much more optimistic about "nonwhite" progress than the discussion in this book would justify. I will not repeat the argument that has already been given. Let me simply state the point baldly: the present rate of economic progress among the minorities is agonizingly slow, and one cannot look for dramatic gains from this direction.

Thus, I would agree with Galbraith that poverty in the sixties has qualities that give it a hardiness in the face of affluence heretofore unknown. As documented and described in this book, there are many special factors keeping the unskilled workers, the minorities, the agricultural poor, and the aged in the culture of poverty. If there is to be a way out, it will come from human action, from political change, not from automatic processes.

But finally, let us suppose that Lampman is correct on every point. In that case a generation of economic growth coupled with some social legislation would find America in 1987 with "only" 10 per cent of the nation impoverished. If, on the other hand, a vast and comprehensive program attacking the culture of poverty could speed up this whole development, and perhaps even abolish poverty within a generation, what is the reason for holding back? This suffering is such an abomination in a society where it is needless that anything that can be done should be done.

In all this, I do not want to depict Robert Lampman as an enemy of the poor. In all seriousness, the very fact that he writes about the subject does him credit: he has social eyes, which is more than one can say for quite a few people in the society. And second, Lampman puts forward "A Program to Hasten the Reduction of Poverty" because of his genuine concern for the poor. My argument with him is not over motive or dedication. It is only that I believe that his theory makes the reduction of poverty too easy a thing, that he has not properly appreciated how deeply and strongly entrenched the other America is.

In any case, and from any point of view, the moral obligation is plain: there must be a crusade against this poverty in our midst.

III

If this research makes it clear that a basic attack upon poverty is necessary, it also suggests the kind of program the nation needs.

First and foremost, any attempt to abolish poverty in the United States must seek to destroy the pessimism and fatalism that flourish in the other America. In part, this can be done by offering real opportunities to these people, by changing the social reality that gives rise to their sense of hopelessness. But beyond that (these fears of the poor have a life of their own and are not simply rooted in analyses of employment chances), there should be a spirit, an élan, that communicates itself to the entire society.

If the nation comes into the other America grudgingly, with the mentality of an administrator, and says, "All right, we'll help you people," then there will be gains, but they will be kept to the minimum; a dollar spent will return a dollar. But if there is an attitude that society is gaining by eradicating poverty, if there is a positive attempt to bring these millions of the poor to the point where they can make their contribution to the United States, that will make a huge difference. The spirit of a campaign against poverty does not cost a single cent. It is a matter of vision, of sensitivity.

Let me give an example to make this point palpable. During the Montgomery bus boycott, there was only one aim in the Negro community of that city: to integrate the buses. There were no speeches on crime or juvenile delinquency. And yet it is reported that the crime rate among Negroes in Montgomery declined. Thousands of people had been given a sense of purpose, of their own worth and dignity. On their own, and without any special urging, they began to change their personal lives; they became a different people. If the same élan could invade the other America, there would be similar results.

Second, this book is based upon the proposition that poverty forms a culture, an interdependent system. In case after case, it has been documented that one cannot deal with the various components of poverty in isolation, changing this or that condition but leaving the basic structure intact. Consequently, a campaign against the misery of the poor should be comprehensive. It should think, not in terms of this or that aspect of poverty, but along the lines of establishing new communities, of substituting a human environment for the inhuman one that now exists.

Here, housing is probably the basic point of departure. If there were the funds and imagination for a campaign to end slums in the United States, most of the other steps needed to deal with poverty could be integrated with it. The vision should be the one described in the previous chapter: the political, economic, and social integration of the poor with the rest of the society. The second nation in our midst, the other America, must be brought into the Union.

In order to do this, there is a need for planning. It is literally incredible that this nation knows so much about poverty, that it has made so many inventories of misery, and that it has done so little. The material for a comprehensive program is already available. It exists in congressional reports and the statistics of Government agencies. What is needed is that the society make use of its knowledge in a rational and systematic way. As this book is being written, there are proposals for a Department of Urban Affairs in the Cabinet (and it will probably be a reality by the time these words are published) . Such an agency could be the coordinating center for a crusade against the other America. In any case, if there is not planning, any attempt to deal with the problem of poverty will fail, at least in part.

Then there are some relatively simple things that could be done, involving the expansion of existing institutions and programs. Every

American should be brought under the coverage of social security, and the payments should be enough to support a dignified old age. The principle already exists. Now it must be extended to those who need help the most. The same is true with minimum wage. The spectacle of excluding the most desperate from coverage must come to an end. If it did, there would be a giant step toward the elimination of poverty itself.

In every subculture of the other America, sickness and disease are the most important agencies of continuing misery. The New York *Times* publishes a list of the "neediest cases" each Christmas. In 1960 the descriptions of personal tragedy that ran along with this appeal involved in the majority of cases the want of those who had been struck down by illness. If there were adequate medical care, this charity would be unnecessary.

Today the debate on medical care centers on the aged. And indeed, these are the people who are in the most desperate straits. Yet it would be an error of the first magnitude to think that society's responsibility begins with those sixty-five years of age. As has been pointed out several times, the ills of the elderly are often the inheritance of the earlier years. A comprehensive medical program, guaranteeing decent care to every American, would actually reduce the cost of caring for the aged. That, of course, is only the hardheaded argument for such an approach. More importantly, such a program would make possible a human kind of existence for everyone in the society.

And finally, it must be remembered that none of these objectives can be accomplished if racial prejudice is to continue in the United States. Negroes and other minorities constitute only 25 per cent of the poor, yet their degradation is an important element in maintaining the entire culture of poverty. As long as there is a reservoir of cheap Negro labor, there is a means of keeping the poor whites down. In this sense, civil-rights legislation is an absolutely essential component in any campaign to end poverty in the United States.

In short, the welfare provisions of American society that now help the upper two-thirds must be extended to the poor. This can be done if the other Americans are motivated to take advantage of the opportunities before them, if they are invited into the society. It can be done if there is a comprehensive program that attacks the culture of poverty at every one of its strong points.

But who will carry out this campaign?

There is only one institution in the society capable of acting to abolish poverty. That is the Federal Government. In saying this, I do not rejoice, for centralization can lead to an impersonal and bureaucratic program, one that will be lacking in the very human quality so essential in an approach to the poor. In saying this, I am only recording the facts of political and social life in the United States.

The cities are not now capable of dealing with poverty, and each day they become even less capable. As the middle class flees the central urban area, as various industries decentralize, the tax base of the American metropolis shrinks. At the same time, the social and economic problems with which the city must deal are on the rise. Thus, there is not a major city in the United States that is today capable of attacking poverty on its own. On the contrary, the high cost of poverty is dragging the cities down.

The state governments in this country have a political peculiarity that renders them incapable of dealing with the problem of poverty. They are, for the most part, dominated by conservative rural elements. In every state with a big industrial population, the gerrymander has given the forces of rural conservatism two or three votes per person. So it is that the state legislatures usually take more money out of the problem areas than they put back into them. So it is that state governments are notoriously weighted in the direction of caution, pinchpenny economics, and indifference to the plight of the urban millions.

The various private agencies of the society simply do not have the funds to deal with the other America. And even the "fringe benefits" negotiated by unions do not really get to the heart of the problem. In the first place, they extend to organized workers in a strong bargaining position, not to the poor. And second, they are inadequate even to the needs of those who are covered.

It is a noble sentiment to argue that private moral responsibility expressing itself through charitable contributions should be the main instrument of attacking poverty. The only problem is that such an approach does not work.

So, by process of elimination, there is no place to look except toward the Federal Government. And indeed, even if there were alternate choices, Washington would have to play an important role, if only because of the need for a comprehensive program and for national planning. But in any case there is no argument, for there is only one realistic possibility: only the Federal Government has the power to abolish poverty.

In saying this, it is not necessary to advocate complete central control of such a campaign. Far from it. Washington is essential in a double sense: as a source of the considerable funds needed to mount a campaign against the other America, and as a place for coordination, for planning, and the establishment of national standards. The actual implementation of a program to abolish poverty can be carried out through myriad institutions, and the closer they are to the specific local area, the better the results. There are, as has been pointed out already, housing administrators, welfare workers, and city planners with dedication and vision. They are working on the local level, and their main frustration is the lack of funds. They could be trusted actually to carry through on a national program. What they lack now is money and the support of the American people.

There is no point in attempting to blueprint or detail the mechanisms and institutions of a war on poverty in the United States. There is information enough for action. All that is lacking is political will.

Thus the difficult, hardheaded question about poverty that one must answer is this: Where is the political will coming from? The other America is systematically underrepresented in the Government of the United States. It cannot really speak for itself. The poor, even in politics, must always be the object of charity (with the major exception of the Negroes, who, in recent times, have made tremendous strides forward in organization).

As a result of this situation, there is no realistic hope for the abolition of poverty in the United States until there is a vast social movement, a new period of political creativity. In times of slow change or of stalemate, it is always the poor who are expendable in the halls of Congress. In 1961, for instance, the laundry workers were dropped out of the minimum wage as part of a deal with the conservatives. Precisely because they are so poor and cruelly exploited, no one had to fear their political wrath. They, and others from the culture of poverty, will achieve the protection of the welfare state when there is a movement in this land so dynamic and irresistible that it need not make concessions.

For that matter, it is much easier to catalogue the enemies of the poor than it is to recite their friends.

All the forces of conservatism in this society are ranged against the needs of the other America. The ideologues are opposed to helping the poor because this can be accomplished only through an expansion of the welfare state. The small businessmen have an immediate self-interest in maintaining the economic underworld. The powerful agencies of the corporate farms want a continuation of an agricultural program that aids the rich and does nothing for the poor.

And now the South is becoming increasingly against the poor. In the days of the New Deal, the Southern Democrats tended to vote for various kinds of social legislation. One of the most outspoken champions of public housing, Burnet Maybank, was a senator from South Carolina. For one thing, there is a Southern tradition of being against Wall Street and big business; it is part of the farmers' hostility to the railroads and the Babylons of the big city. For another, the New Deal legislation did not constitute a challenge to the system of racial segregation in the South.

But in the postwar period, this situation began to change. As industrialization came to the South, there was a growing political opposition to laws like minimum wage, to unions, and to other aspects of social change. The leaders of this area saw their depressed condition as an advantage. They could lure business with the promise of cheap, unorganized labor. They were interested in exploiting their backwardness.

The result was the strengthening of the coalition of Southern Democrats and conservative Northern Republicans. The Northern conservatives went along with opposition to Civil Rights legislation. The Southerners threw their votes into the struggle against social advance. It was this powerful coalition that exacted such a price in the first period of the Kennedy Administration. Many of the proposals that would have benefited the poor were omitted from bills in the first place, and other concessions were made in the course of the legislative battle. Thus poverty in the United States is supported by forces with great political and economic power.

On the other side, the friends of the poor are to be found in the American labor movement and among the middle-class liberals. The unions in the postwar period lost much of the élan that had characterized them in the thirties. Yet on questions of social legislation they remained the most powerful mass force committed to change in general, and to bettering the lot of the poor in particular. On issues like housing, medical care, minimum wage, and social security, the labor movement provided the strongest voice stating the cause of the poor.

Yet labor and the liberals were caught in the irrationalities of the American party system, and this was an enormous disadvantage to the other America. The unionists and their liberal allies are united in the Democratic party with the Southern conservatives. A Democratic victory was usually achieved by appealing to those who were concerned for social change. But at the same time it brought the forces of conservatism powerful positions on the standing committees of the Congress.

Indeed, part of the invisibility of poverty in American life is a result of this party structure. Since each major party contained differences within itself greater than the differences between it and the other party, politics in the fifties and early sixties tended to have an issueless character. And where issues were not discussed, the poor did not have a chance. They could benefit only if elections were designed to bring new information to the people, to wake up the nation, to challenge, and to call to action.

In all probability there will not be a real attack on the culture of poverty so long as this situation persists. For the other America cannot be abolished through concessions and compromises that are almost inevitably made at the expense of the poor. The spirit, the vision that are required if the nation is to penetrate the wall of pessimism and despair that surrounds the impoverished millions cannot be produced under such circumstances.

What is needed if poverty is to be abolished is a return of political debate, a restructuring of the party system so that there can be clear choices, a new mood of social idealism.

These, then, are the strangest poor in the history of mankind.

They exist within the most powerful and rich society the world has ever known. Their misery has continued while the majority of the nation talked of itself as being "affluent" and worried about neuroses in the suburbs. In this way tens of millions of human beings became invisible. They dropped out of sight and out of mind; they were without their own political voice.

Yet this need not be. The means are at hand to fulfill the age-old dream: poverty can now be abolished. How long shall we ignore this underdeveloped nation in our midst? How long shall we look the other way while our fellow human beings suffer? How long?

7. Elinor Graham
The Politics of Poverty

The much-heralded War on Poverty proved, in the words of one analyst,
to be a "minor skirmish." There are many reasons for this. The
deepening war in Southeast Asia drained tens of billions of dollars
from the U.S. treasury. An endless literature has developed that
demonstrates how political critics, the rivalry of competing government
agencies, the vested interests of local officials, and bureaucratic expenses
undermined the potential success of the poverty programs. But in
the perceptive and controversial essay that follows, Elinor Graham, a
political scientist working at the Institute for Policy Studies in
Washington, D.C., when she wrote this analysis, raises profound questions
on the motivations of the leaders who created the programs.

In Graham's interpretation, the Negro liberation movement created
a powerful threat to the traditional ruling groups that then sought a means
to divert its revolutionary implications into controllable channels.
The poverty program was the answer. It "redefined civil rights in a manner
that secures the power positions of white public leaders and places
them in control." Moreover, to repress the moral questions raised by
the existence of racism, "poverty" was substituted for "race": "white
Americans had to raise the poverty issue to relieve the emotional
tension and political impasse created by the racial confrontation."
Implicit in this analysis is the thesis that white America has never
fully confronted the reality of racial conflict, and that this failure
doomed the poverty war to ultimate defeat.

This essay raises many questions. Among them is whether Elinor Graham
has isolated the major reason for the shortcomings of the poverty
programs. Does the essay deal fairly with the emotional travail that
many liberals experienced when first confronted with the issue of
poverty? Have subsequent years and administrations tended to vindicate
or disprove Graham's thesis?

In January 1964, a man familiar to congressional surroundings delivered
his first address to a joint session of Congress in his new role as President
of the United States. As he presented his presidential program to Congress, Lyndon Johnson called for an "unconditional war on poverty," a
government commitment "not only to relieve the symptoms of poverty,
but to cure it; and above all, to prevent it."

The complex of ideological themes and political programs officially recognized and initiated by this address—all under the slogan of a War on Poverty—is the topic of this paper. The analysis developed here views this "war" as a key ingredient in the social and political ideology embraced by President Johnson, his administrative officials, and his advisers. As part of an ideology, it is designed to motivate elements in the society to political action. The language of the War on Poverty and the form of its accompanying social-welfare programs are set within the boundaries of traditional social beliefs, arise from the pressure of political needs, and are molded by the nature of those groups seeking action, as well as by the official bodies from which they must receive approval.

Poverty, consequently, is now a major preoccupation of hundreds of public officials, statisticians and social planners across the nation. In less than a year it has been thrust dramatically into the center of governmental programing on local, regional, and national levels. President Johnson has called for "total victory" in a national War on Poverty—"a total commitment by the President, and this Congress, and this Nation, to pursue victory over the most ancient of mankind's enemies." Joining the administration forces and local and state governments, private social-welfare organizations and institutions normally engaged in nonwelfare activities have increasingly indicated an awareness of possibilities, and a willingness, to engage their organizational resources in "extrainstitutional" activities aimed at the alleviation of poverty. Colleges, churches, and corporations have plunged into a potpourri of activities designed to provide "opportunities" for deserving members of low-income groups in forms, and to an extent, that welfare workers could previously conceive only in their wildest dreams.

Given an "understanding of the enemy" which emphasizes the special characteristics of certain low-income groups that cannot easily be integrated into the market economy, what "strategy of attack" is advocated by the national policymakers? The "war on poverty" proposed in 1964 consisted of a ten-point attack which strikingly resembled the President's entire domestic program: income tax cuts, a civil rights bill, Appalachian regional development, urban and rural community rehabilitation, youth programs, teenage and adult vocational training and basic educational programs, and hospital insurance for the aged. A special "anti-poverty package" was introduced—the Economic Opportunity Act of 1964. The Office of Economic Opportunity created by this legislation was to be the headquarters for the new "war."

Administration of the Economic Opportunity Act and supporting programs, as well as plans for future expansion, indicate that the War on Poverty seeks to mobilize the social services of the nation along three major lines: youth education and employment programs, planned regional and community redevelopment, and vocational training and retraining under the beginnings of a national manpower policy.

Under this "strategy of attack," aid to the poor is, in theory, provided in the nature of a new and expanded "opportunity environment." Such aid is primarily directed toward the youth and employable heads of poor families; it will not reach the really critical poverty categories—the aged, female heads of families, and poor farm families—except in the form of improvements in the surrounding physical and economic environments or the administration of welfare and health services. As the Council of Economic Advisers noted in their 1964 report, the proposed programs are designed "to equip and to permit the poor of the Nation to produce and to earn . . . the American standard of living by their own efforts and contributions." Those Americans who are not in a physical or family position which allows them to earn their way out of poverty will not be immediately aided by the programs under the War on Poverty. This situation simply illustrates the difference between social needs defined in a statistical manner and a political designation of poverty. It does not indicate that the War on Poverty is a political hoax or a hollow slogan to attract votes; on the contrary, its ideology and programs respond to social and political needs of a very real, although very different, nature, than those of poverty per se.

The Sociology of Poverty Programs

It is useful to locate welfare-state programs on two scales, vertically and horizontally, in order to visualize the range and nature of programs open to government planners in formulating the War on Poverty and to understand the implications of the particular path chosen. The vertical scale of our imaginary axes indicates at one end whether the poverty-stricken are singled out of the total society as objects for special aid or, at the opposite pole, social services and income payments are provided to all as a right of citizenship. The latter method is followed in most of the Swedish welfare programs. Family payments, old-age pensions, and health services are provided for all members of the society regardless of their financial position. Most United States welfare programs, including those proposed under the War on Poverty, are located at the opposite pole: programs are focused at a particular low-income category and need must be proven in order to receive aid. The second (and horizontal) scale indicates at one end that aid may be provided in the form of direct income payments and at the other extreme through social services. The major portion of the welfare activities in the United States, and particularly those connected with the War on Poverty, are found in the service category, even though, as was argued above, the nature of American poverty in the sixties indicates an urgent need for consideration of direct income payments to critical poverty-stricken groups.

Certain important implications follow from the need-based and service-oriented nature of the War on Poverty programs. First, separation of the poor from the rest of the society by means of need requirements, increases the visibility of the low-income earners. This is a "war" on *poverty* —the very nature of such a proposal requires an exposure of "the enemy" in its human form. In addition, separation of the poor creates a donor-donee relationship whether it exists between the income-tax-paying middle and upper classes and the low-income earners, or the social worker and his client. In the context of American social philosophy, such a situation enhances the self-image of the well-to-do and places a stigma of failure and dependency upon aid recipients. Above all, it is "the American way" to approach social-welfare issues, for it places the burden of responsibility upon the individual and not upon the socioeconomic system. Social services are preferred to income payments in an ideological atmosphere which abhors "handouts."

Second, a focus upon *poverty* allows for a redefinition of the racial clash into the politically understandable and useful terms of a conflict between the "haves" and the "have-nots." The donor-donee relationship, sharply cast into relief by the poverty label, reasserts and stabilizes the power of the political elite, whose positions have been threatened by enfranchisement of the Negro.

Third, the social-service orientation, particularly the stress upon the "reorganization" and "total mobilization" of existing programs, is strongly supported by the nature of the experimental programs started during the Kennedy years. These programs and, of more importance, the ideas and "method of attack" which they initiated, are vigorously advocated by a well-organized and sophisticated lobby within the administrative branch.

Fourth, the social-service orientation of the War on Poverty is *activity*- and *job*-creating for the middle and upper classes. Provision of social services, as opposed to income payments, requires the formation of new organizations and institutions which in turn are the source of activities and income-paying roles for the nation's expanding number of college-educated individuals. The War on Poverty, its programs and ideology, are a response to the demands of an educated "new class": it provides a legitimate outlet for the energies of a group that poses a greater threat to the political system and moral fabric of the society than the inadequately educated poor who are the official objects of aid.

Ideology and Poverty

A nation which confidently points to its unparalleled level of wealth, the "magnificent abundance" of the American way of life, has been suddenly and surprisingly engaged in the public unveiling of the impoverished degradation of one-fifth of its population. Affluence and poverty confront each other, and the shock of the encounter is reflected in the phrase that acknowledges the "stranger's" presence: a "paradox"—the "paradox of poverty in the midst of plenty." This mysterious stranger is apparently inconsistent with the nation's vision of itself and particularly with its moral notions of equality.

One supposes that there is an element of honest surprise and, with many, disbelief, for they *know* that if you work hard and take advantage of all of the opportunities available, you *can* climb out of poverty and reach the top—well, perhaps not *the top,* but certainly a comfortable level of living. It is axiomatic. Numerous individuals will tediously cite their own life experiences as examples of this general law of dynamics of American society. The following account was provided by a retired educator who sought to establish his qualification to talk about poverty in the sixties:

> . . . *I was born in a homestead on the lowland swamps of Louisiana.
> There were no schools. We lived off the land. And, since I have
> viewed the very sections of the underprivileged and poor people in
> the Appalachian highland, I decided I must have been very poor,
> because those children there have much more now than I had.
> We lived from game, and we had no electric lights. We got food if
> there were plenty of ducks and geese and rabbits . . . I was a
> drop-in at school when they finally got a little one- or two-room
> school. I mean, I dropped in when there were no potatoes to plant or
> corn to pull, or something of that sort. I have three college degrees
> from standard universities, and I never spent a day on a college
> campus during regular session. I belong to the old school. I took
> correspondence; I did some summer terms, and I did extension work,
> traveling sometimes a hundred miles each weekend to take it.
> So I think I know what it means to get an education the hard
> way. . . . I understand the phase in our help to the underprivileged.*

Everyone who is over thirty will say that they know what it is like to be poor because they lived during the Great Depression; that is taken as automatic qualification. When attacked by his Democratic "bretheren" for a lack of understanding of the complexities of the problem, Representative Griffin (R.-Mich.) responded with, "my father worked most of his life in a plant; and I worked my way through school, and I believe I do know a little bit about poverty." Without denying the achievements of the poor boy from the swamps of Louisiana who is now a distinguished educator, or the son of a worker holding the office of U.S. congressman, such accounts and their implications for the "struggling young men" from present-day poor families reflect a general confusion of the income and social-class mobility of an individual with a rising national standard of living. The American dream is substituted for the American reality and evidence drawn from the second is said to be proof of the first.

President Johnson intertwined the two concepts when he declared in his 1964 War on Poverty message that:

With the growth of our country has come opportunity for our people—opportunity to educate our children, to use our energies in productive work, to increase our leisure—opportunity for almost every American to hope that through work and talent he could create a better life for himself and his family.

Traditional themes of the bright boy attaining entrance to the world of wealth through "work and talent" are intermingled with the profit figures of economic growth. In suggesting that the benefits of a rising standard of living include increased opportunity for bettering income and even social-class position, two distinct and different concepts are equated for ideological purposes.

Fusion of dream and actuality in the national vision has been strongly influenced by the American business creed and its image of the relationship between the economic system and the individual. Benefits derived from the economic growth of the nation are not conceived as social products. The idealized "free-enterprise" system produces the national wealth through the efforts of atomized individuals operating within a "free competitive market system with individual freedom." A guarantee of the rights of the individual to insure his freedom and free opportunity are thus essential. Since mythology need not correspond to reality (particularly if believed in strongly enough), equality of opportunity is assumed and is "proved" through the individual success stories which abound in the popular literature. Such "proof" is, however, subject to a great deal of doubt. Citing several sociological studies, the authors of *The American Business Creed* observe that a survey of the overall statistical situation "might well lead to more tempered conclusions about American freedom of opportunity."

With an image of itself that denies the possibility of widespread poverty, a nation bent on "recognizing realities" must squeeze the poor in through the basement window. We are told that we are not faced with extensive conditions of poverty (as are other less fortunate nations). Poverty in the United States is "grinding poverty," found only in "pockets of poverty" and has defied all laws of genetics to acquire an hereditary quality exhibited in the "ruthless pattern" and "cycle of poverty." This is not a case of good old-fashioned poverty, it is a special and uniquely American—1964 brand.

A particularly vivid exposition of this version of poverty can be found in the explanation of the Economic Opportunity Act prepared by Sargent Shriver's office for the first congressional hearings. Much of the credit for the modern version of poverty expounded within its covers must go to the influence of John Kenneth Galbraith's writings. He broke the poor into two groups—those afflicted with *case* poverty and those who are victims of *insular* poverty. Characteristics of the individual afflicted with case poverty prevent him from mastering his environment, while the environment proves to be the handicapping factor for those living in "islands of poverty." In both situations an hereditary factor is introduced either in fact (as a physical tendency toward poor health or mental deficiency) or in effect through the deficiencies of the social environment (as with poor schools, lack of job opportunities, lack of motivation and direction from parents). Whether or not such a view corresponds to reality, it should be recognized that when one maintains that the society is affluent, poverty can hardly be tolerated as a widespread phenomenon and must be of a very special and individual variety. With such a thesis, one is not likely to observe that an average American family with an income of $5665—the median for all families in 1960—may not feel particularly affluent at this "modest but adequate" level.

Where, then, are the roots of poverty in an affluent society? Few combatants in the war of ideologies argue that the fault underlies the American landscape and may be lodged in the economic system. The principle according to which the wealth of the society is divided is left unscathed. On official levels, voices do not openly suggest that a system which distributes economic goods solely upon the basis of the individual's present or past functional role within the economy may be at the source of American poverty now and increasingly so in the future. Although not reflecting official opinion, the statement of the Ad Hoc Committee on the Triple Revolution was a notable exception. This group of distinguished educators, labor leaders, economists, and critics suggested in part that:

The economy of abundance can sustain all citizens in comfort and economic security whether or not they engage in what is commonly reckoned as work. . . . We urge, therefore, that society through its appropriate legal and governmental institutions undertake an unqualified commitment to provide every individual in every family with an adequate income as a matter of right.

Right-wing reaction is clear and quite predictable when the legitimacy of the American economic system is questioned in any context. There was no doubt in the mind of Representative Martin (R.-Neb.) that the suggestions of the committee were of "the same kind of plan worked out in Communist nations." Such a reaction hardly leaves room for political debate.

Where questions regarding "the system" are taboo, those focusing upon the individual are welcome and quite comprehensible to the political protagonists. In acceptable political circles, the causes of poverty are sought in the process through which individuals acquire qualities enabling them to succeed and share in the national wealth. Conservatives argue that the fault lies with the poor for being lazy or stupid and not taking advantage of opportunities to obtain education, good health, a marketable skill, and a stable family life. "The fact is that most people who have no skill, have had no education for the same reason—low intelligence or low ambition!" says Barry Goldwater. On the other hand, liberals maintain that something is wrong with the present means provided for individuals to obtain these desirable attributes—in short, the society is at fault: the poor are the "have-not people of America. They are denied, deprived, disadvantaged, and they are discriminated against," argues Walter Reuther of the United Auto Workers. President Johnson and Sargent Shriver, commander of the poverty forces, bow to both groups. They maintain that it is first necessary to change the attitudes of the poor—to give them achievement motivations by changing "indifference to interest, ignorance to awareness, resignation to ambition, and an attitude of withdrawal to one of participation." At the same time, present education, social-welfare, and job-training programs sponsored at all levels of government and in both the public and private sectors of society, must be coordinated, consolidated and expanded to provide a new "opportunity environment" for the poor.

The emphasis is upon the process by which Americans attain the attributes necessary to achieve economic success rather than the legitimacy of the system to distribute the national wealth. This view is enhanced by the assumption that Americans, and poor Americans in particular, must earn and "want to earn" any social or economic benefits they receive. In our society, states Senator Goldwater, one receives rewards by "merit and not by fiat"—essentially, you earn your keep or you get out (or stay out) :

*I strongly believe that all people are entitled to an opportunity . . .
to get an education and to earn a living in keeping with the
value of their work [emphasis supplied]. . . . But I do not believe
that the mere fact of having little money entitles everybody,*

regardless of circumstance, to be permanently maintained by the taxpayers at an average or comfortable standard of living.

Conservatives make no effort to conceal their reliance on this basic assumption; they quite frankly do not want to change the present distribution of wealth, or potential advantages they may have in gaining a greater future share. They are successful because they deserve to be successful, while others are poor because they are innately incapable of doing any better. This assumption about human nature is an integral part of the business creed, for the idealized economic system is dependent upon the "achievement motivations" of the individual. These crucial motivations could easily be destroyed if people became dependent upon government doles. If this happened, the greatest welfare system of all, the "free-enterprise system," would be destroyed. As the witness from the Chamber of Commerce explained to Representative Edith Green during the House antipoverty hearings, the Chamber does not support "programs for people" because:

. . . *economic measures to improve the efficiency of production and thus to get a larger output for our people from the same input of materials and manpower and capital goods is one of the greatest contributions to wealth that has ever been discovered in the history of mankind and the United States excels among all nations of the world in providing this kind of welfare.*

Despite conservative denunciations, President Johnson eagerly reserves a benevolent role for the federal government, and particularly on an ideological level. He counters conservative views by adding a second act to the drama of the poor struggling young man working his way to the top in the "free-enterprise system." A magnanimous millionaire, glowing with compassion and wisdom, stretches out a benevolent helping hand to enable "Ragged Dick" to make good in the final panel of the American dream. Evoking an image of a goddess of peace and plenty rather than lanky Uncle Sam, Johnson declares that both at home and abroad, "We will extend the helping hand of a just nation to the poor and helpless and the oppressed." In the American reality, however, "we" take care to see that the "helping hand" doesn't contain money or tangible goods—just opportunities to earn a better way of life and opportunities *to learn* to "want to earn" in the American way.

Such a sense of *noblesse oblige* is not inherent in the actual programs and techniques proposed in the War on Poverty, but it plays a part in the language which is inevitably used to describe them (and which is perhaps latent within our "progressive" attitudes toward social welfare). It is also the result of the effective control and administration of the government by the affluent and educated classes. In short, the official government attitude toward poverty should be expected to reflect the views arising from the life-situations of those who have formulated it. In speaking of poverty, no one bothers to deny or to hide the fact that the federal government is an instrumentality of the successful classes. This is assumed. The poor are recognized as not having a significant political voice. The entire War on Poverty was created, inspired, and will be carried out by the affluent. Action by the upper classes and all superior groups is urged on moral grounds, because it is right, because, as Senator Robert Kennedy stated simply, "those of us who are better off, who do not have that problem have a responsibility to our fellow citizens who do."

Without an economic crisis which affects the upper-income groups as well as the poor, the social philosophy of the federal antipoverty programs will necessarily contain this strong moral emphasis. Caught between the language of American social mythology and the attitudes generated by the existing social and political realities of a wealthy nation ruled by a distinct class of successful men, the public debate generated by the proposed "war" can only reveal our poverty of ideology. Conservatives balk at action because the poor are "getting what they deserve," and liberals cannot seem to act without assuming the "white man's burden." The militants of the new "war" look for the enemy and find him all too often in the personal attributes of the poor. The remedy offered for poverty amounts to a middle-class success formula (and, perhaps it *is* the route to success in American society) : education, a stable family life, and above all, the proper attitudes. In short, there appears to be justification for the charge that the War on Poverty can be more accurately characterized as a "war on the poor."

The Politics of Poverty and Race

Confronted with a social ideology which easily obscures the existence of poverty, and lacking a thunderous economic crisis that directly threatens the middle and upper classes, the public concern with poverty of a traditionally reactive government is most remarkable. Why did poverty become a politically important issue in 1964?

When asked the reasons for a War on Poverty, President Johnson and Sargent Shriver presented themselves as puppets of the American people who "are interested in the Government and in themselves making a focused or concentrated effort to attack poverty." A public demand for the elimination of poverty, did not, however, exist before it was deliberately made into an issue by the Johnson Administration in 1964. Government programs were not a response to public protests against conditions of poverty for one-fifth of a nation. (An exception to this was perhaps the March on Washington in the Summer of 1963, which came close to protesting poverty directly with demands for more jobs; but the publicity impact of this event was channeled into exclusive concern with civil rights.)

After President Johnson announced his War on Poverty in his State of the Union address on January 8, 1964, the nation was deluged with vivid descriptions of the life of the poor, statistical accounts of their number and characteristics, and details of their geographic location. Poverty became such a "problem" that, by the time Shriver testified at the congressional hearings, there was a degree of truth to his statement. The power of the presidency to stimulate the news media into undertaking a massive effort to increase public awareness, if not to generate actual demands for government action, was dramatically demonstrated. This achievement should not, however, obscure the fact that demands for action directly focused upon poverty did not exist prior to the time that the administration began to produce its new policy line.

Political power-needs, rather than an articulated public demand, were at the source of the sudden resolution to recognize poverty in 1964. Briefly, the most plausible occasion for the urgency and publicity devoted to poverty by the Executive Office can be found in the political and emotionally disrupting effects of the civil-rights movement, especially in regard to white morality and the white power structure. Emotionally, the nation needed to redefine the racial conflict as a conflict between the "haves" and the "have-nots." Politically, a transmutation of the civil-rights movement secured the threatened power position of whites as whites, and further eased the agonies of the slow political death of the south. The latter, with its implications for the composition of the national political parties, has held special meaning for Johnson in his struggle to unify the Democratic Party and attain congressional compliance with presidential programs. In practical terms, the War on Poverty and its implications for opening a new field of jobs and social status, is the means by which American society will expand to accommodate the Negroes' demands for integration.

For over four years, white America has been forced into a state of acute consciousness of its prejudices and unexamined beliefs. In a white man's world, however, Negroes from the time of their early years live with a racial awareness. They must know and understand this world in a very practical sense in order to survive. But whites "experience race" at a more mature age—they are not "born" with it—and in the past they gained their experience somewhat at their own convenience. Suddenly in the sixties, the Negro has become a political power; he has become a "new" Negro who won't fit into the old images. This forced racial confrontation has caught the white off-guard. He does not possess a cultural reservoir that would allow him to interact—or avoid interaction—easily and unemotionally. Political protests, in short, have resulted in a social dislocation of the Negro and have created a necessity for both races to become aware of themselves and their inter-projective images. Politically, this awareness and the knowledge it can bring, is both necessary and beneficial. But this is an inconvenience for the white, an inconvenience requiring extra effort that may result in heightened tension as well as awareness.

The task of knowing is greatly simplified for the white American if he substitutes "poverty" for "race." He can more easily understand the frustrations of job hunting or unemployment than what it means to possess a black skin. "Poverty" has a comfortable sound to it, it makes "sense" and is not emotionally upsetting. Politically speaking, to *redefine* race and civil rights as a manifestation of conditions of poverty, opens a path for action. Where race and nationalism are vivid, emotion-based issues, not easily resolved through reason and logic, conflict between the "haves" and the "have-nots" is well understood. The Western world has a supply of practical tools and intellectual theories with which this persistent enemy can be explained and controlled. Marxian ideology, liberal benevolence, or a religious morality all allow for practical political action that is denied when confronted by race in and of itself. Whether or not the civil-rights movement dramatized existing conditions of poverty, white Americans had to raise the poverty issue to relieve the emotional tension and political impasse created by the racial confrontation. The dollar costs of a War on Poverty are exchanged for the high emotional price-tag attached to race.

Aside from this exchange of emotion for practicality, poverty redefines civil rights in a manner that secures the power positions of white public leaders and places them in control of a movement which frequently has attempted to exclude them, on racial grounds, from exercising a directing influence. Three groups are the principal beneficiaries of this effect: the white liberal "sympathetic" to the Negro cause, public officials in the large urban centers, and the southern politician.

The white liberal has found himself increasingly excluded from policy-making positions in the civil-rights movement. He has been told that he could contribute his warm body and little else in a revolution which was felt to express legitimately only the suffering of the American Negro. However, when the "movement" is placed in the context of a battle between the wealthy and the poor, between the "power-lords" and the "exploited underdog," it is possible to carve out a legitimate place for whites within a dynamic and powerful social movement. Such a recasting of the Negro struggle cuts across racial boundaries to transform it into a fight for "all humanity." A new struggle is created which has a great potential for rallying sustained activities within accepted political channels. But, also, it may push the Negro to the background once again, for he does not have the same priority for a leading role in the new antipoverty struggle. Professional and respectable, social revolutionaries assume directing positions in a poverty war whereas indigenous leadership was beginning to develop out of the civil-rights struggle.

Public officials in the large urban centers have also found their authority threatened and severely shaken by a ground swell which they had to appease in order to survive. Something had to be offered the angry Negro segment of the populace. They couldn't offer to make a Negro white, or at least they couldn't overtly approach the racial question in this manner, although such an objective may underlie the antipoverty programs offered the Negro, with their emphasis upon instilling white middle-class motivations and values. They could, however, offer to train him, to educate him, and perhaps give him a little more *hope* of obtaining solid employment. In other words, the Negro must be viewed as "poor," as deprived of services which the government apparatus can provide, in order to engage him in political bargaining. The demonstrators are taken off the streets and placed in the hands of the welfare bureaucracies and the new "antipoverty" programs which can placate demands more quickly than the courts. (And, hopefully, in more substantial and lasting manner.) This need exists on the national level, but in its War on Poverty the federal government has left the distribution of public goods and services to the local political leaders, whose positions are most immediately threatened by the volatile protest and developing political power of the Negro.

Reaction to the race riots of previous summers provides ample illustration of the ideological function of an antipoverty slogan and the practical role of its accompanying programs. Immediately after the 1964 riots in New York City, Wagner made a special trip to Washington to see if more antipoverty projects and other federal money could be directed toward the slum areas of the city. As *The New York Times* interpreted the visit:

*It would be highly surprising if Mr. Wagner—Mayor of the city
where the present epidemic of racial disturbances began—did
not mean, as part of his mission, to remind members of the House of
the intimate connection between the battle against poverty and the
battle against riots. . . . The antipoverty bill, in the new perspective
given by the disturbances of this long, hot summer, is also an
anti-riot bill. The members of the House of Representatives will
do well to bear that in mind when the time comes for a vote.*

The fact that Wagner's trip produced few promises for programs and less cash was not as important as the public assurance that something could and would be done. Fortunately, the city had initiated its own anti-poverty planning in the spring and could point to several programs already underway. Both large federal juvenile-delinquency programs, Mobilization for Youth and Haryou-Act, as well as the city's own program, Job Opportunities in Neighborhoods, were paraded before public view. In addition, the city signed a contract providing a $223,225 grant for Youth in Action, Inc., to develop an antipoverty program for youth in Brooklyn's Bedford-Stuyvesant area. A job-finding project for semiskilled and unskilled youngsters was accelerated. Programs of training and basic education conducted under MDTA received personal inspections from the mayor, with attendant publicity.

Not only has the President's War on Poverty provided evidence of sincere efforts to alleviate some of the needs of the low-income Negro ghettos, but it also provided white society with a defense against charges of overt racism. Poverty and racism have joined hands to create the Negro's hell—the effects of one cannot be separated easily from the other. When given the choice, however, white society prefers to attribute the source of Negro resentment and protests to poverty. *The New York Times* employed this defense when it maintained that the race riots were "as much demonstrations against Negro poverty as against discrimination and what some call 'police brutality'." In this respect, we should note the extent to which right-wing politicians ignore the racial aspect of the Negro protest and refer to it almost exclusively as a conflict between the "haves" and the "have-nots." They simply make it clear that they are on the side of the "haves." Morally there may be something wrong with denying privileges on the basis of race, but within the right-wing ideology, there is "nothing wrong" with defending your own property and privileges from someone who is not as successful.

For reasons of a less than morally commendable nature, white America has responded to the Negroes' demands for an integrated society with an antipoverty movement: a response slow in coming and pitifully inadequate at first, but still a response. In terms of realistic social dynamics, integration is not, and will not be, an interpenetration of the old by the new, but will be a process of *expansion* and then assimilation. Societies expand and contract; they do not bend except with passing of generations, and that cannot even be predicted with assurance. Those who are within the socioeconomic structure will not give up their positions to Negroes seeking entrance. New roles must be added to the job structure and new status rungs created in the social ladder.

Such is the function of the War on Poverty. As was pointed out, it is a service-oriented welfare measure. The activity- and job-creating nature of its programs are presently opening and shaping new fields in the social services, a process that is certain to increase its range in the future. New professional positions in community organization and social planning, as well as the clerical and blue-collar jobs created to staff the research institutions and service organizations of the "antipoverty" projects, are particularly accessible to the Negro. This is true, above all, for the now small but increasing ranks of the college educated and professionally trained Negro. The politically dangerous energies of the Negro elite can be molded into socially legitimate channels through the creation of roles in an entirely new area of the nation's job structure.

The Negro asks for integration and receives a War on Poverty: it is perhaps not exactly what he ordered nor in the form he imagined, but it is the first step American society is capable of providing. And it is a step that can lead potentially through jobs and social status toward the dignity and justice he desires.

IV. The Economics
of the Great Society

8. Council of Economic Advisers
The Economic Principles
of the Great Society

An introduction to the three selections included in Part IV and a brief
perspective for evaluating the economics of the Great Society is furnished
in the editor's introductory essay, pages 13–17. It acknowledges that
the economic policies of the Kennedy and Johnson administrations
helped to bring six years of unprecedented growth, a creditable
performance by most traditional standards. But further analysis is needed.
That is the task undertaken in selections 9 and 10.

The four passages in selection 8 are taken from the *Economic Report of
the President* (1965 and 1966), prepared by the Council of Economic
Advisers. The three-man Council was created by the Employment Act
of 1946 and charged with keeping a weather watch on the economy.
Its members in 1965 and 1966 were Gardner Ackley (chairman), Otto
Eckstein, and Arthur Okun. The first official statement outlines the
broad economic goals of the Johnson administration, the second includes
eight basic ideas behind federal fiscal and monetary policies, while the
third explains the desirability of economic expansion. The final
selection delineates several features of the "new economics."

The Principles of Economic Policy

In a time of high prosperity, economic policy faces new problems. But it
is still guided by the basic principles that have served us so well.

Twenty years ago next month, the Employment Act of 1946—which
prescribes this Report—became law. The principles of our policy emerge
from that Act and from our two decades of experience under it.

The essential and revolutionary declaration of the Employment Act
was that the Federal Government must accept a share of responsibility
for the performance of the American economy. The nature of that share
has been more and more clearly defined over the years, by the recommendations of four Presidents and the enactments of ten Congresses.

I see these as the main tasks of Federal economic policy today:

1. To attain full employment without inflation; to use fiscal and monetary policies to help to match total demand to our growing productive po-

The first and fourth selections are from the *Economic Report of the President*
(1966), the second and third from the *Economic Report of the President* (1965).

tential, while helping to speed the growth of that potential through education, research and development, manpower policies, and enlarged private and public investment.

2. To help to open the doors of opportunity to all, through developing human resources and removing barriers of discrimination, ignorance, and ill-health.

3. To help to solve social and economic problems that neither private action nor State and local governments can solve alone—an efficient transportation system, the protection of our environment, the health of our agriculture, the reconstruction of our cities.

4. To achieve and maintain equilibrium in the Nation's external payments, and to press for improvements in the international economic order.

5. To maintain and enhance healthy competition.

6. To achieve national purposes as far as possible by enlisting the voluntary cooperation of business, labor, and other groups.

Recognition of these responsibilities of the Federal Government neither lessens the responsibilities nor impairs the freedoms of individuals and private groups; nor does it challenge the authority of State and local governments.

The tasks involve new and growing problems of an increasingly complex and interdependent economy and society. Only the Federal Government can assume these tasks. But the Federal Government by itself cannot create prosperity, reduce unemployment, avoid inflation, balance our external accounts, restore our cities, strengthen agriculture, eliminate poverty, or make people healthy.

Only through a creative and cooperative partnership of all private interests and all levels of government—a creative Federalism—can our economic and social objectives be attained. This partnership has written the story of American success. And a new vitalization of this partnership and a new confidence in its effectiveness have produced the extraordinary economic and social gains of recent years.

Contribution of Federal Fiscal and Monetary Policies

Federal policies have made a major and continuing contribution to the great achievements of the American economy during the past four years. These policies were not laid down in one master plan early in 1961 and then carried out on a predetermined schedule. There have been delays, surprises, and a need to adapt policies to changing events; but policies have had a unified direction and strategy. They have consistently reflected a number of basic ideas shared by those responsible for Federal economic policies. These basic ideas include the following:

1. A firm belief that the United States must make optimum use of the tremendous productive capacity of its economy; conversely, an abhorrence—for both human and economic reasons—of the waste of resources and opportunities involved in a prolonged underutilization of that capacity.

2. A recognition that Federal purchases, taxes, and transfer payments are a major force, along with monetary policy, in determining the strength of the total market demand for productive resources.

3. A full understanding of the key role of private investment in total market demand and in the long-term growth of incomes, and of the need for adequate profit incentives to stimulate this investment.

4. A recognition that expanding consumption is necessary if increasing investment and over-all growth are to be maintained.

5. A belief that vigorous efforts are necessary to restore equilibrium in the balance of payments.

6. A determination to achieve reasonable price stability in order to preserve equity at home and to improve our international competitive position both at home and abroad.

7. A conviction that, if they are to be effective, policies cannot respond passively to what has already transpired, but must try to foresee and shape future developments, remaining flexible and ready to change speed or direction yet holding to fixed goals.

8. A belief that the American people share these ideas and are ready to support imaginative but carefully considered innovations in public policy.

The Anatomy of the Expansion

The remarkable characteristic of the current expansion is not the degree to which it has carried us toward our objective of full employment. Previous expansions have done as well or better in this respect. Rather, its most remarkable feature is its durability. This can be attributed in important part to the balance maintained among the various components of private demand; to the balance maintained between production and sales, thus avoiding excessive inventory accumulation; to the balance maintained between the expansion of demand and the expansion of productive capacity to satisfy that demand; and to the balance maintained among wages, prices, and productivity. Imbalances in one or more of these respects brought earlier expansions to an end. Some ended when inventories became top-heavy; others when a major industry had expanded too fast, and its retrenchment was not offset elsewhere; still others when growth of demand generally failed to keep pace with growth of capacity. The key to sustained full employment lies in preserving balance as overall demand moves closer to the economy's full capacity.

Since 1961, the expansion of demand has been persistent and pervasive, but production has stayed short of supply capabilities. Placement of orders has advanced only moderately ahead of production and shipments, so that unfilled orders have grown gradually. Capacity has expanded along with production, without bottlenecks or overbuilding.

Businesses have followed a prudent employment policy, avoiding both overstaffing and the need for sudden heavy hiring. This, in turn, partly explains the steady gains in productivity throughout the expansion. Increases in production have been large enough to utilize the net gain in the labor force and to make inroads into unemployment.

With no significant buildup of unfilled orders, and with production not making full use of capacity, price increases from generally excessive demand have remained remote. With wage increases matching productivity gains, labor costs per unit of output have remained unusually stable, and any general upward pressure of costs on prices has been avoided. Thus the purchasing power of personal and business incomes has risen steadily and strongly.

Economic Policy Today

Two decades of economic analysis and policy experience have shaped the development of a revised economic policy. By some, current policy has been labeled the "new economics." It draws heavily on the experience and lessons of the past, and it combines both new and old elements. Current policy represents a coordinated and consistent effort to promote balance of over-all supply and aggregate demand—to sustain steady balanced growth at high employment levels with essential price stability.

This approach to policy has several key aspects, not entirely novel by any means. First, it emphasizes a continuous, rather than a cyclical, framework for analyzing economic developments and formulating policies. Stimulus to demand is not confined to avoiding or correcting recession, but rather is applied whenever needed for the promotion of full-utilization and prosperity. Second, in this way, it emphasizes a preventive strategy against the onset of recession. Third, in focusing on balance of the economy, this policy strategy cannot give top priority to balance in the budget. When private investment threatens to outrun saving at full employment, a Government surplus is needed to increase total saving in the economy while restrictive monetary policy may also be called for to restrain investment outlays. When, as in recent years, private saving at full employment tends to outrun actual private investment, the balance should be corrected by budget deficits and expansionary monetary policy. Fourth, it considers the budget and monetary conditions in the framework of a growing economy, recognizing that revenues expand and thereby exert a fiscal drag on demand unless expansionary actions are taken; similarly, it recognizes that money and credit must expand just to keep interest rates from rising. Fifth, this strategy emphasizes the use of a variety of tools to support expansion while simultaneously pursuing other objectives. Manpower policies, selective approaches to control capital outflows, as well as general fiscal and monetary measures, are all part of the arsenal. Sixth, it calls for responsible price-wage actions by labor and management to prevent cost-inflation from impeding the pursuit of full employment. Finally, it makes greater demands on economic forecasting and analysis. The job of the economist is not merely to predict the upturn or the downturn but to judge continuously the prospects for demand in relation to a growing productive capacity.

9. Leo Huberman and Paul M. Sweezy
The Kennedy–Johnson Boom

The economic growth and prosperity of the Kennedy-Johnson years was
widely praised as a logical consequence of an improved state of economic
intelligence. But Leo Huberman and Paul Sweezy, editors of
Monthly Review (an independent socialist magazine), have shown that
the economic boom can be explained in other ways. Readers of the
April 13, 1963, issue of *Business Week,* a magazine read primarily by
American business executives, were surprised to see an analysis of the
Monthly Review and its editors. They read that Huberman and Sweezy,
ex-university professors at Columbia and Harvard respectively,
and coauthors of *Monopoly Capital: An Essay on the American Economic
and Social Order* (1966), peddle "a brand of socialism that is thoroughgoing and tough-minded, drastic enough to provide the sharp break
with the past that many leftwingers in the underdeveloped countries
see as essential. At the same time they maintain a sturdy independence of
both Moscow and Peking that appeals to neutralists. And their
skill in manipulating the abstruse concepts of modern economics
impresses would-be intellectuals. . . . Their analysis of the troubles of
capitalism is just plausible enough to be disturbing."

Two passages from their writings, "plausible enough to be disturbing,"
are reprinted below. The authors undertake to explain the
underpinnings of the Kennedy-Johnson economic policies and argue
that the giant corporations were its primary beneficiaries. They suggest
that Big Business and the American government concluded a tacit
bargain in which the former agreed to support a government policy
of budget deficits in return for highly favorable tax treatment, the
economic consequences of which are described. The economic program
agreed upon amounted "to using the borrowing power of the
federal government to subsidize corporate profits." Deficit financing was
permissible to increase corporate profits, but not to finance welfare
programs for the needy. The new tax depreciation policies worked but
continued to do so, the authors write, because of the sharp escalation
of the war in Vietnam in the mid-1960s.

On the latter point, Huberman and Sweezy's analysis has received
impressive support and elaboration from Seymour Melman, author of
Pentagon Capitalism (1970). Melman writes:

*In the name of defense, and without announcement or debate, a
basic alteration has been effected in the governing institutions of the*

From *Monthly Review, 16* (February 1965) and *17* (February 1966). Copyright
© 1965, 1966, by Monthly Review, Inc. By permission of Monthly Review, Inc.

United States. An industrial management has been installed in the federal government, under the Secretary of Defense, to control the nation's largest network of industrial enterprises. With the characteristic managerial propensity for extending its power, limited only by its allocated share of the national product, the new state-management combines peak economic, political, and military decision-making. Hitherto, this combination of powers in the same hands has been a feature of statist societies—communist, fascist, and others—where individual rights cannot constrain central rule. (p. 1)

From 1946 to 1969, the federal government spent over $1000 billion on the military, more than half of this during the Kennedy-Johnson years. To this staggering sum must be added the human costs:

1. By 1968, there were 6 million grossly substandard dwellings, mainly in the cities.

2. Ten million Americans suffered from hunger in 1968–1969.

3. The United States ranked 18th at last report (1966) among nations in infant mortality rate (23.7 infant deaths in first year per 1000 live births). In Sweden (1966) the rate was 12.6.

4. In 1967, 40.7 percent of the young men examined were disqualified for military service (28.5 percent for medical reasons).

5. In 1950, there were 109 physicians in the United States per 100,000 population. By 1966 there were 98.

6. About 30 million Americans are an economically underdeveloped sector of the society. (p. 3)

This "human inventory of depletion" identifies some of the concerns that have shaped Huberman and Sweezy's analysis of the American economic system. Is it now settled policy that Big Business must be reconciled to all major government policy decisions on welfare, poverty, war, and taxes? Whatever the answer, how can military spending be cut? When budget cutbacks were announced in the early 1970s, why were they made almost solely in the Great Society welfare programs, leaving military spending untouched—this, at a time when the United States had withdrawn its forces from South Vietnam and had improved its relations with the Soviet Union and the Peoples' Republic of China? Questions such as these, radicals and some liberal analysts argue, cut to the heart of the democratic dilemma in modern American society.

The business-political Establishment which runs this country has digested Keynesian economic theory and has begun to put it into practice. It likes the results. Listen to Douglas Dillon, Wall Street financier turned Secretary of the Treasury, speaking at the Harvard Business School last June 6th:

*In the relatively short span . . . of less than three and one half
years, both American economic policy and practice have taken new
and dramatic turns for the better. Our economy is no longer on
the wane—but surely and strongly on the rise. And we can now look
forward, in all sober confidence, to the continuation of a peacetime
economic recovery of greater durability and strength than in any
comparable period in this century.*

*Equally important, the past three and one half years constitute
a significant watershed in the development of American economic
policy. For they have borne witness to the emergence, first of all,
of a new national determination to use fiscal policy as a dynamic and
affirmative agent in fostering economic growth. Those years have
also demonstrated, not in theory, but in actual practice, how our
different instruments of economic policy—expenditure, tax, debt
management, and monetary policies—can be tuned in concert
toward achieving different, even disparate, economic goals.
In short those years have encompassed perhaps our most significant
advance in decades in the task of forging flexible economic policy
techniques capable of meeting the needs of our rapidly changing
economic scene. (Treasury Department News Release.)*

The achievement of which Mr. Dillon and his colleagues in business
and government are proudest is a continuous and, relative to the immediately preceding years, high rate of growth of Gross National Product
(GNP = total output of goods and services). In 1960, the last Eisenhower year, GNP was $502.6 billion. Estimates for 1964 put the fiigure at
$624 billion. The increase in the four years of the Kennedy-Johnson ad-
ministration was thus 24 percent—or, expressed as an average of the annual increases, 5.6 percent per annum. This is unquestionably high by
relevant historical standards, and it is scarcely surprising that it evokes
hosannas from the Establishment's scribes and pundits. "Americans have
received a $40 billion lift this year," writes Edwin L. Dale, Jr., in the
New York Times of December 26th. [1964] And he continues:

The $40 billion represents the growth in the economy in 1964 over
1963, as measured by the gross national product. . . .
The growth in 1964 is nearly as large as the entire gross national product of Canada, which will be about $45 billion this year.
It is about half the gross national product of France.
It is also . . . probably more than the Soviet Union's economy grew
this year and last year combined, and possibly more than the last three
years combined.

What government policies have contributed to this speeding up of the
overall rate of economic growth? At first blush the answer might seem to
be very simple, and entirely in accordance with Keynesian prescriptions:

deficit financing. The record of federal government cash surpluses $(+)$ and deficits $(-)$ during the last five years is as follows (in billions of dollars) :

1960	$+3.6$
1961	-6.8
1962	-5.7
1963	-4.6
1964	-5.2

That a shift from budgetary surplus to deficit and the continuation of sizable deficits should, other things being equal, produce an acceleration of economic growth has by now attained the status of an axiom; it might seem therefore that the question is answered and there is little more to say except that Keynes and his followers have been proved right.

In reality matters are not quite so simple. The "other things being equal" proviso is an indispensable part of the axiom, and in practice other things rarely are equal. In fact, opponents of Keynesian policies, at least the more sophisticated among them, have always argued that deficit financing, if continued for any length of time, must have an adverse effect on other variables of the system and thus defeat its own ends. In particular, they reason that businessmen are a conservative lot who believe in balanced budgets, perhaps not every year but certainly over a period of years, and that therefore a continuation of deficits is bound to undermine their confidence and precipitate a decline in private investment. This did not happen during the last four years; on the contrary, business expenditures for plant and equipment are estimated to have been a good 25 percent higher in 1964 than in 1960, the last year of a (more than) balanced budget. What explains this apparent enthusiasm of businessmen for the policy of continuing deficits? This is evidently as important a part of the whole picture as the facts of the deficits themselves.

The approved answer to this question is that American businessmen have finally become enlightened. They have, so to speak, studied Samuelson's *Principles of Economics,* and they know that the supposed need to balance the budget is an old wives' tale. And so, when Kennedy brought the Keynesians to Washington with him, the stage was all set for the grand experiment: businessmen were not only ready to acquiesce but actively to cooperate.

There is undoubtedly something to this theory: the men who run the giant corporations which dominate the American economy have certainly shed the blinkers of old-fashioned fiscal orthodoxy. But this is not to say that they are enthusiastic about a policy of deficits as such. It is safe to assume that if at any time either Kennedy or Johnson had proposed to open up a deficit by sharply increasing expenditures of a "welfare state" variety while leaving taxes unchanged, the men of the corporations would have been strongly opposed; and if the program had nevertheless been adopted by the Congress (a most unlikely assumption of course), business confidence and private investment would undoubtedly have suffered in accordance with the anticipations of the traditional anti-Keynesian theory. In other words, it all depends on *what kind* of deficits are at issue. Once we look at the matter from this angle, we shall have little difficulty in understanding the wholehearted enthusiasm of the Big Business community for the Kennedy-Johnson policy of deficits.

In the Harvard Business School speech quoted above, Treasury Secretary Dillon gives an account of the genesis and development of this policy. The problem when the Kennedy administration took office, he says, was "sluggish growth and inadequate incentives for investment. Postwar expansionary forces had been dissipated. Tax rates were siphoning off too much income to allow the private economy to reach full employment. The result was inadequate demand—with increased unemployment and evermore frequent recessions."

Under these conditions, a basic decision was taken to rely on fiscal policy. But this posed the "big question" which was "whether to increase government expenditures or to reduce taxes—or, to come to the heart of the matter: whether to rely upon the latent energies of the private sector or to expand government activity."

The reasoning at this point is crucial to an understanding of all that followed:

Larger government expenditures, if well timed, could, of course, have boosted demand and thereby cut unemployment. But unless such expenditures could be clearly justified on their own merits, their long-run contribution to productivity and investment would be uncertain at best. Thus they seemed to offer less benefit . . . than the path we chose: tax reduction.

The phrase "unless such expenditures could be clearly justified on their own merits" is obviously question begging, but in context its meaning is plain enough: unless those responsible for investment decisions approved, additional government expenditures could not be counted on to produce the desired expansionary effect. From the outset a veto power was conceded to the men of the corporations: the expansion of demand (deficit) would have to be achieved by methods tailored to their interests. Hence tax reduction, and hence also the kind of tax reduction decided upon. We return to this presently.

The decision to rely on tax reduction did not mean the renunciation of all increases in spending. In our system, it takes a long time to pass new tax legislation and still longer for it to begin working as intended. In the meantime, an increase in spending was urgently called for, with the proviso of course that it should be justified in the eyes of Big Business. Fortunately, from Mr. Dillon's point of view, there were in 1961 "overriding national priorities, all of which cost money: the need to bring our military defenses to a higher plateau of readiness, the special requirements of the Berlin crisis, the rapidly expanding space program. And, of course, the interest on the national debt." Yes, of course. These are the expenditures which are "justified on their own merits," and Dillon proudly boasts that the rate of increase of spending for arms, space, and interest on the national debt has been double that of the second Eisenhower administration. For all other purposes, he is equally proud to report, the increase in spending during the Kennedy-Johnson administration comes to "one third less than the comparable increase during the earlier 4-year period." In retrospect, Ike is beginning to look like a rabid pacifist and New Dealer!

While the full tax-cut program was in preparation, certain preliminary steps were taken. Let Dillon tell the story:

It was necessary to get the major increases in defense and space spending behind us before we could safely implement our full program of tax reduction. But rather than wait, we promptly undertook two major moves to improve the climate for business investment—moves that could be instituted without any excessive loss of revenue. They were the Revenue Act of 1962, with its central provision of a 7 percent investment tax credit, and the administrative liberalization of depreciation—both landmarks of progress in our drive to spur the modernization of our capital equipment. Together they increased the profitability of investment in new equipment by more than 20 percent. This was equivalent in terms of incentives to invest to a reduction in the corporate profits tax from 52 percent to 40 percent.

But, says Dillon, the "biggest impediment to a more robust private sector still remained—the high individual and corporate income tax rates." The crowning act of policy was therefore the tax law of 1964, designed to "break the grip of these high tax rates on our economy"—and in the process distributing some $11½ billion of largesse, mostly to the rich but with a sop to the little fellow thrown in as a political lubricant.

As a final assessment, Dillon approvingly cites a study by George Terborgh, an ultra-conservative economist at the Machinery and Allied Products Institute, which shows that the tax measures adopted in 1962 and 1964 by the Kennedy-Johnson administration will together have an effect on after-tax returns to capital comparable either to a cut in corporate income tax rates from 52 percent to 34 or 29 percent (depending on the ratio of equity to total capital) , or to a reduction in the cost of new capital equipment of 16 percent. "It is hardly surprising," Dillon adds, "that investment activity is responding to incentives of this magnitude— even though it will be some time before the cumulative impact is fully re- alized—and that investment spending is now spearheading the recovery." Quite so, it is hardly surprising.

It is also hardly surprising that businessmen are so enthusiastic about *this kind* of deficit spending: boiled down to essentials it amounts simply to using the borrowing power of the federal government to subsidize cor- porate profits. But let no one be so naive as to conclude that some other kind of deficit spending—for example, the use of the government's bor- rowing power to provide decent jobs or incomes for the poverty-stricken, free medical services, good education—would command similar enthusi- asm from the lords of the economy. Deficits incurred for *such* purposes would obviously be wasteful and confidence-destroying. And, as every right-thinking person knows, there could be no greater folly than to harm, or even threaten, that delicate plant which is the confidence of the billionaire corporations and the millionaires who run them.

Against this background, let us examine a little more closely the main characteristics of the great Kennedy-Johnson boom.

In the first place, the real beneficiaries have been, as intended, the cor- porations. Aggregate corporate profits after taxes have increased as fol- lows (in billions of dollars) :

1960	22.0
1961	21.9
1962	25.0
1963	26.7
1964	32.0

This, however, underestimates the real increase, since the liberalization of depreciation rules in 1962 enabled the corporations to shift approxi- mately $2.5 billion from (taxable) profits to (nontaxable) depreciation. If we make a rough adjustment by adding this figure to the totals for 1962 and later years, we find that the increase in profits from 1960 to 1964 was $12.5 billion, or 57 percent. This is more than double the in- crease of GNP which, as noted earlier, was 24 percent in the same peri- od.

Not all industries shared equally in this bonanza, of course. It is there- fore worthwhile to cull out industry profit data from a 12-page news re- lease issued by the White House on October 22nd (less than two weeks before the election) setting forth "a compilation showing some of the economic gains achieved by 12 major industries in the United States during the Kennedy-Johnson administration." The figures are percentage increases in after-tax profits during the four-year period 1961–1964, arranged in descending order of magnitude:

Motor vehicles and parts	120.3
Transportation equipment	89.9
Textiles	80.0
Non-electrical machinery	79.0
Nonferrous metals	46.0
Iron and steel	41.9
Chemicals	35.2
Petroleum	34.8
Paper and paper products	28.5
Electrical utilities	21.3
Food and beverages	17.6

Note: No profit figures are given for mining, which is the twelfth industry.

Wage-earners, even those fortunate enough to hold steady jobs, have done less well than even the least favored of these industries. Average weekly earnings in manufacturing went up only 15.8 percent between 1960 and the first three quarters of 1964. And if this is adjusted to take account of the 5 percent increase in consumer prices which has taken place since 1960, it will be seen that real weekly earnings have gone up only about 11 percent. During the same period labor productivity in the private economy is supposed to have risen by 3.6 percent a year, which aggregates to just over 15 percent for the four years. Overall productivity figures of this sort, throwing together as they do all kinds of productive and unproductive labor, are not very meaningful and certainly vastly understate the increase in productivity of rationally organized production workers. Still they show that from labor's point of view, and judged even by the Establishment's own distorted standards, the Kennedy-Johnson administration could appropriately be labeled the Raw Deal.

But perhaps at any rate some progress has been made toward reducing the distressingly high rate of unemployment which developed in the late 1950's? Unfortunately, no. To be sure, the official unemployment rate shows a modest decline from 5.6 percent in 1960 to 5 percent (seasonally adjusted) in November 1964. But at the same time the number of people looking for work also declined so that what is called the labor force participation rate fell by 1.3 percentage points in the same period. If we assume that most of these dropouts from the labor force are as much unemployed as ever but have given up looking for jobs because they know from experience that none exist, we have to conclude that the true unemployment rate has risen to something over 6 percent after four years of uninterrupted expansion.

Nor are matters much better when it comes to the rate of utilization of the economy's material productive capacity. The McGraw-Hill index of capacity utilization stood at 81 in 1960 and rose slowly to 86 at the latest survey in September, 1964.

Overall, therefore, it appears that the slack in the economy today is as great as it was four years ago. And if we keep in mind the experience of the Second World War—when GNP nearly doubled at the same time that 10 million persons in the most productive age groups were being drafted into the armed forces—we can be sure that the commonly accepted measures of unemployment and unused capacity give no more than a faint inkling of what could be produced at the present time with a full, but not overstrained, utilization of available resources. It is surely well on the conservative side to assume that GNP could be rapidly expanded by $100 billion, an increase of 16 percent over the present level. If this amount were distributed, directly and indirectly, to the two fifths of the nation living in poverty or deprivation, their real income would be doubled. Such is the potential of the American economy. Such could be the *immediately* attainable goal of a real war on poverty.

The reality of course is entirely different. Far from disappearing, the problems of poverty and deprivation have grown along with the magnitude of corporate profits in the years of the Kennedy-Johnson boom. In New York City, for example, where so many of the giant corporations have their headquarters and so much of the nation's wealth is concentrated, the Department of Welfare is asking the city government to approve a budget for the next fiscal year of half a billion dollars, 20 percent more than its current budget and 15 percent of the total proposed expenditure by the city in the coming period. In justifying his department's request, Welfare Commissioner James R. Dumpson explained to the city's Budget Bureau that the larger amount was needed to care for the steadily rising number of people receiving public assistance.

The Commissioner said that the rise, which he put at about 5,850 a month, could be attributed to "chronic unemployment among the unskilled, low wages for many employed persons, the unavailability of sufficient low-cost housing, our failure to achieve open occupancy for all people in available housing, increased cost of care for the medically indigent aged, and the continuing breakdown among families." (New York Times, December 29, 1964.)

But maybe this situation will be changed by President Johnson's war on poverty which, in his State of the Union Message, he promised to double in 1965? Well, maybe—a little. But Commissioner Dumpson has already made full allowance for that possibility. If the federal program is implemented, the rate of increase of welfare caseloads might be reduced by half. "If it were not for that possible reduction, he said, the department would have to ask for $20 million more a year." *(Ibid.)*

The conclusion is inescapable: only the rich gain from the kind of boom which can be induced by methods acceptable to the business-political Establishment which rules this country today. The wages of the employed worker have not kept pace with gains in his own productivity. There are more, not fewer, unemployed. Poverty and deprivation are spreading like an unchecked cancer. There is, in truth, only one group President Johnson could have been referring to when he declared in his State of the Union Message: "We are in the midst of the greatest upward surge of economic well-being in the history of any nation." It is the group to which the multi-millionaire President himself belongs.

What about the future?

It is not our purpose to add one more "forecast" to the collection which crowds the news and financial columns at the turn of the year. It is enough to point out that not even the perennial optimists expect GNP to go on expanding at the rate of the last four years much longer. *Fortune* magazine, capitalism's most ardent apologist, says that "a new period, of subnormal growth, is now in prospect for the U.S. economy after this quarter. Following four years of rapid gains in output . . . this means a real change in trend. . . . The odds are still against recession in the next eighteen months, but the chances of it will be rising in 1966." *(Fortune,* January 1965, p. 27.) Others figure the odds differently, but let us suppose that *Fortune* is right and that what we face now is once again a period of sluggish growth such as characterized the late 1950's.

What cannot be overemphasized is that such a prospect, in the conditions of the 1960's, is little short of catastrophic. The labor force is today growing 50 percent more rapidly than it was a decade ago, and the speedup will continue for years to come. At the same time, automation is penetrating more and more areas of the economy—in no small measure, ironically enough, because of the tax-stimulated investment boom of the last few years—and will certainly be throwing more and more workers into the industrial reserve army in the period ahead. If a five-and-a-half percent rate of growth of GNP has been unable to hold the unemployment line, one can imagine what the consequences will be of a decline to, say, half that figure. Even without a recession, unemployment could easily reach the 10 percent level in the next couple of years. With a recession—and it would not have to be a severe one in terms of total output—we could be back where we were in the 1930's.

The somber truth is that this country is headed into a time of troubles from which there is absolutely no escape within the framework and confines of the capitalist system.

(A year later, in February 1966, Sweezy and Huberman updated their previous analysis of the U.S. economy.)

The Boom Continues

Our last analysis of the state of the United States economy appeared just a year ago. . . . There we diagnosed the long upswing of the Kennedy-Johnson years as the result of a new fiscal policy of deliberate deficits engineered by a combination of higher government spending and lower taxes, chiefly on corporations. We quoted Douglas Dillon, then Secretary of the Treasury, to the effect that the cumulative effect of tax changes in 1962 and 1964 would be equivalent to a reduction of the corporate income tax from 52 percent to 34 or 29 percent (depending on the ratio of equity to total capital) or to a reduction in the cost of new capital equipment of 16 percent. "It is hardly surprising," said Dillon in June of 1964, "that investment activity is responding to incentives of this magnitude . . . and that investment spending is now spearheading the recovery."
As all this implies, the biggest beneficiaries of the boom up to that time had been the corporations. Total corporate profits increased by an estimated 57 percent in the period 1960–1964, while Gross National Product was rising less than half as fast, by 24 percent. Simultaneously, real wages were going up by less than the productivity of labor, and poverty was becoming an increasingly obtrusive and serious problem. We concluded by pointing out—quoting *Fortune* as an example—that most observers of the economic scene anticipated an imminent slow-down in the rate of expansion, and that such a change in the economic climate would bring with it a rapid increase in unemployment.
Looking back from the vantage point of a year later, we can see that these anticipations were wide of the mark. The boom has continued, and even accelerated. Between the third quarter of 1964 and the third quarter of 1965 (the latest for which figures are available at the time of writing) GNP rose by 6.9 percent, well above the average of the preceding four years. At the same time, the basic character of the boom not only has not changed but has become markedly accentuated. In the same period corporate profits went up by no less than 19.5 percent, nearly three times the rate of increase of GNP; and expenditures on plant and equipment, still "spearheading the recovery," were up 12 percent. And once again real wages (weekly earnings of workers in manufacturing adjusted to take account of the rise of consumer prices) lagged behind, rising by only

about 3 percent, which once again is probably lower than the rise in labor productivity. If ever confirmation were needed that this economy and this administration belong to the big corporations, the last year has certainly provided it and with plenty to spare.

There remains, however, the question as to why the predictions of a slowdown, and possibly a recession, in 1965 were wrong. By the end of 1964 the upswing had been under way 46 months, only four months fewer than the longest peacetime expansion on record (1933–1938), and for this reason alone it was surely reasonable to expect a leveling off in the near future. How are we to explain that in fact the upswing has continued through 1965, and at the beginning of 1966 shows few of the usual symptoms of an approaching turning point?

Given the complexity and elementality of capitalist economic processes, no one can answer a question of this kind with any certainty. Nevertheless, two important factors are pretty clearly involved, and it seems plausible that, taken together, they provide the explanation.

In the first place, it now seems obvious that the power of the investment boom initiated by the large tax cuts of 1962 and 1964 was considerably greater than was generally realized a year ago. Huge outlays on Research and Development in recent years—now running, according to a *Fortune* article (September 1964, p. 158), at some $20 billion per annum—have brought all sorts of new technologies to the stage of practicality. Apparently all that was needed to touch off an investment boom of unprecedented magnitude and duration was a substantial reduction in the costs of the equipment embodying these technologies—a reduction which the tax cuts effectively accomplished.

Second, and perhaps even more important, has been the sharp escalation of the war in Vietnam which began with United States bombing of the North in February. In last November's issue of MR we printed a dispatch by *New York Times* financial correspondent M. J. Rossant (taken from the Toronto *Globe and Mail,* since the *Times* was then on strike) which began: "It was a close call. Little by little it has become clear that the longest peacetime expansion in U.S. history was in danger of petering out until the escalation of the war in Vietnam gave it a new lease on life." This may be something of an exaggeration, but there is undoubtedly much truth in it. Not that military spending (euphemistically labeled "National Defense" in the official statistics) has gone up all that much during the past year: the annual rate in the third quarter was only about a billion dollars (or less than 2 percent) more than in the first quarter—certainly not enough in itself to have any decisive effect on the state of the economy. But almost from the beginning of the escalation, it has been clear that the planned scale of the United States intervention in Vietnam would involve the spending of many billions more in the near future. A story in the *Wall Street Journal* of December 21, for example, has the following to say on the outlook for military spending:

In late November, the President announced from Texas that current-fiscal-year [July, 1965, through June, 1966] defense spending, budgeted last January at $49 billion . . . ,would actually wind up at $52 billion to $53 billion. Aides now say it will be closer to $53 billion and, depending on how fast the Pentagon can spend extra billions it will seek in January, could go higher.
For the new fiscal year [ending in mid-1967], most expect the defense figure to be somewhat below the $60 billion now rumored, but admit it's approaching that figure unbelievably fast. Any decision to increase the troop build-up in Vietnam beyond present plans would probably force an increase in total U.S. ground forces, swelling military spending still further.

The apparent certainty of massive increases in government spending of course cannot but play a major part in shaping the expectations of businessmen about future demand, the profitability of new investment, the need for inventories, and so on; and these expectations in turn determine current decisions. It is thus entirely reasonable to assume that the escalation of the war in Vietnam has been an important, and perhaps decisive, factor in keeping the investment boom going and hence in prolonging the upswing.

As to how much longer it may last, we quite frankly would not even hazard a guess. The latest McGraw-Hill survey of investment plans for 1966 (press release of November 5, 1965) indicated that the overall level of spending on plant and equipment would be 8 percent above 1965, and at this writing there is unfortunately no sign of an end to the escalation of the war in Vietnam. Since, despite the long boom, the economy has plenty of unemployed men and idle plant, it is probably safe enough to say that an early end to the upswing is not likely. But beyond that nothing is safe. . . .

10. John Kenneth Galbraith

Market Planning
and the Role of Government

A best-selling author, social critic, Harvard professor, former ambassador
to India, and an eloquent master of the linguistic arts, John Kenneth
Galbraith is also a distinguished economist, perhaps the most read
economist of all time. The latter distinction is the result of a trilogy of
works: *American Capitalism, The Affluent Society,* and *The New
Industrial State.* Like Leo Huberman and Paul Sweezy, but from a different
ideological perspective, Galbraith also unites moral-social criticism
with professional economic analysis. Few men in the past two decades
have operated so resourcefully as a gadfly of orthodox economists,
stuffed shirts, Democrats and Republicans alike. His public activism
brought him the chairmanship of the Americans for Democratic Action in
1967; five years later his professional colleagues elected him president
of the American Economic Association.

"Market Planning and the Role of Government", based on *The New
Industrial State* (1967), discusses the overall working of the large
corporate sector of the economy. The large corporation, primarily
seeking security of earnings and growth instead of maximum profits,
has become the dominant planning agent in the American economy.
It controls prices for the purposes of planning rather than monopolistic
exploitation; it manages consumer demands (mass behavior) in ways
that convince consumers that they enjoy free choice. Throughout
the analysis, Galbraith underscores the intimate intertwining of
government and business. He has never paid obeisance to the twin gods of
competition and consumer demand, which in orthodox theory govern
the pattern of production and sales—an assumption that permits
the easygoing to avoid analysis of the location and concentration of
economic power. Nor has he ever accepted the specious reasoning of
recent government economic advisers that little can be done about
unemployment until inflation is brought under control.

Galbraith is a persuasive writer. Does he overlook problems inherent
in bigness, however? Have advances in technology—including cybernated
systems—made smaller plants economically desirable? Is there a
positive correlation between corporate size and techological progressiveness,
as Galbraith avers? Since Veblen, a small band of dissenting economists
has insisted that business is frequently a saboteur of technological

advances. Others have contended that a large number of inventions have originated with independent inventors. (J. Jewkes, et al., *The Sources of Invention* (1959). With government and big business harnessed tandem, where do reformers break into the system without seriously disrupting the economy? Or should sacrifice on the part of certain groups be acknowledged at the outset, as Rexford Tugwell argued during the early days of the New Deal? What of the question Galbraith himself raises: does the United States tailor its military procurement to what private industry wishes to sell? Finally, does Galbraith minimize the rivalry and competition among the large corporations in our oligopolized industrial system?

In fact since Adam and as a matter of settled doctrine since Adam Smith, the businessman has been assumed to be subordinate to the market. In last month's article I showed that modern highly technical processes and products and associated requirements of capital and time lead inevitably to planning—to the management of markets by those who supply them. It is technology, not ideology, that brings this result. The market serves admirably to supply simple things. But excellent as it may be on muskets, it is very bad on missiles. And not even the supply of components for the modern automobile can be trusted to the market; neither is it safe to assume that the market will absorb the necessary production at a remunerative price. There must be planning here as well.

The principal planning instrument in the modern economy is the large corporation. Within broad limits, it determines what the consumer shall have and at what price he shall have it. And it foresees the need for and arranges the necessary supply of capital, machinery, and materials.

The modern corporation is the direct descendant of the entrepreneur. This has kept us from seeing it in its new role. Had the corporation been an out-growth of the state, which we readily associate with planning, we would not be in doubt. The modern corporation has, in fact, moved into a much closer association with the state than most of us imagine. And its planning activities are extensively and systematically supplemented by those of the state.

Let us consider first the regulation of prices in the modern economy and the means by which public behavior is accommodated to plan. Here, I should warn, we encounter some of the more deeply entrenched folk myths of our time, including a certain vested interest in error on the part of both economists and businessmen. If one takes faith in the market away from the economist, he is perilously barren of belief. So, he defends the market to defend his stock of knowledge. And the large corporate enterprise needs the concept of the market as a cover for the authority it exercises. It has great influence over our material existence and also our beliefs. But accepted doctrine holds that in all of its behavior it is subordinate to the market. It is merely an automaton responding to instructions therefrom. Any complaint as to the use or misuse of power can be met by the answer that there is none.

Control of prices is an intrinsic feature of all planning. And it is made urgent by the special vagaries of the market for highly technical products. In the formally planned economies—that of the Soviet Union, for example—price control is a forthright function of the state, although there has been some tendency in recent times to allow some of the power over prices to devolve on the socialist firm. In the Western-type economies, comprehensive systems of price control have come about by evolution and adaptation. Nobody willed them. They were simply required by circumstance.

The power to set minimum industrial prices exists whenever a small number of firms share a market. The innocent at the universities have long been taught that small numbers of firms in the market—oligopoly, as it is known—accord to sellers the same power in imperfect form that has anciently been associated with monopoly. The principal difference is the imperfect nature of this monopoly power. It does not permit the exploitation of the consumer in quite such efficient fashion as was possible under the patents of monopoly accorded by the first Elizabeth to her favorites or by John D. Rockefeller to himself.

But in fact, the modern market shared by a few large firms is combined, in one of the more disconcerting contradictions of economic theory, with efficient production, expansive output, and prices that are generally thought rather favorable to the public. The consequences of oligopoly (few sellers) are greatly condemned in principle as being like those of monopoly but greatly approved in practice. Professor Paul Samuelson, the most distinguished of contemporary economists, warns in his famous textbook on economics that "to reduce the imperfections of competition" (by which he means markets consisting of a small number of large firms or oligopoly) "a nation must struggle perpetually and must ever maintain vigilance." Since American markets are now dominated by a very small number of very large firms, the struggle, obviously, has been a losing one and is now lost. But the result is that the economy functions very well. Samuelson himself concludes that man-hour efficiency in the United States "can hardly help but grow at the rate of three per cent or more, even if we do not rouse ourselves." A similar conflict between the inefficiency of oligopoly and the efficiency of an economy composed thereof is present in every well-regarded economic textbook. Samuelson agrees that technology and associated capital use are what improve efficiency. But these are precisely what require that there be planning and price control.

And here we have the answer. Prices in the modern economy are controlled not for the purposes of monopolistic exploitation. They are controlled for purposes of planning. This comes about as an effortless consequence of the development of that economy. Modern industrial planning both requires and rewards great size. This means, in turn, that a comparatively small number of large firms will divide the production of most (though not all) products. Each, as a matter of ordinary prudence, will act with full consideration of its own needs and of the common need. Each must have control of its own prices. Each will recognize this to be a requirement of others. Each will foreswear any action, and notably any sanguinary or competitive price-cutting, which would be prejudicial to the common interest in price control. This control is not difficult either to achieve or to maintain. Additionally, one firm's prices are another firm's costs. So, stability in prices means stability in costs.

The fact of control is far most important than the precise level at which prices are established. In 1964 in the United States, the big automobile companies had profits on their sales ranging from 5 percent to over 10 percent. There was security against collapse of prices and earnings for firms at either level. Planning was possible at either level of return. All firms could function satisfactorily. But none could have functioned had the price of a standard model fluctuated, depending on whim and reaction to the current novelties, from, say, $1800 to $3600, with steel, glass, chrome, plastic, paint, tires, stereo music, and labor moving over a similar range.

However, the level of prices is not unimportant. And from time to time, in response to major changes in cost—often when the renegotiation of a wage contract provides a common signal to all firms in the industry —prices must be changed. The prices so established will reflect generally the goals of those who guide the enterprise, not of the owners but of those who make the decisions. Security of earnings will be a prime objective. This is necessary for autonomy—for freedom from interference by shareholders and creditors. The next most important goal will be the growth of the firm. This is almost certainly more important than maximum profits. The professional managers and technicians who direct and guide the modern firm do not themselves get the profits. These accrue mainly to the shareholders. But the managers and technicians do get the benefits of expansion. This brings the prestige which is associated with a larger firm and which is associated with growth as such. And as a very practical matter, it opens up new executive jobs, new opportunities for promotion, and better excuses for higher pay.

Prices, accordingly, will be set with a view to attracting customers and expanding sales. When price control is put in the context of planning, the contradiction between expectation of monopolistic exploitation and expectation of efficiency, which pervades all textbook discussion, disappears. Planning calls for stability of prices and costs, security of return, and expansion. With none of these is the consumer at odds. Reality has, by its nature, advantages of internal consistency.

I must mention here one practical consequence of this argument, namely, its bearing on legal action against monopoly. There is a remarkable discrimination in the way such measures, notably the antitrust laws, are now applied. A great corporation wielding vast power over its markets is substantially immune. It does not appear to misuse its power; accordingly, it is left alone. And in any case, to declare all large corporations illegal is, in effect, to declare the modern economy illegal. That is rather impractical—and would damage any President's consensus. But if two small firms making the same product seek to unite, this corporate union will be meticulously scrutinized. And very possibly, it will be forbidden. This may be so even though the merged firm is miniscule in size or market power as compared with the giant that is already a giant.

The explanation is that the modern antimonopoly and antitrust laws are substantially a charade. Their function is not to prevent exploitation of the public. If great size and great market power led to such exploitation, our case would long since have been hopeless. Their function is to persuade people, liberal economists in particular, that the market still exists, for here is the state vigilantly standing guard. It does so by exempting the large firms and swatting those that seek to become larger.

The French, Germans, and Japanese either do not have or do not enforce such laws. That is because they are not impelled similarly to worship at the altar of the market. They quietly accept the logic of planning and its requirements in size for effective market control. There is no indication that they suffer in consequence.

When prices for a particular product are set by a few large firms, there is little danger of price-cutting. This part of the control is secure. There does remain a danger of uncontrolled price increases.

In particular, when a few large firms bargain with a strong union, conflict can be avoided by acceding to union demands. And there is not much incentive to resist. There is a common understanding among the firms that all will raise their prices to compensate for such a settlement. If demand is strong enough to keep the economy near full employment, it will be strong enough to make such price increases feasible. These price increases, in turn, set in motion demands for further wage increases. Thus, the familiar upward spiral of wages and prices proceeds. And this too is prejudicial to planning. The individual firm, moreover, cannot prevent such price increases; they are beyond its control as a planning unit.

So here, more and more we follow the practice of the formally planned economies. We rely on the state to set maximum wages and prices. In the

United States as in Britain this is done with great caution, circumspection, and diffidence, somewhat in the manner of a Victorian spinster viewing an erotic statue. Such action is held to be unnatural and temporary. Economists accord it little or no standing in economic policy. They say it interferes with the market. Unions also dislike it: they say it interferes with free collective bargaining. Businessmen disapprove: they say it interferes with their natural freedom of decision on prices. But what everyone opposes in principle, all advanced countries end up doing in practice. The answer once more is clear. In a market economy, such ceilings would be unnecessary. But they are an indispensable counterpart of economic planning and of the minimum price control that already exists.

This price- and wage-setting by the state could be dispensed with by having such a shortage of demand that it would be impossible for firms to raise prices and unions to raise wages. That is to say, we could do without such controls by rehabilitating the market for labor and industrial products. It would not then be possible to raise wages in response to prices or prices in response to wages. But that would mean unemployment or greater uncertainty of employment, and it would mean greater market uncertainty for producers—for businessmen. Despite everyone's affection for the market, almost no one wants these results. So we have strong demand, small unemployment, reliable purchases, and the maximum price and wage controls that these require. And we try to avert our eyes from this result. It would be simpler were we to recognize that we have planning and that this control is an indispensable aspect.

This leads to another subject, the management of what people buy at the controlled prices.

The key to the management of demand is effective influence over the purchases of final consumers. The latter include both private individuals and the state. If all such purchases are under effective control, there will then be a reliable demand throughout the system for raw materials, parts, machinery, and other items going into the ultimate product. If the demand for its automobiles is secure, an automobile company can accord its suppliers the certainty of long-term contracts for *their* planning. And, even in the absence of such contracts, there will still be a reliable and predictable flow of orders. How, then, are the individual consumers managed?

As so often happens, change in modern industrial society has made possible what change requires. The need to control consumer behavior arises from the exigencies of planning. Planning, in turn, is made necessary by extensive use of advanced technology and the time and capital this requires. This is an efficient way of producing goods; the result is a very large volume of production. As a further consequence in the economically advanced countries, goods that serve elementary physical sensation—that prevent hunger, protect against cold, provide shelter, suppress pain—include only a small and diminishing part of what people consume. Only a few goods serve needs that are made known to the individual by the palpable discomfort or pain that is experienced in their absence. Most are enjoyed because of some psychic or aesthetic response to their possession or use. They give the individual a sense of personal achievement; they accord him a feeling of equality with his neighbors; they make him feel superior; or they divert his mind from thought or the absence of thought; or they promote or satisfy sexual aspiration; or they promise social acceptability; or they enhance his subjective feelings of health, well-being, and adequate peristalsis; or they are thought to contribute to personal beauty.

Thus it comes about that as the industrial system develops to where it has need for planning and the management of the consumer that this requires, we find it serving wants which are psychological in origin. And these are admirably subject to appeal to the psyche. Hence they can be managed. A man whose stomach is totally empty cannot be persuaded that his need is for entertainment. Physical discomfort will tell him he needs food more. But though a hungry man cannot be persuaded to choose between bread and a circus, a well-fed man can. And he can be persuaded to choose between different circuses and different foods.

By giving a man a ration card or distributing to him the specific commodities he is to consume, the individual can be required to consume in accordance with plan. But this is an onerous form of control, and it is ill adapted to differences in personality. In advanced industrial societies, it is considered acceptable only in times of great stress or for the very poor. (Even in the formally planned economies—the Soviet Union and the Eastern European states—the ration card is a manifestation of failure.) It is easier, and if less precise, still sufficient, to manage people by persuasion rather than by fiat.

Though advertising will be thought of as the central feature of this persuasion, and is certainly important, it is but a part of a much larger apparatus for the management of demand. Nor does this consist alone in devising a sales strategy for a particular product. It often means devising a product, or features of a product, around which a sales strategy can be built. Product design,, model change, packaging, and even performance reflect the need to provide what are called strong selling points. They are as much a part of the process of demand management as the advertising campaign.

The first step in this process, generally speaking, is to ensure a loyal or automatic corps of customers. This is known as building customer loyalty and brand recognition. If successful, it means that the firm has a stable body of customers who are secure against any large-scale defection. Being thus reliable and predictable, they allow planning.

A purely defensive strategy will not, however, suffice. In line with the goals of its directing organization, the firm will want to expand sales. And such effort is necessary to hold a given position. The same will be true of others. Out of these efforts, from firms that have the resources to play the game (another advantage of size), comes a crude equilibrating process which accords to each participant a reasonably reliable share of the market.

Specifically, when a firm is enjoying a steady patronage by its existing customers and recruiting new ones at what seems a satisfactory rate, the existing strategy for consumer management—advertising, selling methods, product design—will be considered satisfactory. The firm will not quarrel with success. However, if sales are stationary or slipping, this will call for a change in selling methods—in advertising, product design, or even in the product itself. Testing and experiment are possible. And sooner or later, a formula providing a suitable response is obtained. This will lead, in turn, to countering action by the firms that are then failing to make gains. And out of this process a rough but reliable equilibrium between the participants is achieved.

It does not always work. There are Edsels. But it is the everyday assumption of those who engage in management of demand that if sales of a product are slipping, a new selling formula can be found that will correct the situation. By and large, the assumption is justified. Means, in other words, can almost always be found to keep the exercise of consumer discretion within safe or planned limits.

Management of the consumer on the scale that I have just outlined requires that there be some comprehensive, repetitive, and compelling communication between the managers of demand and those who are managed. It must be possible to win the attention of those who are being managed for considerable periods of time without great effort on their part.

Technology, once again, solved the problem it created. Coincidentally with rising mass incomes came first radio and then television. In their capacity to hold effortless interest, their accessibility over the entire cultural spectrum, and their independence of any educational qualification, these were superbly suited to mass persuasion. Television was especially serviceable. Not since the invention of speech has any medium of communication appeared which is so readily accommodated to the whole spectrum of mental capacity.

There is an insistent tendency among social scientists, including economists, to think that any institution which features singing commercials, shows the human intestinal tract in full or impaired operation, equates the effortless elimination of human whiskers with the greatest happiness of man, and implies that exceptional but wholesome opportunities for seduction are associated with a particular make of automobile is inherently trivial. This is a great mistake. The modern industrial system is profoundly dependent on this art. What is called progress makes it increasingly so.

And the management of demand so provided is in all respects an admirably subtle arrangement in social design. It works not on the individual but on the mass. An individual of will and determination can, in principle, contract out from under its influence. This being the case, no individual compulsion in the purchase of any product can ever be established. To all who object there is a natural answer: You are at liberty to leave! Yet there is no danger that enough people will ever assert this choice—will ever leave—to impair the management of mass behavior.

In the nonsocialist economy, the modern large corporation is, to repeat, the basic planning unit. For some planning tasks, we see that it is exceedingly competent. It can fix minimum prices. It can sufficiently manage consumer wants. And it can extract from revenues the savings it needs for its own growth and expansion. But some things it cannot do. Though the modern corporation can set and maintain minimum prices, it cannot, we have seen, set maximum prices and wages; it cannot prevent wages from forcing up prices and prices from forcing up wages in the familiar spiral. And while it can manage the demand for individual products, it cannot control total demand—it cannot ensure that total purchasing power in the economy will be equal, or approximately equal, to the supply of goods that can be produced by the current working force.

There are two other planning tasks that the large corporation cannot perform. It cannot supply the specialized manpower that modern technology and complex organization and planning require. It can train, but on the whole, it cannot educate. And it cannot absorb the risks and costs that are associated with very advanced forms of scientific and technical development—with the development of atomic power, or supersonic air transports, or antimissile defenses, or weapons systems to pierce these defenses, or the like requirements of modern civilized living.

This leads to a conclusion of great importance. The shortcomings of the large corporation as a planning instrument define the role of the modern state in economic policy. Wherever the private corporation cannot plan, the state comes in and performs the required function. Wherever the modern corporation can do the job, as in setting minimum prices or managing consumer demand, the state must remain out, usually as a matter of principle. But the corporation cannot fix maximum prices, so we have the state establishing wage and price guideposts or otherwise limiting wage and price increases. The private firm cannot control aggregate demand, so the state comes in to manipulate taxes, public spending, and bank lending—to implement what we call modern Keynesian policy. The private firm cannot supply specialized manpower, so we have a great expansion in publicly supported education. Private firms cannot afford to underwrite supersonic aircraft. So governments—British, French, or American—come in to do so and with no taint of socialism.

Our attitudes on the proper role of the state are firmly fixed by what the private corporation can or cannot do. The latter can set minimum prices for cigarettes, persuade people to buy a new and implausible detergent, or develop a more drastic laxative. This being so, such planning activity is naturally held to be sacred to private enterprise.

The planning functions of the state are somewhat less sacred. Some still have an improvised or *ad hoc* aspect. Thus, restraints on wages and prices are perpetual emergency actions; though fully accepted, Keynesian regulation of aggregate demand is thought to be occasioned by the particular imperatives of full employment and growth; the expansion of education is regarded as the result of a new enlightenment following World War II; the underwriting of especially expensive technology is a pragmatic response to the urgent social need for faster travel, emigration to the moon, bigger explosions, and competition with the Soviet Union.

So to regard matters is to fail to see the nature of modern planning. It is to yield unduly to the desire to avert our eyes from the reality of economic life. The planning functions of the state are not *ad hoc* or separate developments. They are a closely articulated set of functions which supplement and fill the gaps in the planning of the modern large firm. Together these provide a comprehensive planning apparatus. It decides what people should have and then arranges that they will get it and that they will want it. Not the least of its achievements is in leaving them with the impression that the controlling decisions are all theirs.

The Keynesian regulation of aggregate demand also requires only a word. The need for it follows directly from modern industrial planning. As we have seen, corporations decide authoritatively what they will reserve from earnings for reinvestment and expansion. But in the non-Soviet economies, there is no mechanism that ensures that the amounts so withheld for investment will be matched in the economy as a whole by what is invested. So there must be direct action by the state to equate the two. This it does primarily by manipulating private investment (principally in housing) and public spending and taxation. The need to equate the planned savings and the planned investment of the large corporation is not, of course, the only reason for such action. Savings and investment elsewhere in the economy must also be matched. But savings and investment by the large planning corporations are by far the most important in the total.

The successful regulation of demand requires that the quantitative role of the state in the modern economy be relatively large. That is because demand is regulated primarily by increasing or decreasing the expenditures of the state or decreasing or increasing the taxes it collects. Only when the state is large and its revenues are substantial will these changes be large enough to serve. One effective way of ensuring the requisite scale of state activity is to have it underwrite modern technology, which is admirably expensive. Such is the case with modern weaponry, space exploration, even highway and airport design. Though technology helps destroy the market, it does make possible the planning that replaces the market.

The next function of the state is to provide the specialized and trained manpower which the industrial system cannot supply to itself. This has led in our time to a very great expansion in education, especially in higher education, as has been true in all of the advanced countries. In 1900, there were 24,000 teachers in colleges and universities in the United States; in 1920, there were 49,000; by 1970, three years hence, there will be 480,000. This is rarely pictured as an aspect of modern economic development; it is the vanity of educators that they consider themselves the moving force in a new enlightenment. But it may be significant that when industry, at a little earlier stage, required mostly unlettered proletarians, that is what the educational system supplied. As it has come to need engineers, sales executives, copywriters, computer programmers, personnel managers, information retrieval specialists, product planners, and executive panjandrums, these are what the educational system has come to provide.

Once the community or nation that wanted more industry gave first thought to its capital supply and how to reassure the bankers on its reliability. Now it gives first thought to its educational system.

We cannot be altogether happy about education that is so motivated. There is danger that it will be excessively vocational and that we shall have a race of men who are strong on telemetry and space communications but who cannot read anything but a blueprint or write anything but a computer program. There is currently some uneasiness about liberal education in the modern industrial society. But so far this has manifested itself only in speeches by university presidents. In this segment of society, unfortunately a solemn speech is regularly considered a substitute for action.

Much the most interesting of the planning functions of the state is the underwriting of expensive technology. Few changes in economic life have ever proceeded with such explosive rapidity. Few have so undermined conventional concepts of public and private enterprise. In 1962, the U.S.

government spent an estimated $10.6 billion on research and development. This was more than its total dollar outlay for all purposes, military or civilian, before World War II. But this function also includes the underwriting of markets—the provision of a guaranteed demand for billions of dollars worth of highly technical products, from aircraft to missiles to electronic gear to space vehicles. Nearly all of this expenditure, some 80 to 85 percent, goes to the large corporation, which is to say that it is to the planned sector of the American economy. It also brings the modern large corporation into the most intimate association with the state. In the case of such public agencies as NASA, the Atomic Energy Commission, or the Air Force, and the corporations serving them, it is no longer easy to say where the public sector ends and the private sector begins. Individuals and organizations are intimately associated. The private sector becomes, in effect, an extended arm of the public bureaucracy. However, the banner of private enterprise can be quite aggressively flaunted by the firm that does 75 percent of its business with the government and yearns to do more.

In the past, Keynesians have argued that there is nothing very special about government business. Replying to standard Marxian charges that capitalism depends excessively on armaments, they have pointed out that spending for housing, theaters, automobiles, highways to allow more automobiles to exist, and for radios to supply more automobiles to amuse more people while they are sitting in the resulting traffic jams, and for other of the attributes of gracious living will serve to sustain demand just as well as spending on arms. This, we now see, is not the whole story. The expenditures I have just mentioned would not serve to underwrite technology. And this underwriting is beyond the reach of private planning. Replacement of military spending, with its emphasis on underwriting advanced technology, must be by other equally technical outlays if it is to serve the same purpose. Otherwise, technical development will have to be curtailed to that level where corporate planning units can underwrite on their own. And this curtailment under present circumstances would be very, very drastic.

This analysis makes a considerable case for the space race. It is not that exploring the moon, Mars, or even Saturn is of high social urgency. Rather, the space race allows for an extensive underwriting of advanced technology. And it does this in a field of activity where spending is large and where, in contrast with weapons and weapons systems, competition with the Soviets is comparatively safe and benign. At the same time, as in the case of competitive athletics, everyone can easily be persuaded that it is absolutely vital to win.

We now see the modern corporation, in the technological aspects of its activities, moving into a very close association with the state. The state is the principal customer for such technology and the underwriter of major risk. In the planning of tasks and missions, the mapping of development work, and the execution of contracts, there is nowadays a daily and intimate association between the bureaucracy and the large so-called private firm. But one thing, it will be said, keeps them apart. The state is in pursuit of broad national goals, whatever these may be. And the private firm seeks to make money—in the more solemn language of economics, to maximize profits. This difference in goals, it will be said, sufficiently differentiates the state from private enterprise.

But here again reality supplies that indispensable thread of consistency. For power, as I showed in the first of these articles, and in detail in the book on which I am drawing, has passed from the owners of the corporation to the managers and scientists and technicians. The latter now exercise largely autonomous power, and not surprisingly, they exercise it in *their* own interest. And this interest differs from that of the owners. As noted, security of return is more important than the level of total earnings. When earnings fail, the autonomy of the decision-makers is threatened. And growth is more important to managers and technicians than maximum earnings.

But a further and important conclusion follows, for economic security and growth are also prime goals of the modern state. Nothing has been more emphasized in modern economic policy than the prevention of depression or recession. Politicians promise it automatically and without perceptible thought. And no test of social achievement is so completely and totally accepted as the rate of economic growth. It is the common measure of accomplishment of all the economic systems. Transcending political faith, religion, occupation, or all except eccentric philosophical persuasion, it is something on which Americans, Russians, Englishmen, Frenchmen, Germans, Italians, and Yugoslavs, and even Irishmen, all agree.

We have seen that as an aspect of its planning, the modern industrial enterprise accommodates the behavior and beliefs of the individual consumer to its needs. It is reasonable to assume that it has also accommodated our social objectives and associated beliefs to what it needs. In any case, there has been an interaction between state and firm which has brought a unity of goals.

A somber thought will occur to many here. We have seen that the state is necessary for underwriting the technology of modern industrial enterprise. Much of this it does within the framework of military expenditure. In the consumer goods economy, the wants and beliefs of the consumer, including his conviction that happiness is associated all but exclusively with the consumption of goods, are accommodated, in greater or less measure, to producer need. Is this true also of the state? Does it respond in its military procurement to what the supplying firms need to sell—and the technology that they wish to have underwritten? Are images of foreign policy in the planned industrial communities—in the United States, the Soviet Union, Western Europe—shaped by industrial need? Do we have an image of conflict because that serves technological and therewith planning need?

We cannot exclude that possibility; on the contrary, it is most plausible. It is a conclusion that was reached, perhaps a bit more intuitively, by President Eisenhower while he was President of the United States. In his famous valedictory, he warned of the influence on public policy resulting from the "conjunction of an immense military establishment and a large arms industry." This will not be an agreeable thought for those for whom the mind is an instrument for evading reality. Others will see the possibility of a two-way flow of influence. Presumably it will be true of any planned economy, East or West. The image of the foreign policy affects the demand of the state on industry. But the needs of economic planning expressed in the intimate association between industry and the state will affect the state's view of military requirements and of foreign policy. It is a matter where we had best be guided by reality.

V. The War in Vietnam

11. Dean Rusk

American Foreign Policy and International Law

The war in Southeast Asia has been the most unpopular foreign war in American history and the most disruptive in American politics. Its historical roots are deep, and it has involved many nations, some of them no longer belligerents in the conflict. The American involvement was based on a multitude of motives and ideological assumptions going back more than 50 years. The direct American connection began during the early years of the Cold War when the Truman administration ignored appeals from Ho Chi Minh for aid against French colonialism, and then in 1950, following the fall of Chiang Kai-shek in China, decided to underwrite the French war effort with lavish financial aid.

With the defeat of the French forces at Dien Bien Phu in May 1954, and with the Geneva accords (July 1954) viewed as a "disaster" by the National Security Council, the United States undertook unilaterally the economic and military support of South Vietnam, described in the Pentagon Papers as "essentially the creation of the United States." President John F. Kennedy turned the "limited risk" gamble of the Eisenhower administration into a broad commitment to prevent Communist domination in the South. But it was President Lyndon B. Johnson who drastically escalated the conflict in 1965 by ordering a sustained air war (Operation Rolling Thunder) against North Vietnam and by committing U.S. ground troops to fight the war his predecessor had said only the Vietnamese themselves could win. By the time Johnson left office, troop strength had risen to nearly 550,000 men.

In the selection that follows, Dean Rusk, secretary of state under Presidents Kennedy and Johnson, presents one version of the official argument for U.S. intervention in Southeast Asia. It is a typical document of the Cold War, warning of the need to stop Communist aggression, to prevent the concrete unfolding of the domino theory, and to set up dikes against wars of national liberation, defined by Rusk as "any war which furthers the Communist world revolution." It was necessary for Rusk to portray the insurgency in South Vietnam as the result of outside aggression rather than of indigenous rebellion so that U.S. intervention could be interpreted as consistent with international law. In a later address Rusk argued that U.S. policy was designed to prepare for the day "within the next decade or two" when "there will be a billion Chinese on the mainland, armed with nuclear weapons, with no certainty about what their attitude would be towards the rest of Asia."

From *Department of State Bulletin*, Vol. 52, No. 1350, Publication 7883 (May 10, 1965).

A paragraph by paragraph analysis of Rusk's speech, part of an address to the American Society of International Law (April 23, 1965), proves rewarding. It reveals the great differences between the realities of the war and the public statements of American officials. The Pentagon Papers, written not by radicals tuned to the screams of the Indochinese but by technicians who worked in the American military bureaucracy, contain decisive evidence of U.S.-initiated escalation in late 1963 and early 1964 that instigated the full-scale war that developed immediately thereafter. According to intelligence reports the first evidence of regular North Vietnamese units fighting in the South appeared in April 1965. CIA assessments of indigenous support for the Vietcong also contradict Rusk leading the authors of the Pentagon study to say, "Only the Viet Cong had any real support and influence on a broad base in the countryside." The CIA also challenged the domino theory, popular in one form or another within administration circles, which Gabriel Kolko (Gravel Edition, *Pentagon Papers,* Vol. V) defines as "a counterrevolutionary doctrine which defined modern history as a movement of Third World and dependent nations—those with economic and strategic value to the United States or its capitalist associates—away from colonialism or capitalism and toward national revolution and forms of socialism."

The Senator Gravel Edition of *The Pentagon Papers,* Vol. V (Beacon Press, 1972), edited by Noam Chomsky and Howard Zinn, contains critical essays that are helpful in assessing the arguments of Secretary Rusk.

. . . American foreign policy is at once principaled and pragmatic. Its central objective is our national safety and well-being—to "secure the Blessings of Liberty to ourselves and our Posterity." But we know we can no longer find security and well-being in defenses and policies which are confined to North America, or the Western Hemisphere, or the North Atlantic community.

This has become a very small planet. We have to be concerned with all of it—with all of its land, waters, atmosphere, and with surrounding space. We have a deep national interest in peace, the prevention of aggression, the faithful performance of agreements, the growth of international law. Our foreign policy is rooted in the profoundly practical realization that the purposes and principles of the United Nations Charter must animate the behavior of states if mankind is to prosper or is even to survive. Or at least they must animate enough states with enough will and enough resources to see to it that others do not violate those rules with impunity. . . .

Unhappily, a minority of governments is committed to different ideas of the conduct and organization of human affairs. They are dedicated to the promotion of the Communist world revolution. And their doctrine justifies any technique, any ruse, any deceit, which contributes to that end. They may differ as to tactics from time to time. And the two principal Communist powers are competitors for the leadership of the world Communist movement. But both are committed to the eventual communization of the entire world.

The overriding issue of our time is which concepts are to prevail: those set forth in the United Nations Charter or those proclaimed in the name of a world revolution.

Charter Prohibitions on Use of Force

The paramount commitment of the charter is article 2, paragraph 4, which reads:

All Members shall refrain in their international relations from the threat or use of force against the territorial integrity or political independence of any state, or in any other manner inconsistent with the Purposes of the United Nations.

This comprehensive limitation went beyond the Covenant of the League of Nations. This more sweeping commitment sought to apply a bitter lesson of the interwar period—that the threat or use of force, whether or not called "war," feeds on success. The indelible lesson of those years is that the time to stop aggression is at its very beginning.

The exceptions to the prohibitions on the use or threat of force were expressly set forth in the charter. The use of force is legal:

—as a collective measure by the United Nations, or
—as action by regional agencies in accordance with chapter VIII of the charter, or
—in individual or collective self-defense. . . .

What Is a "War of National Liberation"?

What is a "war of national liberation"? It is, in essence, any war which furthers the Communist world revolution—what, in broader terms, the Communists have long referred to as a "just" war. The term "war of national liberation" is used not only to denote armed insurrection by people still under colonial rule—there are not many of those left outside the Communist world. It is used to denote any effort led by Communists to overthrow by force any non-Communist government.

Thus the war in South Viet-Nam is called a "war of national liberation." And those who would overthrow various other non-Communist governments in Asia, Africa, and Latin America are called the "forces of national liberation."

Nobody in his right mind would deny that Venezuela is not only a truly independent nation but that it has a government chosen in a free election. But the leaders of the Communist insurgency in Venezuela are described as leaders of a fight for "national liberation"—not only by themselves and by Castro and the Chinese Communists but by the Soviet Communists.

A recent editorial in *Pravda* spoke of the "peoples of Latin America . . . marching firmly along the path of struggle for their national independence" and said, ". . . the upsurge of the national liberation movement in Latin American countries has been to a great extent a result of the activities of Communist parties." It added:

The Soviet people have regarded and still regard it as their sacred duty to give support to the peoples fighting for their independence. True to their international duty the Soviet people have been and will remain on the side of the Latin American patriots.

In Communist doctrine and practice, a non-Communist government may be labeled and denounced as "colonialist," "reactionary," or a "puppet," and any state so labeled by the Communists automatically becomes fair game—while Communist intervention by force in non-Communist states is justified as "self-defense" or part of the "struggle against colonial domination." "Self-determination" seems to mean that any Communist nation can determine by itself that any non-Communist state is a victim of colonialist domination and therefore a justifiable target for a "war of liberation."

As the risks of overt aggression, whether nuclear or with conventional forces, have become increasingly evident, the Communists have put increasing stress on the "war of national liberation." The Chinese Communists have been more militant in language and behavior than the Soviet Communists. But the Soviet Communist leadership also has consistently proclaimed its commitment in principle to support wars of national liberation. This commitment was reaffirmed as recently as Monday of this week by Mr. Kosygin [Aleksai N. Kosygin, Chairman of the U.S.S.R. Council of Ministers].

International law does not restrict internal revolution within a state or revolution against colonial authority. But international law does restrict what third powers may lawfully do in support of insurrection. It is these restrictions which are challenged by the doctrine, and violated by the practice, of "wars of liberation."

It is plain that acceptance of the doctrine of "wars of liberation" would amount to scuttling the modern international law of peace which the charter prescribes. And acceptance of the practice of "wars of liberation," as defined by the Communists, would mean the breakdown of peace itself.

South Viet-Nam's Right of Self-Defense

Viet-Nam presents a clear current case of the lawful versus the unlawful use of force. I would agree with General Giap [Vo Nguyen Giap, North Vietnamese Commander in Chief] and other Communists that it is a test case for "wars of national liberation." We intend to meet that test.

Were the insurgency in South Viet-Nam truly indigenous and self-sustained, international law would not be involved. But the fact is that it receives vital external support—in organization and direction, in training, in men, in weapons and other supplies. That external support is unlawful for a double reason. First, it contravenes general international law, which the United Nations Charter here expresses. Second, it contravenes particular international law: the 1954 Geneva accords on Viet-Nam and the 1962 Geneva agreements on Laos.

In resisting the aggression against it, the Republic of Viet-Nam is exercising its right of self-defense. It called upon us and other states for assistance. And in the exercise of the right of collective self-defense under the United Nations Charter, we and other nations are providing such assistance.

The American policy of assisting South Viet-Nam to maintain its freedom was inaugurated under President Eisenhower and continued under Presidents Kennedy and Johnson. Our assistance has been increased because the aggression from the North has been augmented. Our assistance now encompasses the bombing of North Viet-Nam. The bombing is designed to interdict, as far as possible, and to inhibit, as far as may be necessary, continued aggression against the Republic of Viet-Nam.

When that aggression ceases, collective measures in defense against it will cease. As President Johnson has declared:

. . . if that aggression is stopped, the people and Government of South Viet-Nam will be free to settle their own future, and the need for supporting American military action there will end. . . .

I continue to hear and see nonsense about the nature of the struggle there. I sometimes wonder at the gullibility of educated men and the stubborn disregard of plain facts by men who are supposed to be helping our young to learn—especially to learn how to think.

Hanoi has never made a secret of its designs. It publicly proclaimed in

1960 a renewal of the assault on South Viet-Nam. Quite obviously its hopes of taking over South Viet-Nam from within had withered to close to zero—and the remarkable economic and social progress of South Viet-Nam contrasted, most disagreeably for the North Vietnamese Communists, with their own miserable economic performance.

The facts about the external involvement have been documented in white papers and other publications of the Department of State. The International Control Commission has held that there is evidence "beyond reasonable doubt" of North Vietnamese intervention.

There is no evidence that the Viet Cong has any significant popular following in South Viet-Nam. It relies heavily on terror. Most of its reinforcements in recent months have been North Vietnamese from the North Vietnamese Army.

Let us be clear about what is involved today in Southeast Asia. We are not involved with empty phrases or conceptions which ride upon the clouds. We are talking about the vital national interests of the United States in the peace of the Pacific. We are talking about the appetite for aggression—an appetite which grows upon feeding and which is proclaimed to be insatiable. We are talking about the safety of nations with whom we are allied—and the integrity of the American commitment to join in meeting attack.

It is true that we also believe that every small state has a right to be unmolested by its neighbors even though it is within reach of a great power. It is true that we are committed to general principles of law and procedure which reject the idea that men and arms can be sent freely across frontiers to absorb a neighbor. But underlying the general principles is the harsh reality that our own security is threatened by those who would embark upon a course of aggression whose announced ultimate purpose is our own destruction.

Once again we hear expressed the views which cost the men of my generation a terrible price in World War II. We are told that Southeast Asia is far away—but so were Manchuria and Ethiopia. We are told that, if we insist that someone stop shooting, that is asking them for unconditional surrender. We are told that perhaps the aggressor will be content with just one more bite. We are told that, if we prove faithless on one commitment, perhaps others would believe us about other commitments in other places. We are told that, if we stop resisting, perhaps the other side will have a change of heart. We are asked to stop hitting bridges and radar sites and ammunition depots without requiring that the other side stop its slaughter of thousands of civilians and its bombings of schools and hotels and hospitals and railways and buses.

Surely we have learned over the past three decades that the acceptance of aggression leads only to a sure catastrophe. Surely we have learned that the aggressor must face the consequences of his action and be saved from the frightful miscalculation that brings all to ruin. It is the purpose of law to guide men away from such events, to establish rules of conduct which are deeply rooted in the reality of experience. . . .

12. Robert S. McNamara

"We have not found the formula"

One of the remarkable features of the Vietnam war was the unflagging confidence of American policy-makers in an early victory. Only Secretary of State Robert S. McNamara, among President Johnson's first-level advisers, lost faith in the war, and even then he lingered in his post until after the devastating Tet offensive of February 1968. McNamara exemplified a type of policy-maker that flourished in Washington, D.C., during the 1960s. "They were not so much liberals as technocrats, men of power rather than passion," who made "a fetish of energy and style," one observer has written. They were accustomed to success.

McNamara's career is instructive in this regard. He had come to the Kennedy Administration with impeccable credentials. After receiving an MBA from the Harvard Business School during the early days of World War II, he was appointed to its faculty. He soon resigned and served as a staff officer during the war. Afterward he joined the "whiz kids," a group of independent business analysts who sold their expertise in managerial efficiency and rational planning to corporations. Assigned to the Ford Motor Company, he so impressed company officials that he was invited to stay on, later becoming president, the first member outside the Ford family so honored. From that position he went directly to Washington, D.C., to serve as President Kennedy's secretary of defense.

He dazzled Pentagon officials and critics alike in bringing order to the vast bureaucracy and numerous power centers of the defense establishment. But he became disillusioned when military success in Vietnam proved elusive, and in 1967 he commissioned the study now known as the Pentagon Papers—a massive secret history of the American involvement in Indochina. One of the researchers in the study reveals that the secretary had gone from "hesitancy" in the winter of 1965 to "perplexity" in the spring of 1966 to "disenchantment" the following fall. It was in this mood that McNamara drafted the following memorandum (October 1966) for President Johnson. The once-confident secretary acknowledged that there was no end in sight to the war. Pacification had failed, and the heavy bombing of North Vietnam had failed either to break the morale of Hanoi or to prevent infiltration from the North. On these matters he included supportive evidence from the intelligence community. His conclusion that the United States should

From *The Pentagon Papers* as published by *The New York Times,* Document # 118. (Bantam Books, Inc., 1971.)

level off operations, particularly in the air war, later occasioned his departure from Johnson's cabinet.

The document is notable also in that it contains no question about the legitimacy or rightness of the American involvement in Indochinese affairs. In each stage of the escalating war, the primary issues were always the size of troop commitments, the effectiveness of the bombing of North Vietnam, and the expansion of the air and ground war in the South. Is it this glaring omission of moral and humane considerations that explains why no top official resigned in protest during the bitter domestic debates over the merits of the war?

---

1. Evaluation of the Situation

In the report of my last trip to Vietnam almost a year ago, I stated that the odds were about even that, even with the then-recommended deployments, we would be faced in early 1967 with a military stand-off at a much higher level of conflict and with "pacification" still stalled. I am a little less pessimistic now in one respect. We have done somewhat better militarily than I anticipated. We have by and large blunted the communist military initiative—any military victory in South Vietnam the Viet Cong may have had in mind 18 months ago has been thwarted by our emergency deployments and actions. And our program of bombing the North has exacted a price.

My concern continues, however, in other respects. This is because I see no reasonable way to bring the war to an end soon. Enemy morale has not broken—he apparently has adjusted to our stopping his drive for military victory and has adopted a strategy of keeping us busy and waiting us out (a strategy of attriting our national will). He knows that we have not been, and he believes we probably will not be, able to translate our military successes into the "end products"—broken enemy morale and political achievements by the GVN.[1]

The one thing demonstrably going for us in Vietnam over the past year has been the large number of enemy killed-in-action resulting from the big military operations. Allowing for possible exaggeration in reports, the enemy must be taking losses—deaths in and after battle—at the rate of more than 60,000 a year. The infiltration routes would seem to be one-way trails to death for the North Vietnamese. Yet there is no sign of an impending break in enemy morale and it appears that he can more than replace his losses by infiltration from North Vietnam and recruitment in South Vietnam.

[1] Government of (South) Vietnam.

Pacification is a bad disappointment. We have good grounds to be pleased by the recent elections, by Ky's 16 months in power, and by the faint signs of development of national political institutions and of a legitimate civil government. But none of this has translated itself into political achievements at Province level or below. Pacification has if anything gone backward. As compared with two, or four, years ago, enemy full-time regional forces and part-time guerrilla forces are larger; attacks, terrorism and sabotage have increased in scope and intensity; more railroads are closed and highways cut; the rice crop expected to come to market is smaller; we control little, if any, more of the population; the VC political infrastructure thrives in most of the country, continuing to give the enemy his enormous intelligence advantage; full security exists nowhere (not even behind the U.S. Marines' lines and in Saigon) ; in the countryside, the enemy almost completely controls the night.

Nor has the ROLLING THUNDER program of bombing the North either significantly affected infiltration or cracked the morale of Hanoi. There is agreement in the intelligence community on these facts (see the attached Appendix) .

In essence, we find ourselves—from the point of view of the important war (for the complicity of the people) —no better, and if anything worse off. This important war must be fought and won by the Vietnamese themselves. We have known this from the beginning. But the discouraging truth is that, as was the case in 1961 and 1963 and 1965, we have not found the formula, the catalyst, for training and inspiring them into effective action.

2. Recommended Actions

In such an unpromising state of affairs, what should we do? We must continue to press the enemy militarily; we must make demonstrable progress in pacification; at the same time, we must add a new ingredient forced on us by the facts. Specifically, we must improve our position by getting ourselves into a military posture that we credibly would maintain indefinitely—a posture that makes trying to "wait us out" less attractive. I recommend a five-pronged course of action to achieve those ends.

a. Stabilize U.S. Force-Levels in Vietnam

It is my judgment that, barring a dramatic change in the war, we should limit the increase in U.S. forces in SVN in 1967 to 70,000 men and we should level off at the total of 470,000 which such an increase would provide. It is my view that this is enough to punish the enemy at the large-unit operations level and to keep the enemy's main forces from interrupting pacification. I believe also that even many more than 470,000 would not kill the enemy off in such numbers as to break their morale so long as they think they can wait us out. It is possible that such a 40 percent increase over our present level of 325,000 will break the enemy's morale in the short term; but if it does not, we must, I believe, be prepared for and have underway a long-term program premised on more than breaking the morale of main force units. A stabilized U.S. force level would be part of such a long-term program. It would put us in a position where negotiations would be more likely to be productive, but if they were not we could pursue the all-important pacification task with proper attention and resources and without the spectre of apparently endless escalation of U.S. deployments.

b. Install a Barrier
A portion of the 470,000 troops—perhaps 10,000 to 20,000—should be devoted to the construction and maintenance of an infiltration barrier. Such a barrier would lie near the 17th parallel—would run from the sea, across the neck of South Vietnam (choking off the new infiltration routes through the DMZ) and across the trails in Laos. This interdiction system (at an approximate cost of $1 billion) would comprise to the east a ground barrier of fences, wire, sensors, artillery, aircraft and mobile troops; and to the west—mainly in Laos—an interdiction zone covered by air-laid mines and bombing attacks pinpointed by air-laid acoustic sensors.

The barrier may not be fully effective at first, but I believe that it can be effective in time and that even the threat of its becoming effective can substantially change to our advantage the character of the war. It would hinder enemy efforts, would permit more efficient use of the limited number of friendly troops, and would be persuasive evidence both that our sole aim is to protect the South from the North and that we intend to see the job through.

c. Stabilize the ROLLING THUNDER Program Against the North
Attack sorties in North Vietnam have risen from about 4,000 per month at the end of last year to 6,000 per month in the first quarter of this year and 12,000 per month at present. Most of our 50 percent increase of deployed attack-capable aircraft has been absorbed in the attacks on North Vietnam. In North Vietnam, almost 84,000 attack sorties have been flown (about 25 percent against fixed targets), 45 percent during the past seven months.

Despite these efforts, it now appears that the North Vietnamese-Laotian road network will remain adequate to meet the requirements of the Communist forces in South Vietnam—this is so even if its capacity could be reduced by one-third and if combat activities were to be doubled. North Vietnam's serious need for trucks, spare parts and petroleum probably can, despite air attacks, be met by imports. The petroleum requirement for trucks involved in the infiltration movement, for example, has not been enough to present significant supply problems, and the effects of the attacks on the petroleum distribution system, while they have not yet been fully assessed, are not expected to cripple the flow of essential supplies. Furthermore, it is clear that, to bomb the North sufficiently to make a radical impact upon Hanoi's political, economic and social structure, would require an effort which we could make but which would not be stomached either by our own people or by world opinion; and it would involve a serious risk of drawing us into open war with China.

The North Vietnamese are paying a price. They have been forced to assign some 300,000 personnel to the lines of communication in order to maintain the critical flow of personnel and material to the South. Now that the lines of communication have been manned, however, it is doubtful that either a large increase or decrease in our interdiction sorties would substantially change the cost to the enemy of maintaining the roads, railroads, and waterways or affect whether they are operational. It follows that the marginal sorties—probably the marginal 1,000 or even 5,000 sorties—per month against the lines of communication no longer have a significant impact on the war. (See the attached excerpts from intelligence estimates.)

When this marginal inutility of added sorties against North Vietnam and Laos is compared with the crew and aircraft losses implicit in the activity (four men and aircraft and $20 million per 1,000 sorties), I recommend, as a minimum, against increasing the level of bombing of North Vietnam and against increasing the intensity of operations by changing the areas or kinds of targets struck.

Under these conditions, the bombing program would continue the pressure and would remain available as a bargaining counter to get talks started (or to trade off in talks). But, as in the case of a stabilized level of U.S. ground forces, the stabilization of ROLLING THUNDER would remove the prospect of ever escalating bombing as a factor complicating our political posture and distracting from the main job of pacification in South Vietnam.

At the proper time, as discussed below, I believe we should consider terminating bombing in all of North Vietnam, or at least in the Northeast zones, for an indefinite period in connection with covert moves toward peace.

d. Pursue a Vigorous Pacification Program

As mentioned above, the pacification (Revolutionary Development) program has been and is thoroughly stalled. The large-unit operations war, which we know best how to fight and where we have had our successes, is largely irrelevant to pacification as long as we do not lose it. By and large, the people in rural areas believe that the GVN when it comes will not stay but that the VC will; that cooperations with the GVN will be punished by the VC; that the GVN is really indifferent to the people's welfare; that the low-level GVN are tools of the local rich; and that the GVN is ridden with corruption.

Success in pacification depends on the interrelated functions of providing physical security, destroying the VC apparatus, motivating the people to cooperate and establishing responsive local government. An obviously necessary but not sufficient requirement for success of the Revolutionary Development cadre and police is vigorously conducted and adequately prolonged clearing operations by military troops, who will "stay" in the area, who behave themselves decently and who show some respect for the people.

This elemental requirement of pacification has been missing.

In almost no contested area designated for pacification in recent years have ARVN[2] forces actually "cleared and stayed" to a point where cadre teams, if available, could have stayed overnight in hamlets and survived, let alone accomplish their mission. VC units of company and even battalion size remain in operation, and they are more than large enough to overrun anything the local security forces can put up.

Now that the threat of a Communist main-force military victory has been thwarted by our emergency efforts, we must allocate far more attention and a portion of the regular military forces (at least half of the ARVN and perhaps a portion of the U.S. forces) to the task of providing an active and permanent security screen behind which the Revolutionary Development teams and police can operate and behind which the political struggle with the VC infrastructure can take place.

The U.S. cannot do this pacification security job for the Vietnamese. All we can do is "Massage the heart." For one reason, it is known that we do not intend to stay; if our efforts worked at all, it would merely postpone the eventual confrontation of the VC and GVN infrastructures. The GVN must do the job; and I am convinced that drastic reform is needed if the GVN is going to be able to do it.

The first essential reform is in the attitude of GVN officials. They are generally apathetic, and there is corruption high and low. Often appointments, promotions, and draft deferments must be bought; and kickbacks on salaries are common. Cadre at the bottom can be no better than the system above them.

The second needed reform is in the attitude and conduct of the ARVN. The image of the government cannot improve unless and until

[2] Army of the Republic of (South) Vietnam.

the ARVN improves markedly. They do not understand the importance (or respectability) of pacification nor the importance to pacification of proper, disciplined conduct. Promotions, assignments and awards are often not made on merit, but rather on the basis of having a diploma, friends or relatives, or because of bribery. The ARVN is weak in dedication, direction and discipline.

Not enough ARVN are devoted to area and population security, and when the ARVN does attempt to support pacification, their actions do not last long enough; their tactics are bad despite U.S. prodding (no aggressive small-unit saturation patrolling, hamlet searches, quick-reaction contact, or offensive night ambushes) ; they do not make good use of intelligence; and their leadership and discipline are bad.

Furthermore, it is my conviction that a part of the problem undoubtedly lies in bad management on the American as well as the GVN side. Here split responsibility—or "no responsibility"—has resulted in too little hard pressure on the GVN to do its job and no really solid or realistic planning with respect to the whole effort. We must deal with this management problem and deal with it effectively.

One solution would be to consolidate all U.S. activities which are primarily part of the civilian pacification program and all persons engaged in such activities, providing a clear assignment of responsibility and a unified command under a civilian relieved of all other duties. Under this approach, there would be a carefully delineated division of responsibility between the civilian-in-charge and an element of COMUSMACV[3] under a senior officer, who would give the subject of planning for and providing hamlet security the highest priority in attention and resources. Success will depend on the men selected for the jobs on both sides (they must be among the highest rank and most competent administrators in the U.S. Government) , on complete cooperation among the U.S. elements, and on the extent to which the South Vietnamese can be shocked out of their present pattern of behavior. The first work of this reorganized U.S. pacification organization should be to produce within 60 days a realistic and detailed plan for the coming year.

From the political and public-relations viewpoint, this solution is preferable—if it works. But we cannot tolerate continued failure. If it fails after a fair trial, the only alternative in my view is to place the entire pacification program—civilian and military—under General Westmoreland. This alternative would result in the establishment of a Deputy COMUSMACV for Pacification who would be in command of all pacification staffs in Saigon and of all pacification staffs and activities in the field; one person in each corps, province and district would be responsible for the U.S. effort.

[3] Commander, U.S. Military Assistance Command, Vietnam.

(It should be noted that progress in pacification, more than anything else, will persuade the enemy to negotiate or withdraw.)

e. Press for Negotiations

I am not optimistic that Hanoi or the VC will respond to peace overtures now (explaining my recommendations above that we get into a level-off posture for the long pull). The ends sought by the two sides appear to be irreconcilable and the relative power balance is not in their view unfavorable to them. But three things can be done, I believe, to increase the prospects:

1. Take steps to increase the credibility of our peace gestures in the minds of the enemy. There is considerable evidence both in private statements by the Communists and in the reports of competent Western officials who have talked with them that charges of U.S. bad faith are not solely propagandistic, but reflect deeply held beliefs. Analyses of Communists' statements and actions indicate that they firmly believe that American leadership really does not want the fighting to stop, and, that we are intent on winning a military victory in Vietnam and on maintaining our presence there through a puppet regime supported by U.S. military bases.

As a way of projecting U.S. bona fides, I believe that we should consider two possibilities with respect to our bombing program against the North, to be undertaken, if at all, at a time very carefully selected with a view to maximizing the chances of influencing the enemy and world opinion and to minimizing the chances that failure would strengthen the hand of the "hawks" at home: First, without fanfare, conditions, or avowal, whether the stand-down was permanent or temporary, stop bombing all of North Vietnam. It is generally thought that Hanoi will not agree to negotiations until they can claim that the bombing has stopped unconditionally. We should see what develops, retaining freedom to resume the bombing if nothing useful was forthcoming.

Alternatively, we could shift the weight-of-effort away from "Zones 6A and 6B"—zones including Hanoi and Haiphong and areas north of those two cities to the Chinese border. This alternative has some attraction in that it provides the North Vietnamese a "face saver" if only problems of "face" are holding up Hanoi peace gestures; it would narrow the bombing down directly to the objectionable infiltration (supporting the logic of a stop-infiltration/full-pause deal) ; and it would reduce the international heat on the U.S. Here, too, bombing of the Northeast could be resumed at any time, or "spot" attacks could be made there from time to time to keep North Vietnam off balance and to require her to pay almost the full cost by maintaining her repair crews in place. The sorties diverted from Zones 6A and 6B could be concentrated on infiltration routes in

Zones 1 and 2 (the southern end of North Vietnam, including the Mu Gia Pass), in Laos and in South Vietnam.[3]

To the same end of improving our credibility, we should seek ways— through words and deeds—to make believable our intention to withdraw our forces once the North Vietnamese aggression against the South stops. In particular, we should avoid any implication that we will stay in South Vietnam with bases or to guarantee any particular outcome to a solely South Vietnamese struggle.

2. Try to split the VC off from Hanoi. The intelligence estimate is that evidence is overwhelming that the North Vietnamese dominate and control the National Front and the Viet Cong. Nevertheless, I think we should continue and enlarge efforts to contact the VC/NLF and to probe ways to split members or sections off the VC/NLF organization.

3. Press contacts with North Vietnam, the Soviet Union and other parties who might contribute toward a settlement.

4. Develop a realistic plan providing a role for the VC in negotiations, postwar life, and government of the nation. An amnesty offer and proposals for national reconciliation would be steps in the right direction and should be parts of the plan. It is important that this plan be one which will appear reasonable, if not at first to Hanoi and the VC, at least to world opinion.

3. The Prognosis

The prognosis is bad that the war can be brought to a satisfactory conclusion within the next two years. The large-unit operations probably will not do it; negotiations probably will not do it. *While we should continue to pursue both of these routes in trying for a solution in the short run, we should recognize that success from them is a mere possibility, not a probability.*

The solution lies in girding, openly, for a longer war and in taking actions immediately which will in 12 to 18 months give clear evidence that the continuing costs and risks to the American people are acceptably limited, that the formula for success has been found, and that the end of the war is merely a matter of time. All of my recommendations will contrib-

---

[3] Any limitation on the bombing of North Vietnam will cause serious psychological problems among the men who are risking their lives to help achieve our political objectives; among their commanders up to and including the JCS (Joint Chiefs of Staff); and among those of our people who cannot understand why we should withhold punishment from the enemy. General Westmoreland, as do the JCS, strongly believes in the military value of the bombing program. Further, Westmoreland reports that the morale of his Air Force personnel may already be showing signs of erosion—an erosion resulting from current operational restrictions.

ute to this strategy, but the one most difficult to implement is perhaps the most important one—enlivening the pacification program. The odds are less than even for this task, if only because we have failed consistently since 1961 to make a dent in the problem. But, because the 1967 trend of pacification will, I believe, be the main talisman of ultimate U.S. success or failure in Vietnam, extraordinary imagination and effort should go into changing the stripes of that problem.

President Thieu and Prime Minister Ky are thinking along similar lines. They told me that they do not expect the Enemy to negotiate or to modify his program in less than two years. Rather, they expect that enemy to continue to expand and to increase his activity. They expressed agreement with us that the key to success is pacification and that so far pacification has failed. They agree that we need clarification of GVN and U.S. roles and that the bulk of the ARVN should be shifted to pacification. Ky will, between January and July 1967, shift all ARVN infantry divisions to that role. And he is giving Thang, a good Revolutionary Development director, added powers. Thieu and Ky see this as part of a two-year (1967–68) schedule, in which offensive operations against enemy main force units are continued, carried on primarily by the U.S. and other Free-World forces. At the end of the two-year period, they believe the enemy may be willing to negotiate or to retreat from his current course of action.

Note: Neither the Secretary of State nor the JCS have yet had an opportunity to express their views on this report. Mr. Katzenbach and I have discussed many of its main conclusions and recommendations—in general, but not in all particulars, it expresses his views as well as my own.

Appendix

Extracts from CIA/DIA[4] Report "An Appraisal of the Bombing of North Vietnam through 12 September 1966"

1. There is no evidence yet of any shortage of POL[5] in North Vietnam and stocks on hand, with recent imports, have been adequate to sustain necessary operations.

2. Air strikes against all modes of transportation in North Vietnam and during the past month, but there is no evidence of serious transport problems in the movement of supplies to or within North Vietnam.

3. There is no evidence yet that the air strikes have significantly weakened popular morale.

[4] Central Intelligence Agency/Defense Intelligence Agency.
[5] Petroleum, oil, and lubricants.

4. Air strikes continue to depress economic growth and have been responsible for the abandonment of some plans for economic development, but essential economic activities continue.

Extracts from a March 16, 1966 CIA Report "An Analysis of the ROLLING THUNDER Air Offensive against North Vietnam"
1. Although the movement of men and supplies in North Vietnam has been hampered and made somewhat more costly (by our bombing), the Communists have been able to increase the flow of supplies and manpower to South Vietnam.

2. Hanoi's determination (despite our bombing) to continue its policy of supporting the insurgency in the South appears as firm as ever.

3. Air attacks almost certainly cannot bring about a meaningful reduction in the current level at which essential supplies and men flow into South Vietnam.

Bomb Damage Assessment in the North by the Institute for Defense Analyses' "Summer Study Group"
What surprised us (in our assessment of the effect of bombing North Vietnam) was the extent of agreement among various intelligence agencies on the effects of past operations and probable effects of continued and expanded Rolling Thunder. The conclusions of our group, to which we all subscribe, are therefore merely sharpened conclusions of numerous Intelligence summaries. They are that Rolling Thunder does not limit the present logistic flow into SVN because NVN is neither the source of supplies nor the choke-point on the supply routes from China and USSR. Although an expansion of Rolling Thunder by closing Haiphong harbor, eliminating electric power plants and totally destroying railroads, will at least indirectly impose further privations on the populace of NVN and make the logistic support of VC costlier to maintain, such expansion will not really change the basic assessment. This follows because NVN has demonstrated excellent ability to improvise transportation, and because the primitive nature of their economy is such that Rolling Thunder can affect directly only a small fraction of the population. There is very little hope that the Ho Chi Minh Government will lose control of population because of Rolling Thunder. The lessons of the Korean War are very relevant in these respects. Moreover, foreign economic aid to NVN is large compared to the damage we inflict, and growing. Probably the government of NVN has assurances that the USSR and/or China will assist the rebuilding of its economy after the war, and hence its concern about the damage being inflicted may be moderated by long-range favorable expectations.

Specifically:

1. As of July 1966 the U.S. bombing of North Vietnam had had no measurable direct affect on Hanoi's ability to mount and support military operations in the South at the current level.

2. Since the initiation of the Rolling Thunder program the damage to facilities and equipment in North Vietnam has been more than offset by the increased flow of military and economic aid, largely from the USSR and Communist China.

3. The aspects of the basic situation that have enabled Hanoi to continue its support of military operations in the South and to neutralize the impact of U.S. bombing by passing the economic costs to other Communist countries are not likely to be altered by reducing the present geographic constraints, mining Haiphong and the principal harbors in North Vietnam, increasing the number of armed reconnaissance sorties and otherwise expanding the U.S. air offensive along the lines now contemplated in military recommendations and planning studies.

4. While conceptually it is reasonable to assume that some limit may be imposed on the scale of military activity that Hanoi can maintain in the South by continuing the Rolling Thunder program at the present, or some higher level of effort, there appears to be no basis for defining that limit in concrete terms, or for concluding that the present scale of VC/NVN activities in the field have approached that limit.

5. The indirect effects of the bombing on the will of the North Vietnamese to continue fighting and on their leaders' appraisal of the prospective gains and costs of maintaining the present policy have not shown themselves in any tangible way. Furthermore, we have not discovered any basis for concluding that the indirect punitive effects of bombing will prove decisive in these respects.

13. Leslie H. Gelb

Vietnam: The System Worked

The disenchantment that McNamara experienced was felt by other
American leaders even though it did not lead them to reverse their
policies. So argues Leslie H. Gelb, a former Defense Department
official who served as project director for the Pentagon Papers, and who is
now a senior fellow of The Brookings Institution in Washington, D.C.
From his invaluable vantage point, Gelb presents an incisive and
subtle analysis that rebuts the "mistake" theory of American intervention.
A long-time opponent of the war himself, Gelb contends that neither
the Kennedy nor the Johnson administration sought military victory in
Vietnam. Not importantly misguided by military and intelligence
reports, both administrations followed policies designed to gain time and
to prevent a Communist victory in South Vietnam. Defeat would
threaten America's international policies, they believed, and would prove
politically disastrous at home. Democrats, especially, feared another
"loss" in Asia and the domestic "nightmare of a McCarthyite garrison
state." These fears led to policies designed to stave off disaster, not to win.
American presidents understood that Vietnam was a quagmire, Gelb
argues, but none saw that "the real stakes—who shall govern Vietnam—
were not negotiable." Continuity, perseverance, and saving
face are important themes in Gelb's analysis. He concludes that "the
system worked" because the presidents did what they wanted to do,
they understood what was happening, and they prevented Communist
domination of South Vietnam.

His position is persuasively argued, but it also raises questions.
As several critics have asked, does Gelb have too limited a conception
of continuity? Does the continuity argument explain President Johnson's
quantum escalation in 1965? If not, what does? Does Gelb assume an
"inevitable" deepening of the American involvement? If President
Kennedy could refuse to send U.S. ground troops, why was his successor
unable to do so? Kennedy, after all, had elected to accept humiliation at
the Bay of Pigs rather than to introduce U.S. troops. What evidence
exists that U.S. leaders did *not* expect counterinsurgency and the bombing
war against North Vietnam to work? (For two responses to Gelb's
essay and the author's reply, see "Letters—1", *Foreign Policy, 4* (Fall
1971), 88–100.)

Other issues remain. Radical analysts have contended that Vietnam
is only the most recent and most costly example of American policies

From "Vietnam: The System Worked" by Leslie H. Gelb, in *Foreign Policy, 3*
(Summer 1971). Copyright © 1971 by National Affairs, Inc.

of anticommunism and counterrevolution abroad. According to the radical analysis, American leaders have believed that the viability of the American political-economic system depends on checking Communist expansion because of its threat to the international capitalist system and its contribution to serious economic and political dislocations. Ultimately, American democracy and prosperity depended on subverting Third World revolutions. In this view, the question of Vietnam is not merely one of tactics and miscalculation of costs but is substantive in nature. Is the domino theory correct? Is economic expansion necessary to preserve capitalism? Was intervention in Indochinese affairs necessary to protect American capitalism? What moral responsibilities accrue to individuals, particularly those who exercise great power?

The story of United States policy toward Vietnam is either far better or far worse than generally supposed. Our Presidents and most of those who influenced their decisions did not stumble step by step into Vietnam, unaware of the quagmire. U.S. involvement did not stem from a failure to foresee consequences.

Vietnam was indeed a quagmire, but most of our leaders knew it. Of course there were optimists and periods where many were genuinely optimistic. But those periods were infrequent and short-lived and were invariably followed by periods of deep pessimism. Very few, to be sure, envisioned what the Vietnam situation would be like by 1968. Most realized, however, that "the light at the end of the tunnel" was very far away—if not finally unreachable. Nevertheless, our Presidents persevered. Given international compulsions to "keep our word" and "save face," domestic prohibitions against "losing," and their personal stakes, our leaders did "what was necessary," did it about the way they wanted, were prepared to pay the costs, and plowed on with a mixture of hope and doom. They "saw" no acceptable alternative.

Three propositions suggest why the United States became involved in Vietnam, why the process was gradual, and what the real expectations of our leaders were:

1. U.S. involvement in Vietnam is not mainly or mostly a story of step by step, inadvertent descent into unforeseen quicksand. It is primarily a story of why U.S. leaders considered that it was vital not to lose Vietnam by force to Communism. Our leaders believed Vietnam to be vital not for itself, but for what they thought its "loss" would mean internationally and domestically. Previous involvement made further involvement more unavoidable, and, to this extent, commitments were inherited. But judgments of Vietnam's "vitalness"—beginning with the Korean War—were sufficient in themselves to set the course for escalation.

2. Our Presidents were never actually seeking a military victory in

Vietnam. They were doing only what they thought was minimally necessary at each stage to keep Indochina, and later South Vietnam, out of Communist hands. This forced our Presidents to be brakemen, to do less than those who were urging military victory and to reject proposals for disengagement. It also meant that our Presidents wanted a negotiated settlement without fully realizing (though realizing more than their critics) that a civil war cannot be ended by political compromise.

3. Our Presidents and most of their lieutenants were not deluded by optimistic reports of progress and did not proceed on the basis of wishful thinking about winning a military victory in South Vietnam. They recognized that the steps they were taking were not adequate to win the war and that unless Hanoi relented, they would have to do more and more. Their strategy was to persevere in the hope that their will to continue—if not the practical effects of their actions—would cause the Communists to relent.

Each of these propositions is explored below.

I. Ends: "We Can't Afford to Lose"

Those who led the United States into Vietnam did so with their eyes open, knowing why, and believing they had the will to succeed. The deepening involvement was not inadvertent, but mainly deductive. It flowed with sureness from the perceived stakes and attendant high objectives. U.S. policy displayed remarkable continuity. There were not dozens of likely "turning points." Each post-war President inherited previous commitments. Each extended these commitments. Each administration from 1947 to 1969 believed that it was necessary to prevent the loss of Vietnam and, after 1954, South Vietnam by force to the Communists. The reasons for this varied from person to person, from bureaucracy to bureaucracy, over time and in emphasis. For the most part, however, they had little to do with Vietnam itself. A few men argued that Vietnam had intrinsic strategic military and economic importance, but this view never prevailed. The reasons rested on broader international, domestic, and bureaucratic considerations.

Our leaders gave the *international* repercussions of "losing" as their dominant explicit reason for Vietnam's importance. During the Truman Administration, Indochina's importance was measured in terms of French-American relations and Washington's desire to rebuild France into the centerpiece of future European security. After the cold war heated up and after the fall of China, a French defeat in Indochina was also seen as a defeat for the policy of containment. In the Eisenhower years,

Indochina became a "testing ground" between the Free World and Communism and the basis for the famous "domino theory" by which the fall of Indochina would lead to the deterioration of American security around the globe. President Kennedy publicly reaffirmed the falling domino concept. His primary concern, however, was for his "reputation for action" after the Bay of Pigs fiasco, the Vienna meeting with Khrushchev, and the Laos crisis, and in meeting the challenge of "wars of national liberation" by counterinsurgency warfare. Under President Johnson, the code word rationales became Munich, credibility, commitments and the U.S. word, a watershed test of wills with Communism, raising the costs of aggression, and the principle that armed aggression shall not be allowed to succeed. There is every reason to assume that our leaders actually believed what they said, given both the cold war context in which they were all reared and the lack of contradictory evidence.

With very few exceptions, then, our leaders since World War II saw Vietnam as a vital factor in alliance politics, U.S.-Soviet-Chinese relations, and deterrence. This was as true in 1950 and 1954 as it was in 1961 and 1965. The record of United States military and economic assistance to fight Communism in Indochina tells this story quite clearly. From 1945 to 1951, U.S. aid to France totaled over $3.5 billion. Without this, the French position in Indochina would have been untenable. By 1951, the U.S. was paying about 40 percent of the costs of the Indochina war and our share was going up. In 1954, it is estimated, U.S. economic and technical assistance amounted to $703 million and military aid totaled almost $2 billion. This added up to almost 80 percent of the total French costs. From 1955 to 1961, U.S. military aid averaged about $200 million per year. This made South Vietnam the second largest recipient of such aid, topped only by Korea. By 1963, South Vietnam ranked first among recipients of military assistance. In economic assistance, it followed only India and Pakistan.

The *domestic* repercussions of "losing" Vietnam probably were equally important in Presidential minds. Letting Vietnam "go Communist" was undoubtedly seen as:

• Opening the floodgates to domestic criticism and attack for being "soft on Communism" or just plain soft.
• Dissipating Presidential influence by having to answer these charges.
• Alienating conservative leadership in the Congress and thereby endangering the President's legislative program.
• Jeopardizing election prospects for the President and his party.
• Undercutting domestic support for a "responsible" U.S. world role.
• Enlarging the prospects for a right-wing reaction—the nightmare of a McCarthyite garrison state.

U.S. domestic politics required our leaders to maintain both a peaceful world and one in which Communist expansion was stopped. In order to have the public support necessary to use force against Communism, our leaders had to employ strong generalized, ideological rhetoric. The price of this rhetoric was consistency. How could our leaders shed American blood in Korea and keep large numbers of American troops in Europe at great expense unless they were also willing to stop Communism in Vietnam?

Bureaucratic judgments and stakes were also involved in defining U.S. interests in Vietnam. Most bureaucrats probably prompted or shared the belief of their leaders about the serious repercussions of losing Vietnam. Once direct bureaucratic presence was established after the French departure, this belief was reinforced and extended. The military had to prove that American arms and advice could succeed where the French could not. The Foreign Service had to prove that it could bring about political stability in Saigon and "build a nation." The CIA had to prove that pacification would work. AID had to prove that millions of dollars in assistance and advice could bring political returns.

The U.S. commitment was rationalized as early as 1950. It was set in 1955 when we replaced the French. Its logic was further fulfilled by President Kennedy. After 1965, when the U.S. took over the war, it was immeasurably hardened.

There was little conditional character to the U.S. commitment—except for avoiding "the big war." Every President talked about the ultimate responsibility resting with the Vietnamese (and the French before them). This "condition" seems to have been meant much more as a warning to our friends than a real limitation. In every crunch, it was swept aside. The only real limit applied to Russia and China. Our leaders were not prepared to run the risks of nuclear war or even the risks of a direct conventional military confrontation with the Soviet Union and China. These were separate decisions. The line between them and everything else done in Vietnam always held firm. With this exception, the commitment was always defined in terms of the objective to deny the Communists control over all Vietnam. This was further defined to preclude coalition governments with the Communists.

The importance of the objective was evaluated in terms of cost, and the perceived costs of disengagement outweighed the cost of further engagement. Some allies might urge disengagement, but then condemn the U.S. for doing so. The domestic groups which were expected to criticize growing involvement always were believed to be outnumbered by those who would have attacked "cutting and running." The question of whether our leaders would have started down the road if they knew this would mean over half a million men in Vietnam, over 40,000 U.S. deaths, and the expenditure of well over $100 billion is historically irrelevant. Only Presidents Kennedy and Johnson had to confront the possibility of these large costs. The point is that each administration was prepared to pay the costs it could foresee for itself. No one seemed to have a better solution. Each could at least pass the baton on to the next.

Presidents could not treat Vietnam as if it were "vital" without creating high stakes internationally, domestically, and within their own bureaucracies. But the rhetoric conveyed different messages:

To the Communists, it was a signal that their actions would be met by counteractions.

To the American people, it set the belief that the President would ensure that the threatened nation did not fall into Communist hands—although without the anticipation of sacrificing American lives.

To the Congress, it marked the President's responsibility to ensure that Vietnam did not go Communist and maximized incentives for legislators to support him or at least remain silent.

To the U.S. professional military, it was a promise that U.S. forces would be used, if necessary and to the degree necessary, to defend Vietnam.

To the professional U.S. diplomat, it meant letting our allies know that the U.S. cared about their fate.

To the President, it laid the groundwork for the present action and showed that he was prepared to take the next step to keep Vietnam non-Communist.

Words were making Vietnam into a showcase—an Asian Berlin. In the process, Vietnam grew into a test case of U.S. credibility—to opponents, to allies, but perhaps most importantly, to ourselves. Public opinion polls seemed to confirm the political dangers. Already established bureaucratic judgments about the importance of Vietnam matured into cherished convictions and organizational interests. The war dragged on.

Each successive President, initially caught by his own belief, was further ensnarled by his own rhetoric, and the basis for the belief went unchallenged. Debates revolved around how to do things better, and whether they could be done, not whether they were worth doing. Prior to 1961, an occasional senator or Southeast Asian specialist would raise a lonely and weak voice in doubt. Some press criticism began thereafter. And later still, wandering American minstrels returned from the field to tell their tales of woe in private. General Ridgway as Chief of Staff of the Army in 1954 questioned the value of Vietnam as against its potential costs and dangers, and succeeded in blunting a proposed U.S. military initiative, although not for the reasons he advanced. Under Secretary of State George Ball raised the issue of international priorities in the summer of 1965 and lost. Clark Clifford as Secretary of Defense openly challenged the winnability of the war, as well as Vietnam's strategic significance, and argued for domestic priorities. But no systematic or serious examination of Vietnam's importance to the United States was ever undertaken within the government. Endless assertions passed for analysis. Presidents neither encouraged nor permitted serious questioning, for to do so would be to foster the idea that their resolve was something less than complete. The objective of a non-Communist Vietnam, and after 1954 a non-Communist South Vietnam, drove U.S. involvement ever more deeply each step of the way.

II. Means: "Take the Minimal Necessary Steps"

None of our Presidents was seeking total victory over the Vietnamese Communists. War critics who wanted victory always knew this. Those who wanted the U.S. to get out never believed it. Each President was essentially doing what he thought was minimally necessary to prevent a Communist victory during his tenure in office. Each, of course, sought to strengthen the anti-Communist Vietnamese forces, but with the aim of a negotiated settlement. Part of the tragedy of Vietnam was that the compromises our Presidents were prepared to offer could never lead to an end of the war. These preferred compromises only served to reinforce the conviction of both Communist and anti-Communist Vietnamese that they had to fight to the finish in their civil war. And so, more minimal steps were always necessary.

Our Presidents were pressured on all sides. The pressures for victory came mainly from the inside and were reflected on the outside. From inside the administrations, three forces almost invariably pushed hard. *First,* the military establishment generally initiated requests for broadening and intensifying U.S. military action. Our professional military placed great weight on the strategic significance of Vietnam; they were given a job to do; their prestige was involved; and of crucial importance (in the 1960's) —the lives of many American servicemen were being lost. The Joint Chiefs of Staff, the MAAG (Military Assistance Advisory Group) Chiefs and later the Commander of U.S. forces in Vietnam were the focal points for these pressures. *Second,* our Ambassadors in Saigon, supported by the State Department, at times pressed for and often supported big steps forward. Their reasons were similar to those of the military. *Thirdly,* an ever-present group of "fixers" was making urgent demands to strengthen and broaden the Saigon government in order to achieve political victory. Every executive agency had its fixers. They were usually able men whose entire preoccupation was to make things better in Vietnam. From outside the administration, there were hawks who insisted on winning and hawks who wanted to "win or get out." Capitol Hill hawks, the conservative press, and, for many years, Catholic organizations were in the forefront.

The pressures for disengagement and for de-escalation derived mostly from the outside with occasional and often unknown allies from within. Small for most of the Vietnam years, these forces grew steadily in strength from 1965 onward. Isolated congressmen and senators led the fight. First they did so on anticolonialist grounds. Later their objections developed moral aspects (interfering in a civil war) and extended to non-winnability, domestic priorities, and the senselessness of the war. Peace organizations and student groups in particular came to dominate headlines and air time. Journalists played a critical role—especially through television reports. From within each administration, opposition could be found: (1) among isolated military men who did not want the U.S. in an Asian land war; (2) among some State Department intelligence and area specialists who knew Vietnam and believed the U.S. objective was unattainable at any reasonable price; and (3) within the civilian agencies of the Defense Department and isolated individuals at State and CIA, particularly after 1966, whose efforts were trained on finding a politically feasible way out.

Our Presidents reacted to the pressures as brakemen, pulling the switch against both the advocates of "decisive escalation" and the advocates of disengagement. The politics of the Presidency largely dictated this role, but the personalities of the Presidents were also important. None were as ideological as many persons around them. All were basically centrist politicians.

Their immediate aim was always to prevent a Communist takeover. The actions they approved were usually only what was minimally necessary to that aim. Each President determined the "minimal necessity" by trial and error and his own judgment. They might have done more and done it more rapidly if they were convinced that: (1) the threat of a Communist takeover were more immediate, (2) U.S. domestic politics would have been more permissive, (3) the government of South Vietnam had the requisite political stability and military potential for effective use and (4) the job really would have gotten done. After 1965, however, the minimal necessity became the maximum they could get given the same domestic and international constraints.

The tactic of the minimally necessary decision makes optimum sense for the politics of the Presidency. Even our strongest Presidents have tended to shy away from decisive action. It has been too uncertain, too risky. They derive their strength from movement (the image of a lot of activity) and building and neutralizing opponents. Too seldom has there been forceful moral leadership; it may even be undemocratic. The small step that maintains the momentum gives the President the chance to gather more political support. It gives the appearance of minimizing possible mistakes. It allows time to gauge reactions. It serves as a pressure-relieving valve against those who want to do more. It can be doled out. Above all, it gives the President something to do next time.

The tactic makes consummate sense when it is believed that nothing will fully work or that the costs of a "winning" move would be too high. This was the case with Vietnam. This decision-making tactic explains why the U.S. involvement in Vietnam was gradual and step by step.

While the immediate aim was to prevent a Communist victory and improve the position of the anti-Communists, the longer term goal was a political settlement. As late as February 1947, Secretary of State Marshall expressed the hope that "a pacific basis of adjustment of the difficulties" between France and the Vietminh could be found. After that, Truman's policy hardened, but there is no evidence to suggest that until 1950 he was urging the French not to settle with the Vietnamese Communists. Eisenhower, it should be remembered, was the President who tacitly agreed (by not intervening in 1954) to the creation of a Communist state in North Vietnam. President Kennedy had all he could do to prevent complete political collapse in South Vietnam. He had, therefore, little basis on which to compromise. President Johnson inherited this political instability, and to add to his woes, he faced in 1965 what seemed to be the prospect of a Communist military victory. Yet, by his standing offer for free and internationally supervised elections, he apparently was prepared to accept Communist participation in the political life of the South.

By traditional diplomatic standards of negotiations between sovereign states, these were not fatuous compromises. One compromise was, in effect, to guarantee that the Communists could remain in secure control of North Vietnam. The U.S. would not seek to overthrow this regime. The other compromise was to allow the Communists in South Vietnam to seek power along the lines of Communist parties in France and Italy, i.e. to give them a "permanent minority position."

But the real struggle in Vietnam was not between sovereign states. It was among Vietnamese. It was a civil war and a war for national independence.

Herein lies the paradox and the tragedy of Vietnam. Most of our leaders and their critics did see that Vietnam was a quagmire, but did not see that the real stakes—who shall govern Vietnam—were not negotiable. Free elections, local sharing of power, international supervision, cease-fires—none of these could serve as a basis for settlement. What were legitimate compromises from Washington's point of view were matters of life and death to the Vietnamese. For American leaders, the stakes were "keeping their word" and saving their political necks. For the Vietnamese, the stakes were their lives and their lifelong political aspirations. Free elections meant bodily exposure to the Communist guerrillas and likely defeat to the anti-Communists. The risk was too great. There was no trust, no confidence.

The Vietnam war could no more be settled by traditional diplomatic compromises than any other civil war. President Lincoln could not settle with the South. The Spanish Republicans and General Franco's Loyalists could not have conceivably mended their fences by elections. None of the post-World War II insurgencies—Greece, Malaya, and the Philippines —ended with a negotiated peace. In each of these cases, the civil differences were put to rest—if at all—only by the logic of war.

It is commonly acknowledged that Vietnam would have fallen to the Communists in 1945–1946, in 1954, and in 1965 had it not been for the intervention of first the French and then the Americans. The Vietnamese Communists, who were also by history the Vietnamese nationalists, would not accept only part of a prize for which they had paid so heavily. The anti-Communist Vietnamese, protected by the French and the Americans, would not put themselves at the Communists' mercy.

It may be that our Presidents understood this better than their critics. The critics, especially on the political left, fought for "better compromises," not realizing that even the best could not be good enough, and fought for broad nationalist governments, not realizing there was no middle force in Vietnam. Our Presidents, it seems, recognized that there was no middle ground and that "better compromises" would frighten our Saigon allies without bringing about a compromise peace. And they believed that a neutralization formula would compromise South Vietnam away to the Communists. So the longer-term aim of peace repeatedly gave way to the immediate needs of the war and the next necessary step.

III. Expectations: "We Must Persevere"

Each new step was taken not because of wishful thinking or optimism about its leading to a victory in South Vietnam. Few of our leaders thought that they could win the war in a conventional sense or that the Communists would be decimated to a point that they would simply fade away. Even as new and further steps were taken, coupled with expressions of optimism, many of our leaders realized that more—and still more—would have to be done. Few of these men felt confident about how it would all end or when. After 1965, however, they allowed the impression of "winnability" to grow in order to justify their already heavy investment and domestic support for the war.

The strategy always was to persevere. Perseverance, it seemed, was the only way to avoid or postpone having to pay the domestic political costs of failure. Finally, perseverance, it was hoped, would convince the Communists that our will to continue was firm. Perhaps, then, with domestic support for perseverance, with bombing North Vietnam, and with inflicting heavy casualties in the South, the Communists would relent. Perhaps, then, a compromise could be negotiated to save the Communists' face without giving them South Vietnam.

Optimism was a part of the "gamesmanship" of Vietnam. It had a purpose. Personal-organizational optimism was the product of a number of motivations and calculations:

• Career services tacitly and sometimes explicitly pressured their professionals to impart good news.
• Good news was seen as a job well done; bad news as personal failure.
• The reporting system was set up so that assessments were made by the implementors.
• Optimism bred optimism so that it was difficult to be pessimistic this time if you were optimistic the last time.
• People told their superiors what they thought they wanted to hear.
• The American ethic is to get the job done.

Policy optimism also sprang from several rational needs:

• To maintain domestic support for the war.
• To keep up the morale of our Vietnamese allies and build some confidence and trust between us and them.
• To stimulate military and bureaucratic morale to work hard.

There were, however, genuine optimists and grounds for genuine optimism. Some periods looked promising: the year preceding the French downfall at Dienbienphu; the years of the second Eisenhower Presidency when most attention was riveted on Laos and before the insurgency was stepped up in South Vietnam; 1962 and early 1963 before the strategic hamlet pacification program collapsed; and the last six months of 1967 before the 1968 Tet offensive.

Many additional periods by comparison with previous years yielded a sense of real improvement. By most conventional standards—the size and firepower of friendly Vietnamese forces, the number of hamlets pacified, the number of "free elections" being held, the number of Communists killed, and so forth—reasonable men could and did think in cautiously optimistic terms.

But comparison with years past is an illusory measure when it is not coupled with judgments about how far there still is to go and how likely it is that the goal can ever be reached. It was all too easy to confuse short-term breathing spells with long-term trends and to confuse "things getting better" with "winning." Many of those who had genuine hope suffered from either a lack of knowledge about Vietnam or a lack of sensitivity toward politics or both.

The basis for pessimism and the warning signals were always present. Public portrayals of success glowed more brightly than the full range of classified reporting. Readily available informal and personal accounts were less optimistic still. The political instability of our Vietnamese allies —from Bao Dai through Diem to President Thieu have always been apparent. The weaknesses of the armed forces of our Vietnamese allies were common knowledge. Few years went by when the fighting did not gain in intensity. Our leaders did not have to know much about Vietnam to see all this.

Most of our leaders saw the Vietnam quagmire for what it was. Optimism was, by and large, put in perspective. This means that many knew that each step would be followed by another. Most seemed to have understood that more assistance would be required either to improve the relative position of our Vietnamese allies or simply to prevent a deterioration of their position. Almost each year and often several times a year, key decisions had to be made to prevent deterioration or collapse. These decisions were made with hard bargaining, but rapidly enough for us now to perceive a preconceived consensus to go on. Sometimes several new steps were decided at once, but announced and implemented piecemeal. The whole pattern conveyed the feeling of more to come.

With a tragic sense of "no exit," our leaders stayed their course. They seemed to hope more than expect that something would "give." The hope was to convince the Vietnamese Communists through perseverance that the U.S. would stay in South Vietnam until they abandoned their struggle. The hope, in a sense, was the product of disbelief. How could a tiny, backward Asian country *not* have a breaking point when opposed by the might of the United States? How could they not relent and negotiate with the U.S.?

And yet, few could answer two questions with any confidence: Why should the Communists abandon tomorrow the goals they had been paying so dear a price to obtain yesterday? What was there really to negotiate? No one seemed to be able to develop a persuasive scenario on how the war could end by peaceful means.

Our Presidents, given their politics and thinking, had nothing to do but persevere. But the Communists' strategy was also to persevere, to make the U.S. go home. It was and is a civil war for national independence. It was and is a Greek tragedy.

IV. After Twenty-Five Years

A quick review of history supports these interpretations. To the Roosevelt Administration during World War II, Indochina was not perceived as a "vital" area. The United States defeated Japan without Southeast Asia, and Indochina was not occupied by the allies until *after* Japan's defeat. FDR spoke informally to friends and newsmen of placing Indochina under United Nations trusteeship after the war, but—aware of French, British and U.S. bureaucratic hostility to this—made no detailed plans and asked for no staff work prior to his death. For all practical purposes, Truman inherited *no* Southeast Asia policy.

In 1946 and 1947, the U.S. acquiesced in the re-establishment of French sovereignty. Our policy was a passive one of hoping for a negotiated settlement of the "difficulties" between Paris and the Vietminh independence movement of Ho Chi Minh. To the south, in Indonesia, we had started to pressure the Dutch to grant independence and withdraw, and a residue of anticolonialism remained in our first inchoate approaches to an Indochina policy as well.

But events in Europe and China changed the context from mid-1947 on. Two important priorities were to rearm and strengthen France as the cornerstone of European defense and recovery in the face of Russian pressure, and to prevent a further expansion of victorious Chinese Communism. The Truman Doctrine depicted a world full of dominoes. In May 1950, before Korea, Secretary of State Acheson announced that the U.S. would provide military and economic assistance to the French and their Indochinese allies for the direct purpose of combating Communist expansion. After years of hesitating, Truman finally decided that anti-Communism was more important than anticolonialism in Indochina.

Acheson admits that U.S. policy was a "muddled hodgepodge":

The criticism, however, fails to recognize the limits on the extent to which one may successfully coerce an ally. . . . Furthermore, the result of withholding help to France would, at most, have removed the colonial power. It could not have made the resulting situation a beneficial one either for Indochina or for Southeast Asia, or in the more important effort of furthering the stability and defense of Europe. So while we may have tried to muddle through and were certainly not successful, I could not think then or later of a better course. One can suggest, perhaps, doing nothing. That might have had merit, but as an attitude for the leader of a great alliance toward an important ally, indeed one essential to a critical endeavor, it had its demerits, too.

Several months after the Korean War began, Acheson recalled the warning of an "able colleague": "Not only was there real danger that our efforts would fail in their immediate purpose and waste valuable resources in the process, but we were moving into a position in Indochina in which 'our responsibilities tend to supplant rather than complement those of the French'." Acheson then remembers: "I decided however, that having put our hand to the plow, we would not look back." He decided this despite the fact that he "recognized as no longer valid an earlier French intention to so weaken the enemy before reducing French forces in Indochina that indigenous forces could handle the situation."

V. The Eisenhower Administration

President Eisenhower inherited the problem. Although, with Vietminh successes, the situation took on graver overtones, he, too, pursued a policy of "minimum action" to prevent the total "loss" of Vietnam to Communism. Sherman Adams, Eisenhower's assistant, explains how the problem was seen in the mid-1950's:

If the Communists had pushed on with an aggressive offensive after the fall of Dienbienphu, instead of stopping and agreeing to stay out of Southern Vietnam, Laos and Cambodia, there was a strong possibility that the United States would have moved against them. A complete Communist conquest of Indochina would have had far graver consequence for the West than a Red victory in Korea.

Apparently the President felt he could live with Communist control in the restricted area of North Vietnam, away from the rest of Southeast Asia.

Eisenhower did not take the minimal necessary step to save *all* of Indochina, but he did take the necessary steps to prevent the loss of most of Indochina. He paid almost all the French war cost, increased the U.S. military advisory mission, supplied forty B-26's to the French, and continued the threat of U.S. intervention, first by "united action" and then by forming SEATO. In taking these actions, Eisenhower was deciding against Vice-President Nixon and Admiral Radford, Chairman of the Joint Chiefs of Staff, who favored U.S. intervention in force, and against General Ridgway, Chief of the Army Staff, who opposed any action that could lead to an Asian land war. He was treading the well-worn middle path of doing just enough to balance off contradictory domestic, bureaucratic, and international pressures. The Vietnamese Communists agreed to the compromise, believing that winning the full prize was only a matter of time.

In public statements and later in his memoirs, President Eisenhower gave glimpses of his reasoning. At the time of Dienbienphu, he noted, ". . . we ought to look at this thing with some optimism and some determination . . . long faces and defeatism don't win battles." Later he wrote, "I am convinced that the French could not win the war because the internal political situation in Vietnam, weak and confused, badly weakened their military position." But he persevered nevertheless, believing that "the decision to give this aid was almost compulsory. The United States had no real alternative unless we were to abandon Southeast Asia."

The Geneva Conference of 1954 was followed by eighteen bleak and pessimistic months as official Washington wondered whether the pieces could be put back together. Despite or perhaps because of the pessimism, U.S. aid was increased. Then, in the fall of 1956, Dulles could say: "We have a clean base there now, without a taint of colonialism. Dienbienphu was a blessing in disguise." The years of "cautious optimism" had begun.

President Eisenhower kept the U.S. out of war because he allowed a territorial compromise with the Communists. More critically, he decided to replace the French and maintain a direct U.S. presence in Indochina. With strong rhetoric, military training programs, support for Ngo Dinh Diem in his refusal to hold the elections prescribed by the Geneva accords, and continuing military and economic assistance, he made the new state or "zone" of South Vietnam an American responsibility. Several years of military quiet in South Vietnam did not hide the smoldering political turmoil in that country nor did it obscure the newspaper headlines which regularly proclaimed that the war in Indochina had shifted to Laos.

VI. The Kennedy Administration

The Administration of John F. Kennedy began in an aura of domestic sacrifice and international confrontation. The inauguration speech set the tone of U.S. responsibilities in "hazardous and dangerous" times.

Vietnam had a special and immediate importance which derived from the general international situation. Kennedy's predictions about dangerous times came true quickly—and stayed true—and he wanted to show strength to the Communists. But it was also the precarious situation in Laos and the "neutralist" compromise which Kennedy was preparing for Laos that were driving the President deeper into Vietnam. In Sorensen's words, Kennedy was "skeptical of the extent of our involvement [in Vietnam] but unwilling to abandon his predecessor's pledge or permit a Communist conquest. . . ."

Kennedy had to face three basic general decisions. First, was top priority to go to political reform or fighting the war? On this issue the fixers, who wanted to give priority to political reform, were arrayed against the military. Second, should the line of involvement be drawn at combat units? On this issue the fixers were more quiet than in opposition. The military and the Country Team pushed hard—even urging the President to threaten Hanoi with U.S. bombing. Some counterweight came from State and the White House staff. Third, should the President make a clear, irrevocable and open-ended commitment to prevent a Communist victory? Would this strengthen or weaken the U.S. hand in Saigon? Would it frighten away the Communists? What would be the domestic political consequences?

Kennedy's tactics and decisions—like Eisenhower's—followed the pattern of doing what was minimally necessary. On the political versus military priority issue, Kennedy did not make increasing military assistance definitively contingent on political reform, but he pointed to the absence of reform as the main reason for limiting the U.S. military role. On the combat unit issue, according to biographer Sorensen, "Kennedy never made a final negative decision on troops. In typical Kennedy fashion, he made it difficult for any of the pro-intervention advocates to charge him privately with weakness." On the third issue, he avoided an open-ended commitment, but escalated his rhetoric about the importance of Vietnam. While he did authorize an increase of U.S. military personnel from 685 to 16,000, he did so slowly, and not in two or three big decisions. He continually doled out the increases. He gave encouragement to bureaucratic planning and studying as a safety valve—a valve he thought he could control. He kept a very tight rein on information to the public about the war. In Salinger's words, he "was not anxious to admit the existence of a real war. . . ." By minimizing U.S. involvement, Kennedy was trying to avoid public pressures either to do more or to do less.

The President would make it "their" war until he had no choice but to look at it in a different light. He would not look at it in another light until Diem, who looked like a losing horse, was replaced. He would not gamble on long odds. But it is not clear what he expected to get as a replacement for Diem.

With the exception of much of 1962, which even the North Vietnamese have called "Diem's year," the principal Kennedy decisions were made in an atmosphere of deterioration, not progress, in Vietnam. This feeling of deterioration explains why Kennedy dispatched so many high-level missions to Vietnam. As Kennedy's biographers have written, the President was not really being told he was winning, but how much more he would have to do.

Writing in 1965, Theodore Sorensen summed up the White House view of events following the Diem coup in November 1963:

The President, while eager to make clear that our aim was to get out of Vietnam, had always been doubtful about the optimistic reports constantly filed by the military on the progress of the war. . . . The struggle could well be, he thought, this nation's severest test of endurance and patience. . . . He was simply going to weather it out, a nasty, untidy mess to which there was no other acceptable solution. Talk of abandoning so unstable an ally and so costly a commitment 'only makes it easy for the Communists,' said the President. 'I think we should stay.'

VII. The Johnson Administration

Lyndon Johnson assumed office with a reputation as a pragmatic politician and not a cold war ideologue. His history on Southeast Asia indicated caution and comparative restraint. And yet it was this same man who as President presided over and led the U.S. into massive involvement.

Three facts conspired to make it easier for Johnson to take the plunge on the assumed importance of Vietnam than his predecessors. First, the world was a safer place to live in and Vietnam was the only continuing crisis. Europe was secure. The Sino-Soviet split had deepened. Mutual nuclear deterrence existed between the two superpowers. Second, the situation in Vietnam was more desperate than it ever had been. If the U.S. had not intervened in 1965, South Vietnam would have been conquered by the Communists. Third, after years of effort, the U.S. conventional military forces were big enough and ready enough to intervene. Unlike his predecessors, Johnson had the military capability to back up his words.

In sum, Vietnam became relatively more important, it was in greater danger, and the U.S. was in a position to do something about it.

At Johns Hopkins in April 1965, the President told the American people what he would do: "We will do everything necessary to reach that objective [of no external interference in South Vietnam], and we will do only what is absolutely necessary." But in order to prevent defeat and in order to keep the faith with his most loyal supporters, the minimum necessary became the functional equivalent of gradual escalation. The Air Force and the Commander in Chief, Pacific (CINCPAC) pressed hard for full systems bombing—the authority to destroy 94 key North Vietnamese targets in 16 days. Johnson, backed and pressured in the other direction by Secretary McNamara, doled out approval for new targets over three years in a painstaking and piecemeal fashion. Johnson accommodated dovish pressure and the advice of the many pragmatists who surrounded him by making peace overtures. But these overtures were either accompanied with or followed by escalation. Johnson moved toward those who wanted three-quarters of a million U.S. fighting men in Vietnam, but he never got there. Guided by judgments of domestic repercussion and influenced again by McNamara, the President made at least eight separate decisions on U.S. force levels in Vietnam over a four-year period. For the "fixers" who felt that U.S. conduct of the war missed its political essence and for the doves who wanted to see something besides destruction, Johnson placed new emphasis on "the other war"— pacification, nation-building, and political development—in February 1966. Johnson referred to this whole complex of actions and the air war in particular as his attempt to "seduce not rape" the North Vietnamese.

The objective of the Johnson Administration was to maintain an independent non-Communist South Vietnam. In the later years, this was rephrased: "allowing the South Vietnamese to determine their own future without external interference." As the President crossed the old barriers in pursuit of this objective, he established new ones. While he ordered the bombing of North Vietnam, he would not approve the bombing of targets which ran the risk of confrontation with China and Russia. While he permitted the U.S. force level in Vietnam to go over one-half million men, he would not agree to call up the Reserves. While he was willing to spend $25 billion in one year on the war, he would not put the U.S. economy on a war-time mobilization footing. But the most important Johnson barrier was raised against invading Cambodia, Laos, and North Vietnam. This limitation was also a cornerstone in the President's hopes for a compromise settlement. He would agree to the permanent existence of North Vietnam—even help that country economically—if North Vietnam would extend that same right to South Vietnam.

In order to sustain public and bureaucratic support for his policy, Johnson's method was to browbeat and isolate his opponents. To the American people, he painted the alternatives to what he was doing as irresponsible or reckless. In either case, the result would be a greater risk of future general war. The bureaucracy used this same technique of creating the bug-out or bomb-out extremes in order to maintain as many of its own members in "the middle road." The price of consensus—within the bureaucracy and in the public at large—was invariably a middle road of contradictions and no priorities for action.

President Johnson was the master of consensus. On Vietnam this required melding the proponents of negotiations with the proponents of military victory. The technique for maintaining this Vietnam consensus was gradual escalation punctuated by dramatic peace overtures. As the war was escalated without an end in sight, the numbers of people Johnson could hold together diminished. The pressures for disengagement or for "decisive military action" became enormous, but with the "hawks" always outnumbering and more strategically placed than the "doves."

Johnson knew he had inherited a deteriorating situation in Vietnam. Vietcong military successes and constant change in the Saigon government from 1964 to 1966 were not secrets to anyone. Throughout the critical year of 1965, he struck the themes of endurance and more-to-come. In his May 4, 1965 requests for Vietnam Supplemental Appropriations he warned: "I see no choice but to continue the course we are on, filled as it is with peril and uncertainty." In his July 28, 1965 press conference he announced a new 125,000 troop ceiling and went on to say: "Additional forces will be needed later, and they will be sent as requested."

Talk about "turning corners" and winning a military victory reached a crescendo in 1967. At the same time a new counterpoint emerged— "stalemate." The message of the stalemate proponents was that the U.S. was strong enough to prevent defeat, but that the situation defied victory. Hanoi would continue to match the U.S. force build-up and would not "cry uncle" over the bombing. The Saigon government and army had basic political and structural problems which they were unlikely to be able to overcome. Stalemate, it was urged, should be used as a basis for getting a compromise settlement with Hanoi.

These arguments were not lost on the President. At Guam in March 1967, while others around him were waxing eloquent about progress, the President was guardedly optimistic, speaking of "a favorable turning point, militarily and politically." But after one of the meetings he was reported to have said: "We have a difficult, a serious, long-drawn-out, agonizing problem that we do not have an answer for." Nor did the President overlook the effects of the 1968 Tet offensive, coming as it did after many months of virtually unqualified optimism by him and by others. He stopped the bombing partially, increased troop strength slightly, made a peace overture, and announced his retirement.

In November 1963, Johnson is quoted as saying: "I am not going to be the President who saw Southeast Asia go the way China went." In the spring of 1965, Lady Bird Johnson quoted him as saying: "I can't get out. I can't finish it with what I have got. So what the Hell can I do?" President Johnson, like his predecessors, persevered and handed the war on to his successor.

VIII. Where Do We Go From Here?

If Vietnam were a story of how the system failed, that is, if our leaders did not do what they wanted to do or if they did not realize what they were doing or what was happening, it would be easy to package a large and assorted box of policy-making panaceas. For example: Fix the method of reporting from the field. Fix the way progress is measured in a guerrilla war. Make sure the President sees all the real alternatives. But these are all third-order issues, because the U.S. political-bureaucratic system did not fail; it worked.

Our leaders felt they had to prevent the loss of Vietnam to Communism, and they have succeeded so far in doing just that. Most of those who made Vietnam policy still believe that they did the right thing and lament only the domestic repercussions of their actions. It is because the price of attaining this goal has been so dear in lives, trust, dollars, and priorities, and the benefits so intangible, remote, and often implausible, that these leaders and we ourselves are forced to seek new answers and new policies.

Paradoxically, the way to get these new answers is not by asking why did the system fail, but why did it work so tragically well. There is, then, only one first-order issue—how and why does our political-bureaucratic system decide what is vital and what is not? By whom, in what manner, and for what reasons was it decided that all Vietnam must not fall into Communist hands?

Almost all of our leaders since 1949 shared this conviction. Only a few voices in the wilderness were raised in opposition. Even as late as mid-1967, most critics were arguing that the U.S. could not afford to lose or be "driven from the field," that the real problem was our bombing of North Vietnam, and that this had to be stopped in order to bring about a negotiated settlement. Fewer still were urging that such a settlement should involve a coalition government with the Communists. Hardly anyone was saying that the outcome in Vietnam did not matter.

There is little evidence of much critical thinking about the relation of Vietnam to U.S. security. Scholars, journalists, politicians, and bureaucrats all seem to have assumed either that Vietnam was "vital" to U.S. national security or that the American people would not stand for the loss of "another" country to Communism.

Anti-Communism has been and still is a potent force in American politics, and most people who were dealing with the Vietnam problem simply believed that the Congress and the public would "punish" those who were "soft on Communism." Our leaders not only anticipated this kind of public reaction, but believed that there were valid reasons for not permitting the Communists to take all of Vietnam by force. In other words, they believed in what they were doing on the national security "merits." The domino theory, which was at the heart of the matter, rested on the widely shared attitude that security was indivisible, that weakness in one place would only invite aggression in others.

What can be done?

The President can do more than Presidents have in the past to call his national security bureaucracy to task. He can show the bureaucracy that he expects it to be more rigorous in determining what is vital or important or unimportant. Specifically, he can reject reasoning which simply asserts that security is indivisible, and he can foster the belief that while the world is an interconnected whole, actions can be taken in certain parts of the world to compensate for actions which are not taken elsewhere. For example, if the real concern about Vietnam were the effect of its loss on Japan, the Middle East and Berlin, could we not take actions in each of these places to mitigate the "Vietnam fallout"?

None of these efforts with the bureaucracy can succeed, however, unless there is a change in general political attitudes as well. If anti-Communism persists as an overriding domestic political issue it will also be the main bureaucratic issue. Altering public attitudes will take time, education, and political courage—and it will create a real dilemma for the President. If the President goes "too far" in re-educating public and congressional opinions about Communism, he may find that he will have little support for threatening or using military force when he believes that our security really is at stake. In the end, it will still be the President who is held responsible for U.S. security. Yet, if our Vietnam experience has taught us anything, it is that the President must begin the process of re-education despite the risks.

14. J. William Fulbright

The Two Americas

The frustrations and futility of the war in Vietnam prompted many Americans to question their nation's foreign policy. How had the United States become the world's policeman? Why was it, beyond the often glib and fatuous explanations offered by politicians, that their nation maintained 429 major and 2972 minor bases totaling several thousand square miles, that American soldiers were stationed on every continent, and that annual defense expenditures reached almost $100 billion? A few, troubled by the stunning technological disparities between the United States and North Vietnam, raised moral objections to the continuance of the war.

One of the leading war critics in the 1960s was Senator J. William Fulbright of Arkansas. A former Rhodes scholar and president of the University of Arkansas, Fulbright is that rare individual with solid roots in both the worlds of learning and politics. Elected to the Senate in 1944, he has been chairman of the important Committee on Foreign Affairs since 1959. It is fitting that Fulbright's essay concludes the section on the war in Vietnam since he discusses the larger purposes and motives behind American foreign policy, inquires into the source of our crusading missionary spirit, and discusses the responsibilities incumbent on great powers.

"The Two Americas" is the conclusion to *The Arrogance of Power* (1966). Puzzling over the reasons for the great wars of history, Fulbright offers his definition of the book's title: ". . . I am inclined to the view that the causes attributed to them [the great wars]—territory, markets, resources, the defense or perpetuation of great principles— were not the root causes at all but rather explanations or excuses for certain unfathomable drives of human nature. For lack of a clear and precise understanding of exactly what these motives are, I refer to them as the "arrogance of power"—as a psychological need that nations seem to have in order to prove that they are bigger, better, or stronger than other nations. Implicit in this drive is the assumption, even on the part of normally peaceful nations, that force is the ultimate proof of superiority—that when a nation shows that it has the stronger army, it is also proving that it has better people, better institutions, better principles, and, in general, a better civilization."

There are two Americas. One is the America of Lincoln and Adlai Stevenson; the other is the America of Teddy Roosevelt and the modern superpatriots. One is generous and humane, the other narrowly egotistical; one is self-critical, the other self-righteous; one is sensible, the other romantic; one is good-humored, the other solemn; one is inquiring, the other pontificating; one is moderate, the other filled with passionate intensity; one is judicious and the other arrogant in the use of great power.

We have tended in the years of our great power to puzzle the world by presenting to it now the one face of America, now the other, and sometimes both at once. Many people all over the world have come to regard America as being capable of magnanimity and farsightedness but no less capable of pettiness and spite. The result is an inability to anticipate American actions which in turn makes for apprehension and a lack of confidence in American aims.

The inconstancy of American foreign policy is not an accident but an expression of two distinct sides of the American character. Both are characterized by a kind of moralism, but one is the morality of decent instincts tempered by the knowledge of human imperfection and the other is the morality of absolute self-assurance fired by the crusading spirit. The one is exemplified by Lincoln, who found it strange, in the words of his second Inaugural Address, "that any man should dare to ask for a just God's assistance in wringing their bread from the sweat of other men's faces," but then added: "let us judge not, that we be not judged." The other is exemplified by Theodore Roosevelt, who in his December 6, 1904, Annual Message to Congress, without question or doubt as to his own and his country's capacity to judge right and wrong, proclaimed the duty of the United States to exercise an "internal police power" in the hemisphere on the ground that "Chronic wrongdoing, or an impotence which results in a general loosening of the ties of civilized society, may in America . . . ultimately require intervention by some civilized nation. . . ." Roosevelt of course never questioned that the "wrongdoing" would be done by our Latin neighbors and we of course were the "civilized nation" with the duty to set things right.

After twenty-five years of world power the United States must decide which of the two sides of its national character is to predominate—the humanism of Lincoln or the arrogance of those who would make America the world's policeman. One or the other will help shape the spirit of the age—unless of course we refuse to choose, in which case America may come to play a less important role in the world, leaving the great decisions to others.

The current tendency is toward a more strident and aggressive American foreign policy, which is to say, toward a policy closer to the spirit of Theodore Roosevelt than of Lincoln. We are still trying to build bridges to the communist countries and we are still, in a small way, helping the poorer nations to make a better life for their people; but we are also involved in a growing war against Asian communism, a war which began and might have ended as a civil war if American intervention had not turned it into a contest of ideologies, a war whose fallout is disrupting our internal life and complicating our relations with most of the world.

Our national vocabulary has changed with our policies. A few years ago we were talking of détente and building bridges, of five-year plans in India and Pakistan, or agricultural cooperatives in the Dominican Republic, and land and tax reform all over Latin America. Today these subjects are still discussed in a half-hearted and desultory way but the focus of power and interest has shifted to the politics of war. Diplomacy has become largely image-making, and instead of emphasizing plans for social change, the policy-planners and political scientists are conjuring up "scenarios" of escalation and nuclear confrontation and "models" of insurgency and counter-insurgency.

The change in words and values is no less important than the change in policy, because words *are* deeds and style *is* substance insofar as they influence men's minds and behavior. What seems to be happening, as Archibald MacLeish has put it, is that "the feel of America in the world's mind" has begun to change and faith in "the idea of America" has been shaken for the world and, what is more important, for our own people. MacLeish is suggesting—and I think he is right—that much of the idealism and inspiration is disappearing from American policy, but he also points out that they are not yet gone and by no means are they irretrievable:

> . . . *if you look closely and listen well, there is a human warmth, a human meaning which nothing has killed in almost twenty years and which nothing is likely to kill. . . . What has always held this country together is an idea—a dream if you will—a large and abstract thought of the sort the realistic and the sophisticated may reject but mankind can hold to.*

The foremost need of American foreign policy is a renewal of dedication to an "idea that mankind can hold to"—not a missionary idea full of pretensions about being the world's policemen but a Lincolnian idea expressing that powerful strand of decency and humanity which is the true source of America's greatness.

Humanism and Puritanism

I am not prepared to argue that mankind is suffering from an excess of virtue but I think the world has endured about all it can of the crusades of high-minded men bent on the regeneration of the human race. Since the beginning of history men have been set upon by zealots and crusaders, who, far from wishing them harm, have wanted sincerely and fervently to raise them from benightedness to blessedness. The difficulty about all this doing of noble deeds has not been in its motives but in the perverseness of human nature, in the regrettable fact that most men are loutish and ungrateful when it comes to improving their souls and more often than not have to be forced into their own salvation. The result has been a great deal of bloodshed and violence committed not in malice but for the purest of motives. The victims may not always have appreciated the fact that their tormentors had noble motives but the fact remains that it was not wickedness that did them in but, in Thackeray's phrase, "the mischief which the very virtuous do."

Who are the self-appointed emissaries of God who have wrought so much violence in the world? They are men with doctrines, men of faith and idealism, men who confuse power with virtue, men who believe in some cause without doubt and practice their beliefs without scruple, men who cease to be human beings with normal preferences for work and fun and family and become instead living, breathing embodiments of some faith or ideology. From the religious wars to the two world wars they have been responsible for much or most of the violence in the world. From Robespierre to Stalin and Mao Tse-tung they have been the extreme practitioners of the arrogance of power—extreme, indeed, in a way that has never been known and, hopefully, never will be known in America.

There are elements of this kind of fanaticism in Western societies but the essential strength of democracy and capitalism as they are practiced in the West is that they are relatively free of doctrine and dogma and largely free of illusions about man and his nature. Of all the intellectual achievements of Western civilization, the one, I think, that is most truly civilized is that by and large we have learned to deal with man as he is or, at most, as he seems capable of becoming, but not as we suppose in the abstract he ought to be. Our economy is geared to human acquisitiveness and our politics to human ambition. Accepting these qualities as part of human character, we have been able in substantial measure both to satisfy them and to civilize them. We have been able to civilize them because we have understood that a man's own satisfaction is more nearly a condition of than an obstacle to his decent behavior toward others. This realism about man may prove in the long run to be our greatest asset over communism, which can deny and denounce but, with all the "Red Guards" of China, cannot remake human nature.

Acceptance of his own nature would seem to be the most natural thing in the world for a man, but experience shows that it is not. Only at an advanced state of civilization do men become tolerant of human shortcomings. Only at an advanced level of civilization, it seems, do men acquire the wisdom and humility to acknowledge that they are not really cut out to play God. At all previous levels of culture men seem to be more interested in the enforced improvement of others than in voluntary fulfillment for themselves, more interested in forcing their fellow creatures to be virtuous than in helping them to be happy. Only under the conditions of material affluence and political democracy that prevail in much of the modern West have whole societies been able and willing to renounce the harsh asceticism of their own past, which still prevails in much of the East, and to embrace the philosophy that life after all is short and it is no sin to try to enjoy it.

Our hold on this philosophy is tenuous. There is a strand in our history and in our national character which is all too congenial to the spirit of crusading ideology. The Puritans who came to New England in the seventeenth century did not establish their faith as a major religion in America but the Puritan way of thought—harsh, ascetic, intolerant, promising salvation for the few but damnation for the many—became a major intellectual force in American life. It introduced a discordant element into a society bred in the English heritage of tolerance, moderation, and experimentalism.

Throughout our history two strands have coexisted uneasily—a dominant strand of democratic humanism and a lesser but durable strand of intolerant puritanism. There has been a tendency through the years for reason and moderation to prevail as long as things are going tolerably well or as long as our problems seem clear and finite and manageable. But when things have gone badly for any length of time, or when the reasons for adversity have seemed obscure, or simply when some event or leader of opinion has aroused the people to a state of high emotion, our puritan spirit has tended to break through, leading us to look at the world through the distorting prism of a harsh and angry moralism.

Communism has aroused our latent puritanism as has no other movement in our history, causing us to see principles where there are only interests and conspiracy where there is only misfortune. And when this view of things prevails, conflicts become crusades and morality becomes delusion and hypocrisy. Thus, for example, when young hoodlums—the so-called "Red Guards"—terrorize and humiliate Chinese citizens who are suspected of a lack of fervor for the teachings of Mao Tse-tung, we may feel reconfirmed in our judgment that communism is a barbarous philosophy utterly devoid of redeeming features of humanity, but before going into transports of moral outrage over the offenses of the "Red Guards," we might recall that no fewer than two hundred thousand, and possibly half a million, people were murdered in the anti-communist terror that swept Indonesia in 1966 and scarcely a voice of protest was heard in America—from our leaders, from the press, or from the general public. One can only conclude that it is not man's inhumanity to man but communist manifestations of it that arouse the American conscience.

One of the most outrageous effects of the puritan spirit in America is the existence of that tyranny over what it is respectable to say and think of which we spoke in Part 1. Those who try to look at the country with some objectivity are often the objects of scorn and abuse by professional patriots who believe that there is something illegitimate about national self-criticism, or who equate loyalty to our fighting men in Vietnam with loyalty to the policy that put them there.

Puritanism, fortunately, has not been the dominant strand in American thought. It had nothing to do with the intelligent and subtle diplomacy of the period of the American Revolution. It had nothing to do with the wise policy of remaining aloof from the conflicts of Europe, as long as we were permitted to do so, while we settled and developed the North American continent. It had nothing to do with the restraint shown by the United States at moments of supreme crisis in the cold war—at the time of the Korean War, for example, in the first Indochina war in which President Eisenhower wisely refused to intervene in 1954, and in the Cuban missile crisis of 1962. And it has had absolutely nothing to do with the gradual relaxation of tensions associated with the test ban treaty and the subsequent improvement of relations with the Soviet Union. I am reminded of "Mr. Dooley's" words about the observance of Thanksgiving: " 'Twas founded by th' Puritans to give thanks f'r bein' presarved fr'm th' Indyans, an' . . . we keep it to give thanks we are presarved fr'm th' Puritans."

The crusading puritan spirit has had a great deal to do with some of the regrettable and tragic events of American history. It led us into needless and costly adventures and victories that crumbled in our hands.

The Civil War is an example. Had the Abolitionists of the North and the hotheads of the South been less influential, the war might have been avoided and slavery would certainly have been abolished anyway, peacefully and probably within a generation after emancipation actually occurred. Had the peace been made by Lincoln rather than the Radical Republicans, it could have been a peace of reconciliation rather than the wrathful Reconstruction which deepened the division of the country, cruelly set back the cause of the Negro, and left a legacy of bitterness for which we are still paying a heavy price.

The puritan spirit was one of the important factors in the brief, unhappy adventure in imperialism that began with the war of 1898. Starting with stirring slogans about "manifest destiny" and a natural sense of moral outrage about atrocities in Cuba—which was fed by a spirited compe-

tition for circulation between the Hearst and Pulitzer newspapers—
America forced on Spain a war that it was willing to pay almost any price
short of complete humiliation to avoid. The war was undertaken to liberate the Cuban people and ended with Cuba being put under an American
protectorate, which in turn inaugurated a half century of American intervention in Cuba's internal affairs. American interference was motivated,
no doubt, by a sincere desire to bring freedom to the Cuban people but it
ended, nonetheless, with their getting Batista and Castro instead.

The crusading spirit of America in its modern form, and the contrast
between the crusading spirit and the spirit of tolerance and accommodation, are illustrated in two speeches made by Woodrow Wilson, one preceding, the other following, America's entry into World War I. In early
1917, with the United States still neutral, he declined to make a clear
moral distinction between the belligerents, and called on them to compromise their differences and negotiate a "peace without victory." In the
spring of 1918, when the United States had been at war for a year, Wilson perceived only one possible response to the challenge of Germany in
the war: "Force, Force to the utmost, Force without stint or limit, the
righteous and triumphant Force which shall make right the law of the
world, and cast every selfish dominion down in the dust."

Even Franklin Roosevelt, who was the most pragmatic of politicians,
was not immune from the crusading spirit. So overcome was he, as were
all Americans, by the treachery of the Japanese attack on Pearl Harbor
that one of America's historic principles, the freedom of the seas, for
which we had gone to war in 1812 and 1917, was now immediately forgotten, along with the explicit commitment under the London Naval
Treaty of 1930 not to sink merchant vessels without first placing passen-
gers, crews, and ships' papers in a place of safety. Within seven hours of
the Japanese attack the order went out to all American ships and planes
in the Pacific: "Execute unrestricted air and submarine warfare against
Japan." Between 1941 and 1945 American submarines sank 1,750 Japanese merchant ships and took the lives of 105,000 Japanese civilians. So
much for the "freedom of the seas."

In January 1943, while meeting with Churchill at Casablanca, President Roosevelt announced that the Allies would fight on until the "unconditional surrender" of their enemies. Roosevelt later said that the
phrase just "popped into his mind" but I think it was dredged up from
the depths of a puritan soul. Its premise was that our side was all virtue
and our enemies were all evil who in justice could expect nothing after
their fall but the righteous retribution of Virtue triumphant.

"Unconditional surrender" was an unwise doctrine. Aside from its ne-
gativism as a war aim and the fact that it may have prolonged the war, we
did not really mean to carry out its implications. As soon as our enemies

delivered themselves into our hands we began to treat them with kindness and moderation, and within a very few years we were treating them as valued friends and allies.

The West has won two "total victories" in this century and it has barely survived them. America, especially, fought the two world wars in the spirit of a righteous crusade. We acted as if we had come to the end of history, as if we had only to destroy our enemies and then the world would enter a golden age of peace and human happiness. Some of the problems that spawned the great wars were in fact solved by our victories; others were simply forgotten. But to our shock and dismay we found after 1945 that history had not come to an end, that our triumph had produced at least as many problems as it had solved, and that it was by no means clear that the new problems were preferable to the old ones.

I do not raise these events of the American past for purposes of national flagellation but to illustrate that the problem of excessive ideological zeal is our problem as well as the communists'. I think also that when we respond to communist dogmatism with a dogmatism of our own we are not merely responding by the necessity, as we are told, of "fighting fire with fire." I think we are responding in a way that is more natural and congenial to us than we care to admit.

The great challenge in our foreign relations is to make certain that the major strand in our heritage, the strand of humanism, tolerance, and accommodation, remains the dominant one. I do not accept the excuse, so often offered, that communist zealotry and intransigence justify our own. I do not accept the view that because they have engaged in subversion, intervention, and ideological warfare, so must we and to the same degree. There is far more promise in efforts to encourage communist imitation of our own more sensible attitudes than in ourselves imitating the least attractive forms of communist behavior. It is of course reasonable to ask why *we* must take the lead in conciliation; the answer is that we, being the most powerful of nations, can afford as no one else can to be magnanimous. Or, to put it another way, disposing as we do of the greater physical power, we are properly called upon to display the greater moral power as well.

The kind of foreign policy I have been talking about is, in the true sense of the term, a *conservative* policy. It is intended quite literally to conserve the world—a world whose civilizations can be destroyed at any time if either of the great powers should choose or feel driven to do so. It is an approach that accepts the world as it is, with all its existing nations and ideologies, with all its existing qualities and shortcomings. It is an approach that purports to change things in ways that are compatible with the continuity of history and within the limits imposed by a fragile human nature. I think that if the great conservatives of the past, such as Burke and Metternich and Castlereagh, were alive today, they would not be true believers or relentless crusaders against communism. They would wish to come to terms with the world as it is, not because our world would be pleasing to them—almost certainly it would not be—but because they believed in the preservation of indissoluble links between the past and the future, because they profoundly mistrusted abstract ideas, and because they did not think themselves or any other men qualified to play God.

The last, I think, is the central point. I believe that a man's principal business, in foreign policy as in domestic policy and in his daily life, is to keep his own house in order, to make life a little more civilized, a little more satisfying, and a little more serene in the brief time that is allotted him. I think that man is qualified to contemplate metaphysics but not to practice it. The practice of metaphysics is God's work.

An Idea Mankind Can Hold To

Favored as it is, by history, by wealth, and by the vitality and basic decency of its diverse population, it is conceivable, though hardly likely, that America will do something that no other great nation has ever tried to do—to effect a fundamental change in the nature of international relations. It has been my purpose in this book to suggest some ways in which we might proceed with this great work. All that I have proposed in these pages—that we make ourselves the friend of social revolution, that we make our own society an example of human happiness, that we go beyond simple reciprocity in the effort to reconcile hostile worlds—has been based on two major premises: first, that, at this moment in history at which the human race has become capable of destroying itself, it is not merely desirable but essential that the competitive instinct of nations be brought under control; and second, that America, as the most powerful nation, is the only nation equipped to lead the world in an effort to change the nature of its politics.

If we accept this leadership, we will have contributed to the world "an idea mankind can hold to." Perhaps that idea can be defined as the proposition that the nation performs its essential function not in its capacity as a *power,* but in its capacity as a *society,* or, to put it simply, that the primary business of the nation is not itself but its people.

Obviously, to bring about fundamental changes in the world we would have to take certain chances: we would have to take the chance that other countries could not so misinterpret a generous initiative on our part as to bring about a calamity; we would have to take a chance that later if not sooner, nations which have been hostile to us would respond to reason and decency with reason and decency. The risks involved are great but they are far less than the risks of traditional methods of international relations in the nuclear age.

If we are interested in bringing about fundamental changes in the world, we must start by resolving some critical questions of our foreign relations: Are we to be the friend or the enemy of the social revolutions of Asia, Africa, and Latin America? Are we to regard the communist countries as more or less normal states with whom we can have more or less normal relations, or are we to regard them indiscriminately as purveyors of an evil ideology with whom we can never reconcile? And finally, are we to regard ourselves as a friend, counselor, and example for those around the world who seek freedom and who also want our help, or are we to play the role of God's avenging angel, the appointed missionary of freedom in a benighted world?

The answers to these questions depend on which of the two Americas is speaking. There are no inevitable or predetermined answers because our past has prepared us to be either tolerant or puritanical, generous or selfish, sensible or romantic, humanly concerned or morally obsessed, in our relations with the outside world.

For my own part, I prefer the America of Lincoln and Adlai Stevenson. I prefer to have my country the friend rather than the enemy of demands for social justice; I prefer to have the communists treated as human beings, with all the human capacity for good and bad, for wisdom and folly, rather than as embodiments of an evil abstraction; and I prefer to see my country in the role of sympathetic friend to humanity rather than its stern and prideful schoolmaster.

There are many respects in which America, if she can bring herself to act with the magnanimity and the empathy which are appropriate to her size and power, can be an intelligent example to the world. We have the opportunity to set an example of generous understanding in our relations with China, of practical cooperation for peace in our relations with Russia, of reliable and respectful partnership in our relations with Western Europe, of material helpfulness without moral presumption in our relations with developing nations, of abstention from the temptations of hegemony in our relations with Latin America, and of the all-around advantages of minding one's own business in our relations with everybody. Most of all, we have the opportunity to serve as an example of democracy to the world by the way in which we run our own society. America, in the words of John Quincy Adams, should be "the well-wisher to the freedom and independence of all" but "the champion and vindicator only of her own."

If we can bring ourselves so to act, we will have overcome the dangers of the arrogance of power. It would involve, no doubt, the loss of certain glories, but that seems a price worth paying for the probable rewards, which are the happiness of America and the peace of the world.

VI. The Politics of Repudiation

15. Barry Goldwater

A Foreign Policy for America

The repudiation of traditional policies and assumptions of American
liberalism became a powerful motif in the politics of the 1960s, even
though the political center held and regularly elected more moderate
candidates in the presidential elections. However, the most disturbing
movement of revolt captured the presidential nomination for Senator
Barry Goldwater in 1964. A member of a prominent Arizona business
family, Goldwater has long been a spokesman for the reactionary
Right. His book, *The Conscience of a Conservative* (1960), called for
the abolition of the graduated income tax, the sale of The Tennessee
Valley Authority, and the elimination of many federal government
programs in social welfare, education, public power, public housing,
and urban renewal.

Because of Cold War anxieties, many Americans found most dangerous
the senator's views on foreign policy, which he outlined in 1961 for
readers of *The National Review,* the foremost journal of conservative
opinion in the United States. The theme of repudiation is ubiquitous,
ranging from rejection of coexistence with the Soviet Union, disarmament,
and a viable United Nations organization to contempt for world
opinion and staunch opposition to nationalist revolutions in Africa. The
article expresses the Cold War fears that set important limits on the
range of political debate throughout the 1960s; it also provides a
contrast to President Richard Nixon's efforts a decade later to reach
an accommodation with the U.S.S.R. and the People's Republic of China.

The senator's article represents, too, the style of thought that
historian Richard Hofstadter, drawing upon Theodore Adorno's prominent
behavioral study, *The Authoritarian Personality* (1950), called the
"pseudoconservative revolt." The term describes those "who, in the
name of upholding traditional American values and institutions
and defending them against more or less fictitious dangers, consciously or
unconsciously aim at their abolition." Until radicals on the Left
emerged with a bold voice in the mid-1960s, the partisans of the extreme
Right articulated the basic political and cultural challenge to the
reigning orthodoxies of American liberalism.

From *National Review* (March 25, 1961). Reprinted by permission of *National
Review.*

I begin by making some assumptions with regard to our national objectives. I do not mean to suggest that these assumptions are self-evident, in the sense that everyone agrees with them. If they were, Walter Lippmann would be writing the same columns as George Sokolsky, and Herblock would have nothing to draw cartoons about. I do mean, however, that *I* take them for granted, and that everything I shall be saying would appear quite idiotic against any contrary assumptions.

Assumption 1. The ultimate objective of American policy is to help establish a world in which there is the largest possible measure of freedom and justice and peace and material prosperity; and in particular—since this is our special responsibility—that these conditions be enjoyed by the people of the United States. I speak of "the largest possible measure" because any person who supposes that these conditions can be universally and perfectly achieved—ever—reckons without the inherent imperfectability of himself and his fellow human beings, and is therefore a dangerous man to have around.

Assumption 2. These conditions are unobtainable—are not even approachable in the qualified sense I have indicated—without the prior defeat of world Communism. This is true for two reasons: because Communism is both doctrinally, and in practice, antithetical to these conditions; and because Communists have the will and, as long as Soviet power remains intact, the capacity to prevent their realization. Moreover, as Communist power increases, the enjoyment of these conditions throughout the world diminishes *pro rata* and the possibility of their restoration becomes increasingly remote.

Assumption 3. It follows that victory over Communism is the dominant, proximate goal of American policy. Proximate in the sense that there are more distant, more "positive" ends we seek, to which victory over Communism is but a means. But dominant in the sense that every other objective, no matter how worthy intrinsically, must defer to it. Peace is a worthy objective; but if we must choose between peace and keeping the Communists out of Berlin, then we must fight. Freedom, in the sense of self-determination, is a worthy objective; but if granting self-determination to the Algerian rebels entails sweeping that area into the Sino-Soviet orbit, then Algerian freedom must be postponed. Justice is a worthy objective; but if justice for Bantus entails driving the government of the Union of South Africa away from the West, then the Bantus must be prepared to carry their identification cards yet a while longer. Prosperity is a worthy objective; but if providing higher standards of living gets in the way of producing sufficient guns to resist Communist aggression, then material sacrifices and denials will have to be made. It may be, of course, that such objectives can be pursued consistently with a policy designed to overthrow Communism; my point is that where conflicts arise they must always be resolved in favor of achieving the indispensable condition for a tolerant world—the absence of Soviet Communist power.

The Uses of Power

This much having been said, the question remains whether we have the resources for the job we have to do—defeat Communism—and, if so, how those resources ought to be used. This brings us squarely to the problem of *power,* and the uses a nation makes of power. I submit that this is the key problem of international relations, that it always has been, that it always will be. And I suggest further that the main cause of the trouble we are in has been the failure of American policy-makers, ever since we assumed free world leadership in 1945, to deal with this problem realistically and seriously.

In the recent political campaign two charges were leveled affecting the question of power, and I think we might begin by trying to put them into proper focus. One was demonstrably false; the other, for the most part, true.

The first was that America had become—or was in danger of becoming—a second-rate military power. I know I do not have to dwell here on the absurdity of that contention. You may have misgivings about certain aspects of our military establishment—I certainly do—but you know any comparison of over-all American strength with over-all Soviet strength finds the United States not only superior, but so superior both in present weapons and in the development of new ones that our advantage promises to be a permanent feature of U.S.-Soviet relations for the foreseeable future.

I have often searched for a graphic way of impressing our superiority on those Americans who have doubts, and I think Mr. Jameson Campaigne has done it well in his new book *American Might and Soviet Myth.* Suppose, he says, that the tables were turned, and we were in the Soviets' position: "There would be more than 2,000 modern Soviet fighters, all better than ours, stationed at 250 bases in Mexico and the Caribbean. Overwhelming Russian naval power would always be within a few hundred miles of our coast. Half of the population of the U.S. would be needed to work on arms just to feed the people." Add this to the unrest in the countries around us where oppressed peoples would be ready to turn on us at the first opportunity. Add also a comparatively primitive industrial plant which would severely limit our capacity to keep abreast of the Soviets even in the missile field which is reputed to be our main strength.

If we look at the situation this way, we can get an idea of Khrushchev's nightmarish worries—or, at least, of the worries he might have if his enemies were disposed to exploit their advantage.

U.S. "Prestige"

The other charge was that America's political position in the world has progressively deteriorated in recent years. The contention needs to be formulated with much greater precision than it ever was during the campaign, but once that has been done, I fail to see how any serious student of world affairs can quarrel with it.

The argument was typically advanced in terms of U.S. "prestige." Prestige, however, is only a minor part of the problem; and even then, it is a concept that can be highly misleading. Prestige is a measure of how other people think of you, well or ill. But contrary to what was implied during the campaign, prestige is surely not important for its own sake. Only the vain and incurably sentimental among us will lose sleep simply because foreign peoples are not as impressed by our strength as they ought to be. The thing to lose sleep over is what people, having concluded that we are weaker than we are, are likely to do about it.

The evidence suggests that foreign peoples believe the United States is weaker than the Soviet Union, and is bound to fall still further behind in the years ahead. This ignorant estimate, I repeat, is not of any interest in itself; but it becomes very important if foreign peoples react the way human beings typically do—namely, by taking steps to end up on what appears to be the winning side. To the extent, then, that declining U.S. prestige means that other nations will be tempted to place their bets on an ultimate American defeat, and will thus be more vulnerable to Soviet intimidation, there is reason for concern.

Still, these guesses about the outcome of the struggle cannot be as important as the actual power relationship between the Soviet Union and ourselves. Here I do not speak of military power where our advantage is obvious and overwhelming but of political power—of influence, if you will—about which the relevant questions are: Is Soviet influence throughout the world greater or less than it was ten years ago? And is Western influence greater or less than it used to be?

Communist Gains

In answering these questions, we need to ask not merely whether Communist troops have crossed over into territories they did not occupy before, and not merely whether disciplined agents of the Cominform are in control of governments from which they were formerly excluded: the success of Communism's war against the West does not depend on such spectacular and definitive conquests. Success may mean merely the displacement of Western influence.

Communist political warfare, we must remember, is waged insidiously and in deliberate stages. Fearful of inviting a military showdown with the West which they could not win, the Communists seek to undermine Western power where the nuclear might of the West is irrelevant—in backwoods guerrilla skirmishes, in mob uprisings in the streets, in parliaments, in clandestine meetings of undercover conspirators, at the United Nations, on the propaganda front, at diplomatic conferences—preferably at the highest level.

The Soviets understand, moreover, that the first step in turning a country toward Communism is to turn it against the West. Thus, typically, the first stage of a Communist takeover is to "neutralize" a country. The second stage is to retain the nominal classification of "neutralist," while in fact turning the country into an active advocate and adherent of Soviet policy. And this may be as far as the process will go. The Kremlin's goal is the isolation and capture, not of Ghana, but of the United States—and this purpose may be served very well by countries that masquerade under a "neutralist" mask, yet in fact are dependable auxiliaries of the Soviet Foreign Office.

To recite the particulars of recent Soviet successes is hardly reassuring.

Six years ago French Indochina, though in trouble, was in the Western camp. Today Northern Vietnam is overtly Communist; Laos is teetering between Communism and Pro-Communist neutralism; Cambodia is, for all practical purposes, neutralist.

Indonesia, in the early days of the Republic, leaned toward the West. Today Sukarno's government is heavily besieged by avowed Communists, and for all of its "neutralist" pretensions, it is a firm ally of Soviet policy.

Ceylon has moved from a pro-Western orientation to a neutralism openly hostile to the West.

In the Middle East, Iraq, Syria and Egypt were, a short while ago, in the Western camp. Today the Nasser and Kassem governments are adamantly hostile to the West, are dependent for their military power on Soviet equipment and personnel; in almost every particular follow the Kremlin's foreign policy line.

A short time ago all Africa was a Western preserve. Never mind whether the Kikiyus and the Bantus enjoyed Wilsonian self-determination: the point is that in the struggle for the world that vast land mass was under the domination and influence of the West. Today, Africa is swerving violently away from the West and plunging, it would seem, into the Soviet orbit.

Latin America was once an area as "safe" for the West as Nebraska was for Nixon. Today it is up for grabs. One Latin American country, Cuba, has become a Soviet bridgehead ninety miles off our coast. In some countries the trend has gone further than others: Mexico, Panama, and Venezuela are displaying open sympathy for Castroism, and there is no country—save the Dominican Republic whose funeral services we recently arranged—where Castroism and anti-Americanism does not prevent the government from unqualifiedly espousing the American cause.

Only in Europe have our lines remained firm—and there only on the surface. The strains of neutralism are running strong, notably in England, and even in Germany.

Opportunities Missed

What have we to show by way of counter-successes? We have had opportunities—clear invitations to plant our influence on the other side of the Iron Curtain. There was the Hungarian Revolution which we praised and mourned, but did nothing about. There was the Polish Revolution which we misunderstood and then helped guide along a course favorable to Soviet interests. There was the revolution in Tibet which we pretended did not exist. Only in one instance have we moved purposively and effectively to dislodge existing Communist power: in Guatemala. And contrary to what has been said recently, we did not wait for "outside pressures" and "world opinion" to bring down that Communist government; we moved decisively to effect an anti-Communist *coup d'état*. We served our national interests, and by so doing we saved the Guatemalan people the ultimate in human misery. If there be doubts, ask the Hungarian people. Ask the Cuban people.

Guatemala is our single triumph. We have held the line in some places —in Lebanon, in Berlin, in the Formosa Straits—but nowhere else in the far-flung battle for the world have we *extended* the influence of the United States and *advanced* the cause of freedom.

Unless radical changes are made on our side, the situation will progressively worsen until the United States is at bay—isolated and besieged by an entirely hostile world. We will have to shed the attitudes and techniques of the Salvation Army, and start behaving like a Great Power. To gain respect, not prestige. I do not mean to disparage the Salvation Army. I do mean, however, that the affairs of nations are not determined by goodwill tours, almsgiving, gestures of self-denial, rehabilitation projects and discussion programs. The affairs of nations are determined— for good or for evil—by power.

The Soviet Union has not gotten where it is today through the attractiveness of its doctrines and practices. It has set its sights on distinct, concrete targets—on geographical areas or power centers which it means to infiltrate and eventually conquer—and then it has turned the full weight of its national power, plus the power of the international apparatus it controls, to these particular targets. The United States has never viewed the world struggle in quite this way—as, in effect, a military campaign where one isolates his objective, marshals his forces, and takes it! Rather, we have proceeded on the tacit assumption that virtue is its own reward, and that our only real problem is to make sure that the world perceives our virtue.

Moreover, we entered this supposed contest for world approval with a kind of guilt complex. I suspect the cause lies deep in America's past. Having been brought up on childish myths about the evil of European power politics, Americans felt uneasy when the rights and duties of the greatest power on earth suddenly fell upon them at the end of the Second World War. In order to prove that we were unlike our predecessors in power—selfish, ambitious, warlike—we began to lean over backwards, and to gear our policies to the opinions of others. There are notable exceptions—as when, for example, we have submitted to the imperatives of self-defense: in Greece, in Korea, in the Formosa Straits, in Berlin. But in theme and thrust and motive American foreign policy has been primarily an exercise in self-ingratiation.

I am, of course, over-simplifying the case; but not, I think, exaggerating it. Foreign aid, deference to the United Nations, cultural exchange programs, Summit conferences, the nuclear test ban, advocacy of general disarmament, the proposal to forego the protection of the Connally Reservation, anti-colonialism, the refusal to intervene in Cuba and the Congo—all of these programs and postures and attitudes have a single common denominator: an effort to please world opinion. Indeed, many of these policies are frankly acknowledged by their proponents to be contrary to the immediate interest of the United States; and yet they must be pursued, we are told, because of the overriding importance of having the world think well of us. This sluggish sentimentality, this obsession for pleasing people, has become a matter of grand strategy; has become no less than the guiding principle of American policy. It is leading us to national and international disaster.

How to Lose Respect

There are three fairly plain reasons—aside from the fact that it is a substitute for a real foreign policy—why deference to world opinion is so harmful to American interests.

First, it is self-defeating in the sense that the very admiration and respect we covet is denied to us the moment we go out and beg for it. The would-be beneficiaries of our concessions and self-denials soon construe them as weaknesses, and want more. Does anyone seriously suppose that our generous decision to permit the Panamanian flag to fly over American territory in the Canal Zone will placate the Panamanian nationalists? The gesture is bound simply to whet the mob's appetite and transfer its sights to bigger targets.

Second, trying to prove one's good faith when it has never really been open to question has the paradoxical effect of raising doubts about that good faith. It is partly a matter of protesting too much; and partly a matter of getting into a propaganda contest with a skunk. When we try to match the Kremlin's professions of love of democracy and peace, and hatred for armaments and colonialism, we invite the world to look upon us, as it looks upon the Soviets, as propagandists with something to hide. By not taking the superiority of ourselves and our cause for granted, we forbid others to take it for granted, and we find ourselves forced to make a new plea before the bar of "world opinion" every time *Pravda* opens its mouth.

Third, in deciding to gear our policies to world opinion, we have chosen the standard that is most vulnerable to manipulation by our enemies. When we talk about world opinion, we are not talking about a consensus of two billion human beings, most of whose opinions we know literally nothing about; we are talking about that tiny segment of the world's population that can make itself heard. Intellectuals, journalists, the organizers of street mobs. But these real sources of world opinion are, historically, prime targets for Communist infiltration because of their critical importance in the kind of struggle we are now witnessing. Thus, it is only natural that Communist influence in such areas should be far out of proportion to Communism's real strength in the world. When we permit world opinion to determine our policy toward Trujillo and Syngman Rhee, we are, in effect, giving our mortal enemies a voice in our own councils.

Five Situations

Let me turn now to five concrete situations, and suggest in broad outline how a nation, fully cognizant of the rights and duties that befall the guardian of Western civilization, might deal with them.

Cuba. We begin by denying that the way to rid the hemisphere of Castro is to break relations with Trujillo. Trujillo is not an enemy and a threat to the United States; Castro and his Communist patrons are, and it is to dangerous enemies that the disciplinary power of the United States is properly addressed. We should, therefore, make it clear in the most explicit terms that Communist governments are not tolerated in this hemisphere—and that the Castro regime, being such a government, will be eliminated.

Since it is better to act in concert with our fellow American Republics, we would try to secure their support by whatever discreet reminders are necessary of America's importance to their economic and political well-being. We would then proceed with the relevant economic embargo against Cuba, supported, if necessary, by a naval blockade. We would anticipate riots in the streets of Rio, Caracas and Mexico City, which we would ignore. And while showing our hand as little as possible, we would groom, and if necessary openly assist, a successor government which we would confidently expect to see in power in six months.

Africa. We begin by asserting that it is a Western protégé and a Western responsibility. We of the West should insist on credit for bringing the African masses this far. Remembering our own early attempts to create a government for ourselves—years of argument and indecision—we must recognize the difficult but necessary task of elevating Africans to the point, culturally, economically, and politically, where they are capable of responsible self-government; but we should add that we do not, for that reason, propose to turn them over to the ravages of Communism.

It may be that native leaders will emerge who are friends of the West and who, with our support, can lead their peoples to some measure of orderly, progressive self-government. Where such leaders have not emerged, the West must hold on. We cannot acquiesce in independence movements where independence means a return to savagery or Communist domination. Much less can we afford to jump on the bandwagon of anti-colonialism and so accelerate the mad rush toward anarchy and Soviet peonage. In areas where Western power still prevails, the full weight of American diplomacy must be employed to sustain it. In areas that have already fallen under Communist influence, we must proceed, overtly and covertly, to restore Western influence.

Perhaps the answer is an interim African Protectorate, administered by an association of Western nations. The purpose of such a protectorate would be to preside over a crash program for preparing the African people economically, politically, and culturally for the responsibilities of self-government in an atmosphere conducive to the triumph of Western concepts of justice and freedom. Such a policy would be denounced in many parts of the world as reactionary, chauvinistic and oppressive. Such recriminations we would have to endure. For there would be no doubt in our minds that the colonial system, even in its present state of development, is better for the African people than the misery and chaos into which they are now plunging headlong.

We would hold on to Africa, in part because Western survival there is essential to victory over Communism; but no less because we know that the privilege of being born in the West carries with it the responsibility of extending our good fortune to others. We are the bearers of Western civilization, the most noble product of the heart and mind of man.

Disarmament. We begin by announcing that we are against it. We are against it because we *need* all the armaments we presently have, and more—the weapons for limited war—that we do not have.

Armament races throughout history have always been a symptom of international friction—not a cause of it. Friction does not disappear by rival nations suddenly deciding to turn their swords into ploughshares. No nation in its right mind will give up the means of defending itself without first making sure that hostile powers are no longer in a position to threaten it. The Communist leaders are, of course, in their right minds. They may preach general disarmament for propaganda purposes. They may also seriously promote mutual disarmament in certain weapons in the knowledge that their superior strength in other weapons would leave them, on balance, decisively stronger than the West. Thus, in the light of the West's weakness in conventional weapons, it might make sense for the Communists to seek disarmament in the nuclear field. If all nuclear weapons suddenly ceased to exist, much of the world would immediately be laid open to conquest by the masses of Russian and Chinese manpower.

I do not suggest that any of our responsible leaders take disarmament seriously: they certainly do not favor unilateral disarmament, and they know the Soviets would not join us in any mutual disarmament that is not to their advantage. What I object to is *saying* we favor disarmament. The danger here is that we become hoist by the petard of our own propaganda.

This has already happened in the critical matter of nuclear tests—so vital to our national security. We originally agreed to suspend our tests, partly on the sentimental notion that the Russians were seriously interested in devising an adequate system of inspection and controls—but mostly because we felt the pressure of a "world opinion" we helped create concerning the dangers of radioactive fallout and the ultimate horrors of a nuclear holocaust. Yet now, when the illusions about Soviet intentions have been dispelled, and though the danger of fallout from the kind of underground and stratospheric testing we propose is non-existent, we *still* find it difficult to resume testing for fear of offending the brooding omnipotence of world opinion.

I fear the same consequences will follow from our attempts to match Soviet propaganda concerning the desirability of general disarmament. Already strong pressures are bearing down upon us to "do something" about it. The function of our propaganda should be to educate the people of the world about the realities of life—not to promote an escape from them. Plain talking on the subject of disarmament would do much to further this education.

The United Nations. We begin by not taking it seriously. The United Nations has its useful functions, but the formulation and conduct of American foreign policy is not among them.

On past occasions, when we have subordinated to United Nations policy our own notions of how to wage the cold war effectively, Western interests have suffered—the Korean War, the Suez crisis, the Iraqi revolution, this year's events in the Congo and many others. This is not surprising when we remember that United Nations policy has been the common denominator of the foreign policies of eighty-odd nations, some mortally hostile to us, some indifferent to our interests, nearly all less determined than we to save the world from Communist domination. Continued American deference to the United Nations in the future will invite the very direst consequences.

I submit that the important event at the recent session of the United Nations was not what Communism did with its right hand: Khrushchev's shoe-banging display and the dirty names he called Western leaders—but what Communism accomplished with its left: the successful campaign to get all of the serious themes of the current Soviet foreign policy line endorsed by allegedly neutral nations. Messrs. Tito, Nkrumah, Sukarno, Nehru and Nasser—though their proposals were pro-Soviet in every particular—became a kind of "centrist" block whose favor we found ourselves earnestly courting. This bizarre turn of events is one indication that the power center of the United Nations has moved sharply to the left.

We must liberate our own people and other people from the superstition that international policies—in order to be "good"—must have the approval of the United Nations. There may be occasions when the United Nations can be utilized to provide a broad base to policies that further Western interests. But when submission of a matter to the United Nations will predictably muddy the waters and obstruct the pursuit of American policy, then we must, as we did in the case of Berlin, quietly insist on settling the problem elsewhere.

Take the Offensive

Eastern Europe. We begin by having serious designs on it. Since Communism is organically expansive, it follows—given the laws of momentum and inertia—that we cannot succeed by attempting, merely, to hold on to what we have. American policy must be geared to the offensive.

Our appetite for Communist territory must be every bit as keen as theirs for non-Communist territory. Our efforts to extend freedom behind the Iron Curtain must be no less vigorous than their never-ending campaign to spread the influence of Communism in the free world.

We should encourage the captive peoples to revolt against their Communist rulers. This policy must be pursued with caution and prudence, as well as courage. The freedom fighters must be made to understand that the time and place and method of such uprisings will be dictated by the needs of an over-all world strategy. To this end we should establish close liaison with underground leaders behind the Iron Curtain, furnishing them printing presses, radios, weapons, instructors: the paraphernalia of a full-fledged Resistance.

We must ourselves be prepared to undertake military operations against vulnerable Communist regimes. Assume we have developed nuclear weapons that can be used in land warfare, and that we have equipped our European divisions accordingly. Assume also a major uprising in Eastern Europe such as occurred in Budapest in 1956. In such a situation, we ought to present the Kremlin with an ultimatum forbidding Soviet intervention, and be prepared, if the ultimatum is rejected, to move a highly mobile task force equipped with appropriate nuclear weapons to the scene of the revolt. Our objectives would be to confront the Soviet Union with superior forces in the immediate vicinity of the uprisings and to compel a Soviet withdrawal. An actual clash between American and Soviet armies would be unlikely; the mere threat of American action, coupled with the Kremlin's knowledge that the fighting would occur amid a hostile population and could easily spread to other areas, would probably result in Soviet acceptance of the ultimatum. The Kremlin would also be put on notice, of course, that resort to long-range bombers and missiles would prompt automatic retaliation in kind. On this level, we would invite the Communist leaders to choose between total destruction of the Soviet Union, and accepting a local defeat. Had we the will and the means for it in 1956, such a policy would have saved the Hungarian Revolution.

Might does not make right, but right cannot survive without might and without using might. History is not the story of the triumph of virtue, though virtue when properly supported has sometimes triumphed. The people of the world and their leaders do not rally instinctively behind good causes: if that were true, the plague of Communism would long since have disappeared from our planet. They do, however, rally behind good causes that are energetically and purposively pressed, and that show promise of winning. If we simply summon the courage of our convictions, the blessings of a moderately tolerable life will soon fall on others, as well as ourselves. And future generations will honor us.

16. George C. Wallace

"What I Believe"

Alabama governor George C. Wallace did not receive the nomination
from either of the two major parties as Senator Goldwater did, but, in
terms of the popular vote, he headed the largest third-party movement since
1860. In the 1968 presidential election, running as the candidate of
the American Independent Party, Governor Wallace drew 13.5 percent
of the votes cast. Impressive as this was for a third party in American
politics, Wallace nevertheless carried only five states (all in the South)
even though the AIP was able to get itself put on the ballot in all
50 states. Beyond the historical reasons for the electoral failures of third
parties, there are others that go to the heart of the Wallace movement.
Perhaps the most important among them was Wallace's inability or
unwillingness to formulate a positive program that transcended the
politics of repudiation. He campaigned throughout much of the
nation lambasting straw men such as "left-wing theoreticians, briefcase
totin' bureaucrats, ivory-tower guideline writers, bearded anarchists,
smart-aleck editorial writers and pointy-headed professors." He
appealed almost entirely to the resentments of Americans who felt that
the Democratic and Republican parties had passed them by. In the
following selection the appeal is heavily antiliberal, antidemonstrations,
antifoundations, and antibusing. Philosophically, Wallace stands against
salient characteristics of modern American society: secularism,
humanism, and ethical relativism.

It was unfortunante, however, that the negativist strain in "Wallaceism"
blinded many American leaders to its important, even poignant,
message. In contrast to Goldwater, who spoke for the new rich, the
privileged middle- and upper-middle classes, and the retired officers corps,
Wallace authentically expressed the thoughts of those whom he calls
the "little people." They are the growing number of citizens who
feel powerless before big government, big corporations, and the big
plans of the social engineers. Perhaps it is understandable that in seeking
to be heard, their message comes across as strident and negative.

Wallace had polled a huge popular vote in the 1972 primaries when he
was shot on May 15 at a shopping center in Laurel, Maryland,
leaving him paralyzed from the waist down. On the following day he
won both the Maryland and Michigan primaries but was too ill to continue

"What I Believe" by the Honorable George C. Wallace first appeared in the
December, 1971 issue of *American Opinion* (Belmont, Massachusetts) and is
reprinted by permission of the publisher.

in the race. "What I Believe" has been chosen to represent Wallace because it summarizes the issues that he exploited so effectively during the 1960s, and because Wallace takes this opportunity to repudiate the Populist label so frequently pinned on him. A devotee of free enterprise, Wallace sees historical populism as too collectivist and socialistic in its message. The essay appeared in *American Opinion* (December 1971), published by Robert Welch, head of the John Birch Society.

In our nearly two hundred years as a nation, we Americans have withstood many crises. But at no time in the past has the United States been so decisively challenged both at home and abroad. It has become increasingly obvious during the past three years that our national leaders have let us down. Their failure to resist effectively the Communist onslaught from abroad, and their wholesale promotion of socialism at home, have heralded a retreat from greatness of which all Americans should be truly ashamed. Yet at precisely the time when good citizens should be rising angry, many appear to be in a state of narcosis.

The primary reason for this is that the incumbent President brought to office with him a reputation as an arch foe of Communism abroad and of the Welfare State at home. You remember how he made statement after statement to that effect, both before and during his Presidential campaign. But the proof of politics is in the practice. And the real Mr. Nixon has proved to be as different from Candidate Nixon as was Mr. Hyde from Dr. Jekyll.

The problem is that millions of Americans who would be highly agitated if Mr. Humphrey were doing what Mr. Nixon is doing are telling each other that nothing can be very wrong because the "Liberals" aren't holding the reins of state. If you think that, I've got news for you: Richard Nixon ran on my platform and is running the country on Hubert Humphrey's.

The major reason that President Nixon has been able to have his cake and eat it too is that the longhairs of the "Liberal" media treat him as if he were still breathing down the neck of Alger Hiss. That was more than twenty years ago, and the anti-Communist days of Richard Nixon are long gone. But radical TV and newspaper journalists continue to provide protective coloring for Mr. Nixon as he moves the country Leftward towards total government.

You know, I think that before America can be returned to sanity and justice, something must be done to bring balance to the giant news media, particularly television. Contrary to what they might think, I don't want to dump the Brinkleys, Cronkites, Reasoners, *et al.*, in some electronic junkyard. It isn't necessary, and I wouldn't do it if it were. I just want to make sure that such overstuffed shirts no longer have a monopoly on television news. Think about it a minute. You've got room for more than a dozen channels on your television dial. Why is it, then, that the only national TV news you get is packaged in but three network newsrooms in New York? When you figure that there are nearly nine hundred television stations in this country, and only about three national TV news reports, you just know that something is mighty wrong!

But every time the TV news monopolists are attacked for their flagrant prejudices and dishonesty they scream that their freedom of speech is being threatened. Nobody is threatening their freedom of speech, and nobody should. I am not a rich man, but I will personally buy soap boxes for every one of them, fly them to Montgomery, and assign a State Trooper to guard them while they stand on those boxes and shout any lie they please. That would be fine. As I say, I'd even pay for it. I just don't like to hear those glib phonies tell lies on television to 70 million Americans.

The government has given the three major networks a virtual license to lie by restricting access to the TV audience through dangerous federal licensing restrictions. It is ironic that those who claim they are most threatened are the very ones who have been most protected.

Meanwhile, independent radio and television stations with Conservative editorial policies have been regularly harassed by the government, and the licenses of some of them have been removed by the bureaucrats in Washington. The solution is not to censor the professionals who distort our news, but to allow access to the airwaves to those who will tell America the truth. What the nation needs is more television stations to assure real freedom of speech. All those who are truly in favor of the free exchange of ideas, and opposed to monopoly, should join me in this stand.

It seems to me that the "Liberals" of the media need a bath in lye soap. They not only concoct every possible alibi to justify Mr. Nixon's kowtowing to the Maoist thugs who have murdered nearly 64 million Chinese, but they trumpet that every crook, punk, and thug in the streets here at home is a victim of an oppressive society in general and of the police in particular. What society in all the world is less "oppressive" than ours? Not one. And because we are so free, America's policemen are the thin blue line between anarchy and the survival of our Christian civilization. Our local police deserve our total support. No lawabiding citizen has anything to fear from our police officers. But if you are a law violator you not only have something to fear, you should have!

As a group, our local police are overworked and underpaid while daily risking their lives to protect our loved ones. Our police are under attack from the Communists, anarchists, and professional demagogues of the Left. They have been handcuffed by venal politicians seeking votes, and by sociology-spouting judges who have more sympathy for the criminal than for his victims. As a result, our police officers are openly gunned down by Communists like Black Panther leader Huey Newton, and our women and children and old people are in danger on the streets of their own neighborhoods.

A basic purpose of government is to protect the life and property of its citizens. No nation can long endure if, for any reason, the government ceases to serve the purpose for which it was created. Certainly the Supreme Court is the worst offender in substituting sociology for justice. Because of this, millions of Americans, trapped in our urban centers and unable to escape to the suburbs and countryside, are regularly made victims of the thugs, punks, and criminals who are allowed to roam free. Today, if you are the victim of an assault in New York, your attacker will probably be out of jail before you even get to the hospital—and his legal bills will be paid by the government. When a person steals a pocketbook, the judge plays social worker and tells him that he can keep the pocketbook if he won't do it again.

There was an old saying that crime doesn't pay. Now, thanks largely to the Supreme Court, it oftens pays very well. The laws of supply and demand being what they are, as the pay goes up so does the supply of criminals. According to the F.B.I.'s *Uniform Crime Reports,* the crime rate in the United States rose 144 percent in the last ten years, with crimes of violence up 156 percent. Women employees leaving many buildings in Washington after dark must often be accompanied by armed guards.

It is not enough for the High Court to refrain from making things worse. The damage has already been done, and it is only a matter of time before that damage destroys our country. In order to reestablish Constitutional government the Attorney General must re-submit cases in areas where the Warren Court handed down radical decisions based upon fuzzy sociology rather than sound jurisprudence. So far the Attorney General has shown no more desire to do this than he has to *prosecute* the revolutionaries and rioters who provided such fruitful rhetoric during the last campaign.

Promoting the breakdown of law and order are whole armies of militants, revolutionaries, anarchists, and Communists. They shoot our police, march many thousands strong in our cities, spit on our flag and burn it, and bomb our public buildings—but the internal threat of Communism is an issue which Mr. Nixon abandoned long ago. When it comes to protecting hard-working, decent colored people in our cities from the terrorism of, say, the Communist Black Panthers, he is silent . . . even as he is silent when top Panther and Communist leaders beat the very path to Peking that he will tread himself.

Meanwhile, Mr. Nixon's highly publicized campaign promises about a "war on crime" have had all the explosive effect of a pop gun. His drum beaters claim that crime is now increasing at a slightly lower rate than it did under President Johnson, implying that crime has been reduced under the Nixon Administration. The F.B.I.'s *Uniform Crime Reports* indicate that is just not true.

And let me tell you something else. Because of the continuing push for coddling criminals in our prisons, in the courts, and everywhere else, there have been some 633 police officers shot dead in our streets in the last ten years. The mass media and the revolutionaries and the "Liberals" have been promoting the idea that our local police are brutal, and need to be punished by civilian review boards, and are pigs—and so criminals figure it's Open Season on policemen. A F.B.I. survey of the killers of those 633 police officers revealed that 71 percent of their murderers had previous criminal arrests; 57 percent had previous convictions; 322 of them had been arrested for violent crimes; 324 had been granted leniency from prior sentences; 199 were on parole or probation when they killed a police officer; and, 20 of those killers of policemen had actually been previously convicted of *murder* and set free to kill again.

During the 1968 campaign our law and order theme was appropriated by both the Republicans and Democrats because it was and is a priority concern of our citizens. During the 1970 mid-term elections even Teddy Kennedy was pressured by public opinion into putting on the sheriff's badge and shootin' irons and making noises like Wyatt Earp. The day after the election the star and the six-guns were tossed off a bridge into the political depths. However, none of the country's political commentators, all so concerned about "the public's right to know," whispered a word about such hypocrisy.

If I run again for national public office I just might come up with an issue that Teddy Kennedy and Richard Nixon can't steal. We might make the "Liberal" Establishment itself a major campaign issue. Can you imagine the Hero of Chappaquiddick and the Great Protector of Peking running campaigns aimed at exposing the "Liberal" Establishment? That would be akin to Mae West denouncing men.

And note that while the Establishment's pointy-headed pseudo-intellectuals and Harvard half-bakes promote the coddling of criminals, they also prescribe an ever-larger dole for able persons unwilling to get off their fat and go to work. Any taxi driver can tell you that if you pay people not to work, more and more people are going to *decide* not to work. Steelworkers, carpenters, truck drivers, policemen, beauticians, and shop-girls figured that out years ago, but it is still a secret unknown to the gurus of the Harvard Sociology Department and unheard of in the *sanctum sanctorum* of the Department of Health, Education and Welfare. Contrary to his campaign promises, our President is meanwhile trying to put 24 million people on a permanent dole through a guaranteed annual income program. He postponed the plot when it became obvious that Congress was for the moment unwilling to swallow it, but he says he means to get those extra 24 million on the welfare rolls one way or another. And you know he'll try!

Although purists from the Foundation for Economic Education may disagree with me, I am not against providing charity to the truly needy; the aged, widows, the blind, and the handicapped. But the amount of money going to people in these categories is a miniscule part of total welfare spending. I believe in help for the needy, not for the lazy and the greedy. Let me tell you, no one moves to Alabama to live off the sweat of the working people who pay the welfare bills.

But, frankly, I do not believe that the federal government should be in the welfare business. When it is, it must inevitably turn elections into vote-buying contests. If charity and relief are handled at the local level, citizens can better keep their eyes peeled for corruption, and politicians who engage in vote-buying schemes will get their comeuppance when business locates in other areas. A federal welfare system only puts the heat on the producers, the business and working people, to provide gravy for loafers.

If our commitment to being a Christian people had not been so undermined, it wouldn't be necessary for the counties and states to handle charity. But, as the reality exists today, the only delivery system capable of making certain that those truly in need are cared for is the local or state government. I don't like it, maybe it won't always be necessary, but I'm not going to see the helpless suffer real pain and hurt by denying the local government the authority to help those who can't help themselves.

I have sponsored pensions for the elderly in Alabama, for example, because many working people who are retired today were, during the height of their productive years, working for fifty cents an hour in an era when bread was seven cents a loaf. The federal government has since produced so much inflation that these people couldn't possibly have saved enough out of their fifty-cent wages even to survive in retirement at today's prices. It is ironic that it was the very "Liberal" politicians who claimed they wanted to help the poor who destroyed the purchasing power of our currency and left those elderly people poverty stricken.

If we are to solve the nation's tremendous welfare problem, we must unwind the mess from the top down, keeping the federal government from turning welfare into the biggest boondoggle in history, and turning it back to the states and private charities. The government *must,* however, make good on its Social Security pensions. Conservatives who oppose the philosophy of Social Security correctly argue that it is mismanaged, deceptive, and not even actuarily sound. But those who have paid into the system must not be made to suffer. In my view, however, it is time that

"Liberal" demagogues stopped using Social Security as a political football. If politicians sincerely want to help the elderly they will stop deficit spending, the cause of the inflation which has deprived our elderly citizens of the purchasing power of their small savings, resulted in the taxing away of their homes, and thrown so many of them on the unmerciful hooks of government charity.

It has been pointed out by my critics that we once borrowed some money in Alabama, and they say that it is therefore unfair of me to criticize the vast deficits of Presidents Johnson and Nixon. I maintain there is a tremendous difference between what Washington is doing and what we have done in Montgomery. In the first place, when a state borrows, it borrows money that is already in existence. This is simply a transfer, and no inflationary new money is created as it is when the federal government pumps out printing-press dollars for its deficit use. Secondly, the federal government goes in debt to give money away to socialist and even Communist countries, to pay for a giant and unnecessary bureaucracy, to destroy local school systems, to subsidize the raising of illegitimate children, and for a myriad other "Liberal" programs. Such money is wasted and gone forever.

We borrowed money in Alabama to create a capital asset—roads. I realize that some libertarian theorists believe that private enterprise should build roads. Someday that may come to pass. But, in the meantime, Alabama desperately needed roads to boost its economy. We borrowed money to build roads because those roads attract industry and tourism, improve marketing, and produce tax revenue. Not only have subsequent improvements in business in Alabama justified the economics involved in our road building program but, as roads have been improved, the percentage of deaths on our highways has dropped. Selling bonds to build roads is the same sound, conservative business practice as a corporation's borrowing funds to buy wealth-producing machinery.

Still, we in Alabama have one of the smallest debt services of any state in the union. Today we pay out less than five percent of our income for debt service—and you know, in these days of the Nixon inflation, any businessman who can operate with less than five percent of his income going for debt service is doing very well indeed. Compare that with the fact that under the current Administration in Washington the third largest Budget expenditure—behind only Defense and Welfare—goes to pay the *interest* on the federal debt. In fact, it is a sum that comes to more than 21 billion dollars!

During my first administration, Alabama jumped to Number One in industrial expansion in the South—and held that position three years in a row. From the time I assumed office until I left office in 1966, Alabama had received a total of 1,304 new and expanded industries representing a capital investment of nearly $2 billion and employing approximately 100,000 people. Industrialists like our attitude toward local government and toward the Free Enterprise system. This attitude towards competitive private enterprise could bring prosperity and full employment to all America if the man in the White House would practice what he preaches. Private enterprise is the only real war on poverty which has ever been fought with any success.

But the revolutionaries, high-heeled "Liberals" of both sexes, and limp-wristed pseudo-intellectuals don't believe in the Free Enterprise system. They believe in socialism, the economic system of Karl Marx. And, strangely enough, many of the super-rich in this country also believe in socialism. They set up tax free foundations which promote socialist programs with the taxes they evade, and then arrange to tax the working man to pay for those programs. Such limousine "Liberals" are not humanitarians. If they were they would lead by example and divide their own wealth instead of hiding it in tax shelters while they promote an ever-increasing tax burden on the middle class. In 1966, for example, the super-rich "Liberal" Nelson Rockefeller paid only $685 in personal income taxes. Honest plumbers and steelworkers paid more than that!

I have filed a suit in the United States Supreme Court to have tax-exemption removed from any foundation that uses tax-free monies to promote socialism or revolution. The "Liberal" mass media have ignored that suit, even as they pose as friends of the common man.

Because I have attacked the fraud inherent in the giant foundations, some have accused me of being a radical or a Populist. In the sense that I have always worked to keep the little man from being shoved around by quasi-governmental interests and monopolies, I am a Populist. Take the utilities, which have a government-granted monopoly and have sometimes formed an unholy alliance with politicians to exploit the people. In Alabama I have taken on those utilities, and the giant banks, and big trucking interests, to make sure they pay an equitable share of the taxes. But while concerned with genuine problems, Populists have traditionally looked to socialism as a solution. In that sense I am not a Populist because it is my view that the Free Enterprise system is the only way effectively to elevate the underprivileged.

Many politicians are now calling themselves "Populists," yet the Establishment opinion makers—who long used that term as an epithet to attack me—have not denounced them as demagogues. They are no threat to the insiders of the Establishment. They can be bought, or manipulated, or controlled. Not everybody agrees with me, but no one doubts that I am my own man and mean exactly what I say. I believe in our country and its free traditions. The pitch of the "New Populists" is an alien one

—it argues that since the rich and the poor are subsidized by the government, the middle class should be also. Come and get it, they say! Get yourself a slot at the trough with the rest of the animals, like some poor serf in a Communist hell. Theirs is really a call for total socialism as an answer to the inequities created by partial socialism.

Such regimentation is the greatest threat the ordinary American faces today. When the bureaucrats try to solve problems with collectivist theories and tyrannical decrees, poverty stays and freedom dies.

Yet America is being socialized and almost everybody knows it. Only a few Conservative Republicans refuse to admit that the President is acting as an agent for the collectivists. They pretend that it is happening because it is somehow inevitable. Let me assure them that socialism is *not* inevitable, though it certainly may seem so when you have as President a Republican whom even John Kenneth Galbraith calls a socialist.

In 1968, Richard Nixon made opposition to big government a major part of his campaign. Yet in his every move since election he has paid lip service to the need for decentralization while increasing federal power over the people. More and more each year the people and the states are coming under the arbitrary power of an army of bureaucrats in Washington who are telling us how to run our schools, our businesses, and even our personal lives. Much of this is done in the name of ending "discrimination." Let me tell you, I believe in the right of people to discriminate. When we say a fine lady is *discriminating*, we are complimenting her as having good taste. The right to discriminate is nothing but the right to choose, and the right to choose is the essence of liberty.

I do not, however, believe the government has the right to discriminate between its citizens on the basis of race, creed, or color—and that is exactly what it is doing through federal programs which set up racial quota systems or force busing for racist balance. The Left says Wallace is a racist. I say, and my record shows, that Wallace is for freedom of choice, and that it is the federal government that is racist!

Indicative of the growing arrogance of the nearly all-powerful government in Washington is the virtual takeover of local schools by the guideline writers at the Department of Health, Education and Welfare. Nationwide polls show that Americans of all races are overwhelmingly opposed to racist busing. It is criminal to move students out of their neighborhoods to distant locations for the sole purpose of satisfying the cattle-car racial lusts of a bunch of jackbooted guideline writers in Washington. While professing to believe in the democratic concepts of majority rule, these bureaucrats are forcing little children to be hauled for fifty miles or more in the interest of a racist experiment in sociology. Millions of dollars which could be spent enriching the education of our children are

going out the exhaust pipes of those diesel motor buses. Worse, the bureaucrats in Washington are treating our little children like a hutch of
guinea pigs in a laboratory.

Mr. Nixon claims to be opposed to all this busing—he swears he really
is—yet he has appointed men to run the H.E.W. whose family crests
might as well be a highway rampant with greyhounds. Richard Nixon appointed those H.E.W. bureaucrats who instituted suits to force busing on
local school boards. They serve at his pleasure. If he meant business he
would have cleaned house! But he doesn't mean what he says, any more
than he meant it when he swore to us that he would never institute a
wage-price freeze or betray our anti-Communist allies on Formosa or
promote a guaranteed annual income for welfare loafers.

School boards, under the Nixon guidelines, have become local appen-
dages and agents of a bureau in Washington, answering only to that bureau, not to the people. If that isn't exactly what Mr. Nixon directed, why
hasn't he fired those who have "disobeyed" his orders? I think the answer
to that is all too clear.

The guideline dictators have gone far beyond the busing issue. In many
places they have ordered that indoctrination replace education. The bureaucrats have ordained that our schools, in effect, are to be turned into
propaganda factories for international socialism. In order for these edicts
to be carried out, history books are being rewritten to conform with alien
doctrines; moral values are being replaced; humanism is becoming the official state religion; traditions, patriotism, responsibility to family and
country, are being subverted; and, the students—our children—are being
regimented to serve the socialist Establishment. Good teachers know
these things are happening, and they are doing their best to stop them,
but the federal Office of Education in Washington carries a very big stick.

Granting control over the education of our children to a central government will guarantee the establishment of a dictatorship in America.
Whatever objections, real or imagined, which may be raised about inade-
quacies or duplications or shortcomings of local schools are insignificant
compared to the threat to the liberties of every American posed by federal control of education. The federal government must get out of the education business if freedom is to survive in America. This means that the
guideline bureaucrats must be stripped of their authority over our local
schools and sent out to earn an honest living doing productive work.

The situation is serious. As a result of the growing power of Washington, we have already become a government-fearing people instead of a
God-fearing people. For decades now, politicians have encouraged us to
look to government for strength instead of to our God. It is no accident
that where the state becomes all-powerful, faith in Christ is no longer carried like a banner by Christian soldiers, workers, mothers, and business-

men. I have accepted Christ as my personal Savior, and that is one important reason why I have pledged my life to opposing tyranny wherever I find it. So long as God gives me the strength, I shall continue to do so.

It has been pointed out by libertarian purists who question my Conservative credentials that as Governor of Alabama I let my state receive federal money. We do this because Alabama pays federal taxes. We know that federal money brings federal guidelines, but the realities of politics and fiscal survival of the states leave us little choice but to participate in federal programs which we would prefer to handle by ourselves. There is no question but that federal funds are bait with which the federal government is attempting to take over the authority of the states and of the people, but this must be stopped at the top by getting Washington out of the subsidy business, not by asking any one state to commit fiscal suicide. The solution for this problem is to be found in Washington, not Montgomery, or Sacramento, or Topeka.

"Liberal" news commentators often characterize me as an "angry man." I plead guilty to that description. For years Americans were the most admired people in the world because of their capacity for righteous indignation. Many Americans still rise to anger at evil, but our pseudo-intellectual leaders have used our colleges and mass media to preach moral and ethical relativism until many of our people have adopted a pretended sophistication and blasé attitude toward corruption, immorality, and even treason. America is in the midst of a full-scale retreat from greatness, and every honest American knows it. That retreat was begun by the treason of the intellectuals who, jaded and morally corrupt, lost their capacity for righteous indignation.

I will tell you that I feel indignant that some American corporations, with the full encouragement of the U.S. Government, have been supplying the Vietcong and North Vietnam, however indirectly, with war materials with which to kill American soldiers. If ever there was an act which deserved the condemnation, contempt, and fury of every American, it is that one. Instead, our knee-jerk intelligentsia have hailed it as a sign of "maturity" and "sophistication" by the "progressive" business community.

Another crime of the pseudo-intellectuals has been to take the natural idealism of youth and to pervert it into hatred of our country. Young people who have desecrated the flag, burned draft cards, and engaged in violent protest over the Vietnam War, did not learn to hate their country, its flag, and our national traditions, from their parents. They learned such hatred from the mental amoebae whose poisonous culture is spewed from the lecterns in our college classrooms.

Young people have been conned into believing that Communism is some kind of worldwide humanitarian movement, instead of an evil conspiracy to conquer the world—a conspiracy already responsible for the murders of over 100 million human beings. When I see how our youths are duped and conned and manipulated by the Establishment Left, my anger rises hot and fresh. Deprived of a solid grounding in history, our own sons and daughters are being used as the cadres of their nation's enemies.

America's youth has never been told that it was the "Liberal" politicians who turned the fruits of victory in World War II over to the Communists, and in doing so condemned tens of millions to perpetual slavery. They do not know that it was the "Liberal" politicians who committed our Armed Forces in Korea, and then tied General MacArthur's hands so that he could not win. They have never learned that it was the "Liberal" politicians who put us into the morass of Vietnam and, as in Korea, again tied the hands of the military. Hundreds of thousands of good men who answered their country's call to the colors will never come home from places like Heartbreak Ridge, the Chosin Reservoir, and Khe Sanh. They gave their lives for their country while our "Liberal" politicians made sure that the only real victors would be the Communists.

I take a solemn oath before Almighty God that if I ever become President of the United States I will never commit American soldiers to action without making every possible effort to ensure their victory. General of the Army Douglas MacArthur was right when he said that there is no substitute for victory. If we had listened to MacArthur, the Communists would not be in Vietnam today and neither would we.

I have always maintained that we should never have let ourselves be drawn into the Vietnam War. If troops are required to contain Communism in Asia, they should be provided by Chiang Kai-shek and other Asian anti-Communists who are more than willing to provide them. But the "Liberals" have consistently refused Chiang's offer of troops. Apparently they prefer to let Americans die instead. Once in, however, we should have won that war and then got out! But you can be sure that Richard Nixon will have lost it before another President is inaugurated.

I think that is cause for righteous indignation. It fills me with anger and shame for my country.

And I do not believe that it is an accident that America has been led from one foreign-policy disaster to another until our retreat from greatness seems a rout. To think that stretches credibility further than Mama Cass would stretch Twiggy's bathing suit.

A little over a decade ago, Scott McLeod, head of the State Department's Bureau of Security and Consular Affairs, notified the Secretary of State of the names and records of some 800 security risks then employed by the State Department. Mr. McLeod noted that of the 800, some 250 were "serious" cases—sixty percent of which were "incumbents in high level assignments," with one-half "assigned to what can be categorized as critical intelligence slots in the Department." McLeod was quickly shipped off to be Ambassador to Ireland, and nothing (repeat: nothing) was done about those security risks. Presumably, they are still there! While campaigning for the Presidency, Richard Nixon promised to clean out the State Department. He repudiated that promise even before he was inaugurated.

I think the President's failure to assure the security of our State Department is cause for righteous indignation, but I don't see any emanating from the "Liberals." Little wonder that Mr. Nixon "lost" the vote to save Free China in the U.N. and is heading for Peking. The fact is that more than one of his China intelligence specialists was on the Scott McLeod list.

America must stop helping her enemies and help herself. Richard Nixon promised America military superiority, and has instead continued to disarm us. For this, the "Liberal" pseudo-intellectuals cheer him. Let me tell you, I have been to war. I have seen close friends killed in battle. I never want to see this country have to go to war again. But I am a realist. I have read enough history to know that if we are weak, if we follow policies of appeasement, we will have war whether we like it or not. Why should the Communists abandon their goal of world conquest when we are in full retreat?

The Communists have such contempt for our "Liberal" politicians and opinion makers that they don't even bother to deny that their goal is world conquest. They affirm it at every opportunity, and all one has to do is look at their own literature to see it written in big bold letters. It is only our "Liberals" who deny that the Communists seek world conquest and claim that the Reds have "mellowed." Such men must be removed from positions of power and influence.

I have fought for this country, and I am still fighting for it. I have travelled America from Augusta to San Diego, and from Miami to Seattle. I have met Americans from every section, from all walks of life, from all strata of society. I love the real, decent, patriotic, and hard-working people who *are* America. I am in love with this country. I love its traditions and its heritage. And I mean to labor to preserve them from those who would destroy the fabric of freedom either by design or from innocent error.

I am not an ideologue. There are a lot of fancy philosophers and libertarian pundits whose books and pamphlets I haven't read and am not likely to read. But I believe that government governs best which governs least, and that whatever the people will have their government do is best done at that level closest to the people. I mean to defend my country against her enemies—foremost of which is the International Communist

Conspiracy. I mean to labor at being the best Christian, and the best citizen, that I can be. And I mean to try to serve my country with an unashamed patriotism. If enough of us do that— if enough of us Stand Up For America—we can stop America's retreat from victory.

But the stakes are high. We know that if we fail, liberty in all the world might flicker and die for a thousand years. America can be the land of the free only so long as it is the home of the brave. Join me, brave friends, and together let us Stand Up For America!

17. Richard M. Scammon and Ben J. Wattenberg

The Social Issue

In an attempt to make sense of the political upheavals of the 1960s, political analysts Richard Scammon and Ben Wattenberg, in 1970, published *The Real Majority*. The book is an exercise in psephology (i.e., the study of voting behavior through the examination of election returns, public opinion polls, demographic indices, and press and radio reports). The authors defend the controversial thesis that in the 1960s the "social issue"—crime, race, lawlessness, civil rights, backlash, and alienation—became as important in American elections as the older economic issues. It is possible, they add, that the social issue will draw the blue-collar working class from the Democrats and provide the basis for a new Republican majority.

Kevin Phillips, top aide in 1968 to John Mitchell (Richard Nixon's campaign manager, later appointed U.S. Attorney–General), extends the Scammon-Wattenberg thesis in contending that the 1960s witnessed the dissolution of the Roosevelt coalition of the South, labor unions, blacks, ethnic minorities, and intellectuals. Crucial to Phillips' argument, which appears in his book *The Emerging Republican Majority* (1969), is the assumption that the Nixon and Wallace votes were really one. Hence the 1968 election marked a watershed with the 60-plus Democratic percentage in 1964 becoming a 60-plus percentage for Republicans in 1968. Republican conservatism is now the vehicle for a new majoritarian consensus.

The Scammon-Wattenberg thesis, with or without Phillips' elaboration, inspires many questions. Does it explain President Nixon's landslide victory over Senator George McGovern in 1972, or are there other, more persuasive explanations? If valid for 1972, will it also hold for the duration of the 1970s and 1980s, as Phillips suggests? Might the decline in the two-party electoral system in the 1960s be instead the result of a deep alienation from the existing political alternatives? As still a further alternative, how important are the strains that voter technology, nationalization of the electorate, heightened minority consciousness, and the multiplication of opinion through television place on the two-party system?

Our investigations lead us first to the three main notions that are discussed in the early parts of this book: a substantive notion, a structural notion, and a strategic notion.

The substantive idea is that many Americans have begun casting their ballots along the lines of issues relatively new to the American scene. For several decades Americans have voted basically along the lines of bread-and-butter economic issues. Now, in addition to the older, still potent economic concerns, Americans are apparently beginning to array themselves politically along the axes of certain social situations as well. These situations have been described variously as law and order, backlash, anti-youth, malaise, change, or alienation. These situations, we believe, constitute a new and potent political issue. We call it the Social Issue, and in our definition, it includes all these facets—and much more. It is an issue that has scared many, and yet, in our judgment, it is an issue that holds potential for good as well as for ill, for success or for defeat—for Democrats, for Republicans, for Wallaceites.

The structural idea concerns the makeup of the American electorate. The great majority of the voters in America are unyoung, unpoor, and unblack; they are middle-aged, middle-class, middle-minded. Understanding these simple demographics of the electorate is vital to any real psephological view of politics. For example, while the advocates of the New Politics in 1968 were reminding one another that half of all Americans were under twenty-five (which is roughly true), the canny psephologist was carefully noting that the average age of all *voters* was forty-seven (which is also true, and far more relevant).

The strategic idea deals with the manner in which candidates for office try to make hay with both the *substance* of an election and the *structure* of the electorate. In American political life this has almost invariably manifested itself as an attempt to capture the center ground of an electoral battlefield. The reason for this tropism toward the center is simple: That is where victory lies. A classic case in point was demonstrated in New York City in the 1969 mayoralty campaign when "law-and-order" candidate Mario Procaccino proclaimed himself liberal, while "liberal" candidate John V. Lindsay reminded one and all how tough he was on law and order. It can safely be said that the only extreme that is attractive to the large majority of American voters is the extreme center. . . .

With this understanding, a fourth major notion begins to emerge, more directly relevant to who may be elected to what in the years to come. When coupled with the three earlier ideas, it provides, we believe, the beginning of a general theory of contemporary elections. Simply put, it says that those politicians who ignore the first three ideas do so at their electoral peril and that there are forces at work within both major parties that seem bent on such peril. It is our view that this hazard will more likely be apparent within the Democratic Party, largely because it is easier for an out party to succumb to a move away from the center and toward an extreme, as the out-party Republicans did in 1964 with their nomination of

Senator Barry Goldwater. If this happens, if Republicans capture the center as Democrats go to the extreme, we may well see Republican Presidents in the White House for a generation.

A New Tide Observed: The Social Issue

In 1964 the first unpleasant political rumblings were heard from what may be a new Voting Issue. Early in the year, Governor George C. Wallace of Alabama challenged President Lyndon Johnson in a series of Democratic state primaries. Wallace, who had made his national reputation as a "segregation now; segregation forever" politician, did surprisingly well against the stand-ins who nominally represented President Lyndon Johnson. In Wisconsin—a state with a long liberal tradition—George Wallace received 34% of the Democratic primary vote against Governor John Reynolds. In Indiana, Wallace received 30% of the party primary vote against Governor Matthew Welsh. In Maryland, Wallace got 43% of the Democratic vote against Senator Daniel Brewster.

In 1964 Wallace was regarded primarily as an antiblack candidate, and the term "backlash" came into the political lexicon, describing a white response to what some whites perceived as "Negroes getting too much, too fast, with too much turmoil."

Lyndon Johnson, of course, didn't see it that way. In fact, in a speech to Congress he later picked up the rallying cry of young blacks seeking equity in America and announced to America and the world that "we shall overcome." Lyndon Johnson did overcome in 1964. When the Wallace candidacy dropped away, the backlash vote found a haven with Barry Goldwater, and Mr. Johnson noted one day that there were many Americans who believed in "frontlash" and a fair deal for blacks. Indeed there were, as the election returns showed.

By any purely statistical standard, the election of 1964 was "tidal." Lyndon Johnson—a then popular, activist President in a prosperous, peaceful time—won with 61% of the vote.

But the main reason behind the vote was a strange, onetime wave in the political ocean: Barry Goldwater. One of the precepts of this book is that American politicians normally drive toward the center of the political spectrum. But Senator Goldwater chose instead to head for the right flank. In so doing, Senator Goldwater showed what happens when a candidate moves away from the center: A political stick of dynamite is lit. As perceived by tens of millions of Americans, Senator Goldwater was that worst of all political types: an extremist. As so perceived, he sought to wreck Social Security, to sell TVA, and to put the decision to use nuclear weapons in the hands of field commanders in Vietnam. Voters were apparently voting neither on "backlash" nor on "frontlash," but on what might be called "otherlash"—*i.e.* Goldwater himself. When the electoral dynamite blew up, Goldwater was still holding the charge, still explaining that what America really wanted was a choice, not an echo.

The Goldwater defeat, however, was a one-shot loss owing mostly to the voters' perception of the candidate as an anticentrist and radical. It was a big electoral wave, but not the sort of continuing tidal phenomenon that we have been chronicling here, such as the tides started by McKinley in 1896 and Franklin Roosevelt in 1932. As evidence, by 1968 no one was talking about junking Social Security, selling TVA, or putting nuclear weapons in the control of field commanders.

But perhaps ironically, perhaps coincidentally, and perhaps neither, it was the perception of Goldwater as an extreme candidate that masked the fact that among national major-party Presidential candidates, he was the first to touch the raw nerve ending of the Social Issue. And as he was losing votes on TVA, "nukes," and Social Security, he was in some places gaining votes on race and crime. In Leake County, Mississippi, Barry Goldwater got 96% of the vote whereas Richard Nixon had received only 9% of the vote four years earlier. Farther north, in the largely "ethnic" Ward 2 of Baltimore, Goldwater got 24% of the vote whereas Nixon had received 15%.

Listen to Barry Goldwater phrase the Social Issue as he addresses the 1964 Republican Convention in San Francisco:

> *. . . Tonight there is violence in our streets, corruption in our highest offices, aimlessness among our youth, anxiety among our elderly, and there's a virtual despair among the many who look beyond material success toward the inner meaning of their lives. . . .*
>
> *The growing menace in our country tonight, to personal safety, to life, to limb and property, in homes, in churches, on the playgrounds and places of business, particularly in our great cities, is the mounting concern of every thoughtful citizen in the United States. Security from domestic violence, no less than from foreign aggression, is the most elementary and fundamental purpose of any government, and a government that cannot fulfill this purpose is one that cannot long command the loyalty of its citizens.*

That Goldwater was speaking to a real issue that rather suddenly was concerning tens of millions of Americans is demonstrated from the following list published by the Gallup organization. It concerns what the American public perceives as "the most important problem" facing the nation, and it covers a full decade. The italics are ours.

1958
Feb. 2   Keeping out of war

Mar. 23	Unemployment
Nov. 16	Keeping out of war
1959	
Feb. 27	Keeping world peace, high cost of living, *integration struggle*
Oct. 16	Keeping out of war, high cost of living
1960	
Mar. 2	Defense "lag"
July 8	Relations with Russia
1961	
Mar. 15	Keeping out of war
1962	
Apr. 29	International tensions, high cost of living, unemployment
1963	
July 21	*Racial problems,* Russia
Oct. 2	*Racial problems*
1964	
Mar. 1	Keeping out of war
May 20	*Racial problems,* foreign affairs
June 3	*Integration,* unemployment
July 29	*Racial problems*
Aug. 21	International problems
Oct. 11	International problems
Nov. 18	Vietnam war, medical care for the aged
1965	
Apr. 16	*Civil rights*
May 9	Education, *crime*
June 11	International problems
Aug. 11	Vietnam war, *civil rights*
Oct. 13	*Civil rights,* Vietnam war
Dec. 1	Vietnam war, *civil rights*
1966	
May 27	Vietnam crisis, threat of war
Sept. 11	Vietnam war, *racial problems,* cost of living
1967	
Oct. 18	High cost of living, taxes, health problems, cost of education, Vietnam war
1968	
Feb. 28	*Crime, civil rights,* high cost of living
May 26	Vietnam war, *crime and lawlessness, race relations,* high cost of living

Aug. 4	Vietnam war, *crime and lawlessness, race relations,* high cost of living
Sept. 8	Vietnam war, *crime, civil rights* and high cost of living
Oct. 30	Vietnam war, *crime, race relations,* high cost of living
1969	
March	Vietnam war, *crime and lawlessness, race relations,* high cost of living
1970	
February	Vietnam war, high cost of living, *race relations, crime*

Suddenly, some time in the 1960's, "crime" and "race" and "lawlessness" and "civil rights" became the most important domestic issues in America.

The nondomestic issue of Vietnam was "more important" but as will be shown later in detail, Americans were not voting primarily on a pro-Vietnam or anti-Vietnam basis despite its "importance." An examination of public opinion polls over recent years shows an extremely ambivalent set of feelings about the Vietnam War, circling around the desire to "get out without bugging out." Insofar as both Presidents Johnson and Nixon stayed roughly close to this position, neither man was gaining or losing massive numbers of votes on the substantive hawk versus dove positions on Vietnam. This will be demonstrated. Some votes in 1968 did swing on a tangential feeling of malaise and nonaccomplishment in the field of foreign affairs generally and Vietnam specifically, but the numbers were not large. Many votes, however, did swing on the domestic side effects of the Vietnam War: disruption, dissention, demonstrations.

Generally speaking, it is the feeling of the authors that Americans vote for candidates largely on the basis of domestic issues, not international issues. The ever-potent Economic Issue always holds a high priority, and in a time of economic crisis—great inflation, depression, deep and lengthy recession—the Economic Issue will likely be the crucial Voting Issue in a national election. This is as it has been, as it is, and as it will likely continue to be.

But now a new element has been added. To the authors, the italicized words above seem to herald the clear emergence of a new and major Voting Issue in America, an issue so powerful that it may rival bimetallism and depression in American political history, an issue powerful enough that under certain circumstances it can compete in political potency with the older economic issues. We call this force the Social Issue, and, as shall now be noted, it is complex, and it deals with more than just race and crime as listed above.

We can begin by recounting some of the events and circumstances of recent years that swept the Social Issue to the forefront of the American political scene. They constitute a unique set of converging factors that acted one upon the other, beating ripples into waves and perhaps moving waves into a tide that will be politically observable for decades to come. There was, first, the "crime wave." From a professional data-gathering point of view, the FBI statistics on crime are probably the worst collection of numbers regularly put between federal covers. Still, in recent years, there can be no doubt that there *has* been a sharp increase in crime, no matter how the statistics are tended. The data concerning "offenses against persons" show a 106% increase from 1960 to 1968. These crimes include the ones that frighten the public the most: murder; rape; robbery; aggravated assault. It is of interest to note that a great deal of the "crime wave" can be attributed to a sharp increase in the numbers of young people in recent years. There were more than half again as many Americans aged fifteen to nineteen in 1968 as there were fifteen years earlier, and these crimes that frighten are precisely the crimes that are disproportionately committed by young people.

But citizens afraid of being mugged weren't buying statistical explanations; they were buying guns for protection. Tens of millions of Americans felt unsafe as they walked the streets of their city neighborhoods at night. That the political jugular ran through these same attitudinal neighborhoods could have been gleaned from the results of the special election in New York City in 1966 concerning the setting up of a civilian review board as a check on alleged police brutality. Almost every major politician and Establishment leader endorsed the plan. Yet the voters turned it down 2 to 1. By August, 1968, when Mr. Nixon delivered his acceptance speech in Miami, he knew full well the potency of the crime issue. He spoke of "cities enveloped in smoke and flame" and of "sirens in the night." And then he said: "Time is running out for the merchants of crime and corruption in American society. The wave of crime is not going to be the wave of the future in the United States of America. We shall reestablish freedom from fear in America. . . ."

Race is certainly a second key element of the Social Issue, and of course, the racial question has always been with America. But in the last decade there has been a sharp, yet apparently paradoxical change in the perceptions that white Americans have of black Americans.

This can perhaps best be seen as a series of three fleeting video scenes flashed upon a television screen.

The first picture shows a young, clean-cut black man seated at a lunch counter in a Southern state. In the already archaic language of the late 1950's the young black is known as a New Negro—college-educated, articulate, neat. As he is seated at the lunch counter, a wiry, slack-jawed white man comes up behind him and pours ketchup on his head. Quietly, and with great dignity, the black man remains in his seat, determined to gain for himself and his people the elementary civil rights so long denied. The second video scene shows buildings aflame, sirens wailing, and mobs of young black youths racing across a city street. We see next a jagged plate-glass window. Through the window comes a grinning young black, excited as at a carnival. He is carrying a television set.

The third scene is at Cornell University. A group of black students emerge from a campus building they have recently "taken over." They are carrying rifles.

It would be wrong to say that these three scenes represent the facts of the recent racial situation in America, but they do represent the perceptions that many Americans had and have, and these perceptions lay at the root of changing white attitudes as the Social Issue emerged. And yet, at the same time that white fear and resentment were growing, white attitudes toward civil rights for blacks were probably *liberalizing*. This paradox is explored later in this book.

In any event, in 1964 Harlem had a riot. In 1965 Watts had a riot. By 1966 every major city in America was asking itself, "Would it happen here?"—and major riots did erupt in Hough and Chicago. The apparent peak of a series of long hot summers was reached in 1967, when first Newark and then Detroit exploded in an orgy of violence, disorder, and looting. In April, 1968, on the night of Martin Luther King's assassination, outbreaks were reported in more than 100 cities, with Washington, Chicago, and Baltimore taking particularly heavy damage. The summers of 1968 and 1969 were quieter, but the electoral damage had been done. The electoral nerve had been rubbed raw. Voters were frightened and angry.

And then there was "kidlash." Among a highly publicized segment of young America, hair got long, skirts got short, foul language became ordinary, drugs became common, respect for elders became limited, the invasion and sacking of offices of college administrators became the initiation rite—and adults became fearful and upset. Again.

A fourth element of the Social Issue might simply be called values. Pornography blossomed with legal sanction; sexual codes became more permissive; priests were getting married; sex education was taught in the schools.

Further, the man who works hard, pays his taxes, rears his children—the man who has always been the hero of the American folk mythology—now found himself living in an era where the glorified man is the antihero; morose, introspective, unconcerned with God, country, family, or tax bill.

Finally, to this already combustible mixture, a new highly flammable element was added: the Vietnam protest movement. Suddenly American boys and girls were seen burning American flags on television; clergymen were pouring containers of blood on draft records; the President was jeered.

All these elements acted on one another and on the American voter. The Social Issue was in full flower. It may be defined as a set of public attitudes concerning the more personally frightening aspects of disruptive social change. Crime frightens. Young people, when they invade the dean's office, or destroy themselves with drugs, or destroy a corporate office with a bomb, frighten. Pornography, nudity, promiscuity are perceived to tear away the underpinnings of a moral code, and this, too, is frightening. Dissent that involves street riots frightens.

Put together, it spelled out great change. It was change that some few Americans perceived as beneficial, but measurably larger numbers did not. Most voters felt they gained little from crime, or integration, or wild kids, or new values, or dissent. Of many of the new facets of American life they were downright fearful. These voters became the core of an anti-dissent dissent, feeling the breath of the Social Issue hot and uncomfortable on their necks. When these voters had a chance to vote against it—in 1968 and again in 1969—they did. Other voters, approving of some of the changes but profoundly disturbed by others, felt only confusion.

Demography Is Destiny: Middle-Aged, Middle-Class Whites

If young, poor, and black are what most voters aren't, let us consider the electorate for what it largely is: white; median family income of $8,622; median age of about forty-seven. In short: middle-aged, middle-class whites.

This middle constituency can also be described as middle-educated. Typically, the middleman in America is a high school graduate, no more, no less:

VOTERS, BY YEARS OF SCHOOL COMPLETED, 1968

Years of School Completed	Percent of Electorate
Elementary school or less	22
High school:	
1–3 years	16
4 years	36
College:	
1–3 years	13
4 years or more	13
	(U.S. Census Bureau)

In other words:

—Almost three in four voters have never set foot in a college class-room (74%).

—Only one in eight voters has been graduated from college—any col-lege—with major fields of study including animal husbandry and physical education (13%). . . .

Accordingly, if we are to add to our categories of unyoung, unpoor, and unblack, we may say that the typical voter is, and will be through the sev-enties, "uncollege."

The typical voter is no "intellectual," if we assume that an intellectual has at least a college degree, but that not all college graduates are neces-sarily intellectual. If we move up the qualification a bit and apply the term only to those with *advanced* college degrees (MA, PhD, and the like) the weight of the oft-discussed "intellectual vote" is ridiculously minuscule.

But if the electorate is not "intellectual," it is most certainly not com-posed of ignoramuses. For a candidate to treat the voters largely as jerks (62% are at least high school graduates) would be as disastrous as con-sidering them largely as intellectuals. Indeed, it might be impressionis-tically noted here that it is the authors' opinion that the inherent wisdom of the American voter is substantial. This point will be elaborated upon later. For now, let us observe rashly that the corporate wisdom of voters is often greater than that of politicians. For a truly shocking statement, it can be said that voters are even wiser than political theorists. . . .

Middle-income, middle-aged, middle-educated, and white, the voters in the middle can also be viewed vocationally as men and women primar-ily "at work with their hands, and not exclusively their minds."

VOTERS BY OCCUPATIONAL STATUS, 1968

	Percent of Total Electorate
High level white-collar workers[a]	19
Manual, service, clerical & sales workers	42
Farm workers	3
Unemployed	1
Not in labor force	
Women (mostly housewives)	28
Men over 65 (mostly retired)	5
Other men	2
	(*U.S. Census Bureau*)

[a] Professional, technical, managerial, officials and proprietors.

Some of the numbers need further explanations:

The number of high-level white-collar workers is climbing. In the 1964 election the percentage was 16% compared to the 19% in 1968. If one allocates a proportionate share of the "housewives" and considers them as the spouses of these high-level white-collar workers, we might estimate that about 27% of the voters are in the *families* of those white-collar workers.

Of course, that leaves about 73% who are *not* in such families, still the vast majority; all *those* voters are in families where the earners are working with their hands. When one realizes that fact, the rhetoric of George Wallace can be fully savored, at least for its demographic accuracy:

Now what are the real issues that exist today in these United
States? It is the trend of pseudo-intellectual government, where a
select, elite group have written guidelines in bureaus and court
decisions, have spoken from some pulpits, some college campuses,
some newspaper offices, looking down their noses at the average man
on the street, the glassworker, the steelworker, the autoworker,
and the textile worker, the farmer, the policeman, the beautician
and the barber, and the little businessman, *saying to him that you do*
not know how to get up in the morning or go to bed at night
unless we write you a guideline. . . .

Furthermore, consider for a moment that "policeman" falls into the "work with hands" category. When the "cops" clashed with the "kids" at the 1968 Democratic Convention in Chicago, the journalists and many liberal politicians (high-level white-collars both), picked up the cry, "They're beating up our children." This was accurate: Most of the "kids" came from high-level white-collar homes. On the other hand, the other 73% of the voters could say, "Those student punks are beating up *our* children, or *our* husbands, or *our* fathers." That, too, would be accurate if one considers the policeman as a respected part of the nonelite.

After the convention, the opinion pollsters asked the public what they thought about the Chicago confrontation, and about two of every three Americans said they thought the police acted correctly, which coincides rather well with the occupational categorizations above. The old political axiom applies: "It depends on whose ox is being gored," or, in other words, "It depends on who is the clobberer and who the clobberee."

The confrontation at Chicago probably etched the lines of social class as sharply as they have ever been drawn in America. The fight in the streets was not between hawks and doves. For many it was perceived as between "elitists" and "plain people." There are more plain people than elitists in America.

Finally, and paradoxically, how do these "high-level" families vote?

Despite all the recent comment about elitist Democratic intellectuals, the cold fact remains that the elite in America has a Republican majority. They are the doctors, bankers, and businessmen, with a good proportion of the lawyers and scientists as well. Only the vocal minority of the high-level voters are generally Democratic leaners. In the 1968 election the "professional and business" group went 56–34% for Nixon over Humphrey. The Democrats, despite the Agnew hoopla about the Democratic elitist establishmentarians, are those "plain people who work with their hands." Manual workers went 50–35% for Humphrey over Nixon.

That the Democrats have held the allegiance of most of the "plain people" has been the critical fact in American Presidential politics for more than a third of a century. That is why Democrats have won so often. Now, upon the shoals of the Social Issue, there seems to be the possibility of a rupture in that pattern. If it happens, it will be bad news for Democrats. If it can be prevented from happening, if it can be reversed, it will be happy days again for Democrats. . . .

Next item: More than half the voters are women—51.9% to be precise. They show up in the preceding table not only as housewives, but as substantial parts of both the large employed groups: clerks, secretaries, teacher, etc. In America today, 43% of the women are working.

Since the advent of woman suffrage, no candidate for President has been solidly identified as a "woman's candidate." Women vote pretty much as their men do, or vice versa. In the last five Presidential elections, the largest margin of variance between men and women voters was 6% in the 1956 election—with women more likely to vote for General Eisenhower than Adlai Stevenson. Curiously, despite the legend building that has gone on about John Kennedy's "appeal to women voters," he would have lost the 1960 election had only women voted. In 1960, men voted 52–48% for JFK; women voted 51–49% for Nixon. As solace to Mr. Nixon, had only women voted in 1968, Hubert Humphrey would have won the popular vote, but the differentials aren't great in either case.

Middle-income, middle-aged, middle-educated, white, and what else? Protestant, mostly:

VOTERS, BY RELIGION

	Percentage
Protestant	68
Catholic	25
Jewish	4

Catholics in America are substantially more likely than Protestants to be first- and second-generation Americans (Italians, Poles, Mexicans, Puerto Ricans) and are more likely to be residents of big cities. Residents of big cities and so-called ethnic Americans have traditionally been more likely to vote Democratic. Accordingly, Catholics are somewhat more likely to vote Democratic than are Protestants, but with the single exception of 1960, when Catholicism itself became an issue, there is little recent evidence that Catholics vote heavily *as* Catholics. Catholics will usually vote a few extra points for a Catholic candidate, but not always:

McCARTHY versus HUMPHREY, JULY, 1968   (Percent)

	McCarthy	Humphrey
National	48	40
Catholics	47	41
Protestants	49	39
(Gallup)		

It is interesting to note how fast an issue can be laid to rest in American politics. Such results—Protestants outvoting Catholics for a Catholic candidate—would have been wholly inconceivable in the years between the defeat of Al Smith in 1928 and the victory of John F. Kennedy in 1960. In November, 1928, a Midwestern newspaper reported the defeat of Al Smith, a Catholic, under the banner headline THANK GOD, AMERICA IS SAVED. Today Catholicism seems thoroughly dead as a political issue. . . .

With the exceptions of blacks and Latin Americans, the Jews in the United States are the most solidly liberal-Democratic bloc in the entire electorate. Thus, in 1968, Jews voted 81% for Humphrey. During the years of Franklin Roosevelt the proportion was even higher, according to the studies of Lawrence H. Fuchs in *The Political Behavior of American Jews.* Jewish voting patterns are generally unique in that the vote is usually a liberal and Democratic one even among the wealthy and well educated. Among the non-Jewish well-to-do the trend among the wealthy and well educated goes the other way: Republican.

The so-called ethnic vote is hard to calculate. For how many generations does an Italian-American family remain under the influence of the first half of the hyphenation? How does one classify the children of a Polish father and an Italian mother who moved recently from an in-city "Little Italy" to a suburban neighborhood called Piney Grove? Or, as the late Joseph P. Kennedy, Sr., said, "How long do I have to live here to be an American?"

Yet the ethnics exist, or at least there are many precincts where 70% or 80% of the voters are of Italian, or Slavic, or Mexican origin. For the most part, ethnics have tended to vote Democratic:

ETHNIC GROUPS, VOTE FOR PRESIDENT, 1968 (Percent)

	Humphrey	Nixon	Wallace
Latin Americans			
East (mostly Puerto Ricans)	81	16	3
South (mostly Mexican Americans)	92	7	1
West (mostly Mexican Americans)	81	17	2
Slavic	65	24	11
Italian	51	39	10
			(NBC data)

The "solid" Democratic-liberal group is clearly the "Latin-American" one.

Of more than passing psephological interest is the fact that ethnics are dying out in America and becoming a smaller percentage of the total population. In 1940, Americans of foreign stock (*i.e.*, first- or second-generation) constituted 26% of the population. Twenty years later, in 1960, the foreign stock constituted 18% of the population. An estimate for 1970 shows the foreign stock at 15%, and in ethnic neighborhoods all over America the remark one hears is the same: "All the kids are moving out to the suburbs."

On the surface of it, at least, this data would tend to say that as the masses of immigrants and their children breed and die out, then it may be said that ethnicism in American political life may be dying out also. A first-generation Polish stevedore from Brooklyn via Krakow may feel "Polish." His grandson, the electrician who lives in Hempstead, Long Island, may feel more like an "electrician from Hempstead" than like a "Pole." But even this is too simple. As Nathan Glazer and Daniel Moynihan have pointed out in *Beyond the Melting Pot*, the ethnic feelings may last for far longer than the point when, after two generations, the Census stops classifying people as "foreign stock." Surely, tens of millions of Americans still feel deep ties and ethnic, racial, or religious allegiance as Poles, Hungarians, Jews, blacks, Italians, Mexicans—as well as "just plain Americans." And frequently they still vote along these ethnic lines, and politicians can still attempt all the ethnic appeals with some success. In certain areas, a politician can do worse than to be found with his mouth full of blintzes and knishes, or kielbasa, or soul food. A middle-aged, middle-income, high-school-educated, white Protestant, who works with his hands, decreasingly ethnic—our portrait of the Middle Voter is beginning to emerge. What else? Generally metropolitan, and increasingly suburban, following the pattern of the American postwar hegira: from farms to cities, from cities to suburbs.

U.S. POPULATION DISTRIBUTION

	1950 %	1960 %	1968 %	Gain in Population, 1950–68
Central cities	35	32	29	6 million
Suburb	24	31	35	32 million (!)
Small cities, towns, and rural	41	37	36	9 million

Those are population figures; the *voting* figures are about the same, but give the suburbanite a one-point bonus for a higher participation rate:

VOTERS BY PLACE OF RESIDENCE, 1968

	Percentage of Electorate
Central cities	29.6
Suburbs	35.6
Small cities, towns, and farms	34.8

Among many of the biggest, and oldest, metropolitan areas the voting figures etch in sharp relief this demographic movement from city to suburb. Comparing the 1948 election to the 1968 election, one finds that New York City *lost* more than half a million voters, while the suburbs around New York City (Westchester, Nassau, and Suffolk counties) gained 750,000 voters. The city of Chicago *lost* 400,000 voters; the Chicago suburbs *gained* 500,000. The city of Minneapolis: down 40,000; the Minneapolis suburbs: up 160,000. The term "central cities" refers to cities with populations of 50,000 or more. Accordingly, 2 of every 3 American voters live in or near (suburb) a large city. About an additional 15% live in cities of between 10,000 and 50,000. Accordingly, it is fair to view most of the American electorate as metropolitan or, alternately, as urban.

Because, at least through 1968, the state has been the basic unit of Presidential politics, it is very important to note in which *states* these metropolitan areas lie. And unless a national popular vote replaces the electoral college, then the *state* will remain of vital importance to political strategists.

There has been much talk of a Southern Strategy, a Border State Strategy, a Sun State Strategy, each supposedly designed to corral enough states to win an election for Republicans. Those are excellent strategies to convince your opponents to use. As for the authors, our geographic strategy is an elementary one called Quadcali. It is the essence of simplicity. If one draws a *quad*rangle from Massachusetts to Washington, D.C., to Illinois, to Wisconsin, and then adds in *Cali*fornia, it includes a majority of Americans. Where Americans live, they vote. Where a majority of them live and vote is where Presidents are elected.

In all, 266 electoral votes are needed to win. It is estimated that Quadcali will comprise about 300 electoral votes after the 1970 census.

Of the sixteen states in Quadcali, all but one (Indiana) are either Democratic or close—the Republican margin of victory being no higher than 4.5% and usually slimmer than that. In a tidal year, all those close states can drop like a row of falling dominoes—a familiar image. Carry Quadcali—win the election. Lose Quadcali—lose the election. Split Quadcali close—and it will be a close election that no book can tell you about in advance.

So there you have it: Middle Voter. A metropolitan Quadcalian, middle-aged, middle-income, middle-educated, Protestant, in a family whose working members work more likely with hands than abstractly with head.

Think about that picture when you consider the American power structure. Middle Voter is a forty-seven-year-old housewife from the outskirts of Dayton, Ohio, whose husband is a machinist. She very likely has a somewhat different view of life and politics from that of a twenty-four-year-old instructor of political science at Yale. Now the young man from Yale may feel that he *knows* more about politics than the machinist's wife from suburban Dayton, and of course, in one sense he does. But he does not know much about politics, or psephology, unless he understands what is bothering that lady in Dayton and unless he understands that her circumstances in large measure dictate her concerns.

To know that the lady in Dayton is afraid to walk the streets alone at night, to know that she has a mixed view about blacks and civil rights because before moving to the suburbs she lived in a neighborhood that became all black, to know that her brother-in-law is a policeman, to know that she does not have the money to move if her new neighborhood deteriorates, to know that she is deeply distressed that her son is going to a community junior college where LSD was found on the campus—to know all this is the beginning of contemporary political wisdom.

VII. Voices in Protest

18. Students for a Democratic Society

The Port Huron Statement

Young people were prominent in the early manifestations of rebellion against the cultural pieties and political complacency characteristic of the 1950s. The resistance began with the activities of liberal and socialist groups at a few universities and picked up momentum as college students swelled the ranks of civil rights demonstrations and sit-ins during 1959 and 1960. In short order, a full panoply of social ills became manifest: materialism, militarism, imperialism, poverty, racism, and political obstructionism.

The first group to mobilize the amorphous dissent with any success (the Left was never well organized during the 1960s) was the Students for a Democratic Society, founded in June 1960 in New York. At first associated with the socialist League for Industrial America, SDS struck out on its own after its national convention held in the summer of 1962 at a United Auto Workers Center in Port Huron, Michigan. Organized by student activists from the University of Michigan, the convention approved a manifesto drafted by Tom Hayden, "The Port Huron Statement," which became an intellectual landmark of the early student Left. The document provides a broad critique of American society and an "agenda for a generation" of radical politics. It is moderate in tone, cautious in its assertions, and nondoctrinaire in ideology. With restraint and dignity, the 1962 statement expresses a desire to overcome alienation and the sense of powerlessness with "participatory democracy," Emersonian self-reliance, a revitalization of community life, and a genuine politics based on issues, dialogue, and social conscience. Rejecting both the ideology of anticommunism and communism itself, it advocates working within existing institutions, the labor movement, and the major political parties.

SDS moved steadily leftward during the 1960s as may be seen by comparing the "Port Huron Statement," parts of which are printed below, with "You Don't Need a Weatherman To Know Which Way the Wind Blows," drafted by the Weatherman faction of SDS in 1969.

Introduction: Agenda for a Generation

We are people of this generation, bred in at least modest comfort, housed now in universities, looking uncomfortably to the world we inherit.

When we were kids the United States was the wealthiest and strongest country in the world; the only one with the atom bomb, the least scarred by modern war, an initiator of the United Nations that we thought would distribute Western influence throughout the world. Freedom and equality for each individual, government of, by, and for the people—these American values we found good, principles by which we could live as men. Many of us began maturing in complacency.

As we grew, however, our comfort was penetrated by events too troubling to dismiss. First, the permeating and victimizing fact of human degradation, symbolized by the Southern struggle against racial bigotry, compelled most of us from silence to activism. Second, the enclosing fact of the Cold War, symbolized by the presence of the Bomb, brought awareness that we ourselves, and our friends, and millions of abstract "others" we knew more directly because of our common peril, might die at any time. We might deliberately ignore, or avoid, or fail to feel all other human problems, but not these two, for these were too immediate and crushing in their impact, too challenging in the demand that we as individuals take the responsibility for encounter and resolution.

While these and other problems either directly oppressed us or rankled our consciences and became our own subjective concerns, we began to see complicated and disturbing paradoxes in our surrounding America. The declaration "all men are created equal . . ." rang hollow before the facts of Negro life in the South and the big cities of the North. The proclaimed peaceful intentions of the United States contradicted its economic and military investments in the Cold War status quo.

We witnessed, and continue to witness, other paradoxes. With nuclear energy whole cities can easily be powered, yet the dominant nation-states seem more likely to unleash destruction greater than that incurred in all wars of human history. Although our own technology is destroying old and creating new forms of social organization, men still tolerate meaningless work and idleness. While two-thirds of mankind suffers undernourishment, our own upper classes revel amidst superfluous abundance. Although world population is expected to double in forty years, the nations still tolerate anarchy as a major principle of international conduct and uncontrolled exploitation governs the sapping of the earth's physical resources. Although mankind desperately needs revolutionary leadership, America rests in national stalemate, its goals ambiguous and tradition-bound instead of informed and clear, its democratic system apathetic and manipulated rather than "of, by, and for the people."

Not only did tarnish appear on our image of American virtue, not only did disillusion occur when the hypocrisy of American ideals was discovered, but we began to sense that what we had originally seen as the American Golden Age was actually the decline of an era. The worldwide outbreak of revolution against colonialism and imperialism, the entrenchment of totalitarian states, the menace of war, overpopulation, international disorder, supertechnology—these trends were testing the tenacity of our own commitment to democracy and freedom and our abilities to visualize their application to a world in upheaval.

Our work is guided by the sense that we may be the last generation in the experiment with living. But we are a minority—the vast majority of our people regard the temporary equilibriums of our society and world as eternally functional parts. In this is perhaps the outstanding paradox: we ourselves are imbued with urgency, yet the message of our society is that there is no viable alternative to the present. Beneath the reassuring tones of the politicians, beneath the common opinion that America will "muddle through," beneath the stagnation of those who have closed their minds to the future, is the pervading feeling that there simply are no alternatives, that our times have witnessed the exhaustion not only of Utopias, but of any new departures as well. Feeling the press of complexity upon the emptiness of life, people are fearful of the thought that at any moment things might be thrust out of control. They fear change itself, since change might smash whatever invisible framework seems to hold back chaos for them now. For most Americans, all crusades are suspect, threatening. The fact that each individual sees apathy in his fellows perpetuates the common reluctance to organize for change. The dominant institutions are complex enough to blunt the minds of their potential critics, and entrenched enough to swiftly dissipate or entirely repel the energies of protest and reform, thus limiting human expectancies. Then, too, we are a materially improved society, and by our own improvements we seem to have weakened the case for further change.

Some would have us believe that Americans feel contentment amidst prosperity—but might it not better be called a glaze above deeply felt anxieties about their role in the new world? And if these anxieties produce a developed indifference to human affairs, do they not as well produce a yearning to believe there *is* an alternative to the present, that something *can* be done to change circumstances in the school, the workplaces, the bureaucracies, the government? It is to this latter yearning, at once the spark and engine of change, that we direct our present appeal. The search for truly democratic alternatives to the present, and a commitment to social experimentation with them, is a worthy and fulfilling human enterprise, one which moves us and, we hope, others today. On such a basis do we offer this document of our convictions and analysis: as an effort in understanding and changing the conditions of humanity in the late twentieth century, an effort rooted in the ancient, still unfulfilled conception of man attaining determining influence over his circumstances of life.

Values

Making values explicit—an initial task in establishing alternatives—is an activity that has been devalued and corrupted. The conventional moral terms of the age, the politician moralities—"free world," "people's democracies"—reflect realities poorly, if at all, and seem to function more as ruling myths than as descriptive principles. But neither has our experience in the universities brought us moral enlightenment. Our professors and administrators sacrifice controversy to public relations; their curriculums change more slowly than the living events of the world; their skills and silence are purchased by investors in the arms race; passion is called unscholastic. The questions we might want raised—what is really important? can we live in a different and better way? if we wanted to change society, how would we do it?—are not thought to be questions of a "fruitful, empirical nature," and thus are brushed aside.

Unlike youth in other countries we are used to moral leadership being exercised and moral dimensions being clarified by our elders. But today, for us, not even the liberal and socialist preachments of the past seem adequate to the forms of the present. Consider the old slogans: Capitalism Cannot Reform Itself, United Front Against Fascism, General Strike, All Out on May Day. Or, more recently, No Cooperation with Commies and Fellow Travelers, Ideologies are Exhausted, Bipartisanship, No Utopias. These are incomplete, and there are few new prophets. It has been said that our liberal and socialist predecessors were plagued by vision without program, while our own generation is plagued by program without vision. All around us there is astute grasp of method, technique—the committee, the *ad hoc* group, the lobbyist, the hard and soft sell, the make, the projected image—but, if pressed critically, such expertise is incompetent to explain its implicit ideals. It is highly fashionable to identify oneself by old categories, or by naming a respected political figure, or by explaining "how we would vote" on various issues.

Theoretic chaos has replaced the idealistic thinking of old—and, unable to reconstitute theoretic order, men have condemned idealism itself. Doubt has replaced hopefulness—and men act out a defeatism that is labeled realistic. The decline of utopia and hope is in fact one of the defining features of social life today. The reasons are various: the dreams of the older left were perverted by Stalinism and never recreated; the congressional stalemate makes men narrow their view of the possible; the specialization of human activity leaves little room for sweeping thought; the horrors of the twentieth century, symbolized in the gas ovens and concentration camps and atom bombs, have blasted hopefulness. To be idealistic is to be considered apocalyptic, deluded. To have no serious aspirations, on the contrary, is to be "tough-minded."

In suggesting social goals and values, therefore, we are aware of entering a sphere of some disrepute. Perhaps matured by the past, we have no sure formulas, no closed theories—but that does not mean values are beyond discussion and tentative determination. A first task of any social movement is to convince people that the search for orienting theories and the creation of human values is complex but worthwhile. We are aware that to avoid platitudes we must analyze the concrete conditions of social order. But to direct such an analysis we must use the guideposts of basic principles. Our own social values involve conceptions of human beings, human relationships, and social systems.

We regard *men* as infinitely precious and possessed of unfulfilled capacities for reason, freedom, and love. In affirming these principles we are aware of countering perhaps the dominant conceptions of man in the twentieth century: that he is a thing to be manipulated, and that he is inherently incapable of directing his own affairs. We oppose the depersonalization that reduces human beings to the status of things—if anything, the brutalities of the twentieth century teach that means and ends are intimately related, that vague appeals to "posterity" cannot justify the mutilations of the present. We oppose, too, the doctrine of human incompetence because it rests essentially on the modern fact that men have been "competently" manipulated into incompetence—we see little reason why men cannot meet with increasing skill the complexities and responsibilities of their situation, if society is organized not for minority, but for majority, participation in decision-making.

Men have unrealized potential for self-cultivation, self-direction, self-understanding, and creativity. It is this potential that we regard as crucial and to which we appeal, not to the human potentiality for violence, unreason, and submission to authority. The goal of man and society should be human independence: a concern not with image of popularity but with finding a meaning in life that is personally authentic; a quality of mind not compulsively driven by a sense of powerlessness, nor one which unthinkingly adopts status values, nor one which represses all threats to its habits, but one which has full, spontaneous access to present and past experiences, one which easily unites the fragmented parts of personal history, one which openly faces problems which are troubling and unresolved; one with an intuitive awareness of possibilities, an active sense of curiosity, an ability and willingness to learn.

This kind of independence does not mean egotistic individualism—the object is not to have one's way so much as it is to have a way that is one's own. Nor do we deify man—we merely have faith in his potential.

Human relationships should involve fraternity and honesty. Human interdependence is contemporary fact; human brotherhood must be willed, however, as a condition of future survival and as the most appropriate form of social relations. Personal links between man and man are needed, especially to go beyond the partial and fragmentary bonds of function that bind men only as worker to worker, employer to employee, teacher to student, American to Russian.

Loneliness, estrangement, isolation describe the vast distance between man and man today. These dominant tendencies cannot be overcome by better personnel management, nor by improved gadgets, but only when a love of man overcomes the idolatrous worship of things by man. As the individualism we affirm is not egoism, the selflessness we affirm is not self-elimination. On the contrary, we believe in generosity of a kind that imprints one's unique individual qualities in the relation to other men, and to all human activity. Further, to dislike isolation is not to favor the abolition of privacy; the latter differs from isolation in that it occurs or is abolished according to individual will.

We would replace power rooted in possession, privilege, or circumstance by power and uniqueness rooted in love, reflectiveness, reason, and creativity. As a *social system* we seek the establishment of a democracy of individual participation, governed by two central aims: that the individual share in those social decisions determining the quality and direction of his life; that society be organized to encourage independence in men and provide the media for their common participation.

In a participatory democracy, the political life would be based in several root principles:

That decision-making of basic social consequence be carried on by public groupings.

That politics be seen positively, as the art of collectively creating an acceptable pattern of social relations.

That politics has the function of bringing people out of isolation and into community, thus being a necessary, though not sufficient, means of finding meaning in personal life.

That the political order should serve to clarify problems in a way instrumental to their solution; it should provide outlets for the expression of personal grievance and aspiration; opposing views should be organized so as to illuminate choices and facilitate the attainment of goals; channels should be commonly available to relate men to knowledge and to power so that private problems—from bad recreation facilities to personal alienation—are formulated as general issues.

The economic sphere would have as its basis the principles:

That work should involve incentives worthier than money or survival. It should be educative, not stultifying; creative, not mechanical; self-directed, not manipulated, encouraging independence, a respect for others, a sense of dignity and a willingness to accept social responsibility, since it is this experience that has crucial influence on habits, perceptions and individual ethics.

That the economic experience is so personally decisive that the individual must share in its full determination.

That the economy itself is of such social importance that its major resources and means of production should be open to democratic participation and subject to democratic social regulation.

Like the political and economic ones, major social institutions—cultural, educational, rehabilitative, and others—should be generally organized with the well-being and dignity of man as the essential measure of success.

In social change or interchange, we find violence to be abhorrent because it requires generally the transformation of the target, be it a human being or a community of people, into a depersonalized object of hate. It is imperative that the means of violence be abolished and the institutions —local, national, international—that encourage nonviolence as a condition of conflict be developed.

These are our central values, in skeletal form. It remains vital to understand their denial or attainment in the context of the modern world.

The Students

In the last few years, thousands of American students demonstrated that they at least felt the urgency of the times. They moved actively and directly against racial injustices, the threat of war, violations of individual rights of conscience and, less frequently, against economic manipulation. They succeeded in restoring a small measure of controversy to the campuses after the stillness of the McCarthy period. They succeeded, too, in gaining some concessions from the people and institutions they opposed, especially in the fight against racial bigotry.

The significance of these scattered movements lies not in their success or failure in gaining objectives—at least not yet. Nor does the significance lie in the intellectual "competence" or "maturity" of the students involved—as some pedantic elders allege. The significance is in the fact the students are breaking the crust of apathy and overcoming the inner alienation that remain the defining characteristics of American college life.

If student movements for change are still rareties on the campus scene, what is commonplace there? The real campus, the familiar campus, is a place of private people, engaged in their notorious "inner emigration." It is a place of commitment to business-as-usual, getting ahead, playing it cool. It is a place of mass affirmation of the Twist, but mass reluctance toward the controversial public stance. Rules are accepted as "inevitable," bureaucracy as "just circumstances," irrelevance as "scholarship," selflessness as "martyrdom," politics as "just another way to make people, and an unprofitable one, too."

Almost no students value activity as citizens. Passive in public, they are hardly more idealistic in arranging their private lives: Gallup concludes they will settle for "low success, and won't risk high failure." There is not much willingness to take risks (not even in business), no setting of dangerous goals, no real conception of personal identity except one manufactured in the image of others, no real urge for personal fulfillment except to be almost as successful as the very successful people. Attention is being paid to social status (the quality of shirt collars, meeting people, getting wives or husbands, making solid contacts for later on) ; much, too, is paid to academic status (grades, honors, the med school rat race). But neglected generally is real intellectual status, the personal cultivation of the mind.

"Students don't even give a damn about the apathy," one has said. Apathy toward apathy begets a privately constructed universe, a place of systematic study schedules, two nights each week for beer, a girl or two, and early marriage; a framework infused with personality, warmth, and under control, no matter how unsatisfying otherwise.

Under these conditions university life loses all relevance to some. Four hundred thousand of our classmates leave college every year.

But apathy is not simply an attitude; it is a product of social institutions, and of the structure and organization of higher education itself. The extracurricular life is ordered according to *in loco parentis* theory, which ratifies the administration as the moral guardian of the young.

The accompanying "let's pretend" theory of student extracurricular affairs validates student government as a training center for those who want to spend their lives in political pretense, and discourages initiative from the more articulate, honest, and sensitive students. The bounds and style of controversy are delimited before controversy begins. The university "prepares" the student for "citizenship" through perpetual rehearsals and, usually, through emasculation of what creative spirit there is in the individual.

The academic life contains reinforcing counterparts to the way in which extracurricular life is organized. The academic world is founded on a teacher-student relation analogous to the parent-child relation which characterizes *in loco parentis*. Further, academia includes a radical separation of the student from the material of study. That which is studied, the social reality, is "objectified" to sterility, dividing the student from life

—just as he is restrained in active involvement by the deans controlling student government. The specialization of function and knowledge, admittedly necessary to our complex technological and social structure, has produced an exaggerated compartmentalization of study and understanding. This has contributed to an overly parochial view, by faculty, of the role of its research and scholarship, to a discontinuous and truncated understanding, by students, of the surrounding social order; and to a loss of personal attachment, by nearly all, to the worth of study as a humanistic enterprise.

There is, finally, the cumbersome academic bureaucracy extending throughout the academic as well as the extracurricular structures, contributing to the sense of outer complexity and inner powerlessness that transforms the honest searching of many students to a ratification of convention and, worse, to a numbness to present and future catastrophes. The size and financing systems of the university enhance the permanent trusteeship of the administrative bureaucracy, their power leading to a shift within the university toward the value standards of business and the administrative mentality. Huge foundations and other private financial interests shape the under-financed colleges and universities, not only making them more commercial, but less disposed to diagnose society critically, less open to dissent. Many social and physical scientists, neglecting the liberating heritage of higher learning, develop "human relations" or "morale-producing" techniques for the corporate economy, while others exercise their intellectual skills to accelerate the arms race. . . .

There are no convincing apologies for the contemporary malaise. While the world tumbles toward the final war, while men in other nations are trying desperately to alter events, while the very future qua future is uncertain—America is without community, impulse, without the inner momentum necessary for an age when societies cannot successfully perpetuate themselves by their military weapons, when democracy must be viable because of the quality of life, not its quantity of rockets.

The apathy here is, first, *subjective*—the felt powerlessness of ordinary people, the resignation before the enormity of events. But subjective apathy is encouraged by the *objective* American situation—the actual structural separation of people from power, from relevant knowledge, from pinnacles of decision-making. Just as the university influences the student way of life, so do major social institutions create the circumstances in which the isolated citizen will try hopelessly to understand his world and himself.

The very isolation of the individual—from power and community and ability to aspire—means the rise of a democracy without publics. With the great mass of people structurally remote and psychologically hesitant with respect to democratic institutions, those institutions themselves attenuate and become, in the fashion of the vicious circle, progressively less accessible to those few who aspire to serious participation in social affairs. The vital democratic connection between community and leadership, between the mass and the several elites, has been so wrenched and perverted that disastrous policies go unchallenged time and again.

Politics without Publics

The American political system is not the democratic model of which its glorifiers speak. In actuality it frustrates democracy by confusing the individual citizen, paralyzing policy discussion, and consolidating the irresponsible power of military and business interests.

A crucial feature of the political apparatus in America is that greater differences are harbored within each major party than the differences existing between them. Instead of two parties presenting distinctive and significant differences of approach, what dominates the system is a natural interlocking of Democrats from Southern states with the more conservative elements of the Republican Party. This arrangement of forces is blessed by the seniority system of Congress which guarantees Congressional committee domination by conservatives—ten of seventeen committees in the Senate and thirteen of twenty-one in the House of Representatives are chaired currently by Dixiecrats.

The party overlap, however, is not the only structural antagonist of democracy in politics. First, the localized nature of the party system does not encourage discussion of national and international issues: thus problems are not raised by and for people, and political representatives usually are unfettered from any responsibilities to the general public except those regarding parochial matters. Second, whole constituencies are divested of the full political power they might have: many Negroes in the South are prevented from voting, migrant workers are disenfranchised by various residence requirements, some urban and suburban dwellers are victimized by gerrymandering, and poor people are too often without the power to obtain political representation. Third, the focus of political attention is significantly distorted by the enormous lobby force, composed predominantly of business interests, spending hundreds of millions each year in an attempt to conform facts about productivity, agriculture, defense, and social services, to the wants of private economic groupings.

What emerges from the party contradiction and insulation of privately held power is the organized political stalemate: calcification dominates flexibility as the principle of parliamentary organization, frustration is the expectancy of legislators intending liberal reform, and Congress becomes less and less central to national decision-making, especially in the area of foreign policy. In this context, confusion and blurring is built into the formulation of issues, long-range priorities are not discussed in the rational manner needed for policy-making, the politics of personality and "image" become a more important mechanism than the construction of issues in a way that affords each voter a challenging and real option. The American voter is buffeted from all directions by pseudo-problems, by the structurally initiated sense that nothing political is subject to human mastery. Worried by his mundane problems which never get solved, but constrained by the common belief that politics is an agonizingly slow accommodation of views, he quits all pretense of bothering.

A most alarming fact is that few, if any, politicians are calling for changes in these conditions. Only a handful even are calling on the President to "live up to" platform pledges; no one is demanding structural changes, such as the shuttling of Southern Democrats out of the Democratic Party. Rather than protesting the state of politics, most politicians are reinforcing and aggravating that state. While in practice they rig public opinion to suit their own interests, in word and ritual they enshrine "the sovereign public" and call for more and more letters. Their speeches and campaign actions are banal, based on a degrading conception of what people want to hear. They respond not to dialogue, but to pressure: and knowing this, the ordinary citizen sees even greater inclination to shun the political sphere. The politician is usually a trumpeter to "citizenship" and "service to the nation," but since he is unwilling to seriously rearrange power relationships, his trumpetings only increase apathy by creating no outlets. Much of the time the call to "service" is justified not in idealistic terms, but in the crasser terms of "defending the free world from Communism"—thus making future idealistic impulses harder to justify in anything but Cold War terms.

In such a setting of status quo politics, where most if not all government activity is rationalized in Cold War anti-Communist terms, it is somewhat natural that discontented, super-patriotic groups would emerge through political channels and explain their ultra-conservatism as the best means of Victory over Communism. They have become a politically influential force within the Republican Party, at a national level through Senator Goldwater, and at a local level through their important social and economic roles. Their political views are defined generally as the opposite of the supposed views of Communists: complete individual freedom in the economic sphere, non-participation by the government in the machinery of production. But actually "anti-Communism" becomes an umbrella by which to protest liberalism, internationalism, welfareism, active civil rights and labor movements. It is to the disgrace of the United

States that such a movement should become a prominent kind of public participation in the modern world—but, ironically, it is somewhat to the interests of the United States that such a movement should be a public constituency pointed toward realignment of the political parties, demanding a conservative Republican Party in the South and an exclusion of the "leftist" elements of the national GOP. . . .

19. Noam Chomsky
The Responsibility
of Intellectuals

Noam Chomsky, Ward Professor of Linguistics at the Massachusetts
Institute of Technology, is interested in the nature of language, how we
acquire it, and how we use it. His theories on these and related problems,
developed in *Syntactic Structures, Aspects of the Theory of Syntax,* and
Cartesian Linguistics, have brought about what is known as the
Chomskyan Revolution. Chomsky challenges the empirical explanation
for language, dominant for nearly three centuries, believing instead
that the principles of language are present in the mind at birth.
"Knowledge of language," Chomsky is careful to say, "results from the
interplay of initially given structures of the mind, maturational processes
and interaction with the environment." From this position in linguistics
Chomsky has also become one of the country's most penetrating
critics of behaviorism which, in this century, has been the major orthodoxy
in American psychology.

But Noam Chomsky is best known to the public as an anti-Vietnam
war activist. It was indicative of the radicalization of an important
sector of the academic community when Chomsky, highly successful and
prestigious in his field of learning, suddenly emerged in the mid-1960s
as the antiwar movement's foremost intellectual. Participating in
peace demonstrations, debates, teach-ins, and writing prolifically against
the war, the MIT scholar became both a political and moral force.
Using a series of articles written by Dwight Macdonald at the close of
World War II as a springboard for his own views, Chomsky, in the
selection that follows, discusses the responsibilities of intellectuals. They
include the duty to insist upon the truth and to expose the lies of
government, to analyze the reigning ideologies and to create new ones,
and to locate events in historical perspective. All too often, Chomsky finds,
American intellectuals have distorted the truth on Vietnam, tolerated
abuses of the democratic process, rationalized the imperial policies of the
U.S. government, and have offered their expertise to the alleged
imperatives of a value-free technology. In criticizing the role of technician-
intellectuals, Chomsky, by his own example, offers an alternative role—
that of the activist humanist-scholar, uneasy in the world of power,
who likes to think about the moral code that governs society. This mode
of intellectual activity includes the judging of, as well as description
of, society; it is done not in a spirit of self-righteousness or as a simpleton

but out of the conviction that the crucial issues of life—war, peace, poverty, racism, justice, and love—are in essense moral and religious questions.

The essay reprinted here is a revised and abridged version of a talk given at Harvard in 1966; other revisions have been published in several places. The essay raises questions about the social role of experts and their relation to decision making. How persuasively does Chomsky discuss the attitudes behind American terror in Vietnam? In a technological society what are the advantages and dangers of relinquishing key decisions to experts? Should intellectuals of Chomsky's persuasion be willing to take government positions? If not, can they expect leadership to be practiced with the sensitivity they demand?

Twenty years ago, Dwight Macdonald published a series of articles in *Politics* on the responsibilities of peoples, and specifically, the responsibility of intellectuals. I read them as an undergraduate, in the years just after the war, and had occasion to read them again a few months ago. They seem to me to have lost none of their power or persuasiveness. Macdonald is concerned with the question of war guilt. He asks the question: To what extent were the German or Japanese people responsible for the atrocities committed by their governments? And, quite properly, he turns the question back to us: To what extent are the British or American people responsible for the vicious terror bombings of civilians, perfected as a technique of warfare by the Western democracies and reaching their culmination in Hiroshima and Nagasaki, surely among the most unspeakable crimes in history? To an undergraduate in 1945–1946—to anyone whose political and moral consciousness had been formed by the horrors of the 1930s, by the war in Ethiopia, the Russian purge, the "China incident," the Spanish Civil War, the Nazi atrocities, the Western reaction to these events and, in part, complicity in them—these questions had particular significance and poignancy.

With respect to the responsibility of intellectuals, there are still other, equally disturbing questions. Intellectuals are in a position to expose the lies of governments, to analyze actions according to their causes and motives and often hidden intentions. In the Western world at least, they have the power that comes from political liberty, from access to information and freedom of expression. For a privileged minority, Western democracy provides the leisure, the facilities, and the training to seek the truth lying hidden behind the veil of distortion and misrepresentation, ideology, and class interest through which the events of current history are presented to us. The responsibilities of intellectuals, then, are much deeper than what Macdonald calls the "responsibility of peoples," given the unique privileges that intellectuals enjoy.

The issues that Macdonald raised are as pertinent today as they were twenty years ago. We can hardly avoid asking ourselves to what extent the American people bear responsibility for the savage American assault on a largely helpless rural population in Vietnam, still another atrocity in what Asians see as the "Vasco da Gama era" of world history. As for those of us who stood by in silence and apathy as this catastrophe slowly took shape over the past dozen years, on what page of history do we find our proper place? Only the most insensible can escape these questions. I want to return to them, later on, after a few scattered remarks about the responsibility of intellectuals and how, in practice, they go about meeting this responsibility in the mid-1960s.

It is the responsibility of intellectuals to speak the truth and to expose lies. This, at least, may seem enough of a truism to pass without comment. Not so, however. For the modern intellectual, it is not at all obvious. Thus we have Martin Heidegger writing, in a pro-Hitler declaration of 1933, that "truth is the revelation of that which makes a people certain, clear, and strong in its action and knowledge"; it is only this kind of "truth" that one has a responsibility to speak. Americans tend to be more forthright. When Arthur Schlesinger was asked by the *New York Times,* in November 1965, to explain the contradiction between his published account of the Bay of Pigs incident and the story he had given the press at the time of the attack, he simply remarked that he had lied; and a few days later, he went on to compliment the *Times* for also having suppressed information on the planned invasion, in "the national interest," as this was defined by the group of arrogant and deluded men of whom Schlesinger gives such a flattering portrait in his recent account of the Kennedy administration. It is of no particular interest that one man is quite happy to lie in behalf of a cause which he knows to be unjust; but it is significant that such events provoke so little response in the intellectual community—no feeling, for example, that there is something strange in the offer of a major chair in humanities to a historian who feels it to be his duty to persuade the world that an American-sponsored invasion of a nearby country is nothing of the sort. And what of the incredible sequence of lies on the part of our government and its spokesmen concerning such matters as negotiations in Vietnam? The facts are known to all who care to know. The press, foreign and domestic, has presented documentation to refute each falsehood as it appears. But the power of the government propaganda apparatus is such that the citizen who does not undertake a research project on the subject can hardly hope to confront government pronouncements with fact.

The deceit and distortion surrounding the American invasion of Vietnam are by now so familiar that they have lost their power to shock. It is therefore well to recall that although new levels of cynicism are constantly being reached, their clear antecedents were accepted at home with quiet toleration. It is a useful exercise to compare government statements at the time of the invasion of Guatemala in 1954 with Eisenhower's admission—to be more accurate, his boast—a decade later that American planes were sent "to help the invaders." Nor is it only in moments of crisis that duplicity is considered perfectly in order. "New Frontiersmen," for example, have scarcely distinguished themselves by a passionate concern for historical accuracy, even when they are not being called upon to provide a "propaganda cover" for ongoing actions. For example, Arthur Schlesinger describes the bombing of North Vietnam and the massive escalation of military commitment in early 1965 as based on a "perfectly rational argument": ". . . so long as the Vietcong thought they were going to win the war, they obviously would not be interested in any kind of negotiated settlement." The date is important. Had the statement been made six months earlier, one could attribute it to ignorance. But this statement appeared after months of front-page news reports detailing the United Nations, North Vietnamese, and Soviet initiatives that preceded the February 1965 escalation and that, in fact, continued for several weeks after the bombing began, after months of soulsearching by Washington correspondents who were trying desperately to find some mitigating circumstances for the startling deception that had been revealed. (Chalmers Roberts, for example, wrote with unconscious irony that late February 1965 "hardly seemed to Washington to be a propitious moment for negotiations [since] Mr. Johnson . . . had just ordered the first bombing of North Vietnam in an effort to bring Hanoi to a conference table where bargaining chips on both sides would be more closely matched.") Coming at this moment, Schlesinger's statement is less an example of deceit than of contempt—contempt for an audience that can be expected to tolerate such behavior with silence, if not approval. . . .

[There has also been a] failure of skepticism. Consider the remarks of Henry Kissinger in concluding his presentation in a Harvard-Oxford television debate on American Vietnam policies. He observed, rather sadly, that what disturbs him most is that others question not our judgment but our motives—a remarkable comment on the part of one whose professional concern is political analysis, that is, analysis of the actions of governments in terms of motives that are unexpressed in official propaganda and perhaps only dimly perceived by those whose acts they govern. No one would be disturbed by an analysis of the political behavior of Russians, French, or Tanzanians, questioning their motives and interpreting their actions in terms of long-range interests, perhaps well concealed behind official rhetoric. But it is an article of faith that American motives are pure and not subject to analysis. Although it is nothing new in American intellectual history—or, for that matter, in the general history of imperialist apologia—this innocence becomes increasingly distasteful as the power it serves grows more dominant in world affairs and more capable, therefore, of the unconstrained viciousness that the mass media present to us each day. We are hardly the first power in history to combine material interests, great technological capacity, and an utter disregard for the suffering and misery of the lower orders. The long tradition of naiveté and self-righteousness that disfigures our intellectual history, however, must serve as a warning to the Third World, if such a warning is needed, as to how our protestations of sincerity and benign intent are to be interpreted. . . .

Let us, however, return to the war in Vietnam and the response that it has aroused among American intellectuals. A striking feature of the recent debate on Southeast Asian policy has been the distinction that is commonly drawn between "responsible criticism," on the one hand, and "sentimental" or "emotional" or "hysterical" criticism, on the other. There is much to be learned from a careful study of the terms in which this distinction is drawn. The "hysterical critics" are to be identified, apparently, by their irrational refusal to accept one fundamental political axiom, namely, that the United States has the right to extend its power and control without limit, insofar as is feasible. Responsible criticism does not challenge this assumption, but argues, rather, that we probably can't "get away with it" at this particular time and place.

A distinction of this sort seems to be what Irving Kristol has in mind, for example, in his analysis of the protest over Vietnam policy, in *Encounter*, August 1965. He contrasts the responsible critics, such as Walter Lippmann, the *New York Times*, and Senator Fulbright, with the "teach-in movement." "Unlike the university protesters," he maintains, "Mr. Lippmann engages in no presumptuous suppositions as to 'what the Vietnamese people really want'—he obviously doesn't much care—or in legalistic exegesis as to whether, or to what extent, there is 'aggression' or 'revolution' in South Vietnam. His is a *realpolitik* point of view; and he will apparently even contemplate the possibility of a *nuclear* war against China in extreme circumstances." This is commendable, and contrasts favorably, for Kristol, with the talk of the "unreasonable, ideological types" in the teach-in movement, who often seem to be motivated by such absurdities as "simple, virtuous 'anti-imperialism,' " who deliver "harangues on 'the power structure,' " and who even sometimes stoop so low as to read "articles and reports from the foreign press on the American presence in Vietnam." Furthermore, these nasty types are often psychologists, mathematicians, chemists, or philosophers (just as, incidentally, those most vocal in protest in the Soviet Union are generally physicists, literary intellectuals, and others remote from the exercise of power), rather than people with Washington contacts, who of course realize that "had they a new, good idea about Vietnam, they would get a prompt and respectful hearing" in Washington.

I am not interested here in whether Kristol's characterization of protest and dissent is accurate, but rather in the assumptions that it expresses with respect to such questions as these: Is the purity of American motives a matter that is beyond discussion, or that is irrelevant to discussion? Should decisions be left to "experts" with Washington contacts—that is, even if we assume that they command the necessary knowledge and principles to make the "best" decision, will they invariably do so? And, a logically prior question, is "expertise" applicable—that is, is there a body of theory and of relevant information, not in the public domain, that can be applied to the analysis of foreign policy or that demonstrates the correctness of present actions in some way that the psychologists, mathematicians, chemists, and philosophers are incapable of comprehending? Although Kristol does not examine these questions directly, his attitudes presuppose answers, answers which are wrong in all cases. American aggressiveness, however it may be masked in pious rhetoric, is a dominant force in world affairs and must be analyzed in terms of its causes and motives. There is no body of theory or significant body of relevant information, beyond the comprehension of the layman, which makes policy immune from criticism. To the extent that "expert knowledge" is applied to world affairs, it is surely appropriate—for a person of any integrity, quite necessary—to question its quality and the goals that it serves. These facts seem too obvious to require extended discussion.

A corrective to Kristol's curious belief in the administration's openness to new thinking about Vietnam is provided by McGeorge Bundy in a recent article. As Bundy correctly observes, "on the main stage . . . the argument on Viet Nam turns on tactics, not fundamentals," although, he adds, "there are wild men in the wings." On stage center are, of course, the President (who in his recent trip to Asia had just "magisterially reaffirmed" our interest "in the progress of the people across the Pacific") and his advisers, who deserve "the understanding support of those who want restraint." It is these men who deserve the credit for the fact that "the bombing of the North has been the most accurate and the most restrained in modern warfare"—a solicitude which will be appreciated by the inhabitants, or former inhabitants, of Nam Dinh and Phu Ly and Vinh. It is these men, too, who deserve the credit for what was reported by Malcolm Browne as long ago as May 1965: "In the South, huge sectors of the nation have been declared 'free bombing zones,' in which anything that moves is a legitimate target. Tens of thousands of tons of bombs, rockets, napalm and cannon fire are poured into these vast areas each week. If only by the laws of chance, bloodshed is believed to be heavy in these raids."

Fortunately for the developing countries, Bundy assures us, "American democracy has no enduring taste for imperialism," and "taken as a whole, the stock of American experience, understanding, sympathy and simple knowledge is now much the most impressive in the world." It is true that "four-fifths of all the foreign investing in the world is now done by Americans" and that "the most admired plans and policies . . . are no better than their demonstrable relation to the American interest"— just as it is true, so we read in the same issue of *Foreign Affairs,* that the plans for armed action against Cuba were put into motion a few weeks after Mikoyan visited Havana, "invading what had so long been an almost exclusively American sphere of influence." Unfortunately, such facts as these are often taken by unsophisticated Asian intellectuals as indicating a "taste for imperialism." For example, a number of Indians have expressed their "near exasperation" at the fact that "we have done everything we can to attract foreign capital for fertilizer plants, but the American and the other Western private companies know we are over a barrel, so they demand stringent terms which we just cannot meet," while "Washington . . . doggedly insists that deals be made in the private sector with private enterprise." But this reaction, no doubt, simply reveals once again how the Asian mind fails to comprehend the "diffuse and complex concepts" of Western thought.

It may be useful to study carefully the "new, good ideas about Vietnam" that are receiving a "prompt and respectful hearing" in Washington these days. The United States Government Printing Office is an endless source of insight into the moral and intellectual level of this expert advice. In its publications one can read, for example, the testimony of Professor David N. Rowe, director of graduate studies in international relations at Yale University, before the House Committee on Foreign Affairs. Professor Rowe proposes that the United States buy all surplus Canadian and Australian wheat, so that there will be mass starvation in China. These are his words: "Mind you, I am not talking about this as a weapon against the Chinese people. It will be. But that is only incidental. The weapon will be a weapon against the Government because the internal stability of that country cannot be sustained by an unfriendly Government in the face of general starvation." Professor Rowe will have none of the sentimental moralism that might lead one to compare this suggestion with, say, the *Ostpolitik* of Hitler's Germany. Nor does he fear the impact of such policies on other Asian nations, for example Japan. He assures us, from his "very long acquaintance with Japanese questions," that "the Japanese above all are people who respect power and determination." Hence "they will not be so much alarmed by American policy in Vietnam that takes off from a position of power and intends to seek a solution based upon the imposition of our power upon local people that we are in opposition to." What would disturb the Japanese is "a policy of indecision, a policy of refusal to face up to the problems [in China and Vietnam] and to meet our responsibilities there in a positive way," such as the way just cited. A conviction that we were "unwilling to use the power that they know we have" might "alarm the Japanese people very intensely and shake the degree of their friendly relations with us." In fact, a full use of American power would be particularly reassuring to the Japanese, because they have had a demonstration "of the tremendous power in action of the United States . . . because they have felt our power directly." This is surely a prime example of the healthy *"realpolitik* point of view" that Irving Kristol so much admires.

But, one may ask, why restrict ourselves to such indirect means as mass starvation? Why not bombing? No doubt this message is implicit in the remarks to the same committee of the Reverend R. J. de Jaegher, regent of the Institute of Far Eastern Studies, Seton Hall University, who explains that like all people who have lived under Communism, the North Vietnamese "would be perfectly happy to be bombed to be free."

Of course, there must be those who support the Communists. But this is really a matter of small concern, as the Honorable Walter Robertson, Assistant Secretary of State for Far Eastern Affairs from 1953 to 1959, points out in his testimony before the same committee. He assures us that "The Peiping regime . . . represents something less than 3 percent of the population."

Consider, then, how fortunate the Chinese Communist leaders are, compared to the leaders of the Vietcong, who, according to Arthur Goldberg, represent about "one-half of one percent of the population of South Vietnam," that is, about one half the number of new Southern recruits for the Vietcong during 1965, if we can credit Pentagon statistics.

In the face of such experts as these, the scientists and philosophers of whom Kristol speaks would clearly do well to continue to draw their circles in the sand.

Having settled the issue of the political irrelevance of the protest movement, Kristol turns to the question of what motivates it—more generally, what has made students and junior faculty "go left," as he sees it, amid general prosperity and under liberal, welfare state administrations. This he notes, "is a riddle to which no sociologist has as yet come up with an answer." Since these young people are well off, have good futures, etc., their protest must be irrational. It must be the result of boredom, of too much security, or something of this sort.

Other possibilities come to mind. It might be, for example, that as honest men the students and junior faculty are attempting to find out the truth for themselves rather than ceding the responsibility to "experts" or to government; and it might be that they react with indignation to what they discover. These possibilities Kristol does not reject. They are simply unthinkable, unworthy of consideration. More accurately, these possibilities are inexpressible; the categories in which they are formulated (honesty, indignation) simply do not exist for the tough-minded social scientist.

In this implicit disparagement of traditional intellectual values, Kristol reflects attitudes that are fairly widespread in academic circles. I do not doubt that these attitudes are in part a consequence of the desperate attempt of the social and behavioral sciences to imitate the surface features of sciences that really have significant intellectual content. But they have other sources as well. Anyone can be a moral individual, concerned with human rights and problems; but only a college professor, a trained expert, can solve technical problems by "sophisticated" methods. Ergo, it is only problems of the latter sort that are important or real. Responsible, nonideological experts will give advice on tactical questions; irresponsible "ideological types" will "harangue" about principle and trouble themselves over moral issues and human rights, or over the traditional problems of man and society, concerning which "social and behavioral science" have nothing to offer beyond trivialities. Obviously, these emotional, ideological types are irrational, since, being well off and having power in their grasp, they shouldn't worry about such matters.

At times this pseudoscientific posing reaches levels that are almost pathological. Consider the phenomenon of Herman Kahn, for example. Kahn has been both denounced as immoral and lauded for his courage. By people who should know better, his *On Thermonuclear War* has been described "without qualification . . . [as] . . . one of the great works of our time" (Stuart Hughes) . The fact of the matter is that this is surely one of the emptiest works of our time, as can be seen by applying to it the intellectual standards of any existing discipline, by tracing some of its "well-documented conclusions" to the "objective studies" from which they derive, and by following the line of argument, where detectable. Kahn proposes no theories, no explanations, no empirical assumptions that can be tested against their consequences, as do the sciences he is attempting to mimic. He simply suggests a terminology and provides a façade of rationality. When particular policy conclusions are drawn, they are supported only by *ex cathedra* remarks for which no support is even suggested (e.g., "The civil defense line probably should be drawn somewhere below $5 billion annually" to keep from provoking the Russians—why not $50 billion, or $5?) . What is more, Kahn is quite aware of this vacuity; in his more judicious moments he claims only that "there is no reason to believe that relatively sophisticated models are more likely to be misleading than the simpler models and analogies frequently used as an aid to judgment." For those whose humor tends towards the macabre, it is easy to play the game of "strategic thinking" à la Kahn, and to prove what one wishes. For example, one of Kahn's basic assumptions is that "an all-out surprise attack in which all resources are devoted to counter-value targets would be so irrational that, barring an incredible lack of sophistication or actual insanity among Soviet decision makers, such an attack is highly unlikely." A simple argument proves the opposite. Premise 1: American decision makers think along the lines outlined by Herman Kahn. Premise 2: Kahn thinks it would be better for everyone to be red than for everyone to be dead. Premise 3: If the Americans were to respond to an all-out counter-value attack, then everyone would be dead. Conclusion: The Americans will not respond to an all-out counter-value attack, and therefore it should be launched without delay. Of course, one can carry the argument a step further. Fact: The Russians have not carried out an all-out counter-value attack. It follows that they are not rational. If they are not rational, there is no point in "strategic thinking." Therefore . . .

Of course this is all nonsense, but nonsense that differs from Kahn's only in the respect that the argument is of slightly greater complexity than anything to be discovered in his work. What is remarkable is that serious people actually pay attention to these absurdities, no doubt because of the façade of toughmindedness and pseudoscience. . . .

When we consider the responsibility of intellectuals, our basic concern must be their role in the creation and analysis of ideology. And in fact, Kristol's contrast between the unreasonable ideological types and the responsible experts is formulated in terms that immediately bring to mind Daniel Bell's interesting and influential essay on the "end of ideology," an essay which is as important for what it leaves unsaid as for its actual content. Bell presents and discusses the Marxist analysis of ideology as a mask for class interest, in particular quoting Marx's well-known description of the belief of the bourgeoisie "that the *special* conditions of its emancipation are the *general* conditions through which alone modern society can be saved and the class struggle avoided." He then argues that the age of ideology is ended, supplanted, at least in the West, by a general agreement that each issue must be settled on its own individual terms, within the framework of a welfare state in which, presumably, experts in the conduct of public affairs will have a prominent role. Bell is quite careful, however, to characterize the precise sense of "ideology" in which "ideologies are exhausted." He is referring only to ideology as "the conversion of ideas into social levers," to ideology as "a set of beliefs, infused with passion, . . . [which] . . . seeks to transform the whole of a way of life." The crucial words are "transform" and "convert into social levers." Intellectuals in the West, he argues, have lost interest in converting ideas into social levers for the radical transformation of society. Now that we have achieved the pluralistic society of the welfare state, they see no further need for a radical transformation of society; we may tinker with our way of life here and there, but it would be wrong to try to modify it in any significant way. With this consensus of intellectuals, ideology is dead.

There are several striking facts about Bell's essay. First, he does not point out the extent to which this consensus of the intellectuals is self-serving. He does not relate his observation that, by and large, intellectuals have lost interest in "transforming the whole way of life" to the fact that they play an increasingly prominent role in running the welfare state; he does not relate their general satisfaction with the welfare state to the fact that, as he observes elsewhere, "America has become an affluent society, offering place . . . and prestige . . . to the onetime radicals." Secondly, he offers no serious argument to show that intellectuals are somehow "right" or "objectively justified" in reaching the consensus to which he alludes, with its rejection of the notion that society should be transformed. Indeed, although Bell is fairly sharp about the empty rhetoric of the "New Left," he seems to have a quite utopian faith that technical experts will be able to come to grips with the few problems that still remain; for example, the fact that labor is treated as a commodity, and the problems of "alienation."

It seems fairly obvious that the classical problems are very much with us; one might plausibly argue that they have even been enhanced in severity and scale. For example, the classical paradox of poverty in the midst of plenty is now an ever increasing problem on an international scale. Whereas one might conceive, at least in principle, of a solution within national boundaries, a sensible idea as to how to transform international society in such a way as to cope with the vast and perhaps increasing human misery is hardly likely to develop within the framework of the intellectual consensus that Bell describes.

Thus it would seem natural to describe the consensus of Bell's intellectuals in somewhat different terms than his. Using the terminology of the first part of his essay, we might say that the welfare state technician finds justification for his special and prominent social status in his "science," specifically, in the claim that social science can support a technology of social tinkering on a domestic or international scale. He then takes a further step, proceeding, in a familiar way, to claim universal validity for what is in fact a class interest: he argues that the special conditions on which his claims to power and authority are based are, in fact, the general conditions through which alone modern society can be saved; that social tinkering within a welfare state framework must replace the commitment to the "total ideologies" of the past, ideologies which were concerned with a transformation of society. Having found his position of power, having achieved security and affluence, he has no further need for ideologies that look to radical change. The scholar-expert replaces the "free-floating intellectual" who "felt that the wrong values were being honored, and rejected the society," and who has now lost his political role (now, that is, that the right values are being honored).

Conceivably, it is correct that the technical experts who will (or hope to) manage the "postindustrial society" will be able to cope with the classic problems without a radical transformation of society. Just so, it is conceivably true that the bourgeoisie was right in regarding the special conditions of its emancipation as the general conditions through which alone modern society would be saved. In either case, an argument is in order, and skepticism is justified where none appears.

Within the same framework of general utopianism, Bell goes on to pose the issue between welfare state scholar-experts and Third World ideologists in a rather curious way. He points out, quite correctly, that there is no issue of Communism, the content of that doctrine having been "long forgotten by friends and foes alike." Rather, he says, "the question is an older one: whether new societies can grow by building democratic institutions and allowing people to make choices—and sacrifices—voluntarily, or whether the new elites, heady with power, will impose totalitarian means to transform their countries." The question is an interesting one; it is odd, however, to see it referred to as "an older one." Surely he cannot be suggesting that the West chose the democratic way—for example, that in England during the industrial revolution, the farmers voluntarily made the choice of leaving the land, giving up cottage industry, becoming an industrial proletariat, and voluntarily decided, within the framework of the existing democratic institutions, to make the sacrifices that are graphically described in the classic literature on nineteenth-century industrial society. One may debate the question whether authoritarian control is necessary to permit capital accumulation in the underdeveloped world, but the Western model of development is hardly one that we can point to with any pride. It is perhaps not surprising to find a Walt Rostow referring to "the more humane processes [of industrialization] that Western values would suggest." Those who have a serious concern for the problems that face backward countries and for the role that advanced industrial societies might, in principle, play in development and modernization must use somewhat more care in interpreting the significance of the Western experience.

Returning to the quite appropriate question, whether "new societies can grow by building democratic institutions" or only by totalitarian means, I think that honesty requires us to recognize that this question must be directed more to American intellectuals than to Third World ideologists. The backward countries have incredible, perhaps insurmountable problems, and few available options; the United States has a wide range of options, and has the economic and technological resources, though evidently neither the intellectual nor the moral resources, to confront at least some of these problems. It is easy for an American intellectual to deliver homilies on the virtues of freedom and liberty, but if he is really concerned about, say, Chinese totalitarianism or the burdens imposed on the Chinese peasantry in forced industrialization, then he should face a task that is infinitely more significant and challenging—the task of creating, in the United States, the intellectual and moral climate, as well as the social and economic conditions, that would permit this country to participate in modernization and development in a way commensurate with its material wealth and technical capacity. Massive capital gifts to Cuba and China might not succeed in alleviating the authoritarianism and terror that tend to accompany early stages of capital accumulation, but they are far more likely to have this effect than lectures on democratic values. It is possible that even without "capitalist encirclement" in its varying manifestations, the truly democratic elements in revolutionary movements—in some instances soviets and collectives, for example—might be undermined by an "elite" of bureaucrats and technical intelligentsia; but it is a near certainty that the fact of capitalist encirclement, which all revolutionary movements now have to face, will guarantee this result. The lesson, for those who are concerned to strengthen the democratic, spontaneous, and popular elements in developing societies, is quite clear. Lectures on the two-party system, or even the really substantial democratic values that have been in part realized in Western society, are a monstrous irrelevance in the face of the effort that is required to raise the level of culture in Western society to the point where it can provide a "social lever" for both economic development and the development of true democratic institutions in the Third World—and for that matter, at home as well.

A good case can be made for the conclusion that there is indeed something of a consensus among intellectuals who have already achieved power and affluence, or who sense that they can achieve them by "accepting society" as it is and promoting the values that are "being honored" in this society. And it is also true that this consensus is most noticeable among the scholar-experts who are replacing the free-floating intellectuals of the past. In the university, these scholar-experts construct a "value-free technology" for the solution of technical problems that arise in contemporary society, taking a "responsible stance" towards these problems, in the sense noted earlier. This consensus among the responsible scholar-experts is the domestic analogue to that proposed, in the international arena, by those who justify the application of American power in Asia, whatever the human cost, on the grounds that it is necessary to contain the "expansion of China" (an "expansion" which is, to be sure, hypothetical for the time being)—to translate from State Department Newspeak, on the grounds that it is essential to reverse the Asian nationalist revolutions, or at least to prevent them from spreading. . . .

If it is the responsibility of the intellectual to insist upon the truth, it is also his duty to see events in their historical perspective. Thus one must applaud the insistence of the Secretary of State on the importance of historical analogies, the Munich analogy, for example. As Munich showed, a powerful and aggressive nation with a fanatic belief in its manifest destiny will regard each victory, each extension of its power and authority, as a prelude to the next step. The matter was very well put by Adlai Stevenson, when he spoke of "the old, old route whereby expansive powers push at more and more doors, believing they will open, until, at the ultimate door, resistance is unavoidable and major war breaks out." Herein lies the danger of appeasement, as the Chinese tirelessly point out to the Soviet Union, which they claim is playing Chamberlain to our Hitler in Vietnam. Of course, the aggressiveness of liberal imperialism is not that of Nazi Germany, though the distinction may seem rather academic to a Vietnamese peasant who is being gassed or incinerated. We do not want to occupy Asia; we merely wish, to return to Mr. Wolf, "to help the Asian countries progress toward economic modernization, as relatively 'open' and stable societies, to which our access, as a country and as individual citizens, is free and comfortable." The formulation is appropriate. Recent history shows that it makes little difference to us what form of government a country has as long as it remains an "open society," in our peculiar sense of this term—a society, that is, which remains open to American economic penetration or political control. If it is necessary to approach genocide in Vietnam to achieve this objective, then this is the price we must pay in defense of freedom and the rights of man. . . .

In pursuing the aim of helping other countries to progress towards open societies, with no thought of territorial aggrandizement, we are breaking no new ground. Hans Morgenthau has aptly described our traditional policy towards China as one of favoring "what you might call freedom of competition with regard to the exploitation of China." In fact, few imperialist powers have had explicit territorial ambitions. Thus in 1784, the British Parliament announced that "to pursue schemes of conquest and extension of dominion in India are measures repugnant to the wish, honor, and policy of this nation." Shortly after, the conquest of India was in full swing. A century later, Britain announced its intentions in Egypt under the slogan "Intervention, Reform, Withdrawal." It is unnecessary to comment on which parts of this promise were fulfilled, within the next half century. In 1936, on the eve of hostilities in North China, the Japanese stated their Basic Principles of National Policy. These included the use of moderate and peaceful means to extend her strength, to promote social and economic development, to eradicate the menace of Communism, to correct the aggressive policies of the great powers, and to secure her position as the stabilizing power in East Asia. Even in 1937, the Japanese government had "no territorial designs upon China." In short, we follow a well-trodden path.

It is useful to remember, incidentally, that the United States was apparently quite willing, as late as 1939, to negotiate a commercial treaty with Japan and arrive at a *modus vivendi* if Japan would "change her attitude and practice towards our rights and interests in China," as Secretary Hull put it. The bombing of Chungking and the rape of Nanking were rather unpleasant, it is true, but what was really important was our rights and interests in China, as the responsible, unhysterical men of the day saw quite clearly. It was the closing of the Open Door by Japan that led inevitably to the Pacific war, just as it is the closing of the Open Door by "Communist" China itself that may very well lead to the next, and no doubt last, Pacific war.

Quite often, the statements of sincere and devoted technical experts give surprising insight into the intellectual attitudes that lie in the background of the latest savagery. Consider, for example, the following comment by economist Richard Lindholm, in 1959, expressing his frustration over the failure of economic development in "free Vietnam": ". . . the use of American aid is determined by how the Vietnamese use their incomes and their savings. The fact that a large portion of the Vietnamese imports financed with American aid are either consumer goods or raw materials used rather directly to meet consumer demands is an indication that the Vietnamese people desire these goods, for they have shown their desire by their willingness to use their piasters to purchase them."

In short, the Vietnamese *people* desire Buicks and air conditioners, rather than sugar-refining equipment or road-building machinery, as they have shown by their behavior in a free market. And however much we may deplore their free choice, we must allow the people to have their way. Of course, there are also those two-legged beasts of burden that one stumbles on in the countryside, but as any graduate student of political science can explain, they are not part of a responsible modernizing elite, and therefore have only a superficial biological resemblance to the human race.

In no small measure, it is attitudes like this that lie behind the butchery in Vietnam, and we had better face up to them with candor, or we will find our government leading us towards a "final solution" in Vietnam, and in the many Vietnams that inevitably lie ahead.

Let me finally return to Macdonald and the responsibility of intellectuals. Macdonald quotes an interview with a death-camp paymaster who bursts into tears when told that the Russians would hang him. "Why should they? What have I done?" he asked. Macdonald concludes: "Only those who are willing to resist authority themselves when it conflicts too intolerably with their personal moral code, only they have the right to condemn the death-camp paymaster." The question "What have I done?" is one that we may well ask ourselves, as we read, each day, of fresh atrocities in Vietnam—as we create, or mouth, or tolerate the deceptions that will be used to justify the next defense of freedom.

20. Eldridge Cleaver

Open Letter to Ronald Reagan

Born in Little Rock, Arkansas, in 1935, Eldridge Cleaver has been in jail or in exile during much of his adult life. At the age of 22 he was sentenced to California's Folsom State Prison for possession of marijuana. Later, on different charges, he was imprisoned at San Quentin, Soledad, and the California Medical Facility. Eldridge Cleaver is best known as the Minister of Information of the Black Panther party. Deeply influenced by the Black Muslims and by Malcolm X, he describes himself as "a full-time revolutionary in the struggle for black liberation in America." As such he has had to share the fate of other Panthers and militant black leaders such as Huey Newton, Bobby Seale, David Hilliard, George Jackson, Angela Davis, Stokely Carmichael, Fred Hampton, and H. Rap Brown. By the end of the decade all had been harassed by local and federal authorities, jailed, forced into exile, or killed.

With his book *Soul on Ice* (1968), Cleaver emerged as a talented observer of American customs (Ofay watching) and an eloquent articulator of a black soul that had been "colonized" by the oppressive institutions of white society. His "Open Letter to Ronald Reagan," published in *Post-Prison Writings and Speeches,* describes the circumstances of his confinement in 1968 and lays before the public the harassment of the Black Panther party by the Oakland Police Department.

California Medical Facility
Vacaville, California
May 13, 1968

The Honorable Ronald Reagan
Governor of the State of California
Sacramento, California

Honorable Sir:

In writing you this letter, I want first of all to make one thing clear: I do not write it to ask a favor of you; I do not write it seeking mercy; I do not write it to complain. Rather, I am writing to you to call to your atten-

From *Eldridge Cleaver: Post-Prison Writings and Speeches,* edited by Robert Sheer. Copyright © 1967, 1968, 1969 by Eldridge Cleaver. Reprinted by permission of Random House, Inc.

tion that certain persons who are responsible to you have conspired to violate my rights and are now holding me as a political prisoner at Vacaville Medical Facility, one of the chain of prisons operated by the California Department of Corrections, a state agency, under your control. As the Chief Executive of the State of California, I thought you might want to know what the people whom you have appointed to the California Adult Authority have done. And whether you in fact want to know about it or not, as the Chief Executive it is your duty to see to it that the agencies under your control carry out their functions in such a manner as not to violate the rights of any citizen of the State of California, or of any other state or jurisdiction, for that matter. I want to speak to you about a clear instance in which my rights have been violated in a most flagrant and indefensible manner. So it is from that point of view that I write this letter, and it is in that spirit that I hope you will receive it, look into the matter, and then act, or not act, as your reason, conscience, and advisors move you.

I am a political prisoner, and an examination of the circumstances resulting in my imprisonment will reveal this fact to you or to anybody else. I realize that I have asserted an awkward claim, because I know that other people have already examined the circumstances of which I speak and have drawn the conclusion that, indeed, I should be right where I am. But I do not intend to argue their side of the story, which I not only consider wrong, but perfidious and criminal. Because certain people had to do certain things in order for me to be, at this moment, sitting in this cell. People talked about me and my activities and then they issued orders. Other people moved to carry out those orders. Those who fastened the handcuffs to my wrists, the shackles around my legs, the chain around my body, put me into a car, transported me to this place and turned me over to the keepers here, were mere functionaries, automatons, carrying out their "duties" in Adolf Eichmann's spirit. I speak, rather, of the decision makers, those whom you have appointed and charged with making decisions in this area. They are the guilty ones, the conspirators, whose decisions and orders I bring to your attention.

I was on parole in San Francisco, after serving nine years of a fourteen-year sentence in San Quentin, Folsom, and Soledad. I was released on December 12, 1966. My parole agent was Mr. R. L. Bilideau. I was given four years' parole by the California Adult Authority, presumably because, according to their lights, I had been rehabilitated. According to my own lights, I had.

Having gone to prison from Los Angeles, I decided to take my parole to San Francisco, to start anew in a brand new locale, there to stand or fall on my own merit, and to build a brand new life. I did this with ease, with a thirst for life, a driving hunger to be involved in life, the real life that I had watched for so long from the sidelines of a stagnant, deadening, artificial world. I found love, and married it. Her name is Kathleen, my darling wife. While in prison I decided that, upon my release, I would find a way to relate to the struggle of my people for a better life, to plunge myself into that struggle and contribute of myself what I possessed that could be used, without reservation: my life, my fortune, and my sacred honor which, through my struggles to survive the soul-murder of my stay in prison, I found.

After a few false starts, I encountered the Black Panther Party, which I quickly joined, and after proving myself, was appointed to the position of Minister of Information. It is a position which I still hold and of which I am as proud, Governor, as I imagine you are of the office you hold. You may have heard of my party, and I certainly have heard of yours. We visited you in Sacramento last year on May 2nd, and, if I may say so, were very badly received. As I understand it, this was because some of us brought our guns with us, even though your men had theirs with them. Moreover, your men turned their guns on us, although we did not do the same thing to them. We were told that your men had the right to have their guns but that ours didn't. We argued the point, of course, but evidently our arguments fell on deaf ears, because our men with guns were arrested and some of them had to serve a jail sentence. I was arrested also, but quickly released with all charges dropped. Then a judge discovered that I should not have been arrested in the first place because I was there as a reporter, with proper credentials, for *Ramparts* magazine, of which I was then and still am, a staff writer; because I did not have a gun; and because, in reference to my being on parole, I had the written consent of my parole agent to be there. That was the only time in my eighteen months on parole that I was ever arrested. Since that situation was resolved as it was, I think it would be fair to say, Governor, that in those eighteen months I was never arrested for cause.

If the truth were to be told, I was a model parolee, although I gather that I was something of a headache to my parole agent. This was through no fault of my own, but because he was caught up in the contradiction between the presumptions of the parole department and my human rights and my Constitutional rights to engage in political activity. He was always telling me that, although I had a perfect right to be a Black Panther, there were politicians in Sacramento who did not approve of the party. It was his advice that if I wanted to be successful on parole, I be cool. *Be cool?* For nine long years I had been on *ice*. Shit. I was being cool. In fact I was still thawing out, trying to warm up, so that I could really do my thing. Besides, legality was on my side. As for politicians, I was one myself. (I guess I forgot that politics, especially when they start to get deep, get dirty. You can't really count on anything, not even, as in my own case, the Constitution of the United States. Still, I was not *really* counting on that, being aware as I was that some politicians, in the name of upholding the Constitution, violate it, yea, rub it in the mud.)

But I am Minister of Information of the Black Panther Party. And what would be the quality of my soul, politics, and value to my party, to my comrades, and to the people we represent, if (through mere fear of hostile politicians) I abdicated the responsibilities I had accepted and pledged myself to fulfill? Having yourself taken an oath of office, Governor, I'm sure you can understand that. Suppose Jesse Unruh sent you a threatening message demanding that you resign as governor. I know what you would do: you would tell Big Daddy where to go. Well, I did more or less the same thing, but that was, at least it was *supposed* to be, just between me and my parole agent. I chose to stick to my guns. Anyway, I thought that the politicians in Sacramento had better things to do than to be fucking around with parolees, and the party didn't have any plans for visiting the State Capital again. Dispensing information seemed innocuous enough, and besides, I was so busy that I didn't have much time to worry about it.

Huey P. Newton, Minister of Defense of the Black Panther Party, was uptight, on Death Row, and he needed me: District Attorney Coakley of Alameda County was prosecuting my leader for murder, in the name of the People of the State of California, so it was very clear to me that the people needed some information they didn't seem to have: about Huey, about the Black Panther Party, about the Oakland Police Department, about District Attorney Coakley, about black people, about 1968, and the black response to white racism (this was before LBJ decided to give me a hand by issuing his Civil Disorders Report), and about politics—and about how all that jazz was mixed up, interrelated with welfare, police brutality, bad housing, the war in Vietnam—all that shit. All that shit had to be put into a perspective from which the people could see, and understand, and join in the demand that Huey Must Be Set Free! Come See About Huey!

Whew! To tell you the truth, Governor, that shit was wearing me out. I was getting old before my time: I'm twenty-two years old, the age I was when I went to prison, because when I got out, there was a great big gap in my soul that had to be filled. I filled it with the Black Revolution. In practical terms, I filled it with Huey, because Huey is the incarnation of the Black Revolution, if you can dig that.

And then along came the Peace and Freedom Party. Politics. What the hell. We had called them, hadn't we? "Come See About Huey, but the rest of you don't come." No, we were serious, and there was very little time. The Black Revolution was at stake, and we needed every hand we could get, because the people needed information.

O.K. We had asked for it, and here it was: the Peace and Freedom Party. Politics. How do we relate to it? Shit. Do you think we had a hard time coming up with the answer, Governor? If you do, you are as wrong as two left shoes, because it was as simple as "States' Rights" is to George Wallace. He, by the way, came along with his National States' Rights Party, the American Independence Party, at the same time as the Peace and Freedom Party, as I'm sure you are aware. But they didn't come to see about Huey. I think they went to see about the Oakland Police Department and D. A. Coakley. The Peace and Freedom people only needed a little information because they already had a lot of their own. In fact, it would be fair to say that we exchanged information with them. After that, it was just a question of apportioning the work load, which we did, at the Richmond Auditorium, at the Founding Convention of the Peace and Freedom Party. That was in March, and a grand coalition was formed between Browns (Brown Caucus), Whites (White Caucus), and Blacks (Black Caucus)—that's a little complicated, Governor, I know, but let me leave it like that. If you want more information on that subject, contact the Peace and Freedom people or the Black Panthers or the Mexican-Americans, and they will fill you in. If I could leave here, I would be glad to go get that information for you, because you really should know about it, it's a brand new bag; but this joint I'm in sort of cramps my style. Information-wise.

The notorious, oppressive, racist, and brutal Oakland Police Department is at the heart of the matter. This gestapo force openly and flagrantly terrorizes the black people of Oakland. The Black Panther Party took a position against what the OPD was and is doing to black people. As one of the chief spokesmen for the party, I became well known to the OPD and I was hated by them. I know that they hated me; I've seen murderous hatred burning in their eyes. They hated the whole idea of a Black Panther Party, and they were out to destroy it. We were out, on the other hand, to organize the black community so that it could put an end to the terror. We saw no reason why we shouldn't do this, and nobody else seemed to be doing anything about it. If they were, it was not showing, because things were getting worse and not better. The OPD had increased its patrols of the black community to the saturation point, and become like a sword buried in the heart of the people. The Black Panther Party intended to remove that sword.

In its effort to counter the party's drive, the OPD launched a systematic campaign of harassment by arrest of party members, particularly its leaders. Take a look at the rap sheets of Huey P. Newton, our Minister of Defense, or David Hilliard, our National Captain, or Bobby Seale, our Chairman. You will find a string of phony cases as long as your arm. On October 28, 1967, they attempted to murder Huey, then charged him with murder when one of their own men came up dead. On April 6, 1968, they attempted to murder me, shot me, and did murder a member of our party—Bobby Hutton, seventeen years old. And then they charged me with attempting to murder them!

Governor Reagan, I would call to your attention an old saying: that where there is smoke there is fire; because there is a lot of smoke around the Oakland Police Department. I submit that the smoke is from the frequent use of their guns against the black community. It deserves looking into. As the Governor of the State of California, you would not be stepping out of your place if you looked into Oakland. Besides, it may be easier for you to look into Oakland than for anybody else. I understand that you have many friends and supporters in Oakland and that recently you received a warm welcome by the Republican convention there.

Well, on the night that I was shot and arrested, the OPD came up with the paranoid, fantastic notion that other members of the Black Panther Party *might* invade the jail and rescue me. (Shit. Anybody *might* do anything!) So they got in touch with the California Adult Authority (did they, I wonder, get in touch with you?) and asked them to come get me and take me to San Quentin. The OPD communicated its own panic to the Adult Authority, because at the absurd hour of 4 a.m., Sunday morning, April 7, two of its members (a quorum meeting over the telephone; voices groggy from sleep) ordered my parole revoked and I was taken to San Quentin, and from there to Vacaville. I have at last been served by the Adult Authority with three reasons for revoking my parole. Here they are:

1. Eldridge Cleaver violated his parole by being in possession of a gun.

2. Eldridge Cleaver violated his parole by associating with people of bad reputation.

3. Eldridge Cleaver violated his parole by failing to cooperate with his parole agent.

Are you outraged, Governor? I am, and I think you should be. Let me point out why. On what do they base the first charge? The impeccable word of the Oakland Police Department! (After the Surgeon General of the United States said to stop, after the Chiefs of Police of both San Francisco and Los Angeles issued orders to stop, the OPD still hasn't said that it will stop using mace on the citizens of the state you govern.) This charge by the Adult Authority amounts to nothing more nor less than an invasion into the province of the Judiciary. I have been imprisoned without a trial; I have entered a plea of Not Guilty to the charge in the Superior Court; but the Adult Authority has already convicted and sentenced me. Am I not entitled to a trial?

The second charge—that I associated with people of bad reputation—is fantastic. Now I realize that all black people have a bad reputation in the eyes of certain racists, but the Adult Authority here refers to members of the Black Panther Party. My parole officer, Mr Bilideau, told me, and I quote him, that "it's all right with us if you are a Black Panther." We had a full discussion of the matter and he merely cautioned me about Sacramento politicians who don't like the Panthers. My question is, in whose opinion does the Black Panther Party have a bad reputation? Certainly not in the opinion of the black community, and not in the opinion of all white people. So what's this shit about reputation? Hundreds of people, all over the Bay Area, all over the state, across the nation, and around the world, have cried out against the persecution of the Black Panther Party by the Oakland Police Department. As a matter of fact, if we are going to speak of reputations, the Oakland Police Department has the worst reputation of any police department in the State of California, and can only be compared to the racist police in Mississippi and South Africa. So what is the Adult Authority doing associated with this disreputable police force? Ah, they have a regular thing going. The prisons of California are bursting with people handed over by the Oakland Police Department. Pure and simple, this bad reputation jazz is nothing but political opinion, uninformed at that.

The third and last charge, that I failed to cooperate with my parole officer, turns my stomach inside out, because it is a lie. Like the other charges, it is an afterthought, conjured up as justification for the precipitous action of ordering me back to prison. (Why is it that when some people see that they have made a serious mistake, instead of moving to correct it and offer relief to the victim of their mistake, they move to fabricate a justification? I know a boxcarful of convicts who are better men than that, who are more than willing to admit that they were wrong.) The last time I saw my parole officer, just a few days before I was arrested, we shook hands, and his parting words to me were: "I want you to do me a favor, Eldridge. When I get a copy of your book, will you autograph it for me?" We both laughed, and I said, "Isn't this a fantastic turn of events? Just think of it: all these years I have been dependent on you guys signing things for me, and now I get a chance to sign something for you! It will be a pleasure!"

I do not know whether or not my parole officer actually submitted such a lying report against me, or whether the Adult Authority merely charged me in his name, because failure to cooperate with one's parole officer is a routine charge lodged against men whose paroles are revoked. It is a cliche, tossed in for good measure. And the Adult Authority operates in such a secret fashion, is cloaked with such an impenetrable shroud of darkness, that nobody knows what goes on in its Star Chamber proceedings. However, if my parole officer did submit that lie, I would be more hurt than surprised, because in my time I have seen enough of the organization men of the Department of Corrections so that nothing they do could surprise me, no matter how nauseating. But you know, Governor, when you have frequent contact with another person for eighteen months, something between you is built up. You get to know each other on a human level, you learn to see inside each other's personalities, and there are certain things that human beings naturally expect from each other, like not to be stabbed in the back. But, alas, it is not so, or else why and from what depth of a sense of betrayal, could Caesar say, Et tu Brute? *Et tu Bilideau?*

Well, there you are, Governor, that is more or less the substance of what I wanted to lay before you. But permit me to add a few remarks. I am finished with the California Department of Correction, with the Adult Authority, with parole officers, with prisons, and all of their world of restraint, confinement, and punishment. I can't relate to them anymore, because I am free. I am a free man, Governor, and I no longer know how to submit and play the part of a debtor to society. What I owe to society is the work that I must do outside these stone walls. My work can't wait, it won't wait, it should not wait. And you, Governor, should welcome me back to my job, becuase I was dealing with some of the most pressing problems facing not only the State of California but this nation and the world. And the people you can't reach, the dispossessed and oppressed people—whom you can't even talk to, whom you can't understand, and who neither trust nor understand you—are the very people with whom I am on the best of terms, for I am of them, I am one of them. You and I, Governor, have both been working on the same problems, except that you are working from the top down and I am working from the bottom up. The bottom of the world is in motion, Governor, and Bobby Dylan's "empty handed beggar" is at the door, except that his hand is not empty any more. He's got a gun in that hand. And he's stopped begging. In fact, he's nearly stopped talking, because it's becoming clear to him that hardly anybody is listening. When he finally stops talking altogether, he is going to start shooting. This brings to a conclusion what I wanted to talk to you about, and I have nothing else to say, except one question: Have you been listening to me, Governor?

> Respectfully submitted,
>
> Eldridge Cleaver,
> Minister of Information
> Black Panther Party.

21. Marlene Dixon

Why Women's Liberation?

The Women's Liberation Movement delivered the last major blow to
traditional cultural orthodoxies in the 1960s. Appearing late in the
decade, the movement was a revival of a long history of feminist agitation,
largely dormant after World War II. Some young women activists joined
in hopes of broadening the struggle for human equality pursued
earlier through radical and civil rights groups. Others discovered that
revolutionists did not always shuck off masculine prejudices and decided to
pursue equality along sex lines. During the Columbia student uprising,
for example, women were assigned housekeeping and cooking chores (a
practice in keeping with Che Guevara's manual) until they rebelled
and forced a more truly revolutionary division of duties.

Working women joined the movement as they became aware of and
troubled by discrimination in the work place, especially in pay. The
Bureau of the Census (Consumer Income, P-60, no. 75, December 14,
1970) reported at the close of the decade that whereas full-time white
male workers received an average income of almost $9650, white
women received only $5339. For nonwhites, the story was similar, but
at an appallingly low level: nonwhite men received $6021, and nonwhite
women only $4299. Other exploitive practices, from the manipulations
of advertisers to the biases of psychologists, were documented by
Betty Friedan in *The Feminine Mystique* (1963), a runaway best seller
that exposed the vacuity of the lives of many suburban housewives. She
described the American home as a "comfortable concentration camp"
where, as the "mystique" had it, housekeeping plus children plus
sex plus consumption equalled happiness. Friedan's successors demanded
an end to the cultural and commercial exploitation of women as
domestics and sexual objects, and, by calling for abortion on demand,
insisted on sovereignty over their own bodies.

In the following essay, Marlene Dixon, a sociologist now at McGill
University in Canada, discusses the causes of the Women's Liberation
Movement and analyzes several sources of women's oppression. She
concludes that significant improvement in the position of women depends
on radical social change, with some sort of socialism a minimum
requirement.

Professor Dixon's provocative article has not gone unchallenged.

From *Ramparts* magazine, *8* (December 1969). Copyright © Noah's Ark, Inc.
(for *Ramparts* magazine), 1969. By permission of the editors.

Black liberationists have questioned the usefulness of sex as a basis for a broad human-rights movement. Some suggest race instead. For many white radicals, the most crucial element uniting all oppressed groups is not sex but class and economic issues. Dixon's reconsiderations, incorporating these criticisms, may be found in a later article, "Public Ideology and the Class Composition of Women's Liberation (1966–1969)" *(Berkeley Journal of Sociology, XVI* [1971–1972]).

Other questions remain. How pervasive and damaging to human rights is sexual discrimination and can it be entirely separated from economic issues? Can marriage in its present form survive the liberation of women (and men)? To achieve real equality of roles, should attention be devoted equally to the liberation of men from the cultural and biological myths that enslave them? How should "social equality" of the sexes be defined?

The 1960's has been a decade of liberation; women have been swept up by that ferment along with blacks, Latins, American Indians and poor whites—the whole soft underbelly of this society. As each oppressed group in turn discovered the nature of its oppression in American society, so women have discovered that they too thirst for free and fully human lives. The result has been the growth of a new women's movement, whose base encompasses poor black and poor white women on relief, working women exploited in the labor force, middle class women incarcerated in the split level dream house, college girls awakening to the fact that sexiness is not the crowning achievement in life, and movement women who have discovered that in a freedom movement they themselves are not free. In less than four years women have created a variety of organizations, from the nationally-based middle class National Organization of Women (NOW) to local radical and radical feminist groups in every major city in North America. The new movement includes caucuses within nearly every New Left group and within most professional associations in the social sciences. Ranging in politics from reform to revolution, it has produced critiques of almost every segment of American society and constructed an ideology that rejects every hallowed cultural assumption about the nature and role of women.

As is typical of a young movement, much of its growth has been underground. The papers and manifestos written and circulated would surely comprise two very large volumes if published, but this literature is almost unknown outside of women's liberation. Nevertheless, where even a year ago organizing was slow and painful, with small cells of six or ten women, high turnover, and an uphill struggle against fear and resistance, in 1969 all that has changed. Groups are growing up everywhere with women eager to hear a hard line, to articulate and express their own rage and bitterness. Moving about the country, I have found an electric atmosphere of excitement and responsiveness. Everywhere there are doubts, stirrings, a desire to listen, to find out what it's all about. The extent to which groups have become politically radical is astounding. A year ago the movement stressed male chauvinism and psychological oppression; now the emphasis is on understanding the economic and social roots of women's oppression, and the analyses range from social democracy to Marxism. But the most striking change of all in the last year has been the loss of fear. Women are no longer afraid that their rebellion will threaten their very identity as women. They are not frightened by their own militancy, but liberated by it. Women's Liberation is an idea whose time has come.

The old women's movement burned itself out in the frantic decade of the 1920's. After a hundred years of struggle, women won a battle, only to lose the campaign: the vote was obtained, but the new millennium did not arrive. Women got the vote and achieved a measure of legal emancipation, but the real social and cultural barriers to full equality for women remained untouched.

For over 30 years the movement remained buried in its own ashes. Women were born and grew to maturity virtually ignorant of their own history of rebellion, aware only of a caricature of blue stockings and suffragettes. Even as increasing numbers of women were being driven into the labor force by the brutal conditions of the 1930's and by the massive drain of men into the military in the 1940's, the old ideal remained: a woman's place was in the home and behind her man. As the war ended and men returned to resume their jobs in factories and offices, women were forced back to the kitchen and nursery with a vengeance. This story has been repeated after each war and the reason is clear: women form a flexible, cheap labor pool which is essential to a capitalist system. When labor is scarce, they are forced onto the labor market. When labor is plentiful, they are forced out. Women and blacks have provided a reserve army of unemployed workers, benefiting capitalists and the stable male white working class alike. Yet the system imposes untold suffering on the victims, blacks and women, through low wages and chronic unemployment.

With the end of the war the average age at marriage declined, the average size of families went up, and the suburban migration began in earnest. The political conservatism of the '50s was echoed in a social conservatism which stressed a Victorian ideal of the woman's life: a full womb and selfless devotion to husband and children.

As the bleak decade played itself out, however, three important social developments emerged which were to make a rebirth of the women's struggle inevitable. First, women came to make up more than a third of the labor force, the number of working women being twice the prewar figure. Yet the marked increase in female employment did nothing to better the position of women, who were more occupationally disadvantaged in the 1960's than they had been 25 years earlier. Rather than moving equally into all sectors of the occupational structure, they were being forced into the low paying service, clerical and semi-skilled categories. In 1940, women had held 45 per cent of all professional and technical positions; in 1967, they held only 37 per cent. The proportion of women in service jobs meanwhile rose from 50 to 55 per cent.

Second, the intoxicating wine of marriage and suburban life was turning sour; a generation of women woke up to find their children grown and a life (roughly 30 more productive years) of housework and bridge parties stretching out before them like a wasteland. For many younger women, the empty drudgery they saw in the suburban life was a sobering contradiction to adolescent dreams of romantic love and the fulfilling role of woman as wife and mother.

Third, a growing civil rights movement was sweeping thousands of young men and women into a moral crusade—a crusade which harsh political experience was to transmute into the New Left. The American Dream was riven and tattered in Mississippi and finally napalmed in Viet-Nam. Young Americans were drawn not to Levittown, but to Berkeley, the Haight-Ashbury and the East Village. Traditional political ideologies and cultural myths, sexual mores and sex roles with them, began to disintegrate in an explosion of rebellion and protest.

The three major groups which make up the new women's movement —working women, middle class married women and students—bring very different kinds of interests and objectives to women's liberation. Working women are most concerned with the economic issues of guaranteed employment, fair wages, job discrimination and child care. Their most immediate oppression is rooted in industrial capitalism and felt directly through the vicissitudes of an exploitative labor market.

Middle class women, oppressed by the psychological mutilation and injustice of institutionalized segregation, discrimination and imposed inferiority, are most sensitive to the dehumanizing consequences of severely limited lives. Usually well educated and capable, these women are rebelling against being forced to trivialize their lives, to live vicariously through husbands and children.

Students, as unmarried middle class girls, have been most sensitized to the sexual exploitation of women. They have experienced the frustration of one-way relationships in which the girl is forced into a "wife" and companion role with none of the supposed benefits of marriage. Young women have increasingly rebelled not only against passivity and dependency in their relationships but also against the notion that they must function as sexual objects, being defined in purely sexual rather than human terms, and being forced to package and sell themselves as commodities on the sex market.

Each group represents an independent aspect of the total institutionalized oppression of women. Their differences are those of emphasis and immediate interest rather than of fundamental goals. All women suffer from economic exploitation, from psychological deprivation, and from exploitive sexuality. Within women's liberation there is a growing understanding that the common oppression of women provides the basis for uniting across class and race lines to form a powerful and radical movement.

Racism and Male Supremacy

Clearly, for the liberation of women to become a reality it is necessary to destroy the ideology of male supremacy which asserts the biological and social inferiority of women in order to justify massive institutionalized oppression. Yet we all know that many women are as loud in their disavowal of this oppression as are the men who chant the litany of "a woman's place is in the home and behind her man." In fact, women are as trapped in their false consciousness as were the mass of blacks 20 years ago, and for much the same reason.

As blacks were defined and limited socially by their color, so women are defined and limited by their sex. While blacks, it was argued, were preordained by God or nature, or both, to be hewers of wood and drawers of water, so women are destined to bear and rear children, and to sustain their husbands with obedience and compassion. The Sky-God tramples through the heavens and the Earth/Mother-Goddess is always flat on her back with her legs spread, putting out for one and all.

Indeed, the phenomenon of male chauvinism can only be understood when it is perceived as a form of racism, based on stereotypes drawn from a deep belief in the biological inferiority of women. The so-called "black analogy" is no analogy at all; it is the same social process that is at work, a process which both justifies and helps perpetuate the exploitation of one group of human beings by another.

The very stereotypes that express the society's belief in the biological inferiority of women recall the images used to justify the oppression of blacks. The nature of women, like that of slaves, is depicted as dependent, incapable of reasoned thought, childlike in its simplicity and warmth, martyred in the role of mother, and mystical in the role of sexual partner. In its benevolent form, the inferior position of women results in paternalism; in its malevolent form, a domestic tyranny which can be unbelievably brutal.

It has taken over 50 years to discredit the scientific and social "proof" which once gave legitimacy to the myths of black racial inferiority. Today most people can see that the theory of the genetic inferiority of blacks is absurd. Yet few are shocked by the fact that scientists are still busy "proving" the biological inferiority of women.

In recent years, in which blacks have led the struggle for liberation, the emphasis on racism has focused only upon racism against blacks. The fact that "racism" has been practiced against many groups other than blacks has been pushed into the background. Indeed, a less forceful but more accurate term for the phenomenon would be "social Darwinism." It was the opinion of the social Darwinists that in the natural course of things the "fit" succeed (i.e. oppress) and the "unfit" (i.e. the biologically inferior) sink to the bottom. According to this view, the very fact of a group's oppression proves its inferiority and the inevitable correctness of its low position. In this way each successive immigrant group coming to America was decked out in the garments of "racial" or biological inferiority until the group was sufficiently assimilated, whereupon Anglo-Saxon venom would turn on a new group filling up the space at the bottom. Now two groups remain, neither of which has been assimilated according to the classic American pattern: the "visibles"—blacks and women. It is equally true for both: "it won't wear off."

Yet the greatest obstacle facing those who would organize women remains women's belief in their own inferiority. Just as all subject populations are controlled by their acceptance of the rightness of their own status, so women remain subject because they believe in the rightness of their own oppression. This dilemma is not a fortuitous one, for the entire society is geared to socialize women to believe in and adopt as immutable necessity their traditional and inferior role. From earliest training to the grave, women are constrained and propagandized. Spend an evening at the movies or watching television, and you will see a grotesque figure called woman presented in a hundred variations upon the themes of "children, church, kitchen" or "the chick sex-pot."

For those who believe in the "rights of mankind," the dignity of man," consider that to make a woman a person, a human being in her own right, you would have to change her sex: imagine Stokely Carmichael "prone and silent"; imagine Mark Rudd as a Laugh-In girl; picture Rennie Davis as Miss America. Such contradictions as these show how pervasive and deep-rooted is the cultural contempt for women, how difficult it is to imagine a woman as a serious human being, or conversely, how empty and degrading is the image of woman that floods the culture.

Countless studies have shown that black acceptance of white stereo-types leads to mutilated identity, to alienation, to rage and self-hatred. Human beings cannot bear in their own hearts the contradictions of those who hold them in contempt. The ideology of male supremacy and its ef-fect upon women merits as serious study as has been given to the effects of prejudice upon Jews, blacks, and immigrant groups.

It is customary to shame those who would draw the parallel between women and blacks by a great show of concern and chest beating over the suffering of black people. Yet this response itself reveals a refined combi-nation of white middle class guilt and male chauvinism, for it overlooks several essential facts. For example, the most oppressed group within the feminine population is made up of black women, many of whom take a dim view of the black male intellectual's adoption of white male attitudes of sexual superiority (an irony too cruel to require comment). Neither are those who make this pious objection to the racial parallel addressing themselves very adequately to the millions of white working class women living at the poverty level, who are not likely to be moved by this middle class guilt-ridden one-upmanship while having to deal with the boss, the factory, or the welfare worker day after day. They are already dangerous-ly resentful of the gains made by blacks, and much of their "racist back-lash" stems from the fact that they have been forgotten in the push for social change. Emphasis on the real mechanisms of oppression—on the commonality of the process—is essential lest groups such as these, which should work in alliance, become divided against one another

White middle class males already struggling with the acknowledgment of their own racism do not relish an added burden of recognition: that to white guilt must soon be added "male." It is therefore understandable that they should refuse to see the harshness of the lives of most women —to honestly face the facts of massive institutionalized discrimination against women. Witness the performance to date: "Take her down off the platform and give her a good fuck," "Petty Bourgeois Revisionist Running Dogs," or in the classic words of a Berkeley male "leader," "Let them eat cock."

Among whites, women remain the most oppressed—and the most un-organized—group. Although they constitute a potential mass base for the radical movement, in terms of movement priorities they are ignored; in-deed they might as well be invisible. Far from being an accident, this omission is a direct outgrowth of the solid male supremist beliefs of white radical and left-liberal men. Even now, faced with both fact and agita-tion, leftist men find the idea of placing any serious priority upon women so outrageous, such a degrading notion, that they respond with a viru-lence far out of proportion to the modest requests of movement women.

This only shows that women must stop wasting their time worrying about the chauvinism of men in the movement and focus instead on their real priority: organizing women.

Marriage: Genesis of Women's Rebellion

The institution of marriage is the chief vehicle for the perpetuation of the oppression of women; it is through the role of wife that the subjugation of women is maintained. In a very real way the role of wife has been the genesis of women's rebellion throughout history.

Looking at marriage from a detached point of view one may well ask why anyone gets married, much less women. One answer lies in the economics of women's position, for women are so occupationally limited that drudgery in the home is considered to be infinitely superior to drudgery in the factory. Secondly, women themselves have no independent social status. Indeed, there is no clearer index of the social worth of a woman in this society than the fact that she has none in her own right. A woman is first defined by the man to whom she is attached, but more particularly by the man she marries, and secondly by the children she bears and rears —hence the anxiety over sexual attractiveness, the frantic scramble for boyfriends and husbands. Having obtained and married a man the race is then on to have children, in order that their attractiveness and accomplishments may add more social worth. In a woman, not having children is seen as an incapacity somewhat akin to impotence in a man.

Beneath all of the pressures of the sexual marketplace and the marital status game, however, there is a far more sinister organization of economic exploitation and psychological mutilation. The housewife role, usually defined in terms of the biological duty of a woman to reproduce and her "innate" suitability for a nurturant and companionship role, is actually crucial to industrial capitalism in an advanced state of technological development. In fact, the housewife (some 44 million women of all classes, ethnic groups and races) provides, unpaid, absolutely essential services and labor. In turn, her assumption of all household duties makes it possible for the man to spend the majority of his time at the workplace.

It is important to understand the social and economic exploitation of the married women, since the real productivity of her labor is denied by the commonly held assumption that she is dependent on her husband, exchanging her keep for emotional and nurturant services. Margaret Benston, a radical women's liberation leader, points out: "In sheer quantity, household labor, including child care, constitutes a huge amount of socially necessary production. Nevertheless, in a society based on commodity production, it is not usually considered even as 'real work' since it is outside of trade and the marketplace. This assignment of household work as the function of a special category 'women' means that this group *does* stand in a different relationship to production. . . . The material basis for the inferior status of women is to be found in just this definition of women. In a society in which money determines value, women are a group who work outside the money economy. Their work is not worth money, is therefore valueless, is therefore not even real work. And women themselves, who do this valueless work, can hardly be expected to be worth as much as men, who work for money."

Women are essential to the economy not only as free labor, but also as consumers. The American system of capitalism depends for its survival on the consumption of vast amounts of socially wasteful goods, and a prime target for the unloading of this waste is the housewife. She is the purchasing agent for the family, but beyond that she is eager to buy because her own identity depends on her accomplishments as a consumer and her ability to satisfy the wants of her husband and children. This is not, of course, to say that she has any power in the economy. Although she spends the wealth, she does not own or control it—it simply passes through her hands.

In addition to their role as housewives and consumers, increasing numbers of women are taking outside employment. These women leave the home to join an exploited labor force, only to return at night to assume the double burden of housework on top of wage work—that is, they are forced to work at two full-time jobs. No man is required or expected to take on such a burden. The result: two workers from one household in the labor force with no cutback in essential female functions—three for the price of two, quite a bargain.

Frederick Engels, now widely read in women's liberation, argues that, regardless of her status in the larger society, within the context of the family the woman's relationship to the man is one of proletariat to bourgeoisie. One consequence of this class division in the family is to weaken the capacity of men and women oppressed by the society to struggle together against it.

In all classes and groups, the institution of marriage functions to a greater or lesser degree to oppress women; the unity of women of different classes hinges upon our understanding of that common oppression. The 19th century women's movement refused to deal with marriage and sexuality, and chose instead to fight for the vote and elevate the feminine mystique to a political ideology. That decision retarded the movement for decades. But 1969 is not 1889. For one thing, there now exist alternatives to marriage. The most original and creative politics of the women's movement has come from a direct confrontation with the issue of marriage and sexuality. The cultural revolution—experimentation with lifestyles, communal living, collective child-rearing—have all come from the rebellion against dehumanized sexual relationships, against the notion of women as sexual commodities, against the constriction and spiritual strangulation inherent in the role of wife.

Lessons have been learned from the failures of the earlier movement as well. The feminine mystique is no longer mistaken for politics, nor gaining the vote for winning human rights. Women are now all together at the bottom of the work world; and the basis exists for a common focus of struggle for all women in American society. It remains for the movement to understand this, to avoid the mistakes of the past, to respond creatively to the possibilities of the present.

Women's oppression, although rooted in the institution of marriage, does not stop at the kitchen or the bedroom door. Indeed, the economic exploitation of women in the workplace is the most commonly recognized aspect of the oppression of women.

Most women who enter the labor force do not work for "pin money" or "self-fulfillment." Sixty-two per cent of all women working in 1967 were doing so out of economic need (i.e., were either alone or with husbands earning less than $5000 a year). In 1963, 36 per cent of American families had an income of less than $5000 a year. Women from these families work because they must; they contribute 35 to 40 per cent of the family's total income when working full-time, and 15 to 20 per cent when working part-time.

Despite their need, however, women have always represented the most exploited sector of the industrial labor force. Child and female labor were introduced during the early stages of industrial capitalism, at a time when most men were gainfully employed in crafts. As industrialization developed and craft jobs were eliminated, men entered the industrial labor force, driving women and children into the lowest categories of work and pay. Indeed, the position of women and children industrial workers was so pitiful, and their wages so small, that the craft unions refused to organize them. Even when women organized themselves and engaged in militant strikes and labor agitation—from the shoemakers of Lynn, Massachusetts, to the International Ladies' Garment Workers and their great strike of 1909—male unionists continued to ignore their needs. As a result of this male supremacy in the unions, women remain essentially unorganized, despite the fact that they are becoming an ever larger part of the labor force.

The trend is clearly toward increasing numbers of women entering the work force: women represented 55 per cent of the growth of the total labor force in 1962, and the number of working women rose from 16.9 million in 1957 to 24 million in 1962. There is every indication that the number of women in the labor force will continue to grow as rapidly in the future.

Job discrimination against women exists in all sectors of work, even in occupations which are predominantly made up of women. This discrimination is reinforced in the field of education, where women are being short-changed at a time when the job market demands higher educational levels. In 1962, for example, while women constituted 53 per cent of the graduating high school class, only 42 per cent of the entering college class were women. Only one in three people who received a B.A. or M.A. in that year was a woman, and only one in ten who received a Ph.D. was a woman. These figures represent a decline in educational achievement for women since the 1930's, when women received two out of five of the B.A. and M.A. degrees given, and one out of seven of the Ph.Ds. While there has been a dramatic increase in the number of people, including women, who go to college, women have not kept pace with men in terms of educational achievement. Furthermore, women have lost ground in professional employment. In 1960 only 22 per cent of the faculty and other professional staff at colleges and universities were women—down from 28 per cent in 1949, 27 per cent in 1930, 26 per cent in 1920. 1960 does beat 1919 with only 20 per cent—"you've come a long way, baby"—right back to where you started! In other professional categories: 10 per cent of all scientists are women, 7 per cent of all physicians, 3 per cent of all lawyers, and 1 per cent of all engineers.

Even when women do obtain an education, in many cases it does them little good. Women, whatever their educational level, are concentrated in the lower paying occupations. The figures in Chart A tell a story that most women know and few men will admit: most women are forced to work at clerical jobs, for which they are paid, on the average, $1600 less per year than men doing the same work. Working class women in the service and operative (semi-skilled) categories, making up 30 per cent of working women, are paid $1900 less per year on the average than are men. Of all working women, only 13 per cent are professionals (including low-pay and low-status work such as teaching, nursing and social work), and they earn $2600 less per year than do professional men. Household workers, the lowest category of all, are predominantly women (over 2 million) and predominantly black and third world, earning for their labor barely over $1000 per year.

Not only are women forced onto the lowest rungs of the occupational ladder, they are in the lowest income levels as well. The most constant and bitter injustice experienced by all women is the income differential. While women might passively accept low status jobs, limited opportunities for advancement, and discrimination in the factory, office and university, they choke finally on the daily fact that the male worker next to them earns more, and usually does less. In 1965 the median wage or salary income of year-round full-time women workers was only 60 per cent that of men, a 4 per cent loss since 1955. Twenty-nine per cent of working women earned less than $3000 a year as compared with 11 per cent of the men; 43 per cent of the women earned from $3000 to $5000 a year as compared with 19 per cent of the men; and 9 per cent of the women earned $7000 or more as compared with 43 per cent of the men.

CHART A
COMPARATIVE STATISTICS FOR MEN AND WOMEN IN THE LABOR FORCE, 1960

Occupation	Percentage of Working Women in Each Occupational Category	Income of Year Round Full Time Workers		Numbers of Workers in Millions	
		Women	Men	Women	Men
Professional	13	$4358	$7115	3	5
Managers, Officials and Proprietors	5	3514	7241	1	5
Clerical	31	3586	5247	7	3
Operatives	15	2970	4977	4	9
Sales	7	2389	5842	2	3
Service	15	2340	4089	3	3
Private household	10	1156	—	2	—

Sources. U.S. Department of Commerce, Bureau of the Census: "Current Population Reports," P-60, No. 37, and U.S. Department of Labor, Bureau of Labor Statistics and U.S. Department of Commerce, Bureau of the Census.

What most people do not know is that in certain respects, women suffer more than do non-white men, and that black and third world women suffer most of all.

CHART B
MEDIAN ANNUAL WAGES FOR MEN AND WOMEN BY RACE, 1960

Workers	Median Annual Wage
Males, white	$5137
Males, nonwhite	3075
Females, white	2537
Females, nonwhite	1276

Source. U.S. Department of Commerce, Bureau of the Census. Also see: President's Commission on the Status of Women, 1963.

Women, regardless of race, are more disadvantaged than are men, including non-white men. White women earn $2600 less than white men and $1500 less than non-white men. The brunt of the inequality is carried by 2.5 million non-white women, 94 per cent of whom are black. They earn $3800 less than white men, $1900 less than non-white men, and $1200 less than white women.

There is no more bitter paradox in the racism of this country than that the white man, articulating the male supremacy of the white male middle class, should provide the rationale for the oppression of black women by black men. Black women constitute the largest minority in the United States, and they are the most disadvantaged group in the labor force. The further oppression of black women will not liberate black men, for black women were never the oppressors of their men—that is a myth of the liberal white man. The oppression of black men comes from institutionalized racism and economic exploitation: from the world of the white man. Consider the following facts and figures.

The percentage of black working women has always been proportionately greater than that of white women. In 1900, 41 per cent of black women were employed, as compared to 17 per cent for white women. In 1963, the proportion of black women employed was still a fourth greater than that of whites. In 1960, 44 per cent of black married women with children under six years were in the labor force, in contrast to 29 per cent for white women. While job competition requires ever higher levels of education, the bulk of illiterate women are black. On the whole, black women—who often have the greatest need for employment—are the most discriminated against in terms of opportunity. Forced by an oppressive and racist society to carry unbelievably heavy economic and social burdens, black women stand at the bottom of that society, doubly marked by the caste signs of color and sex.

The rise of new agitation for the occupational equality of women also coincided with the re-entry of the "lost generation"—the housewives of the 1950s—into the job market. Women from middle class backgrounds, faced with an "empty nest" (children grown or in school) and a widowed or divorced rate of one-fourth to one-third of all marriages, returned to the workplace in large numbers. But once there they discovered that women, middle class or otherwise, are the last hired, the lowest paid, the least often promoted, and the first fired. Furthermore, women are more likely to suffer job discrimination on the basis of age, so the widowed and divorced suffer particularly, even though their economic need to work is often urgent. Age discrimination also means that the option of work after child-rearing is limited. Even highly qualified older women find themselves forced into low-paid, unskilled or semi-skilled work—if they are lucky enough to find a job in the first place.

The realities of the work world for most middle class women—that they become members of the working class, like it or not—are understandably distant to many young men and women in college who have never had to work, and who tend to think of the industrial "proletariat" as a revolutionary force, to the exclusion of "bourgeois" working women. Their image of the "pampered middle class woman" is factually incorrect and political naive. It is middle class women forced into working class life who are often the first to become conscious of the contradiction between the "American Dream" and their daily experience.

Faced with discrimination on the job—after being forced into the lower levels of the occupational structure—millions of women are inescapably presented with the fundamental contradictions in their unequal treatment and their massive exploitation. The rapid growth of women's liberation as a movement is related in part to the exploitation of working women in all occupational categories.

Male supremacy, marriage, and the structure of wage labor—each of these aspects of women's oppression has been crucial to the resurgence of the women's struggle. It must be abundantly clear that radical social change must occur before there can be significant improvement in the social position of women. Some form of socialism is a minimum requirement, considering the changes that must come in the institutions of marriage and the family alone. The intrinsic radicalism of the struggle for women's liberation necessarily links women with all other oppressed groups.

The heart of the movement, as in all freedom movements, rests in women's knowledge, whether articulated or still only an illness without a name, that they are not inferior—not chicks, nor bunnies, nor quail, nor cows, nor bitches, nor ass, nor meat. Women hear the litany of their own dehumanization each day. Yet all the same, women know that male supremacy is a lie. They know they are not animals or sexual objects or commodities. They know their lives are mutilated, because they see within themselves a promise of creativity and personal integration. Feeling the contradiction between the essentially creative and self-actualizing human being within her, and the cruel and degrading less-than-human role she is compelled to play, a woman begins to perceive the falseness of what her society has forced her to be. And once she perceives this, she knows that she must fight.

Women must learn the meaning of rage, the violence that liberates the human spirit. The rhetoric of invective is an equally essential stage, for in discovering and venting their rage against the enemy—and the enemy in everyday life is men—women also experience the justice of their own violence. They learn the first lessons in their own latent strength. Women must learn to know themselves as revolutionaries. They must become hard and strong in their determination, while retaining their humanity and tenderness.

There is a rage that impels women into a total commitment to women's liberation. That ferocity stems from a denial of mutilation; it is a cry for life, a cry for the liberation of the spirit. Roxanne Dunbar, surely one of the most impressive women in the movement, conveys the feelings of many: "We are damaged—we women, we oppressed, we disinherited. There are very few who are not damaged, and they rule. . . . The oppressed trust those who rule more than they trust themselves, because self-contempt emerges from powerlessness. Anyway, few oppressed people believe that life could be much different. . . . We are damaged and we have the right to hate and have contempt and to kill and to scream. But for what? . . . Do we want the oppressor to admit he is wrong, to withdraw his misuse of us? He is only too happy to admit guilt—then do nothing but try to absorb and exorcize the new thought. . . . That does not make up for what I have lost, what I never had, and what all those others who are worse off than I never had. . . . Nothing will compensate for the irreparable harm it has done to my sisters. . . . How could we possibly settle for anything remotely less, even take a crumb in the meantime less, than total annihilation of a system which systematically destroys half its people. . . ."

22. Robert Coles

The Middle Americans

Young radicals, intellectuals, blacks, and women held no monopoly on
discontent in the 1960s; it was also expressed by Middle Americans—
the "plain people" or "average people" or "ordinary people" as
they are apt to call themselves. Who are they? Robert Coles, a child
psychiatrist on the staff of the Harvard University Health Services, writes
that they are "not black, not red, not brown, not unemployed, not eligible
for or desirous of welfare, not intellectuals, not hippies, not members
of a drug scene, a youth cult, a 'counterculture,' not in general against
our military position in the world, not rich, not professional men,
not 'big businessmen,' not individuals exceptionally well-born, well-to-do,
well educated." Instead, the Middle Americans consist of families headed
by factory workers, policemen, firemen, construction workers, telephone
repairmen, clerks, small farmers, and small storekeepers,"—people
whom politicians frequently term the "silent majority" or the "forgotten
Americans."

Robert Coles has lived among them for many years in hopes of
learning what they believe and hope for in life. His contribution does
not consist of the presentation of statistical analyses, the construction
of "theoretical models," or the discovery of a "social type"; instead, his task
has been to see and listen in a manner reminiscent of the now classic
depression documentary, *Let Us Now Praise Famous Men* (1941),
written by James Agee and Walker Evans. Photographs taken by Jon
Erikson and effectively correlated with Coles' commentary, add insight to
this sensitive study of mainstream America. Contrary to the previous
selections in this section, the dominant note is one of uncertainty and
ambivalence in relation to corporate power, blacks and civil rights,
and education.

The Middle Americans sheds light on numerous questions that have
engaged the attention of academics, sociologists, journalists, politicians,
and public relations men alike. Why do so many Americans feel left out,
confused, ignored, and enraged? In what ways are these millions of
Americans peculiarly vulnerable in modern technocratic society? What is
the basis for the distrust of blacks so prominent among Middle
Americans? Precisely when do cultural issues supersede the traditional
economic issues in their voting patterns? Is the selection from Scammon
and Wattenberg, *The Real Majority*, helpful on this point? As Coles
phrases it, are middle Americans best thought of as socially insecure,
economically marginal, politically unorganized, or what?

"We are proud of ourselves, that's what I'd like to say. We're not sure of things, though; we're uncertain, I'm afraid, and when you're like that—worried, it is—then you're going to lose a little respect for yourself. You're not so proud anymore." There he goes, like a roller coaster; he is up one minute, full of self-confidence and glad that he is himself and no one else, and the next minute he is down, enough so to wish he somehow could have another chance at his life, start in again and avoid the mistakes and seize the opportunities and by God, "get up there."

Now, where is "there" for him? In the observer's mind the question is naturally asked, but the man who speaks like that about his destination would not understand why anyone would feel the need to do so, require a person to say the most obvious things in the world. In fact, if the question were actually asked, the man would have one of his own in return, which out of courtesy he might keep to himself: you mean you don't know? And that would be as far as the man would want to take the discussion. He has no interest in talking about life's "meanings," about his "goals" and his "values." At least, he has no interest in a direct and explicitly acknowledged discussion of that kind. He feels more comfortable when he slides into such matters, when he is talking about something quite concrete and of immediate concern and then for a few minutes finds himself "going off." It is not that he minds becoming introspective or philosophical or whatever; he likes to catch himself "getting carried away" with ideas and observations. What he dislikes is the self-consciousness and self-congratulation and self-display that go with "discussions." Perhaps he is "defensive" about his lack of a college education. Perhaps he feels "inferior," suffers from a poor "self-image." Sometimes a visitor slides into that way of looking at a person, even as sometimes the person being branded and pinioned comes up with considerably more than the self-justifications he at first seems intent upon offering: "Maybe we should ask ourselves more questions, Doris and me, like you do. I don't have time for questions; and neither does my wife. Mind you, I'm not objecting to yours. They're not bad questions. I'll have to admit, there'll be a few seconds here and there when I'll put them to myself. I'll say, Joe, what's it all about, and why in hell kill yourself at two jobs? I'll ask myself what I want out of life. My dad, he'd do the same, I can remember."

He can indeed remember. At forty-three he can remember the thirties, remember his father's vain efforts to find work. He can remember those three letters, WPA; he can remember being punished, shouted at, and grabbed and shouted at some more, because he dropped an ice-cream cone. Did he know what a nickel meant, or a dime? Did he know how few of them there are, how hard they are to come by? Now, his youngest son has a toolbox, and once in a while tries to pound a nail through a nickel or a dime, or even a quarter. The father gets a little nervous about such activities, but soon his apprehension gives way to those memories —to an amused, relaxed moment of recall. Indeed, it is just such ironies, both personal and historic, that get him going. And that is how he often does get going, with an ironic disclaimer: "I don't want to go on and on about the depression. My dad will do that at the drop of a hat. We've never had another one so bad since the Second World War started, so I don't believe we're in danger. But you can't forget, even if you were only a kid then. When my kids start complaining, I tell them they should know what their grandfather went through. I start telling them what it was like in America then; but they don't take in what you say. They listen, don't get me wrong. No child of mine is going to walk away from me when I'm talking. I have them looking right at me. But they think I'm exaggerating. I know they do. My wife says it's because they were born in good times, and that's all they've ever known. Maybe she's right. But even now for the workingman, the average guy, it's no picnic. That's what I really want my kids to know: it's no picnic. Life, it's tough. You have to work and work and work."

Then he adds that he likes work. No, he *loves* work. What would he do without it? He'd be sitting around. He'd go crazy. He'd last maybe a few weeks, then go back and be glad to be back. True, he'd like to get rid of his second job. That's not work, what he does in the evenings—after supper, or on weekends and some holidays. He needs the extra money. The bills have mounted and mounted. Prices are not merely "up"; they are "so high it's a joke, the kind of joke that makes you want to cry." So, he finds "odd jobs," one after the other, but when he talks about them he doesn't talk about his *work;* he refers to the *jobs,* and often enough, the damned jobs. . . .

Joe and Doris see no reason to make lists of "criteria" that characterize the people they feel comfortable with, or on the contrary don't; but upon occasion they will spell things out rather clearly. Joe will talk about "brainy people." One of his friends has a son who is just studying and studying, not in order to become a doctor or a lawyer (which is fine) but to stay out of the draft (Joe thinks) and "because he's so shy he can't talk to people, so he lives in the library." The subject of libraries and the universities that own them leads to other matters. Joe and Doris want those libraries and universities for their children, and indeed, their oldest son is in his first year of college. But no one can be snobbier, more arrogant and condescending than "a certain kind of professor" or a lot of those "professional students," which means students who are not content to study and to learn, but make nuisances of themselves, flaunt themselves before the public, disrupt things, behave like fools. He gets angry as he gets further into the discussion, but his wife slows him down, and even manages to cause a partial reversal of his views. After all, she insists, he is always complaining about certain things that are wrong with the country. He is always saying that the rich are getting richer, and the ordinary man, he can barely keep up with himself. Someone has to do more than complain; someone has to say unpopular things. Doris herself does so, says unpopular things, at least at certain times—though only to her husband, when they are having a talk. And soon Joe switches, says maybe, says yes, says it is true that some of the students are good, mean well, are on the workingman's side against the big corporations.

They don't like those big corporations; Joe and Doris don't, and their neighbors don't. If the students are at different times called vulgar, wild, crazy, insulting, and obscene, the corporations are declared clever, wily, treacherous, dishonest, and powerful beyond belief. Doris believes in "balancing things," and she believes in keeping her cool. She wants her husband, also, to have a certain distance on events. When he takes after college students, she reminds him that they have one in the family, hope to have more in the family as the years go by. And she brings up the corporations, and the way they "behave." They are decorous and restrained, but in Doris's mind they are no less outrageous than "the bad element" among the students, the ones who "look so awful" and make her and everyone she knows feel uncomfortable and puzzled and really, at a loss.

After a while one can see that Doris and Joe are just that: at a loss to figure certain things out, at a loss to know how their own various opinions can ever become reconciled into some consistent, believable and coherent viewpoint. To some extent, they well know, the task is hopeless, because like the proudest, most knowing social critic, they are thoroughly aware of the ambiguities and ironies they, we, everyone must face: "I try to slow Joe down. He'll be watching the news, and he shouts at the demonstrators, you know. He doesn't like the colored very much. He says they're pushing too hard on the rest of us. I agree, but I think we ought to be careful, because the children will hear, and they'll repeat what they listen to us saying in Sunday School, and that's no good. Our son wants to be an engineer. He is in college. He is a sensible boy. He'll never be a radical or a militant. But he tells his father to go easy, and I agree. Where I go wild is on prices. They go up and up and no one seems to want to stop them. I voted Republican for the first time last year, because I thought they'd do something. But they're like the Democrats. They're all the same. They're all a bunch of politicians, every one of them. Joe says I'm as nutty when I talk about politicians and the prices in the supermarket as he is when he talks about the colored and the college students.

"There are times when I wonder who really runs this country. It's not people like us, that I know. We vote, we do what we're supposed to do and we go fight in the wars—I lost a brother in the Second World War and a cousin in the Korean War, and I hope to God my son doesn't end up in Vietnam, like my nephew, his cousin—but we don't get any place for being good citizens. There are some big people, in Washington I guess, and they make all the decisions; and then it's left for us to go and send our boys to fight, and try to pay the high prices that the politicians have caused us to have. Don't ask me more. I don't know who the big people are. But it's a clique. They own the stocks in the banks and the corporations. It's up to them, what the country does. We get these letters from our Congressman, that he sends around, and it's just a lot of talk. . . .

"I'm bitter. You bet your goddamn dollar I'm bitter. It's people like us who give up our sons for the country. The business people, they run the country and make money from it. The college types, the professors, they go to Washington and tell the government what to do. Do this, they say; do that. But their sons, they don't end up in the swamps over there, in Vietnam. No sir. They're deferred, because they're in school. Or they get sent to safe places. Or they get out with all those letters they have from their doctors. Ralph told me. He told me what went on at his physical. He said most of the kids were from average homes; and the few rich kids there were, they all had big-deal letters saying they weren't eligible. They looked eligible to Ralph. Let's face it: if you have a lot of money, or if you have the right connections, you don't end up on a firing line in the jungle over there, not unless you *want* to. Ralph had no choice. He didn't want to die. He wanted to live. They just took him—to 'defend democracy,' that's what they keep on saying. Hell, I wonder. If I was a colored kid, they couldn't get me to go over there. I'd sooner go to prison. Let them 'defend democracy' right here at home. Those big-shot American officials ought to ride their military helicopters over their own country, and see the mess *it's in.*

"I shouldn't be talking like this; I know it. I'm strong for this country. It's the best country in the world. Where else could a guy like me, who didn't even finish high school, live the way I do? I'm not floating in cash; actually, every week we wonder if we'll make it to the next, the way prices are. But we're not starving to death, and we have a nice little house here. And I can say what I've just said. No one's carting me off to jail. I think they *should* take some of those draft-resister types and put them in jail. What right do they have to demoralize the country, when our boys are over there, overseas, fighting. Every night it seems they announce new deaths. More and more innocent kids are killed. For what? I ask you, for what? I watch the news every night. I see some of those faces, the people who decide things in Washington. They're full of talk and talk and more talk. They've got their ideas and their plans, more and more of them. The President, he has one man, I read someplace, sitting around all day making new plans for what we're supposed to do here, there and everywhere, all over the lousy, rotten world. There's plan A for this country and plan B for that one, in case they go against us, the different countries. Then we'll send our Ralphs over. The President's adviser, he's not going over there to fight. His big brain stays home, and the Ralphs of America—it's *the Ralphs of America* who pay every time. Do they pay!" . . .

Not that she or her husband spend much time talking about such frustrating, mystifying and upsetting issues. By and large they shun what Doris calls "current events." There is more than enough to do from day to day. Joe works almost all the time. Doris does, too. She has four children to look after. She has a house to keep clean, very clean. She has her aged mother to visit, who lives nearby with Doris's older sister. And then of late Doris has also had to find work. She doesn't "always" work, but she "helps out" at a luncheonette for two hours, eleven to one, five days a week. Her husband did not want her to do so, but she insisted, and she got her way. She rather likes the work, serving the crowded tables. She gets a view of the outside world. She meets people. She hears people talk, and she learns what is on their minds. She makes a few dollars. She feels more independent. She feels that time goes by more quickly. And much as she dislikes talking about all the world's problems, she finds herself listening rather intently to what others have to say about those problems: "I can't help it. I'll be coming over to a table with the food, and serving it, and I'll hear them, the men on their lunch hour, and the women, too. They all talk the same way, when you come right down to it. They're worried about where the country is going. Yesterday I waited on a man who lost his son in Vietnam. You know how I know? I heard him telling his friend that the boy died so we could be safe over here. I'm sure he's right. I couldn't help wondering what I'd say if it happened to me, if I lost my son. I guess I'd say what he did, that man. My husband says there's nothing else you *can* say. You have to believe your own government. I mean, if you start turning on your own country, then what have you got left? The answer is nothing, I guess.

"I don't think the country is being run the way it should be. Don't ask me how I'd do better, but everyone I know agrees we're in trouble: boys dying every day over there in the jungle, and here the criminals taking over. There's the big gangsters, the Mafia, and there's the demonstrators, and downtown there's the colored—little boys, no more than ten or twelve a lot of them, looking for things to steal. I've seen them steal in the department stores. They knock down women and run away with their pocketbooks. I don't even carry one any more when I go shopping in town. And I only go there to do holiday shopping, because most of the stores have branches out in our plaza. Why don't the students and the college people demonstrate against the criminals? My sister-in-law was knocked down by three colored boys. They had a knife! They said they'd kill her. They took her pocketbook and ran. And you hear the Negro people asking for more, more, more!"

She would go so far and no further. She would never use the word "nigger." Her husband does, all the time he does; but when he goes further, starts cussing and swearing, starts sending people to hell, starts making sweeping, utterly unqualified judgments, she tries to stop him, and usually manages to succeed. She even gets him to reverse himself somewhat—which means, she gets him to say a number of *other* things he believes. For example, he believes that at birth "we're all just about the same," and he believes "it's the education a child gets that makes the difference," and he believes that "if a child is born poor and he doesn't get good food, then he's going to pay for it later."

As a matter of fact when he is feeling reflective and not pushed into a liberal corner by anyone, Joe will come up with some rather strong-minded rebuttals of his own assertions: "I can see how the niggers feel cheated out of things. If I was a Negro, I'd be madder than hell. I'd stand up to anyone who tried to keep me away from my share. We have a couple of them, carpenters, working with us on the job now. They're the best guys you could want. They work hard, and they're smart. They speak good, as good as anyone I know. If all the Negro people were like those two, then I can't believe we'd be having the trouble we are. A man is a man, that's what I believe; I don't care what his skin color is, or where he goes to church. This country has every kind of people in it; and it's all to the good, because that way no one group runs the show. The thing that bothers me about the Negro people is this: they're not like the rest of us, and I don't mean because their skin is a different color. I drive through their neighborhood. I've worked in the buildings where they live. I've listened to them talking, when they didn't even know I was listening. I'd be working on the pipes and I'd hear them from another apartment or down in the cellar. (The sound carries!) If you ask me, they're slow, that's what I think. They're out for a good time. They want things made easy for them —maybe not all of them, but plenty of them. They actually want relief. They think they're entitled to it!"

He stops. He lifts his head up, ever so slightly but noticeably nevertheless, and significantly. He is about to reminisce. After several years of visiting his home and getting to know him and his family, one can anticipate at least that much, the several directions his mind will pursue, if not the particular message he will deliver on a given day. So, he takes a slightly longer swallow of beer, and waits a few seconds, as if to pull them all together, all his memories. And then he is on his way: "I remember my father, how it killed him to take money from the government, the WPA, you know. I remember him crying. He said he wished he was never born, because it's not right that a man shouldn't be able to earn a living for his family. He could have stayed on relief longer, but he got off as fast as he could. He hated every day he didn't work. I guess they made some work for people, the WPA did; but no one was fooled, because it was phony work. When a man really wants to do something, and instead he's raking leaves and like that, he's even worse off than sitting on his porch all day—except that without the money, I guess we all would have starved to death.

"Now with the niggers it's different. They want all they can get—for free. They don't really like to work. They do work, a lot of them, I know. But it's against their wish, I believe. They seem to have the idea that they're entitled to something from the rest of us. That's the big thing with them: they've suffered, and we should cry our heads off and give them the country, lock, stock and barrel, because we've been bad to them, white people were. I have friends, a lot of them; and let me tell you, not one of them goes along with that way of thinking. You know why? It's an insult, it's an insult to you and me and everyone, including the niggers themselves. If I was a Negro, and someone came up to me and told me how sorry he was—sorry for what he'd done, his people had, and sorry for the Negro people—I'd tell him to get away fast, real fast, if he wanted to keep his good health. Pity is for the weak; my grandfather used to tell us kids that. But your niggers, a lot of them want pity; and they get it. You know who gives it to them? The rich ones out in the fancy suburbs, they're the ones—the bleeding hearts, always ready to pat people on the head and say you're wonderful, and we love you, and just sit back, we'll take care of you, with welfare and the rest, just like we do with our pet dogs."

There is more, much more. He fires himself up as he gets deeper and deeper into the subject, the issue, the argument he is setting forth. He reaches for more beer, and his wife gets slightly worried, then obviously nervous, then somewhat alarmed. She wants him to stop. She wants us to change the subject. She doesn't necessarily disagree with the thrust of his remarks; but the more he speaks, the longer the exposition, the more explicit the references and criticisms and illustrative examples, the more uncomfortable she feels. Why? What bothers her about her husband's ideas? He asks her that. She has told him that he is getting "carried away." He says yes, he is getting carried away with the truth, and if that is wrong, it is also rare "in this country, today." He invokes the "credibility gap." He reminds us that politicians and businessmen tell lies all the time. He insists that "a lot of very proper types" delude themselves and fool others. It is hard to be honest, and for that reason most of us shirk saying what we know "in our hearts" is true. People are afraid to speak out, say certain things, because they know they'll be called "prejudiced," and in fact they are not at all that; rather they are "letting the chips fall where they do."

But yes, he goes on to acknowledge, she is right, his wife; she always is, as a matter of fact. What is the point of working oneself up into a virtual frenzy over people who themselves never let anything really trouble them? In his own words and manner he says that he actually rather accepts his wife's disapproval—and anticipates exactly why she "really" was made anxious: "She doesn't want the kids to hear that kind of talk. They admire this minister, and he's always worrying out loud over someone, or some problem." Joe dislikes all those sermons; they make him feel uncomfortable, accused, a criminal of sorts. The minister can talk as he wishes, and if need be, move on to another church; whereas people like Joe and Doris have to stay—or so Joe feels. And anyway, ministers have a way of making things much too simple and stark and apocalyptic: "To hear him talk on Sunday, you'd think we were on the verge of ruin, America, unless we solve every problem we have and especially the race problem. He's got the Negro people on his brain, our minister. He must dream about them every night. He says we're to blame, the white people, for all that's happened. I went up once after the sermon and asked him what I've done that's to blame. He said he didn't mean any one person, just the whole white world. I didn't know how I could answer him. I said I'd never wanted to hurt a Negro, all I wanted was for them to leave me alone and I'd leave them alone. But that got him going again, and I pretended that I had to leave, because we had to be somewhere. On the way home I told Doris I'm ready to start shopping for a new church, but she and the children like him, the minister. They say he's 'dynamic.' He either makes me mad or puts me to sleep. So you see, we don't agree on *everything* in this house."

Joe is at times envious. His sister is married to a schoolteacher who is a Catholic. In the Catholic Church, he believes, one is spared those sermons. In the Catholic Church one goes for mass, for communion, not to be lectured at over and over again. But his sister and brother-in-law disagree. They have also had to sit through sermons, and they have their misgivings about the direction the church is taking. Here is what his sister says: "It's not any one church, it's them all. I listen to my neighbors talk. A lot of church people are always scolding the ordinary man. If you ask me, the rich people and the college professors have too much influence with the cardinal. Even the Catholic Church can be pushed around. All of a sudden, these last few years, we've been hearing these letters from him, the cardinal. He tells us this is wrong and that is wrong, and it seems all he has on his mind is the colored people. I'm sick and tired of them and their complaining. And they've stirred up everyone; my husband tells me the children in junior high school are 'organizing.' That's what they call it. They have 'grievances,' and they want to talk about them with the teachers and the principal. I'd give them the back of my hand. I'd read them the riot act. But no, the principal is afraid that if they get 'too strict,' the teachers, then the kids will get even more aroused, and there wil be more trouble. Can you imagine that? And he's talking with them—hour after hour, I hear.

"There's something wrong, that's what I say; and it all started with this civil rights business, the demonstrations, and then the college radicals and on and on. It used to be that you could go to church and pray for your family and country. Now they're worried about colored people and you even get the feeling they care more about the enemy, the people killing our boys in Vietnam, than our own soldiers. And the schools, the radicals and the colored are both trying to destroy the schools—I mean, take them over, that's what. They don't like what's being taught, and they don't like the teachers, and a day doesn't go by that they don't have something bad to say, or a new threat for us to hear. My husband says he'd quit tomorrow if he didn't have so much seniority, and if he could get another job. It's pretty bad for you these days if you're just a law-a-biding, loyal American and you believe in your country, and in people being happy with their own kind, and doing their best to keep us the first in the world. And, God forbid, if you say we need to keep the streets safe, and stop those riots and marches, then the priest will pull you aside and tell you that you don't 'understand.' But I do, that's the point. I understand what's happening. We're losing our freedom. We can't be ourselves anymore. There are those that want to change the country completely. They are dictators. A lot of priests are with us; but some have been fooled, and two of them are in our parish, I'll tell you."

There are differences, of course, in the two families. A teacher is not a steam fitter. Once the teacher felt himself "higher," a man of education, a man who wears a suit to work. Now the teacher feels hard pressed and bitter. His salary has for a decade been inadequate, and for half a decade he has had to work in the evenings and on weekends, even as his brother-in-law does. The high school children seem harder to control. The educational critics are constantly saying bad things about people like him, or so he feels. And everyone's sympathy seems to go elsewhere: "The priests, a lot of them feel sorry for the Negroes and the North Vietnamese. The college students love Asians and Africans, love to go work in the ghetto. Their professors keep on saying how bad our schools are. College professors make three and four times what we do, and they have the nerve to say we're not 'motivated' enough, and we don't teach the way we should. They can cry with sympathy for some insolent, fresh-talking Negro demonstrator, who wants the world delivered into his hands within twenty-four hours, but if we even try to explain our problems, they start telling us how wrong we are, and how we need to learn how to be 'open' with the children, and 'accepting,' and how we are 'rigid' and 'prejudiced,' and everything bad. I've heard them on television.

"No one asks people like me to be on television. I'm a teacher, but no educational television people come and ask me my opinion. They get these writers and 'experts' and let them say one bad thing after the other, and we're supposed to say: that's right, that's absolutely right. Not one of them impresses me as anything but a sensationalist. They love tearing things down. And you know who eats it all up, don't you: the intellectuals, the rich people out in the suburbs, the people who send their children to private schools, and then say it's awful, how we're treating the Negroes, and not keeping up with all those 'progressive' ideas, which (mind you) change every other year." . . .

More than any other expression, though, the people themselves (as we have mentioned) like to use "ordinary man" or "average American" or "plain person." Again and again one hears those words, all the time spoken with pride and conviction and a touch of sadness, a touch of worry—as if the country has not learned to appreciate such people, and maybe even makes them pay for the sins of others, pay with their lives, their savings, their energies. And they have indeed paid. They have seen their savings mean less, or disappear, as inflation gets worse and worse. They have had to take second jobs to keep up with prices. They have sent their sons abroad, and thousands of them have died—all of which an observer knows and reads and repeats to himself from time to time and then is likely to forget.

Is it, then, a certain vulnerability that they share, those "ordinary people"? Are they best thought of as socially insecure, economically marginal, politically unorganized, hence weak? Ought we be talking about millions and millions of people in such a way; that is, do they all lend themselves to the generalizations that social scientists, journalists and politicians persist in using? Needless to say, statistics and indices of one kind or another certainly do tell a lot; they quite precisely tell us how much money comes into homes, how much is spent and by whom—that is, people employed where and of what educational "level" or background. But again, one must ask whether expressions like "social class" quite explain what it is that so many Americans have in common when they call themselves "ordinary." Money is part of the answer; they have some, enough to get by, *just* get by, *barely* get by, *fairly* comfortably get by. (Qualifications like "just" or "barely" or "fairly" are always there and say a good deal.) But there are other things that matter to people. How much schooling did I get? How much do I wish I'd had? How much do I want for my children? What kind of work do I do, apart from the money I make, and what kind would I like to do? Where do I live? Where would I prefer to live, if I could have my choice? Which church do I attend? How do I like to dress? And finally, do I feel at ease about my life and my future, even though I live in a good, strong house, well supplied with gadgets and appliances on the inside and surrounded by a nicely tended lawn on the outside?

VIII. A New Theology

23. John A. T. Robinson

The End of Theism?

How can belief in God exist in a secular and scientific age? This question has been one of the major dilemmas facing religious thinkers since the publication more than a century ago of Charles Darwin's *Origin of Species*. But in the 1960s, theology was taken out of its old academic and clerical seclusion. Popular humanist writers, iconoclasts, and even theologians questioned the historic modes of "god-talk" and—finally—questioned the subject of theology itself. The "new theology" quickly became a subject of popular news magazines, television programs, thousands of sermons, even jokes. Its sensational impact was partly a consequence of the general public's unfamiliarity with recent intellectual trends in theology, for example, Paul Tillich's *The Shaking of the Foundations* (1949) and Dietrich Bonhoeffer's *Letters and Papers from Prison* (1953). Tillich had called for a radical self-criticism by all the churches of their historic conservatism and dogmatism, their promise of miracle through sacrament and priestcraft, their frequent defiance of reason and knowledge, and their tendency to sanctify the values of ruling classes. Bonhoeffer had called for a "religionless Christianity" to humanize and redeem a "world come of age."

During the 1960s it became clear that a new theological climate had emerged in which "neo-orthodoxy", prominent for a generation in the United States, was found wanting. In a fairly conservative statement, Bishop John A. T. Robinson writes of the end of supranaturalism, the end of theism, meaning popular Christianties' belief in a personal God, wholly separate from man, dwelling at the top of a three-story universe. He doubts not the presence of God, but the popular understanding of Him. The enthusiastic reception given to *Honest to God* by the laity suggests the continuing relevance of traditional questions: What is religion? What do we believe? What are the uses of "myth" in the religious view of the world? What do contemporary answers to these and similar questions tell us about society, about man himself?

Must Christianity be 'Supranaturalist'?

Traditional Christian theology has been based upon the proofs for the existence of God. The presupposition of these proofs, psychologically if not logically, is that God might or might not exist. They argue from some-thing which everyone admits exists (the world) to a Being beyond it who could or could not be there. The purpose of the argument is to show that he must be there, that his being is 'necessary'; but the presupposition be-hind it is that there is an entity or being 'out there' whose existence is problematic and has to be demonstrated. Now such an entity, even if it could be proved beyond dispute, would not be God: it would merely be a further piece of existence, that might conceivably not have been there— or a demonstration would not have been required.

Rather, we must start the other way round. God is, by definition, ulti-mate reality. And one cannot argue whether ultimate reality *exists*. One can only ask what ultimate reality is like—whether, for instance, in the last analysis what lies at the heart of things and governs their working is to be described in personal or impersonal categories. Thus, the funda-mental theological question consists not in establishing the 'existence' of God as a separate entity but in pressing through in ultimate concern to what Tillich calls 'the ground of our being'.

What he has to say at this point is most readily summarized in the opening pages of the second volume of his *Systematic Theology,* where he restates the position he has argued in the first volume and defends it against his critics.

The traditional formulation of Christianity, he says, has been in terms of what he calls 'supranaturalism'. According to this way of thinking, which is what we have all been brought up to, God is posited as 'the high-est Being'—out there, above and beyond this world, existing in his own right alongside and over against his creation. As Tillich puts it elsewhere, he is

*a being beside others and as such part of the whole of reality. He
certainly is considered its most important part, but as a part
and therefore as subjected to the structure of the whole . . . He
is seen as a self which has a world, as an ego which is related to
a thou, as a cause which is separated from its effect, as having a
definite space and an endless time. He is a being, not being-itself*[1]

The caricature of this way of thinking is the Deist conception of God's relation to the world. Here God is the supreme Being, the grand Archi-tect, who exists somewhere out beyond the world—like a rich aunt in Australia—who started it all going, periodically intervenes in its running, and generally gives evidence of his benevolent interest in it.

It is a simple matter to shoot down this caricature and to say that what *we* believe in is not Deism but Theism, and that God's relationship to the world is fully and intimately personal, not this remote watchmaker rela-

[1] *The Courage to Be* (1952), p. 175.

tionship described by the Deists. But it is easy to modify the *quality* of the relationship and to leave the basic structure of it unchanged, so that we continue to picture God as a Person, who looks down at this world which he has made and loves from 'out there'. We know, of course, that he does not exist in space. But we think of him nevertheless as defined and marked off from other beings *as if* he did. And this is what is decisive. He is thought of as *a* Being whose separate existence over and above the sum of things has to be demonstrated and established.

It is difficult to criticize this way of thinking without appearing to threaten the entire fabric of Christianity—so interwoven is it in the warp and woof of our thinking. And, of course, it *is* criticized by those who reject this supranaturalist position as a rejection of Christianity. Those who, in the famous words of Laplace to Napoleon, 'find no need of this hypothesis' attack it in the name of what they call the 'naturalist' position. The most influential exponent of this position in England today, Professor Julian Huxley, expressly contrasts 'dualistic supernaturalism' with 'unitary naturalism'. The existence of God as a separate entity can, he says, be dismissed as superfluous; for the world may be explained just as adequately without positing such a Being.

The 'naturalist' view of the world identifies God, not indeed with the totality of things, the universe, *per se,* but with what gives meaning and direction to nature. In Tillich's words,

The phrase deus sive natura, *used by people like Scotus Erigena and Spinoza, does not say that God is identical with nature but that he is identical with the* natura naturans, *the creative nature, the creative ground of all natural objects. In modern naturalism the religious quality of these affirmations has almost disappeared, especially among philosophising scientists who understand nature in terms of materialism and mechanism.*[2]

Huxley himself has indeed argued movingly for religion as a necessity of the human spirit. But any notion that God really exists 'out there' must be dismissed: 'gods are peripheral phenomena produced by evolution'. True religion (if that is not a contradiction in terms, as it would be for the Marxist) consists in harmonizing oneself with the evolutionary process as it develops ever higher forms of self-consciousness.

'Naturalism' as a philosophy of life is clearly and consciously an attack on Christianity. For it 'the term "God" becomes interchangeable with the term "universe" and therefore is semantically superfluous'. But the God it is bowing out is the God of the 'supranaturalist' way of thinking. The real question is how far Christianity is identical with, or ultimately committed to, this way of thinking.

[2] *Systematic Theology,* Vol. II. p. 7.

Must Christianity be 'Mythological'?

Undoubtedly it has been identified with it, and somewhere deep down in ourselves it still is. The whole world-view of the Bible, to be sure, is unashamedly supranaturalistic. It thinks in terms of a three-story universe with God up there, 'above' nature. But even when we have refined away what we should regard as the crudities and literalism of this construction, we are still left with what is essentially a mythological picture of God and his relation to the world. Behind such phrases as 'God created the heavens and the earth', or 'God came down from heaven', or 'God sent his only-begotten Son', lies a view of the world which portrays God as a person living in heaven, *a* God who is distinguished from the gods of the heathen by the fact that 'there is no god beside me'.

In the last century a painful but decisive step forward was taken in the recognition that the Bible does contain 'myth', and that this is an important form of religious truth. It was gradually acknowledged, by all except extreme fundamentalists, that the Genesis stories of the Creation and Fall were representations of the deepest truths about man and the universe in the form of myth rather than history, and were none the less valid for that. Indeed, it was essential to the defence of Christian truth to recognize and assert that these stories were *not* history, and not therefore in competition with the alternative accounts of anthropology or cosmology. Those who did not make this distinction were, we can now see, playing straight into the hands of Thomas Huxley and his friends.

In this century the ground of the debate his shifted—though in particular areas of Christian doctrine (especially in that of the last things) the dispute that raged a hundred years ago in relation to the first things has still to be fought through to its conclusion, and the proper distinction established between what statements are intended as history and what as myth. But the centre of today's debate is concerned not with the relation of particular myths to history, but with how far Christianity is committed to a mythological, or supranaturalist, picture of the universe at all. Is it necessary for the Biblical faith to be expressed in terms of this worldview, which in its way is as primitive philosophically as the Genesis stories are primitive scientifically? May it not be that the truth of Christianity can be detached from the one as much as from the other—and may it not be equally important to do so if it is to be defended properly today? In other words, is the reaction to naturalism the rehabilitation of supranaturalism, or can one say that Julian Huxley is performing as valuable a service in detaching Christianity from the latter as we now see his grandfather was in shaking the Church out of its obscurantism in matters scientific?

This is the problem to which Bultmann has addressed himself. And he answers boldly, 'There is nothing specifically Christian in the mythical view of the world as such. It is simply the cosmology of a pre-scientific age.' The New Testament, he says, presents redemption in Christ as a supranatural event—as the incarnation from 'the other side' of a celestial Being who enters this earthly scene through a miraculous birth, performs signs and wonders as an indication of his heavenly origin, and after an equally miraculous resurrection returns by ascent to the celestial sphere whence he came. In truth, Bultmann maintains, all this language is not, properly speaking, describing a supranatural transaction of any kind but is an attempt to express the real depth, dimension and significance of the *historical* event of Jesus Christ. In this person and event there was something of ultimate, unconditional significance for human life—and that, translated into the mythological view of the world, comes out as 'God' (a Being up there) 'sending' (to 'this' world) his only-begotten 'Son'. The transcendental significance of the historical event is 'objectivized' as a supranatural transaction.

I do not wish here to be drawn into the controversy which Bultmann's programme of demythologizing has provoked. Much of it has, I believe, been due to elements in his presentation which are to some extent personal and fortuitous. Thus,

a. Bultmann is inclined to make statements about what 'no modern man' could accept (such as 'It is impossible to use electric light and the wireless and believe . . .') which reflect the scientific dogmatism of a previous generation. This gives to some of his exposition an air of old-fashioned modernism.

b. The fact that he regards *so much* of the Gospel history as expendable (e.g., the empty tomb *in toto*) is due to the fact that purely in his capacity as a New Testament critic he is extremely, and I believe unwarrantably, distrustful of the tradition. His historical scepticism is not necessarily implied in his critique of mythology.

c. His heavy reliance on the particular philosophy of (Heidegger's) Existentialism as a replacement for the mythological world-view is historically, and indeed geographically, conditioned. He finds it valuable as a substitute for the contemporary generation in Germany; but we are not bound to embrace it as the only alternative.

One of the earliest and most penetrating criticisms of Bultmann's original essay was made by Bonhoeffer, and to quote it will serve as a transition to his own contribution. 'My view of it today', he writes from prison in 1944,

would be not that he went too far, as most people seem to think, but that he did not go far enough. It is not only the mythological conceptions such as the miracles, the ascension and the like (which are not in principle separable from the conceptions of God, faith and so on) that are problematic, but the 'religious' conceptions themselves. You cannot, as Bultmann imagines, separate God and miracles, but you do have to be able to interpret and proclaim both of them in a 'nonreligious' sense.[3]

Must Christianity be 'Religious'?

What does Bonhoeffer mean by this startling paradox of a non-religious understanding of God?

I will try to define my position from the historical angle. The movement beginning about the thirteenth century (I am not going to get involved in any arguments about the exact date) towards the autonomy of man (under which head I place the discovery of the laws by which the world lives and manages in science, social and political affairs, art, ethics and religion) has in our time reached a certain completion. Man has learned to cope with all questions of importance without recourse to God as a working hypothesis. In questions concerning science, art, and even ethics, this has become an understood thing which one scarcely dares to tilt at any more. But for the last hundred years or so it has been increasingly true of religious questions also: it is becoming evident that everything gets along without 'God', and just as well as before. As in the scientific field, so in human affairs generally, what we call 'God' is being more and more edged out of life, losing more and more ground.

Catholic and Protestant historians are agreed that it is in this development that the great defection from God, from Christ, is to be discerned, and the more they bring in and make use of God and Christ in opposition to this trend, the more the trend itself considers itself to be anti-Christian. The world which has attained to a realization of itself and of the laws which govern its existence is so sure of itself that we become frightened. False starts and failures do not make the world deviate from the path and development it is following; they are accepted with fortitude and detachment as part of the bargain, and even an event like the present war is no exception. Christian apologetic has taken the most varying forms of opposition to this self-assurance. Efforts are made to prove to a world thus come of age that it cannot live without the tutelage of 'God'. Even though there has been surrender on all secular problems, there still remain the so-called ultimate questions—death, guilt—on which only 'God' can furnish an

---

[3] *Letters and Papers from Prison* (1953), p. 125.

*answer, and which are the reason why God and the Church and the
pastor are needed. Thus we live, to some extent by these ultimate
questions of humanity. But what if one day they no longer exist as
such, if they too can be answered without 'God'? . . .
The attack by Christian apologetic upon the adulthood of the
world I consider to be in the first place pointless, in the second
ignoble, and in the third un-Christian. Pointless, because it looks to
me like an attempt to put a grown-up man back into adolescence,
i.e. to make him dependent on things on which he is not in fact
dependent any more, thrusting him back into the midst of problems
which are in fact not problems for him any more. Ignoble, because
this amounts to an effort to exploit the weakness of man for
purposes alien to him and not freely subscribed to by him.
Un-Christian, because for Christ himself is being substituted one
particular stage in the religiousness of man.*[4]

Bonhoeffer speaks of the God of 'religion' as a *deus ex machina.* He
must be 'there' to provide the answers and explanations beyond the point
at which our understanding or our capacities fail. But such a God is constantly pushed further and further back as the tide of secular studies advances. In science, in politics, in ethics the need is no longer felt for such
a stop-gap or long-stop; he is not required in order to guarantee anything,
to solve anything, or in any way to come to the rescue. In the same vein
Julian Huxley writes:

*The god hypothesis is no longer of any pragmatic value for the
interpretation or comprehension of nature, and indeed often stands
in the way of better and truer interpretation. Operationally,
God is beginning to resemble not a ruler but the last fading smile
of a cosmic Cheshire Cat.
It will soon be as impossible for an intelligent, educated man or
woman to believe in a god as it is now to believe that the earth
is flat, that flies can be spontaneously generated, that disease is a
divine punishment, or that death is always due to witchcraft. Gods
will doubtless survive, sometimes under the protection of vested
interests, or in the shelter of lazy minds, or as puppets used by
politicians, or as refuges for unhappy and ignorant souls.*[5]

And it is in this final haunt, says Bonhoeffer, that the God who has
been elbowed out of every other sphere has a 'last secret place', in the
private world of the individual's need. This is the sphere of 'religion' and
it is here that the Churches now operate, doing their work among those
who feel, or can be induced to feel, this need.

---

[4] *Ibid.,* pp. 145–147.
[5] *Religion Without Revelation,* 2nd ed., pp. 58, 62. Cf. S. Freud, *The Future of an
Illusion* (1928), pp. 76f.

The only people left for us to light on in the way of 'religion' are a few 'last survivals of the age of chivalry', or else one or two who are intellectually dishonest. Would they be the chosen few? Is it on this dubious group and none other that we are to pounce, in fervour, pique, or indignation, in order to sell them the goods we have to offer? Are we to fall upon one or two unhappy people in their weakest moment and force upon them a sort of religious coercion?[6]

Bonhoeffer's answer is that we should boldly discard 'the religious premise', as St Paul had the courage to jettison circumcision as a precondition of the Gospel, and accept 'the world's coming of age' as a God-given fact. 'The only way to be honest is to recognize that we have to live in the world *etsi deus non daretur*—even if God is not 'there'. Like children outgrowing the secure religious, moral and intellectual framework of the home, in which 'Daddy' is always there in the background, 'God is teaching us that we must live as men who can get along very well without him'.

The God who makes us live in this world without using him as a working hypothesis is the God before whom we are ever standing. Before God and with him we live without God. God allows himself to be edged out of the world, and that is exactly the way, the only way, in which he can be with us and help us. . . . This is the decisive difference between Christianity and all religions. Man's religiosity makes him look in his distress to the power of God in the world; he uses God as a Deus ex machina. The Bible however directs him to the powerlessness and suffering of God; only a suffering God can help. To this extent we may say that the process we have described by which the world came of age was an abandonment of a false conception of God, and a clearing of the decks for the God of the Bible, who conquers power and space in the world by his weakness. This must be the starting point for our 'worldly' interpretation.[7]

Transcendence for Modern Man

Bonhoeffer here touches on what he would put in the place of what he has demolished, and to this we shall return in the chapters that follow. This chapter has been concerned with 'clearing the decks' and it has inevitably therefore been destructive. I have called it 'The End of Theism?', following Tillich's lead. For, as he says, theism as ordinarily understood 'has made God a heavenly, completely perfect person who resides above the world and mankind'. Classical Christian theology has not in fact spo-

[6] *Letters,* p. 122.
[7] *Ibid.,* p. 164.

ken of God as 'a person' (partly because the term was already pre-empt-
ed for the three 'persons' of the Trinity) , and the Church's best theologians have not laid themselves open to such attack. They would have been
content with the essential orthodoxy of Professor Norman Pittenger's description of God as 'the Reality undergirding and penetrating through the
whole derived creation'. Yet popular Christianity has always posited such
a supreme personality. And Julian Huxley cannot be blamed for seeing
'humanity in general, and religious humanity in particular', as 'habituated
to thinking' of God 'mainly in terms of an external, personal, supernatural, spiritual being'. Indeed, If I understand them aright, it is still about the
existence or non-existence of such a Being that our contemporary linguistic philosophers, for all their sophistication, continue to do battle. 'The
theist', says I. M. Crombie, 'believes in God as a transcendent *being*', and
G. F. Woods regards R. W. Hepburn as stating the issue 'concisely and
accurately' when he writes, 'The language of "transcendence", the
thought of God as a personal being, wholly other to man, dwelling in
majesty—this talk may well collapse into meaninglessness, in the last
analysis. And yet to sacrifice it seems at once to take one quite outside
Christianity.'

It is precisely the identification of Christianity—and transcendence—
with this conception of theism that I believe we must be prepared to
question. Does the Gospel stand or fall with it? On the contrary, I am
convinced that Tillich is right in saying that 'the protest of atheism
against such a highest person is correct'. And this protest, which today is
made in the name of the 'meaninglessness' of any such metaphysical
statement, has seemed to others a matter of much greater existential concern. And to understand them we should be prepared to see how it looks
to them. Huxley contents himself with saying, 'For my own part, the
sense of spiritual relief which comes from rejecting the idea of God as a
supernatural being is enormous'. But, earlier, men like Feuerbach and
Nietzsche, whom Proudhon correctly described as 'antitheists' rather than
atheists, saw such a supreme Person in heaven as the great enemy of
man's coming of age. This was the God they must 'kill' if man was not to
continue dispossessed and kept in strings. Few Christians have been able
to understand the vehemence of their revolt because for them he has not
been the tyrant they portrayed, who impoverishes, enslaves and annihi-
lates man. Indeed, for most non-Christians also he has been more of a
Grandfather in heaven, a kindly Old Man who could be pushed into one
corner while they got on with the business of life. But the nature of his
character is here secondary. What is important is whether such a Being
represents even a distorted image of the Christian God. Can he be rehabilitated, or is the whole conception of that sort of a God, 'up there', 'out
there', or however one likes to put it, a projection, an idol, that can and
should be torn down?

For an answer to that question I should like to end not with a theological analysis but with a personal testimony—from John Wren-Lewis, who believes that it was just such a superstition from which he was delivered in order to become a Christian:

I cannot emphasize too strongly that acceptance of the Christian faith became possible for me only because I found I did not have to go back on my wholesale rejection of the superstitious beliefs that had hitherto surrounded me. The faith I came to accept was not merely different from what I had hitherto believed Christianity to be—it was utterly opposed to it, and I still regard that sort of 'religion' as an unmitigated evil, far, far more anti-Christian than atheism. This is a truth to which I do not think religious apologists pay nearly enough attention. There is a misplaced sense of loyalty which makes many Christians feel reluctant to come out in open opposition to anything that calls itself by the same name, or uses words like 'God' and 'Christ'; even Christians who in practice dislike superstition as much as I do still often treat it as a minor aberration to be hushed up rather than a radical perversion to be denounced. For example, Christian writers whose positive views are, as far as I can judge, very similar to my own, even though they may use different language to express them, still feel constrained to produce 'refutations' of the Freudian case against religion, although in fact a very large proportion of what passes for religion in our society is exactly the sort of neurotic illness that Freud describes, and the first essential step in convincing people that Christianity can be true in spite of Freud is to assert outright that belief based on the projection-mechanisms he describes is false, however much it may say 'Lord, Lord'. It is not enough to describe such beliefs as childish or primitive, for this implies that the truth is something like them, even though much more 'refined' or 'enlightened', whereas in reality nothing like the 'God' and 'Christ' I was brought up to believe in can be true. It is not merely that the Old Man in the Sky is only a mythological symbol for the Infinite Mind behind the scenes, nor yet that this Being is benevolent rather than fearful: the truth is that this whole way of thinking is wrong, and if such a Being did exist, he would be the very devil.[8]

That, I believe, is an exaggeration. To speak thus one is in danger, like the Psalmist, of condemning a whole generation—indeed many, many generations—of God's children. It is still the language of most of his children—and particularly his older children. There is nothing intrinsically wrong with it, any more than there was with the symbolism of a localized heaven. There will be many—and indeed most of us most of the time—

[8] *They Became Anglicans,* ed. Dewi Morgan, pp. 168f.

for whom it presents no serious difficulties and no insuperable barriers to belief. In fact, its demolition will be the greater shock to faith and will appear to leave many people bereft and 'without God in the world'. Nevertheless, I am firmly convinced that this whole way of thinking can be the greatest obstacle to an intelligent faith—and indeed will progressively be so to all except the 'religious' few. We shall eventually be no more able to convince men of the existence of a God 'out there' whom they must call in to order their lives than persuade them to take seriously the gods of Olympus. If Christianity is to survive, let alone to recapture 'secular' man, there is no time to lose in detaching it from this scheme of thought, from this particular theology or *logos* about *theos,* and thinking hard about what we should put in its place. We may not have a name yet with which to replace 'theism': indeed, it may not prove necessary or possible to dispense with the term (hence the query in the title of this chapter). But it is urgent that we should work away at framing a conception of God and the Christian Gospel which does not depend upon that projection. And to this, very tentatively, I now turn.

But before turning to it it will be well to say at once that our concern will not be simply to substitute an immanent for a transcendent Deity, any more than we are implying that those who worked with the previous projection thought of him as being *only* 'out there' and denied his immanence. On the contrary, the task is to validate the idea of transcendence for modern man. But this means restating its reality in other than what Bultmann has called the 'objectivized', mythological terms which merely succeed in making nonsense of it to him. For, as Professor R. Gregor Smith has said, 'The old doctrine of transcendence is nothing more than an assertion of an outmoded view of the world'. Our concern is in no way to change the Christian doctrine of God but precisely to see that it does not disappear with this outmoded view.

24. William Hamilton

The Death of
God Theologies Today

The most radical and most popularized assault on the religious and
cultural authority of God came from a group of young theologians who
affirmed that "God is dead." The inprecision of the phrase muddied the
waters of discourse and at times blinded opponents to its positive
contributions. William Hamilton, professor of theology at Colgate
Rochester Divinity School when he wrote the article that follows, and a
leader of the movement, has isolated several usages of the "death of
God," among them the following: (1) there is no God and there
never has been; (2) our idea of God is in need of radical reformulation;
(3) the culturally conditioned ways in which people have experienced
God have become eroded; (4) our language of God is always inadequate
and imperfect; and (5) there once was a God to whom adoration and
praise were appropriate, but now there is no such God.

The final statement most closely approximates what Hamilton
understands by the death of God. In the following essay he discusses
the work of fellow radicals Thomas J. J. Altizer and Paul Van Buren as
a prelude to his own point of view. Convinced that the brilliant
premonitions of Nietzsche's madman have come of age, Hamilton rejects
Bishop Robinson's view as too moderate and inappropriate to a genuine
understanding of the world. "My Protestant," he writes, "has no God,
has no faith in God, and affirms both the death of God and the death of
all forms of theism." Christians should move away from the security and
order of the church and into the world that is so frequently rejected
in modern literature—"the world of technology, power, money, sex,
culture, race, poverty and the city."

Most theologians have not been attracted to the death of God theology.
Among the many criticisms of it are the following: the "death of God"
is more a commentary upon the present predicament of man than
upon God; its proponents have too cavalierly dismissed the symbols of
art and literature by which men live; its proponents have overenthusiastic-
ally welcomed secular, technocratic society; the death of God is
unconsciously affirmed so as to take the sting out of the death of man.
Religious humanists also have expressed reservations. Typical of their
concern is this paragraph from an essay by David L. Edwards, published
in *The Student World* (No. 2, 1966) :

*The riddle of human existence remains, and many eminent
humanists remain interested in this riddle. True humanism, I*

should say, believes that the most important business of man in his days on earth is to pierce the great riddle by the symbols of art and by storytelling, and in the light gained to live in peace and love. When that day of true humanism comes, the present impatient ignorance of philosophical and mystical theology, and the present bored refusal to study the subtle character of religious belief and religious language, will be seen as immature. It seems to me that those of us who remain religious believers, having accepted many rebukes, now have every right to call on our fellow humanists to be braver in their own dedication to the mature dignity of human wisdom. A book needs to be written called Beyond the Secular.

Other critiques may be found in Bernard Murchland, ed., *The Meaning of the Death of God* (1967) ; Will Herberg, "The Death of God Theology," *National Review* (August 9, 1966) ; and Langdon Gilkey, "Is God Dead?" *The Voice: Bulletin of Crozer Theological Seminary* (January 1965) .

Complacencies of the peignoir, and late
Coffee and oranges in a sunny chair,
And the green freedom of a cockatoo
Upon a rug mingle to dissipate
The holy hush of ancient sacrifice.
She dreams a little, and she feels the dark
Encroachment of that old catastrophe. . . .

What is divinity if it can come
Only in silent shadows and in dreams?
Shall she not find in comforts of the sun,
In pungent fruit and bright, green wings, or else
In any balm of beauty of the earth,
Things to be cherished like the thought of heaven?
Divinity must live within herself. . . .

Wallace Stevens, "Sunday Morning"

We have been aware for some time that modern atheism has become a subject of special theological concern to Christians, but only recently has it moved so close to the center of theology and faith itself. The British publication of Bishop Robinson's *Honest to God* partly created and partly released forces that may well be coming together into a new theological movement in that country. And there is an American counterpart to this British movement, though it goes back in time a bit before *Honest to God*. This American movement is the death of God theology. It is a movement, though until quite recently there was no communication between the participants. But they have begun to talk to each other and to discover that there are a handful of people here and there who one day may all contribute to a common theological style. Right now, the American death of God movement seems to be more radical than the British "radicals," more radical on each of the three main points of *Honest to God*—God, ethics and the church. To the death of God theologian, Robinson is far too confident about the possibility of God-language. To use Paul van Buren's terms, Robinson is perfectly right to reject objectified theism, but he is wrong to think that his non-objectified theism is any more satisfactory. Van Buren would claim that modern philosophy has done away with both possibilities.

But unlike many American theologians, the death of God people do not patronize *Honest to God*. They take its publication as an important event in the life of the church, and they note particularly its enthusiastic reception by the laity as a sign that they may have a theological vocation in the church after all, in spite of the fact that their writing has up to now given more ecclesiastical offense than they expected. In any case, the purpose here is not to study the British radicals but to describe this American theological tradition and to ask under what conditions it might become part of the very lively theological discussion going on right now in this country.

What is meant by the phrase "death of God"? My colleague, Thomas Altizer, likes to say, for example, that the death of God is an historical event, that it has happened in our time and that we should welcome, even will it, not shrink from it. But if we call it an event, it is so in a special or odd sense, for it has not been experienced in any regular or ordinary way. The reference to Nietzsche's *Gay Science* is deliberate, and perhaps we ought to have the relevant material before us.

The Madman.—*Have you ever heard of the madman who on a bright morning lighted a lantern and ran to the marketplace calling out unceasingly: "I seek God! I seek God!"—As there were many people standing about who did not believe in God, he caused a great deal of amusement. Why! is he lost? said one. Has he strayed away like a child? said another. Or does he keep himself hidden? Is he afraid of us? Has he taken a sea-voyage? Has he emigrated?— the people cried out laughingly, all in a hubbub. The insane man jumped into their midst and transfixed them with his glances. "Where is God gone?" he called out. "I mean to tell you!* We have killed him,—*you and I! We are all his murderers! But how have we done it? How were we able to drink up the sea? Who gave us the sponge to wipe away the whole horizon? What did we do when we loosened this earth from its sun? Whither does it now move? Whither do we move? Away from all suns? Do we not dash on unceasingly? Backwards,*

sideways, forwards, in all directions? Is there still an above and
below? Do we not stray, as through infinite nothingness? Does
not empty space breathe upon us? Has it not become colder? Does
not night come on continually, darker and darker? Shall we not
have to light lanterns in the morning? Do we not hear the noise of
the grave-diggers who are burying God? Do we not smell the divine
putrefaction?—for even gods putrefy! God is dead! God remains
dead! And we have killed him! How shall we console ourselves, the
most murderous of all murderers? The holiest and the mightiest that
the world has hitherto possessed, has bled to death under our
knife,—who will wipe the blood from us? With what water could
we cleanse ourselves? What lustrums, what sacred games shall we
have to devise? Is not the magnitude of this deed too great for
us? Shall we not ourselves have to become Gods, merely to seem
worthy of it? There never was a greater event,—and on account of it,
all who are born after us belong to a higher history than any
history hitherto!"—Here the madman was silent and looked again at
his hearers; they also were silent and looked at him in surprise.
At last he threw his lantern on the ground, so that it broke in pieces
and was extinguished. "I come to early," he then said, "I am
not yet at the right time. This prodigious event is still on its way,
and is travelling,—it has not yet reached men's ears. Lightning
and thunder need time, the light of the stars needs time, deeds need
time, even after they are done, to be seen and heard. This deed is
*as yet further from them than the furthest star,—*and yet they have*
done it!" It is further stated that the madman made his way into
different churches on the same day, and there intoned his Requiem
aeternam deo. *When led out and called to account, he always*
gave the reply: "What are these churches now, if they are not the
tombs and monuments of God?" . . .

What does it mean to say that God is dead? Is this any more than a
rather romantic way of pointing to the traditional difficulty of speaking
about the holy God in human terms? Is it any more than a warning
against all idols, all divinites fashioned out of human need, human ideologies? Does it perhaps not just mean that "existence is not an appropriate word to ascribe to God, that therefore he cannot be said to exist, and
he is in that sense dead"? It surely means all this, and more. The hypothetical meanings suggested still all lie within the safe boundaries of the
neo-orthodox or biblical-theology tradition, and the death of God group
wants clearly to break away from that. It used to live rather comfortably
there, and does so no longer. Perhaps we can put it this way; the neo-orthodox reconstruction of the Christian doctrine of revelation seems to
have broken down for some. It used to be possible to say: we cannot
know God but he has made himself known to us, and at that point analo-

gies from the world of personal relations would enter the scene and help us. But somehow, the situation has deteriorated; as before, we cannot know, but now it seems that he does not make himself known, even as enemy. This is more than the old protest against natural theology or metaphysics; more than the usual assurance that before the holy God all our language gets broken and diffracted into paradox. It is really that we do not know, do not adore, do not possess, do not believe in God. It is not just that a capacity has dried up within us; we do not take all this as merely a statement about our frail psyches, we take it as a statement about the nature of the world and we try to convince others, God is dead. We are not talking about the absence of the experience of God, but about the experience of the absence of God. Yet the death of God theologians claim to be theologians, to be Christians, to be speaking out of a community to a community. They do not grant that their view is really a complicated sort of atheism dressed in a new spring bonnet. Let us look more carefully at their work.

I

Thomas Altizer's book, *Mircea Eliade and the Dialectic of the Sacred,* was published late in 1963 and has so far attracted very little attention. In the book Altizer has not decided whether to do a book on Eliade (to whom he owes a profound debt) or an original piece of theological exposition. He comes up with a little of both, and the result is not structurally satisfactory. But it is a brilliant book in many ways and an important piece of material in the movement.

Altizer begins by declaring that his basic presupposition is the death of God in our history, for us, now. A theology of the word can ignore this death, he says, but only by keeping the word quite untouched by the reality of modern existence. So Altizer lays out the problems raised for him by the death of God in terms of the sacred and the profane, and this enables him to make interesting use of Eliade's studies of the meaning of the sacred in archaic and modern religion. Altizer's question becomes, then, how to recover that connection with the sacred that modern men have lost. He grants that gnosticism, the negation of the profane, is a powerful temptation at this point, and he tries very hard to reject it. We must not, he says, seek for the sacred by saying "no" to the radical profanity of our age, but by saying "yes" to it. Thus, he writes, "the task of the theologian becomes the paradoxical one of unveiling religious meaning in a world that is bathed in the darkness of God's absence."

This statement suggests that Altizer, like Nietzsche, finds it a painful thing to have to affirm the death of God, and it is clear that he wishes things were otherwise. But he refuses to follow Eliade's tempting advice to return to some sort of precosmic primitivism and to recover the sacred in the way archaic religion did. How does the sacred become a possibility for a man who refuses to think himself out of his radically profane contemporary existence, who refuses in other words to archaize himself, with Eliade into primitivism or with Barth into the strange new world of the Bible?

Apparently the answer comes in Altizer's use of the Kierkegaardian idea of dialectic, or—what comes to the same thing—in his reading of Eliade's version of the myth of the coincidence of opposites. This means that affirming something passionately enough—in this case the full reality of the profane, secular, worldly character of modern life—will somehow deliver to the seeker the opposite, the sacred, as a gift he does not deserve. At times, Altizer walks very close to the gnostic nay-sayer whose danger he ordinarily perceives. His interest in the religious writing, such as it is, of Norman O. Brown is a sign of his own religious-gnostic temptations. Brown not only mounts an undialectical Freudian attack on the profane and the secular, he sees both history and ordinary genital sexuality as needing to be radically spiritualized and transcended. His religious vision, both at the end of *Life Against Death* and in his more recent thought, is mystical, spiritual and apocalyptic. This temptation is not a persistent one in Altizer, and in one important section of his book he makes the most ungnostic remark that the sacred will be born only when Western man combines a willing acceptance of the profane with a desire to change it. . . .

For Altizer men do not solve the problem of the death of God by following Jesus, but, it seems, by being liberated from history by him. In spite of his insight that ethics (or transforming the profane) can be a real way of handling the problem of the ambiguity of the profane realm, Altizer ultimately prefers the categories of neither Christology nor ethics but of mysticism. Thus his vision, beginning with man accepting, affirming, even willing the death of God in a radical sense, ends with man willing to participate in the utter desolation of the secular or the profane, willing to undergo the discipline of darkness, the dark night of the soul (here Altizer's affinity with the religious existentialists, who may not have God but who don't at all like not having him, is clearest) , while the possibility of a new epiphany of the sacred, a rebirth of the possibility of having God once more is awaited. Sometimes Altizer would have us wait quietly without terror; more often it seems he would have us attack the profane world with a kind of terrible hostility so that it might give up its sacred secret.

Altizer's vision is an exciting one, logically imprecise, calculated to make empiricists weep, but imaginatively and religiously it is both sophisticated and powerful.

II

The work of Paul van Buren says something about the rather strange sense of community that one finds in the death of God group that two such different personalities as van Buren and Altizer could have a common theological vocation. Altizer is all *élan*, wildness, excessive generalization, brimming with colorful, flamboyant, and emotive language. Van Buren is ordered, precise, cool. While he has certainly moved beyond the position of his book, it is in fact his book, *The Secular Meaning of the Gospel,* that has placed him firmly in the death of God camp, and we must briefly recall its major emphases.

Van Buren begins by citing Bonhoeffer's plea for a non-religious interpretation of the Gospel, appropriate to the world come of age. The title of his book reflects this Bonhoefferean concern, though the book as a whole does not, and the Bonhoeffer introduction is really extraneous to his argument.

He next moves on to a consideration of the method he proposes for his non-religious theology, and it turns out to be a certain species of linguistic analysis, but the theological context within which van Buren puts his method to work is, after all, that created by Bultmann and his demythologizing project, and van Buren very clearly sees the sense in which Bultmann, taken seriously, means the end of the rhetoric of neo-orthodoxy and the so-called biblical theology.

The mythological view of the world has gone, and with it went the possibility of speaking seriously of a Heilsgeschichte: *a historical "drama of salvation," in which God is said to have acted at a certain time in this world to change the state of human affairs.*

He rejects Barth who is described as forfeiting the world as we live in it today (precisely the reason for Altizer's rejection of the theologies of the word), and he rejects also the left-wing Bultmannians who have, he justly remarks, given up the historical basis of faith for an idea of authentic existence. In van Buren's debate with a left-wing Bultmannian like Schubert Ogden we can see what he is after. What he attacks in Ogden is the belief that there is *any* trustworthy language about God at all, either analogical language or retranslations such as the odd one Ogden uses: God as "experienced non-objective reality."

Van Buren is inclined to assume that analytical philosophy has made all language about God impossible. He is not talking about the deterioration of our experience of God, and he is not talking about the loss of the sacred. He is talking about words, and how hard it is to find the right ones. "Simple literal theism" is out, he says, but so is the kind of sophisticated and qualified non-objective theism that he finds in Ogden, Tillich, Karl Jaspers, and that he ought to find in Bishop Robinson.

It is not necessary to raise the question as to whether Van Buren is guilty of taking this philosophical tradition too seriously, of receiving the impressive blows it is able to deliver with too radical a retreat. The fact remains that he has set about to do his theological work without God. There is something remaining in the vacated space, and perhaps the idea of one's historical perspective or point of view can be used to rebuild the old notion of faith as *assensus* and *fiducia* before God. Perhaps. But apart from this, we do without God and hold to Jesus of Nazareth.

Thus, the urban[e] and methodologically scrupulous van Buren joins hands with Altizer the ecstatic and complex proclaimer of the death of God. The tone of voice is quite different; indeed the languages are not the same, but the meaning is unmistakable in both: God is dead. For Altizer the disappearance of the sacred is a sort of cosmic event; for van Buren it can be more precisely described: the rise of technology and modern science, the need in our thinking to stick pretty close to what we can experience in ordinary ways. Both are referring to something that has happened to them, not to someone else or to modern man in some generalized sense, and they are willing to admit it.

Altizer comes finally to depend on mystical categories to deal with the death of God, to save himself from undialectical atheism. Van Buren is too loyal an erstwhile Barthian to want to use mystical categories: for him ethical terms will do. When the theisms have gone, literal or fancy, as they must, and after faith has been Ramseyed and Hared, Christianity still stands as an ethic, public and private, and its character is largely derived from the sovereign freedom of Jesus the Lord. The Christian without God is a waiting man for Altizer, daring to descend into the darkness, grappling with all that is profane to wrest from it its potential sacral power. The Christian without God for van Buren is Jesus' man, perfectly free lord of all, subject to none.

Altizer and van Buren, thus, may be said to share a common vision which we have been calling the death of God, though this actual phrase is doubtless more congenial to the fiery Altizer than to the lucid van Buren. Both men, furthermore, deny that this vision disqualifies them as religious or Christian men. It may cripple, it may weaken or threaten, but they are both inside the circle. And each uses a different strategy to deal with the problem raised by the vision. Altizer, as we have seen, uses images from the world of mysticism: waiting, darkness, a new epiphany, the dialectic of opposites. Van Buren does without and does not really need God, preferring to point to Jesus as a way of standing before the neighbor. We will meet later in the book this distinction between mysticism and a Christological ethic as different ways of living in the time of the death of God.

III

My own point of view belongs in this general tradition. If Altizer begins with the cosmic event of the disappearance of the sacred, and if van Buren begins with the language problem, my starting point may be said to have two parts, one negative, the other positive.

The negative part is the perception, already referred to, of the deterioration of the portrait of the God-man relation as found in biblical theology and the neo-orthodox tradition. This theological tradition was able to portray a striking and even heroic faith, a sort of holding on by the fingernails to the cliff of faith, a standing terrified before the enemy-God, present to man as terror or threat, comforting only in that he kept us from the worse terrors of life without him. This God, we used to say, will never let us go. But he has, or we have him, or something, and in any case this whole picture has lost its power to persuade some in our time.

But our negations are never very important or interesting. There is a positive affirmation or starting point by which I enter into the country inhabited by the death of God settlers. It has to do with the problem of the Reformation or being a Protestant today. At the end of the last century the Reformation was interpreted as a victory for the autonomous religious personality, freed from the tyranny of hierarchy and institution, while man's relation to God was described as unmediated and available to all. This is what the Reformation means, for example, in A. von Harnack's *What is Christianity?* It was characteristic of liberal Protestantism as a whole, and it achieves its symbolic expression in Luther, standing alone at Worms, refusing to go against his conscience.

As the century wore on, and wars, depressions, bombs and anxieties came our way, we found ourselves seeing the Reformation in a new light. The old approach was not wrong, it was just that the new approach fitted our experience better. In this new approach, which we might call yesterday's understanding of the Reformation, the central fact was not the autonomous religious personality; it was the theological discovery of the righteous God. In that portion of our century when men and nations knew trouble, sin and guilt, we needed to receive this theological truth of the Reformation, just as earlier the psychological truth needed to be heard. Thus, we learned to say that the Reformation was a theological event. It centered in Luther's discovery of the meaning of justification or forgiveness, and its symbol proved to be Luther, storming about his room in Wittenberg, cursing the God who demands righteousness of men.

Today we may need to look at the Reformation in a third sense, no more or less true than the earlier approaches, but perhaps needing special emphasis just now and fitting new experiences in both church and world. This approach is more ethical than psychological or theological, and its focus is not on the free personality or on justification by faith, but on the movement from the cloister to the world. Of course, there is no specific event in Luther's life that can be so described, but the movement is there in his life nonetheless, and it is a movement we need to study. From cloister to world means from church, from place of protection and security, of order and beauty, to the bustling middle-class world of the new university, of politics, princes and peasants. Far more important than any particular ethical teaching of Luther is this fundamental ethical movement. Here I touch some of Alitzer's concerns, but I am not as anxious to recover the sacred, since I am starting with a definition of Protestantism as a movement away from the sacred place.

This view of the Reformation, along with my preliminary negative comment, does allow a kind of picture of faith. It is not, this time, holding on by the fingernails, and it is not a terror-struck confession before the enemy God. It is not even a means of apprehending God at all. This faith is more like a place, a being with or standing beside the neighbor. Faith has almost collapsed into love, and the Protestant is no longer defined as the forgiven sinner, the *simul justus et peccator,* but as the one beside the neighbor, beside the enemy, at the disposal of the man in need. The connection between holding to the neighbor and holding to Jesus will be dealt with in a moment.

Here I reflect the thought of the later Bonhoeffer more than either van Buren or Altizer wants or needs to. My Protestant has no God, has no faith in God, and affirms both the death of God and the death of all the forms of theism. Even so, he is not primarily a man of negation, for if there is a movement away from God and religion, there is the more important movement into, for, toward the world, worldly life, and the neighbor as the bearer of the wordly Jesus. We must look more carefully at these two movements: towards the world and away from religion.

IV

We need to be very careful in how we put this Protestant "yes" to the world. It is not the same kind of "yes" that one finds in that tradition of theology of culture today that makes use of the world as illustrations for its doctrines of sin and redemption. This "yes" is also in considerable tension with a number of themes in modern literature. Recently, Lionel Trilling called attention to Thomas Mann's remark that all his work was an effort to free himself from the middle class, and to this Trilling added the comment that all truly modern literature can be so described. Indeed, he goes on, modern literature is not only asking for a freedom from the middle class, but from society itself. It is this conception of the modern, I am saying, that should be opposed by the Protestant. Who are the characteristically modern writers in this sense I am criticising? Any such list would surely include Henry James, Eliot, Yeats, Pound, Joyce, Lawrence, Kafka, Faulkner, Beckett. Is it possible to affirm the value of the technological revolution, the legitimacy of the hopes and claims of the dispossessed, most of all, of the moral centrality of the Negro revolution in America today—is it possible to affirm all these values and still to live comfortably in the modern world as these writers portray it? Surely not, in some important senses.

To say there is something in the essence of Protestantism itself that drives us into the world is not to say that we are driven to the world of these "modern" writers. But in many ways it is into the world they reject—to the world of technology, power, money, sex, culture, race, poverty and the city—that we are driven. Lawrence's protest against the mechanization of life now seems a bit archaic and piquant, and his aristo-cratic hostility to the democratic ethos of Christianity is rather more than piquant, it is irrelevant and false. In a way, I am describing not a move away from Puritanism, but a move to it, and to the middle class and to the city. Perhaps the time has come when Protestants no longer need to make ritual acts of hostility to Puritanism, moralism, and to all the hy-pocrisies and prohibitions of middle-class culture. The chronicle of mid-dle-class hypocrisy may well be complete, with no more work on it nec-essary. There are those in our world today who would like to be a little closer to the securities of middle-class existence so they too might be-come free to criticize them, and who must indeed be granted political, economic, and psychological admission to that world. Attacks on the silli-ness of middle-class morality have almost always had an a-political char-acter, and it is to that element in the modern sensibility that the Protes-tant takes exception. Thus the worldliness affirmed by Protestanism has a post-modern, pro-bourgeois, urban and political character. This may mean a loosening of the ties between the Protestant intellectual and avant-garde modernism and it might even mean the start of some inter-esting work in the shaping of a contemporary radical ethic.

The Protestant protest against religion is related to, but it must not be confused with, this affirmation of the world. (Both are clearly implied by our formula, from church to world.) Assertions that Protestantism is against religion, or that Christianity or revelation is an attack on religion, have, of course, been with us for a considerable time now, and nearly every-body has had a word to say on the subject. Karl Barth's long discussion in *Church Dogmatics* I/2 has had a massive and perhaps undeserved in-fluence. Barth defines religion, in his attack on it, as something like man's arrogant and grasping attempt to become God, so it is hard to see what all the posturing is about. If by definition religion equals sin, and you then say revelation ought to be against religion, you may bring some delight to careless readers, but you have not forwarded theological clarity very much.

More immediate in influence, of course, is the plea for a religionless

Christianity in the prison letters of Bonhoeffer. We really don't know what Bonhoeffer meant by religion, and our modern study of the problem of religionlessness must be carried on quite independent of the task, probably fruitless, of establishing just what Bonhoeffer meant.

There are two schools of interpretation of Protestant religionlessness. In the moderate, Honest-to-God, ecclesiastical school of interpretation, religion generally means "religious activities" like liturgy, counselling, going to church, saying your prayers. To be religionless in this sense is to affirm that the way we have done these things in the past may not be the only way, or may not be worth doing at all, and that radical experiments ought to be attempted in the forms of the church and ministry. Bishop Robinson's lectures on "The New Reformation" delivered in America in the spring of 1964 are an able presentation of this moderate radicalism. A good deal of the material out of New York, Geneva, and the denominational headquarters on the church and ministry reflects this promising line, and a good many religious sociologists and radical religious leaders on the race issue tend to use Bonhoeffer and religionlessness in this way.

This is an important trend, and we need more and not less experimentation on these matters of the ministry, for we are well into the opening phase of the breakdown of organized religion in American life, well beyond the time when ecumenical dialogues or denominational mergers can be expected to arrest the breakdown.

The religionlessness I wish to defend, however, is not of this practical type. At no point is the later Bonhoeffer of greater importance to the death of God theology than in helping us work out a truly theological understanding of the problem of religionlessness. I take religion to mean not man's arrogant grasping for God (Barth) and not assorted Sabbath activities usually performed by ordained males (the moderate radicals), but any system of thought or action in which God or the gods serve as fulfiller of needs or solver of problems. Thus I assert with Bonhoeffer the breakdown of the religious *a priori* and the coming of age of man.

The breakdown of the religious *a priori* means that there is no way, ontological, cultural or psychological, to locate a part of the self or a part of human experience that needs God. There is no God-shaped blank within man. Man's heart may or may not be restless until it rests in God. It is not necessarily so. God is not in the realm of the necessary at all; he is not necessary being, he is not necessary to avoid despair or self-righteousness. He is one of the possibles in a radically pluralistic spiritual and intellectual milieu.

This is just what man's coming of age is taken to mean. It is not true to say, with Luther, *entweder Gott oder Abgott*. It is not true to say, with Ingmar Bergman, "Without God, life is an outrageous terror." It is not true to say that there are certain areas, problems, dimensions to life today that can only be faced, solved, illumined, dealt with, by a religious perspective.

Religion is to be defined as the assumption in theology, preaching, apologetics, evangelism, counselling, that man needs God; and that there are certain things that God alone can do for him. I am denying that religion is necessary and saying that the movement from the church to the world that we have taken as definitive of Protestantism not only permits but requires this denial. To assert that we are men moving from cloister to world, church to world, to say that we are secular men, is to say that we do not ask God to do for us what the world is qualified to do. Really to travel along this road means that we trust the world, not God, to be our need fulfiller and problem solver, and God, if he is to be for us at all, must come in some other role. . . .

By way of a provisional summary: the death of God must be affirmed; the confidence with which we thought we could speak of God is gone, and our faith, belief, experience of him are very poor things indeed. Along with this goes a sharp attack on religion which we have defined as any system using God to meet a need or to solve a problem, even the problem of not having a God. Our waiting for God, our godlessness, is partly a search for a language and a style by which we might be enabled to stand before him once again, delighting in his presence.

In the time of waiting we have a place to be. It is not before an altar, it is in the world, in the city, with both the needy neighbor and the enemy. This place really defines our faith, for faith and love have come together in the interim of waiting. This place, as we shall see, is not only the place for the waiting for God, it is also a way to Jesus Christ. . . .

V

[The] combination of waiting and attention on the concrete and personal is the theological point I have been trying to make. Waiting here refers to the whole experience I have called "the death of God," including the attack on religion and the search for a means by which God, not needed, may be enjoyed. We have insisted all along that "death of God" must not be taken as symbolic rhetoric for something else. There really is a sense of not-having, of not-believing, of having lost, not just the idols or the gods of religion, but God himself. And this is an experience that is not peculiar to a neurotic few, nor is it private or inward. Death of God is a public event in our history.

Thus we wait, we try out new words, we pray for God to return, and we seem to be willing to descend into the darkness of unfaith and doubt that something may emerge on the other side. In this way, we have tried to interpret and confirm the mystical images that are so central to the thought of Altizer.

But we do more than play the waiting game. We concentrate our energy and passion on the specific, the concrete, the personal. We turn from the problems of faith to the reality of love. We walk away from the inner anguish of a Hamlet or an Oedipus and take up our worldly responsibility with Prospero and Orestes. As Protestants, we push the movement from church to world as far as it can go and become frankly worldly men. And in this world, as we have seen, there is no need for religion and no need for God. This means that we refuse to consent to that traditional interpretation of the world as a shadow-screen of unreality, masking or concealing the eternal which is the only true reality. This refusal is made inevitable by the scientific revolution of the seventeenth century, and it is this refusal that stands as a troublesome shadow between ourselves and the Reformation of the sixteenth. The world of experience is real, and it is necessary and right to be actively engaged in changing its patterns and structures.

This concentration on the concrete and the worldly says something about the expected context of theology in America today. It means that the theological work that is to be truly helpful—at least for a while—is more likely to come from worldly contexts than ecclesiastical ones, more likely to come from participation in the Negro revolution than from the work of faith and order. But this is no surprise, for ever since the Civil War, ever since the Second Inaugural of Lincoln, the really creative American theological expressions have been worldly rather than ecclesiastical: the work of Walter Rauschenbusch and the work of Reinhold Niebuhr are surely evidence for this. (It is not yet clear how the civil rights movement is going to take on its theological significance, but it has begun, as the radical, southern Negro student comes out of the movement to seminary. He brings a passionate interest in the New Testament doctrines of discipleship and following Jesus and very little interest in the doctrine of sin. One of the most pressing intellectual responsibilities of the Negro student and minister today is that of working out some of the ethical and theological clues that the Negro revolution is teaching him and us all.)

The death of God Protestant, it can be seen, has somewhat inverted the usual relation between faith and love, theology and ethics, God and the neighbor. We are not proceeding from God and faith to neighbor and love, loving in such and such a way because we are loved in such and such a way. We move to our neighbor, to the city and to the world out of a sense of the loss of God. We set aside this sense of loss or death, we note it and allow it to be, neither glad for it, nor insistent that it must be so for all, nor sorry for ourselves. And, for the time of our waiting we place ourselves with our neighbor and enemy in the world.

There is something more than our phrase "waiting for God" that keeps this from sheer atheist humanism. Not only our waiting but our worldly work is Christian too, for our way to our neighbor is not only mapped out by the secular social and psychological and literary disciplines, it is mapped out as well by Jesus Christ and his way to his neighbor. Our ethical existence is partly a time of waiting for God and partly an actual Christology. Our being in the world, in the city, is not only an obedience to the Reformation formula, from church to world, it is an obedience to Jesus himself. How is this so? How is Jesus being disclosed in the world, being found in the world in our concrete work?

First, Jesus may be concealed in the world, in the neighbor, in this struggle for justice, in that struggle for beauty, clarity, order. Jesus is in the world as masked, and the work of the Christian is to strip off the masks of the world to find him, and, finding him, to stay with him and to do his work. In this sense, the Christian life is not a longing and is not a waiting, it is a going out into the world. The self is discovered, but only incidentally, as one moves out into the world to tear off the masks. Life is a masked ball, a Halloween party, and the Christian life, ethics, love, is that disruptive task of tearing off the masks of the guests to discover the true princess.

In the parable of the last judgment (Matthew 25:34 ff.) the righteous did not know it was Jesus they were serving. The righteous today don't need to know it either, unless they are Christian, in which case they will say that what they are doing is not only service, work, justified for this and that structural reason; it is also an act of unmasking, a looking for, a finding and a staying with Jesus.

In this first sense, the Christian life, ethics, love, is public, outward, visible. It is finding Jesus in your neighbor: "as you did it to one of the least of these my brethren, you did it to me" (Matthew 25:40) .

There is another form of the presence of Jesus Christ in the world. Here, we no longer talk about unmasking Jesus who is out there in the world somewhere, we talk about becoming Jesus in and to the world. Here, the Christian life, ethics, love, is first a decision about the self, and then a movement beyond the self into the world.

The form, if not the content, of the parable of the Good Samaritan should be recalled. Jesus is asked a question: which one, among all the many claimants out there, is my neighbor? Jesus answers the question with one of his characteristic non-answers: "Don't look for the neighbor, be one." Or, to put the form of his answer to work on our problem: "Don't look for Jesus out there, in scripture, tradition, sacraments, Ingmar Bergman movies, in the world behind a mask—become Jesus." Become a Christ to your neighbor, as Luther put it.

In this form, the Christian life is not a looking outwards to the world and its claims, it is first a look within in order to become Jesus. "For me to live," cried Paul in one of his most daring utterances, "is Christ." Ethics and love are first a dangerous descent into the self. And in this form, the Christian life, ethics, love, are not so active or worldly. At this point the Christian is the passive man, and doubtless tempted into all of the easily noted dangers of confusing the self with Jesus.

The Christian life as the discernment of Jesus beneath the worldly masks can be called work or interpretation or criticism; while the Christian life as becoming Jesus looks a little different. At this point the Christian is the sucker, the fall guy, the jester, the fool for Christ, the one who stands before Pilate and is silent, the one who stands before power and power-structures and laughs.

Whichever of the paths one takes to find or define Jesus in the world, and perhaps some of us are called to choose both ways, and some only one, the worldliness of the Protestant can never, because of this, have an utterly humanistic form. I may be proposing a too simple marriage between Christology and ethics, a too narrowly ethical approach to Christological problems, but it should at least be noted that however acute the experience of the death of God may be for us, however much silence and loneliness are entailed during our time of waiting for the absent God, we are not particularly cast down or perplexed by this. A form of obedience remains to us in our time of deprivation. We dechristianize no one, we make no virtue of our defects, and we even dare to call men into the worldly arena where men are in need and where Jesus is to be found and served.

IX. Science and Human Nature

25. René Dubos

Science and Man's Nature

On the last day of his life Socrates related to friends that he had once had a prodigious appetite for the study of natural science. But his eager expectations soon lay in ruins because his reputable teachers persisted in talking only of air and water and ether and other eccentricities. They neglected the truly important questions of life, leaving the soul unattended. Thorstein Veblen, in a brilliant essay ("The Place of Science in Modern Civilization") written at the beginning of this century, concluded that science had become the dominant note of Western culture. This he found congenial, but warned: "the normal man, such as his inheritance has made him, has . . . good cause to be restive under its dominion."

These suspicions, common to all ages, found many new voices in the 1960s, enough to constitute a major challenge to the reigning cultural authority of science. Eloquent criticism from within the scientific establishment came from René Dubos, microbiologist, Pulitzer prize winner and, for nearly 50 years, a professor at Rockefeller University. Having made important discoveries leading to the control of pneumonia and tuberculosis, and commonly acknowledged as a person who could bridge the gap between scientist and humanist, his words have carried more than ordinary force. He contends that scientific knowledge is alienating man from his own nature, meaning the instinctive, psychological, moral, and physiological attributes that make up man's being. For thousands of years the applications of science have enabled man to modify his environment, yet today science is inextricably allied with a monstrous technology that threatens to extinguish human life. Within the scientific community, Dubos laments, overwhelming concern with technique and with the elementary fragments of living organisms has led to a loss of interest in the whole of nature. The consequence is a rupture between the interests and needs of the professional scientists and the public, a rupture that has occasioned a growing antiscience movement.

But Dubos has not despaired, as readers of his books *A God Within* (1972) and *So Human an Animal* (awarded a Pulitzer Prize in 1969) will discover. Science must be understood as indispensible but not omnicompetent, he has written. A society able to internalize that understanding in its institutional and ideological structures has a good chance of survival.

Reprinted by permission of *Daedalus*, Journal of the American Academy of Arts and Sciences, Boston, Mass. (Winter 1965, *Science and Culture*.)

The Shaping of Modern Culture by Science

Words have dictionary meanings, but more importantly they have undertones which are determined by the history, beliefs and hopes of the people who use them. The word culture, for example, denotes very different attitudes and contents depending upon the kind of civilization to which it is applied. For civilizations of the Arcadian type, based on the belief that life was happy in the past, the role of culture is to preserve and transmit experience and traditions as faithfully as possible. In contrast, civilizations of the Utopian type, which believe that happiness can be realized only in New Jerusalem, demand that culture prepare man for the mastery of nature and for the creation of a better world.

Most men, in any period of history, have been at times Arcadians and at times Utopians. There is no doubt, however, that the world as a whole is now losing its belief in Arcadia and that the concept of culture is changing accordingly. Whereas traditional civilizations put a premium on the transfer of beliefs and customs from one generation to another, modern societies tend to regard the heritage of the past as but a matter of entertainment for leisure time, and to consider that the forces which are creating the world of tomorrow are the really serious concern of culture. One of the consequences of this shift of emphasis has been the progressive recognition that the natural sciences constitute as legitimate a component of culture as the traditional knowledge of man, of his history, and of his artistic creations.

It goes without saying that many varied social forces other than science have played and continue to play an immense role in shaping modern life. The invention of tools and of agriculture by prehistoric man, the emergence of social groups and especially of large cities, the development of laws and of the various religions, are but a few among the non-scientific forces which have determined the evolution of human nature and of the ways of life. Today, however, science and the technologies derived from it constitute the forces which affect most profoundly the environment in which men have to function and to evolve. Either by choice or from necessity, the cultural evolution of man will be molded in the future by scientific concepts and technological forces. Even more important probably is the fact that science is accelerating the rate of environmental and conceptual changes.

The horse remained the most rapid means of locomotion until the invention of the railroad, but we have moved from the propeller to the supersonic aircraft in one generation. All civilizations have until recently considered the earth as the center of the universe and man as the highest form of life, but we now seriously think about ways of communicating with other thinking and highly evolved creatures that we assume to exist in many parts of the universe. Science is the most characteristic aspect of our civilization precisely because it provides the mental and physical apparatus for rapid changes in our ways of life and even more perhaps in our conceptual views of creation. Indeed, the tempo at which man changes the environment and his views of himself is now so rapid that the rules of conduct for the good life must be changed from one generation to the other. In many fields, the wisdom of the father is now of little use to his son.

The immense role of science in the practical affairs of the modern world is recognized by all, even by its detractors, but surprisingly its influence on culture is often questioned, even by its champions. The following statement is typical of this skeptical attitude concerning the modern mind as it confronts science: "Our lives are changed by its handiwork, but the population of the West is as far from understanding the nature of this strange power as a remote peasant of the Middle Ages may have been from understanding the theology of Thomas Aquinas." I shall attempt later in this essay to consider some of the factors which contribute to the estrangement of the scientific enterprise from the human condition. But it may be useful to emphasize first that science has influenced modern thought and culture much more profoundly than is usually admitted. In fact, it is probable that most educated men have now incorporated concepts derived from theoretical science in their daily thoughts even more effectively than medieval or Renaissance Europeans ever incorporated Thomas Aquinas in their cosmologies or their ethics.

The rate of acquisition of new knowledge was so slow in the distant past, and indeed until the advent of experimental science, that ancient civilizations found it difficult to conceive of the possibility of progress. Men whose lives depended entirely on the course of natural events were bound to be more aware of the recurrence of daily and seasonal phenomena, year after year, then of the continuous process of change which we now take for granted. Seeing that natural events repeat themselves endlessly, they tended to extrapolate from these cosmic cycles to human history. For them, the myth of eternal return seemed to apply to the affairs of man just as it did to the cycles of nature and the motions of stars. The known conditions of the present seemed to them but one stage in the endless ebb and flow of events.

It is difficult, of course, to determine with precision at what time the myth of eternal return was displaced in the Western mind by the concept of progress, namely, by the belief in a continuous process of change toward a new state different not only from the present, but also from anything in the past, and hopefully better. The philosophical teachings of the Renaissance and of the Enlightenment certainly helped to formulate the concept and make it intellectually acceptable. But there is no doubt that the philosophy of progress became part of collective consciousness in the Western world approximately at the time when experimental science first began to prosper. Men like Condorcet or Franklin wrote of progress as a theoretical possibility, and placed their hopes for its realization in the future developments of science. However, it was the doctrine of biological evolution which eventually provided the theoretical basis for the concept of progressive historical change. The doctrine of evolution therefore provides one of the most striking examples of the influence of scientific knowledge on modern culture.

Few laymen, it is true, have an exact understanding of the scientific mechanisms involved in biological evolution. Nevertheless, practically all of them now accept as a fact that everything in the cosmos—heavenly bodies as well as living organisms—has developed and continues to develop through a process of historical change. In the Western world, most great religions have come to accept a progressive historical view of creation.

Enlightened laymen tacitly apply evolutionary concepts not only to living organisms and to man, but also to his social institutions, his customs, and his arts. Yet the general acceptance of this evolutionary view is rather recent, dating only from the post Darwinian era. Evolutionary concepts were still either ignored, ridiculed, or almost universally opposed less than one hundred years ago. In contrast, they appear so obvious today that most orthodox churches, political parties, and schools of sociology, history, or art, teach them and indeed make them the basis of their doctrines. It can be said without exaggeration that theoretical biology has thus introduced into human thought a new element which pervades all aspects of traditional culture.

Cosmology, or the physicochemical sciences, could probably be used just as well as the theory of evolution to illustrate how much modern thought is being influenced by scientific knowledge. But since I am a biologist ignorant of these fields, I must act here as a representative of the lay public whose views concerning the cosmos and the structure of matter are progressively being transformed by a kind of knowledge that I do not really understand. Like every human being, for example, I have been puzzled by the concept of the divisibility of matter. I cannot imagine that the division of matter into smaller and smaller fragments can go on indefinitely, but neither can I imagine how this division can come to an end since I can always carry out one further dividing operation in my mind. Fortunately, I begin to sense that this paradox is not entirely beyond human comprehension. Although I know nothing of the theories or practices of elementary particle physics, I can apprehend that when sufficient energy is applied to elementary particles in the big accelerators, the particles are changed not by a process of true division but by a transmutation of energy into matter; every particle can be transformed into any other if the energy applied is sufficiently great.

In the preceding paragraph, I have mentioned on purpose a kind of phenomenon completely foreign to my knowledge in order to illustrate the manner in which science becomes incorporated into the cultural tradition. Science shapes culture not necessarily through its technical aspects, but rather by providing new points of views and by facilitating new attitudes. That the earth is round, and that all living creatures that we know have a common ancestry, is not obvious either to my senses or my common sense, yet these concepts have become integrated in my daily thoughts and thus constitute part of the fabric of my culture. It would be surprising if the general concepts of elementary particle physics and of relativity theory did not in some way become integrated in the general culture of the next generation.

The integration of scientific knowledge into general culture will probably be accelerated by the fact that there is a wide public awareness of some of the basic assumptions of science. Many lay persons have come to realize that each particular field of science develops as if it were a self-contained structure, with its own body of facts and its own inner logic. Students of matter investigate elementary particles and the laws which govern the primordial stuff of which these particles might be but the transient manifestations; their information is derived from recent experiments in high energy physics carried out with the aid of complex hardware. Students of human evolution trace the origin of man, step by step, to some small creature which lived in trees at the beginning of the Paleocene period; their conclusions are derived from the comparative study of ancient fossils found here and there in many parts of the world. It is obvious enough that the structure of matter and the evolution of man constitute two fields of science which have developed independently, each with its own techniques, points of view and goals. In this light, it would appear as if there were no such thing as science, but only a multiplicity of unrelated fields of knowledge. But while it is a fact that each field of science has its own characteristics and displays its own pattern of development, it is also true, and probably far more important, that no incompatibility has ever been found between one field of science and another; the laws of one do not violate the laws of the other.

The remarkable compatibility between all fields of science, whether they deal with inanimate objects or with living things, has implications which affect deeply the culture of our times. The validity of these implications is supported by the fact that the various scientific disciplines strengthen each other when, perchance, they can establish contact. Despite the immense diversity of creation, we all accept that there exists in nature a profound underlying unity. The search for this unity provides the motivation for the lives of many different men, some who like Einstein search for it in general natural laws, and others who like Teilhard de Chardin would trace cosmic evolution to a divine origin.

So general is the belief in the unity of nature, and in the power of the scientific approach, that this method is now applied to most areas of human concern, from the natural sciences to the historical sciences, from the analysis of the human fabric to the appreciation of human arts, naive as it may be to hope that methods developed for the study of inanimate objects can be applied to the much more complex and qualitatively different problems of social human life. But despite their premature character, the attempts to apply the scientific method as used by the natural sciences to problems for which it is not suited are of interest because they reveal a general awareness that we have under cultivation only a small area of the fields which can be exploited by science.

The Antiscience Movement

Since the various scientific fields include all the subjects on which reasonable men can converse objectively and exchange verifiable information, it is difficult if not impossible to state in words where science ends and where the humanities begin. The paradox, however, is that this semantic difficulty hardly ever causes any confusion in human behavior. The immense majority of the lay public shows by its reading habits that it sharply differentiates between science and non-science; this differentiation also appears in the fact that concert halls and art museums have more popular appeal than science exhibits. The "two cultures" may be an illusion, but in practice science is still regarded in our communities as a kind of foreign god, powerful and useful, yes, but so mysterious that it is feared rather than known and loved.

It is healthy to acknowledge that scientists themselves generally behave like the lay public when they function outside their areas of professional specialization. The student of plasma physics or of plasma proteins is not likely to select books on marsupials for his bedside reading, nor is the organic chemist inclined to become familiar with problems of population genetics. Most scientists, it is true, are interested at present in radiation fallout and in the hidden surface of the moon, but so are many members of the Rotary Club. Winston Churchill, Pablo Picasso and Ernest Hemingway are much more frequently discussed at the luncheon tables of scientific research institutes than are the Nobel prize winners in physics, chemistry, or biology of the same generation. And if Linus Pauling or

Robert Oppenheimer is mentioned, it is less likely with regard to either's achievements as chemist or physicist than because their behavior makes them interesting and vital human beings. In brief, while scientists are deeply committed to their own specialized fields, they generally turn to non-scientific topics when they move outside their professional spheres.

The priority of general "human" concerns over purely scientific interests acquires particular importance in education. Whatever historians and philosophers of science may say concerning the fundamental similarities between science and the humanities as intellectual and creative pursuits, the high school or college student soon discovers from his personal experience that the two kinds of learning and activities are different as far as he is concerned. He will probably like one and despise the other; and science commonly loses in the comparison. A recent study of high school students selected for extremely high scholastic aptitude (only one per cent of the total student population!) revealed that the percentage of those selecting science decreased from 37.77 per cent in 1958 to 28.87 per cent in 1963. Even more serious was the finding that among those who had originally selected science 55.2 per cent of the males and 58.9 per cent of the females changed to other fields during their college years. The significance of these figures becomes the greater when it is realized that the trend away from science occurred during a period when great social pressure was being exerted on young people to induce them to go into scientific careers.

The difficulty of scientific courses, and the shortage of gifted scientific teachers devoted to the training of undergraduates, may account in part for this disturbing rejection of science. But to be satisfied with such obvious explanations seems to be unwarranted, and unwise. At the risk of oversimplifying the problem and exaggerating its gravity, I incline to the view that the attitude of the lay public and of many young people toward science is at bottom one of hostility arising from anxiety. In my opinion, this anxiety is in part the result of a breakdown in the system of relationships between human nature and the scientific creations of man.

Throughout this essay, the expression human nature is used in the French sense of *nature humaine,* which encompasses much more than does the English phrase. By human nature I mean not only the instinctive, psychological and moral attributes which are characteristic of man, but also all the physiological needs and urges which are woven into his very fabric, and which he has retained from his evolutionary past. In other words, I shall have in mind man's total nature rather than the limited aspects of it usually denoted by the expression human nature. In the light of this larger view of man's nature, it may be easier to understand how scientific knowledge, although it enables man to manipulate his environment, paradoxically leaves him an outsider in the world he is creating. While man is progressively mastering nature, his own nature has not so far surrendered to the scientific and technological onslaught.

Mankind has, of course, always known anxiety. The doctrine of original sin may well be merely a symbol for the uneasiness man experienced when he first realized that he was alienating himself from the rest of creation. From ancient times many have been those who believed that the world is out of joint, and it is not at all certain that their percentage numbers are larger than in the past. What is beyond doubt is that the gap between man's nature and the rest of nature is constantly becoming wider, hence the ambivalent attitude of modern man toward science. He wants the benefits of scientific technology, but he feels uneasy and indeed apprehensive about scientific knowledge *per se*. Despite much writing on the miracles of science, public fear and mistrust of scientists is probably on the increase and is certainly becoming more vocal. More and more frequently the emphasis is on the potential dangers of technological innovations, and even on horror stories concerning them.

The attitude of uneasiness has been increased, of course, by the fear of nuclear warfare, and of certain technologies which threaten the health of man. Popular articles entitled "The truth about. . . ." almost uniformly refer to the dangers of medical and technological procedures, and hint at the social irresponsibility of scientists. However, the origins of the antiscience movement are more complex and more profound than would appear from recent developments. There was already much talk of the "bankruptcy" of science during the 19th century. Science was then accused of destroying religious and philosophic values without substituting for them any other guide to behavior, or any convincing picture of the universe and of human destiny. This dissatisfaction is pungently expressed in Dewey's warning that "a culture which permits science to destroy traditional values, but which distrusts its power to create new ones, is destroying itself." The malaise has now extended to the scientific community itself, as recently acknowledged in a public lecture by a distinguished professor of chemistry in the United States. "Science is only one branch of philosophy . . . if we do make claims for support because of our rather immediate relation to industrial technology, we may well be making value-judgments concerning technology that we are, by virtue of our training, ill-equipped to make."

Admittedly, the meaning of the word "value" is so poorly defined that most scientists would probably deny that it has any usefulness as a basis either for discussion or for action. Yet, the word is so charged with the hopes of mankind, its impact on the relationships between the world of science and the rest of society is so great, that it must be recognized as a real force. I would not presume to formulate values or propose a solution to the dilemma stated by Dewey. I shall instead limit myself to a consideration of several aspects of the scientific enterprise which contribute to its progressive estrangement from the human condition, and thereby to incoherence in modern life.

Man and his Future

A symposium entitled "Man and His Future" was held in London in 1963. Its purpose was to examine the consequences of the fact that "research is creating and promising methods of interference with natural processes which could destroy or could transform every aspect of human life which we value."

The participants in the symposium found it rather easy to discuss the role of science in several current problems, such as: how to feed the billions of hungry people in the world; how to maintain an adequate supply of raw materials and of energy; how to accelerate the process of learning; how to prepare man for space travel. There was a tacit agreement among them that by using the proper scientific approach "almost everything one can imagine possible will in fact be done, if it is thought to be desirable." In contrast, the participants found no basis for common discourse when the discussions turned to the physical, psychological, emotional, cultural, or ethical traits which are desirable for human betterment. Indeed, the sheer diversity of views concerning what constitutes the good life led one of them to conclude that the only possible social policy for science as well as for human institutions was "piecemeal social engineering," that scientists must forego ambitious social plans and dedicate themselves instead to limited goals.

History shows, however, that human institutions cannot merely drift if they are to survive. Each civilization is characterized by the special kind of problems which it elects to emphasize. Furthermore, all societies operate on certain assumptions, and move toward certain goals. Despite our pathetic attempt at objectivity, we as scientists are in fact highly subjective in the selection of our activities, and we have goals in mind when we plan our work. We make *a priori* decisions concerning the kind of facts worth looking for; we arrange these facts according to certain patterns of thought which we find congenial; and we develop them in such a manner as to promote social purposes which we deem important. The most sweeping assumption in our communities at the present time is that the good life will automatically emerge if we focus our scientific efforts on the production of things and on the manipulation of the body machine, even though a large percentage of scientists probably believe that such an attitude is responsible for incoherence in technological civilization.

One might argue, of course, that incoherence is not objectionable *per se*, that incoherence may even be a symbol of intellectual integrity, and a necessary condition for the evolutionary development of mankind, since no one knows how to formulate either the ultimate truth, or the good life, or even the intermediary goals on the way to these ideals. In practice, however, there are limits to the amount of incoherence that man and his societies can tolerate; the popular success of anti-utopian and anti-scientific literature at the present time may indicate that we are approaching the breaking point.

I shall attempt in the following pages to discuss several disturbing aspects of the interplay between man's nature and the environment created by scientific knowledge. First to be considered will be the fact that, while the external environment and the ways of life are being revolutionized by technology, biological man remains fundamentally the same as he was when he emerged from his animal past. Outwardly, man makes adjustments to the new conditions of life; inwardly, however, he has so far failed to make true adaptations to them, and this discrepancy creates physiological and psychological conflicts which threaten to become increasingly traumatic.

Another cause of incoherence in our societies is that modern knowledge, especially scientific knowledge, relates less and less to human experience. In many cases, the technical apparatus of knowledge reaches into aspects of reality which are beyond human grasp. There is a disjunction between scientific knowledge and direct human experience.

Because science and technology are now advancing without the guidance of a well thought out philosophy of natural and social values, they achieve results and produce effects which in many cases no longer correspond to real human needs. Man, through science, has released disruptive forces which he has not yet learned to control. In front of his eyes, these forces are undermining the relationships slowly built through evolutionary processes between nature, the works of reason, and the hidden aspects of man's nature.

H. G. Wells pointed out in *A Modern Utopia* that ours is an adaptive civilization, incompatible with static social structures. Since we transform the external world through technology, we must also change our societies and ways of life because the maintenance of adaptive fitness is as essential for the survival of institutions as it is for the survival of living things. As presently formulated, however, evolutionary and social concepts give but an inadequate picture of man's relation to his environment. Their inadequacy comes from the fact that human societies and ways of life are rapidly changing while certain fundamental components of man's nature remain essentially unaltered.

Ever since the Neolithic revolution, man has become increasingly proficient in controlling the external world—beasts, forests, floods, climate, and many other natural forces. He has also developed enough knowledge of his own body and behavior to exercise some measure of control over certain obvious aspects of his life. Indeed, his confidence that he can modify and improve not only external nature, but also his own nature, constitutes the rationalistic basis for modern technological civilization. In Western countries, at least, technology has transformed the external world, medicine is learning to manipulate the body and the mind, social institutions are striving to establish universal respect for human dignity. Thus, ways of life are undergoing profound adaptive changes in an attempt to keep *social* man in tune with the rapid changes in the environment which are brought about by technological innovations.

In contrast, many important aspects of man's fundamental nature are not changing at all, or change so slowly that they are out of phase with the modern world. Biological evolutionary mechanisms are far too slow to keep pace with social evolution. For example, most functions of the body continue to exhibit diurnal and seasonal cycles, as well perhaps as cycles of other periodicities. Even though the ideal of technology is to create a constant and uniform environment, physiological functions still undergo cyclic changes because they are linked to the cosmic forces under which human evolution took place. When modern life carries the day into the night, maintains the same temperature and food supply throughout the year, and imposes rapid changes of latitude in a jet aircraft, it creates physiological conflicts because man's body machine continues to function according to the cosmic order. Anyone who travels by jet aircraft has a direct perception of the physiological disturbances caused in his body by the change of latitude. The immediate effects of the conflict between the paleolithic constitution of man and the exigencies of modern life can be documented by chemical, physiological and psychological measurements, but little is known of their long range consequences. There is no doubt, however, that many physiological disturbances have their origin in the conflict between the modern environment and the paleolithic ordering of physiological functions.

The so-called fight and flight response constitutes another manifestation of very ancient hidden forces which are still operating in modern man. It consists in a series of physiological and chemical processes which are rapidly mobilized in the body under conditions of threat, and which were certainly useful in the past. When prehistoric man encountered an enemy or a wild beast, a variety of hormonal processes placed his body in readiness either for combat or for running away. Today, the same processes are still set in motion under circumstances which modern man symbolizes as a threat, for example during social conflicts at the office or at a cocktail party. The physiological consequences of the fight and flight response, however, are no longer useful and indeed are probably noxious, since the proprieties of civilized life require the subjugation of the direct, physical response, and thus prevent the expenditure of physical energy. Many other ancestral mechanisms which persist in modern man must find some outlet, even though they no longer correspond to a necessity of life. Just as a kind of hunting activity remains a need for the house cat even when it is well fed at home, similarly man has retained from his evolutionary past certain needs which no longer have a place in the world he has created, yet which must be satisfied. Ancient civilizations were aware of the profound effects that hidden physiological and psychological forces exert on human behavior and they commonly symbolized these forces by a ferocious bull struggling against reason. In fact, most people have developed empirical procedures to let these occult forces manifest themselves under somewhat controlled conditions. As shown by Dodds in *The Greeks and the Irrational*, the Dionysian celebrations, the Eleusinian mysteries, and many other myths and rituals, served as release mechanisms for fundamental human urges which did not find adequate expression in the rational and classical aspects of Greek life; even Socrates found it wise to participate in the Corybantic rites. Many such ancient traditions still persist in the advanced countries of Western culture, even though in a distorted form. In the most modern city, as among the hills of Arcadia three thousand years ago, men and women perceive in springtime that nature is awakening and at work in their bodies, just as it is in the beasts and trees. Carnival is still celebrated when the sap starts running.

Scientific knowledge of the persisting ancestral aspects of man's nature hardly goes beyond a vague awareness of their existence. Limited though it is, this knowledge is nevertheless sufficient to make it clear that medical and social philosophies are based on assumptions which should be reexamined. Some of these assumptions have come to light in their simplest and perhaps crudest forms during discussions on the medical problems posed by the necessity to make man more effective in the technological age, and also to prepare astronauts for life in space capsules.

At the London symposium mentioned above, the participating scientists each had his own formula for modifying man by mechanical protheses, organ grafting, drug action, or eugenic control. But they hardly concerned themselves with the effects of these alterations on the aspects of man's nature which Dodds grouped under the adjective "irrational." A similar indifference appears in a recent article by a physician specialized in problems of space medicine. According to him, the sensible solution of these problems is to drastically modify man; the easiest approach being, in his view, to replace certain organs by mechanical parts more efficient for dial reading and better suited to electronic control. Natural, ordinary man could thus be converted into an "optiman."

Needless to say, the efficiency that biotechnologists aim at fostering in the various forms of "optiman" has little to do with the ancient but still vigorous biological human urges. Commentators in the daily press and in magazines have pointed out in many humorous or scornful articles that some scientists appear to be unaware of these fundamental needs of man's nature. The lay public has pragmatically recognized that man retains from his ancestral past certain needs and drives which, even though scientifically ill defined, nevertheless cry out for some form of expression.

There are also many tacit assumptions in the belief that the goal of technology, including medicine, should be to provide man with a sheltered environment in which he is protected as completely as possible from traumatic experiences. This assumption is dangerous because of the fact that many important traits of man's nature cannot develop normally, or remain in a healthy state, without constant stimulation and challenge. Life at constant temperaure through air conditioning, learning made effortless through mechanical aids, avoidance of conflicts through social adjustment, are examples of the means by which modern life eliminates or minimizes physiological or psychological effort, but by the same token causes an atrophy of man's adaptive mechanisms. Thus, while protection from stresses and effort may add to the pleasure or at least comfort of the moment, and while emotional neutrality minimizes social conflicts, the consequences of an excessively sheltered life are certainly unfavorable in the long run. They are even dangerous in that the human jelly fish becomes adjusted to a particular place and time, but loses his ability to readjust as surroundings change.

Scientific Knowledge and Human Experience

In contrast with the arts, science is usually identified with logic and reason. Indeed, a large part of scientific history obviously consists in the progressive unfolding of a logical process; each particular field of science has its own inner logic, which makes one fact derive from another. It is also true, on the other hand, that the growth of science presents many aspects which are essentially independent of logic. At any given period, scientists are profoundly influenced by the assumptions which they accept as a basis for their work, and by the goals which they pursue consciously or more often unconsciously. To a large extent, these assumptions and these goals are those of the social community as a whole.

The most influential assumption of modern science is that the best and indeed the only scientific approach to the study of natural phenomena and of living organisms is to divide them into fragments and to investigate elementary structures and properties in greater and greater detail. While it is repeatedly, and properly, pointed out that this analytical approach has been immensely fruitful in discoveries, there is far too little recognition of the disturbing fact that it has led to the neglect of other fields of science. Although everyone recognizes that the very existence of natural phenomena and of living organisms is the manifestation of the interplay between their constituent parts under the influence of environmental factors, hardly anything is known of the mechanisms through which natural systems function is an integrated manner.

In the course of reductionist analysis, the scientist tends to become so much involved intellectually and emotionally in the elementary fragments of the system, and in the analytical process itself, that he loses interest in the organism or the phenomenon which had been his first concern. For example, the student of man who starts from a question singled out because of its relevance to human life is likely to progress seriatim to the organ or function involved, then to the single cell, then to the cellular fragments, then to the molecular groupings or reactions, then to the individual molecules and atoms; and he would happily proceed if he knew enough to the elementary particles where matter and energy become indistinguishable. Problems of great interest obviously arise at each step in the disintegration of the original phenomenon. But in practically all cases the phenomenon itself is lost on the way, and the knowledge acquired in the course of its analysis usually throws little light on its determinants and modalities—let alone on the approach to its control. Scientists might find it useful now and then to evaluate their professional activities in the light of Kant's admonition, "To yield to every whim of curiosity, and to allow our passion for inquiry to be restrained by nothing but the limits of our ability, this shows an eagerness of mind not unbecoming to scholarship. But it is wisdom that has the merit of selecting from among the innumerable problems which present themselves, those whose solution is important to mankind."

Loss of interest in phenomena as they occur in Nature is found in practically all fields of science. It would be out of place to discuss here the consequences of this aspect of scientific professionalism for the advancement of knowledge. But it is relevant to the present theme to suggest that therein lies in part the cause of the estrangement of the general public from science. The primary interest of the public is in the phenomena of nature or in the living organisms, whereas the deepest commitment of the professional scientist is to the results of his analytical processes. In consequence, the scientist generally loses his public as he loses sight of the original problem.

Furthermore, whereas science was at first a method to deal with the world of matter and of life as man perceives it through his senses, much of the scientist's knowledge is now acquired through technical and mental processes which operate outside the range of immediate human experience. Emile Gilson stated in his William James Lectures at Harvard that "Every scientist naturally has the temper and the tastes of a specialist . . . . the natural tendency of science is not towards unity, but towards an ever more complete disintegration." This statement certainly describes a state of affairs which is increasingly prevalent, but it does not, in my opinion, deal with the most important aspect of the problem. A more disturbing aspect of modern science is that the specialist himself commonly loses contact with the aspect of reality which was his primary concern, whether it was matter, life or man.

In his own experience of the physical world, the physicist does not use his specialized knowledge for a richer or more subtle contact with reality; nor is the biologist rendered capable of perceiving the living experience more acutely because he is familiar with intermediate metabolism or x-ray diffraction patterns of contractile fibers. The theoretical physicist apparently finds it difficult to convert the mathematical formulae on which he depends into experiences or thoughts meaningful to his own senses and reason. The general biologist finds no trace of the creativeness of life in the macromolecules he isolates from the cell. The student of consciousness cannot relate the operations of the sense organs or of the nerve impulse to the emotion elicited by a fragrant rose or a romantic sunset.

There has been much talk during recent years of the lack of communication between the humanistic and the scientific aspects of knowledge. In reality, however, this disjunction is not so critical as is often suggested. Each and every one of us can and does learn many facts and concepts pertaining to areas of knowledge totally different from the one in which he is a specialist. The breakdown in communication is complete only when the concepts cannot be related to human experience. The physicist, the biologist, the humanist, and the layman can all find a common ground for discourse if they talk about matter, life, or man as perceived by the senses, or as apprehended in the form of images, analogies, and responses. But discussions of matter in terms of mathematical symbolism, or of life and man in terms of disintegrated components, cannot be related to any form of direct experience. Specialists must return to the original human basis of their work if they want to converse with mankind.

Science and Technology as Independent Forces

Just as scientific knowledge is becoming alienated from human experience, so are its technological applications becoming increasingly alienated from human needs. Although modern technology appears at first sight but a spectacular extension of what it started out to be in the 18th and 19th centuries, in reality it is moving toward other goals. This change of focus is contributing to the disjunction between science and mankind.

The natural philosophers and sociologists of the Age of Reason were concerned with a few well defined problems of obvious importance for the welfare of the human race. Everywhere they saw misery and disease caused by acute shortages of food and of elementary conveniences; they observed that ignorance of the natural forces generates terror, superstitions and often acts of cruelty. The task they set for science was therefore to abolish the threat of scarcity, and to gain enough knowledge to help man face the natural world without fear. These goals were within the range of human experience. By making it possible to reach them, science was truly acting as a servant of mankind.

In contrast, science and the technologies derived from it now often function as forces independent of human goals. In many cases, as we have seen, knowledge creates concepts that man cannot restate in terms of his experience; and increasingly technology creates services and products that man does not really need. All too often, knowledge and technology pursue a course which is not guided by a pre-determined social philosophy. The knowledge of ionizing radiations and of atomic structure was developed by men with the highest ideals who can be regarded as saints of science, yet immense harm has come from their creations. The guilt for this harm cannot be placed on villains with selfish interests or bent on hurting mankind; it results rather from a political and social process which allows science to move blindly in the social arena.

Even though dangers are also inherent in the knowledge concerning automation, synthetic chemicals, or almost any other new technology, surprisingly little is done to evaluate the possible social consequences of these innovations. One dramatic illustration of this negligence is the research budget of the State Department. Science, lavishly endowed by public funds, produced nuclear weapons—the means by which man can now destroy himself. The problem of preventing this catastrophe is primarily the State Department's responsibility. Yet its total budget for policy research studies is negligible. Indeed, there is very little federal support for any kind of scholarly work on the explosive international issues now facing the world. Nor is there much recognition of the fact that the recent advances in medicine have created vast new problems which are essentially social, political, and economic rather than scientific. As E. M. Forster predicted in "The Machine Stops," technology moves on, but not on our lines; it proceeds, but not to our goals. It is urgent that science and technology be given goals of significance and value to man lest the sorcerer's apprentice be converted from a literary symbol into a terrifying reality.

The Industrial Revolution, with mass production of energy and its rapid injection into all aspects of social life, is everywhere beginning to disrupt the great dynamic processes which have so far maintained the earth in a state compatible with human life. Disruption of the water cycle is speeding water on its way to the sea and increasing its destructive action on land surfaces; denudation of the soil is creating dust bowls all over the earth; pollution of the air and of water is beginning to upset the biological balance and to damage human health. The medical sciences themselves are becoming so effective that they can affect unfavorably the fate of immense numbers of people and of their descendants, often creating new pathological processes as they control old diseases. Their greatest impact, probably, will be not so much on the size of the world population as on its genetic qualities, and on its other qualitative characteristics.

Needless to say, there is nothing fundamentally new in the fact that technology alters the relationship between man and nature. For many thousand years, man has modified his environment by using fire, farming the land, building houses, opening roads, and even controlling his reproduction. The all important difference, however, is that many modern applications of science have nothing to do with human biological needs and aim only at creating new demands, even though these be inimical to health, to happiness, or to the aspirations of mankind. Technology allowed to develop for its own sake often acts as a disruptive force which upsets the precarious relationships upon which civilizations have been built in the past. It creates new environmental conditions to which man finds it difficult to adapt, and which destroy some of the most valuable human attributes.

A process of adaptation is of course going on continuously between man and the new world he is creating. As we have seen, however, some important traits which are built into the fabric of man's nature are not likely to be eliminated, or significantly modified, despite all the changes which occur in his societies and ways of life. Even when man becomes an automated and urbane city dweller, his physiological processes remain geared to the daily rotation of the earth around its axis and to its annual rotation around the sun; the paleolithic bull which survives in his inner self still paws the earth whenever a threatening gesture is made on the social scene. The tragic paradox is that science fosters ways of life and manners of response which are often determined by technological expediency, whereas it hardly concerns itself with the fundamental characteristics and needs of man's nature.

While most human beings believe that the proper study of mankind is man, the scientific establishment has not tooled itself for this task. The great scientific institutions are geared for the analytical description of the body machine, which they approach in much the same spirit as they do simple inanimate objects. They pay little heed to the scientific study of man as a functioning entity, exhibiting all the complex responses that living entails. Nor do they pay much attention to the environmental factors which condition the manifestations of human life.

The disjunction between man's nature and the creations of science and technology inevitably manifests itself in social disturbances. In principle, these disturbances are not beyond the scope of scientific study; in practice, however, they have a low order of priority in the world of learning. The study of man as an integrated unit, and of the ecosystems in which he functions, is grossly neglected because it is not in the tradition which has dominated experimental science since the 17th century. Such a study would demand an intellectual approach, as well as research techniques and facilities, different from those which are fashionable and professionally profitable in the academic establishment.

Two historical reasons account for the tendency of scientists to neglect the problems posed by the complex situations found in the real world. One is that the simpler problems are more likely to yield clear results and rapid professional advance. The other reason is that until recently, the applications of science were direct and on the whole beneficial. Only during the past few decades has science become such a powerful force that any technological intervention affects simultaneously many aspects of human life.

Land conservation, water resources, urban development, the physiological and mental qualities of the human race are but a few among the immense problems created by the impact of scientific technology. It is therefore a moral obligation for the scientific establishment to devote itself in earnest to the study of ecosystems, both those of nature and those created by man. But ecosystems cannot be studied by the use of the oversimplified models which constitute the stock in trade of orthodox experimental science.

The urgency to escape from shackles of the scientific past is particularly apparent when attention turns to man himself. One of the strangest assumptions of present day biology is that knowledge of living man will automatically follow from so called "fundamental" studies of the elementary structures and reactions of fragments derived from living things. In reality, a very different kind of knowledge is needed to understand the nature of the cohesive forces which maintain man in an integrated state, physically, psychologically, and socially, and enable him to relate successfully to his environment. Hardly anything is known of man's adaptive potentialities, of the manner in which he responds to the stimuli which impinge on him early in his development and throughout his life, of the long range consequences of these responses not only for himself but for his descendants. There are countless problems ranging from those posed by the earlier sexual maturity of children to those involved in urban planning, which should and could be studied scientifically, yet have hardly any place in the curriculum of universities or research institutes.

Science for Man

Incoherence implies the breakdown of integrative relationships. One remedial measure is of course to establish better understanding and communication within the scientific community itself and between it and the public. But there is no knowledge of how this can be done effectively. At most, it is known that a few scientific books of distinction have been widely read, or at least have had a wide influence and are often quoted. A study of the reason for their success might provide some insight into the determinants of the public response to science, and indirectly into the aspects of science which have human values.

There are good reasons to believe that conceptual views of the world, even if purely theoretical, can have as much general appeal as utilitarian applications, and it is obvious of course that the appeal is even greater when the facts have some relevance to the problems which have always preoccupied mankind, whether these be concerned with the place of man in the cosmos or with his survival and welfare. But in any case, scientific communication demands more than the description of facts or the reporting of news. In science, just as in any other field, man can communicate with man only through the channels of shared experiences, or still better, through mutual hopes.

Through its emphasis on over-simplified models, the scientific community is betraying the very spirit of its vocation—namely, its professed concern with reality. Nature exists only in the form of complex ecosystems, and these constitute the environment which man perceives, and to which he responds. As human life becomes more dependent on technology, it will become more vulnerable to the slightest miscarriage or unforeseen consequence of innovations, hence the need for studies directed to the problems of interrelationships within complex ecosystems. Science will remain an effective method for the acquisition of knowledge meaningful to man, and consequently for social service only if its orthodox techniques can be supplemented by others which come closer to the human experience or reality, and to a kind of social action designed for fundamental human needs.

The study of natural and man-made ecosystems, as well as of man's responses to environmental forces, has as much intellectual dignity and deserves as much academic support as the study of isolated particles and elementary reactions. Only through a scientific knowledge of man's nature and of the ecosystems in which he functions can technology be usefully and safely woven into the fabric of society. Indeed, a truly human concept of technology might well constitute the force which will make science once more part of the universal human discourse, because technology at its highest level must integrate knowledge of the external world and of man's nature.

Since each particular field of science has its inner logic of growth, the scientific enterprise can long continue to move on its own momentum even though it becomes increasingly indifferent to man. Lacking worthwhile social goals, however, science may soon find itself floundering in a sea of irrelevancies. Eventually, it might even be rejected by ordinary men if they were to decide that its values are irrelevant and dangerous. "It seems to me entirely possible," stated recently a Sigma Xi lecturer, "that our society, which, for whatever motives, has invested not only immense sums of money but large amounts of spiritual faith in what it uninformedly conceives science to be, may become as thoroughly disillusioned and rebellious toward scientific and technological authoritarianism as early societies became rebellious towards regal authoritarianism."

Despite its spectacular successes, science is not yet firmly established in the human mind. Its increasing alienation from the problems which are of deepest concern for mankind might well transform the anti-utopian outbursts so characteristic of our time from a literary exercise into an anti-science crusade. In its mildest form, such a crusade will at least continue to clamor for a moratorium on science, under the pretext that knowledge is accumulating faster than it can be digested and therefore is becoming dangerous. In reality, of course, there cannot be any retreat from science. Rather, public apprehension and hostility point to the need for an enlargement of science. Scientists must take more to heart the questions which deeply concern human beings; they must learn to give greater prominence to large human values when formulating their problems and their results. Fortunately, this is probably easier than is commonly believed because, as emphasized earlier, history shows that the broad implications of science can become integrated in the intellectual fabric of modern societies. Human cultures, like organisms and societies, depend for survival on their internal integration, an integration which can be achieved only to the extent that science remains meaningful to the living experience of man.

26. Theodore Roszak

The Myth of
Objective Consciousness

Growing numbers of social critics, intellectuals, and students stand
convinced that René Dubos' criticism of science does not go far enough.
Among them is Theodore Roszak, a member of the history department
of California State College at Hayward, who believes that dissenters within
the scientific establishment fail to confront fully the terrors of their own
handiwork, particularly in relation to the powerful technocracy, or if
they do, nevertheless fail to comprehend the psychological and
epistemological limitations of the scientific world view. By technocracy
he means an industrial society that is highly integrated organizationally.
It legitimizes the rule of experts who modernize, update, and plan,
and who value efficiency, social security, and coordination. Their
vocabulary runs from structures, variables, parameters, correlations,
inputs, and outputs to systems analysis, optimizations, escalations, kill
ratios, and body counts. The myth of objective consciousness, the belief
that reality can be understood through the "objective" and one-dimensional
method of science, is a crucial element of the ideology supporting the
technocracy. Roszak attempts to show, however, that science only
remythologizes life, it does not demythologize it. As such it is yet another
single path to truth whose pretensions require unmasking if man is to
find psychological and spiritual liberation.

"The Myth of Objective Consciousness" forms part of Roszak's popular
study, *The Making of a Counter Culture* (1969). This thoughtful and
often arresting book examines the counter culture and its heroes who have
begun the intellectual dismantling of the technocracy by calling into
question the conventional scientific world view upon which it rests.
It has inspired considerable discussion. Is the scientific consciousness
as deeply rooted in American society as Roszak assumes? Dubos, for
one, argues that it is not. Are science and technology so inextricably
coupled and deeply imbedded in our thinking that a thorough
change is virtually impossible without an accompanying social and
economic revolution of American society? Can science and technology
be separated? Has Roszak ignored possible changes in science? One
view of current scientific activity is that the scientist is no longer
a truth seeker but a spinner of artificially created hypotheses and models
of which he asks only that they work. If science and technology
cannot be trusted to usher in the good society, where shall men look?
It seems certain that answers to these questions must be found if
Americans are to regain a portion of their world that has been lost
to democracy and to civilized values.

If there is one especially striking feature of the new radicalism we have been surveying, it is the cleavage that exists between it and the radicalism of previous generations where the subjects of science and technology are concerned. To the older collectivist ideologies, which were as given to the value of industrial expansion as the capitalist class enemy, the connection between totalitarian control and science was not apparent. Science was almost invariably seen as an undisputed social good, because it had become so intimately related in the popular mind (though not often in ways clearly understood) to the technological progress that promised security and affluence. It was not foreseen even by gifted social critics that the impersonal, large-scale social processes to which technological progress gives rise—in economics, in politics, in education, in every aspect of life—generate their own characteristic problems. When the general public finds itself enmeshed in a gargantuan industrial apparatus which it admires to the point of idolization and yet cannot comprehend, it must of necessity defer to those who are experts or to those who own the experts; only they appear to know how the great cornucopia can be kept brimming over with the good things of life.

Centralized bigness breeds the regime of expertise, whether the big system is based on privatized or socialized economies. Even within the democratic socialist tradition with its stubborn emphasis on workers' control, it is far from apparent how the democratically governed units of an industrial economy will automatically produce a general system which is not dominated by co-ordinating experts. It is both ironic and ominous to hear the French Gaullists and the Wilson Labourites in Great Britain—governments that are heavily committed to an elitist managerialism—now talking seriously about increased workers' "participation" in industry. It would surely be a mistake to believe that the technocracy cannot find ways to placate and integrate the shop floor without compromising the continuation of super-scale social processes. "Participation" could easily become the god-word of our official politics within the next decade; but its reference will be to the sort of "responsible" collaboration that keeps the technocracy growing. We do well to remember that one of the great secrets of successful concentration camp administration under the Nazis was to enlist the "participation" of the inmates.

It is for this reason that the counter culture, which draws upon a profoundly personalist sense of community rather than upon technical and industrial values, comes closer to being a radical critique of the technocracy than any of the traditional ideologies. If one starts with a sense of the person that ventures to psychoanalytical depths, one may rapidly arrive at a viewpoint that rejects many of the hitherto undisputed values of industrialism itself. One soon begins talking about "standards of living" that transcend high productivity, efficiency, full employment, and the work-and-consumption ethic. Quality and not quantity becomes the touchstone of social value.

The critique is pushed even further when the counter culture begins to explore the modes of non-intellective consciousness. Along this line, questions arise which strike more deeply at technocratic assumptions. For if the technocracy is dependent on public deference to the experts, it must stand or fall by the reality of expertise. But what *is* expertise? What are the criteria which certify someone as an expert?

If we are foolishly willing to agree that experts are those whose role is legitimized by the fact that the technocratic system needs them in order to avoid falling apart at the seams, then of course the technocratic status quo generates its own internal justification: the technocracy is legitimized because it enjoys the approval of experts; the experts are legitimized because there could be no technocracy without them. This is the sort of circular argument student rebels meet when they challenge the necessity of administrative supremacy in the universities. They are invariably faced with the rhetorical question: but who will allocate room space, supervise registration, validate course requirements, coordinate the academic departments, police the parking lots and dormitories, discipline students, etc., if not the administration? Will the multiversity not collapse in chaos if the administrators are sent packing? The students are learning the answer: yes, the multiversity will collapse; but *education* will go on. Why? Because the administrators have nothing to do with the reality of education; their expertise is related to the illusory busywork that arises from administrative complexity itself. The multiversity creates the administrators and they, in turn, expand the multiversity so that it needs to make place for more administrators. One gets out of this squirrel cage only by digging deep into the root meaning of education itself.

The same radicalizing logic unfolds if, in confronting the technocracy, we begin looking for a conception of expertise which amounts to something more than the intimidating truism that tells us experts are those in the absence of whom the technocracy would collapse.

An expert, we say, is one to whom we turn because he is in control of reliable knowledge about that which concerns us. In the case of the technocracy, the experts are those who govern us because they know (reliably) about all things relevant to our survival and happiness: human needs, social engineering, economic planning, international relations, invention, education, etc. Very well, but what is "reliable knowledge"? How do we know it when we see it? The answer is: reliable knowledge is knowledge that is scientifically sound, since science is that to which modern man refers for the definitive explication of reality. And what in turn is it that characterizes scientific knowledge? The answer is: objectivity. Scientific knowledge is not just feeling or speculation or subjective ruminating. It is a verifiable description of reality that exists independent of any purely personal considerations. It is true . . . real . . . dependable. . . . It works. And that at last is how we define an expert: he is one who *really* knows what is what, because he cultivates an objective consciousness.

Thus, if we probe the technocracy in search of the peculiar power it holds over us, we arrive at the myth of objective consciousness. There is but one way of gaining access to reality—so the myth holds—and this is to cultivate a state of consciousness cleansed of all subjective distortion, all personal involvement. What flows from this state of consciousness qualifies as knowledge, and nothing else does. This is the bedrock on which the natural sciences have built; and under their spell all fields of knowledge strive to become scientific. The study of man in his social, political, economic, psychological, historical aspects—all this, too, must become objective: rigorously, painstakingly objective.. At every level of human experience, would-be scientists come forward to endorse the myth of objective consciousness, thus certifying themselves as experts. And because they know and we do not, we yield to their guidance.

But to speak of "mythology" in connection with science would seem at first glance to be a contradiction in terms. Science, after all, purports to be precisely that enterprise of the mind which strips life of its myths, substituting for fantasy and legend a relationship to reality based, in William James' phrase, on "irreducible and stubborn facts." Is not scientific knowledge, indeed, that residue which is left when all the myths have been filtered away? One might in fact argue that this is exactly what distinguishes the scientific revolution of the modern West from all previous cultural transitions. In the past, when one cultural epoch has displaced another, the change frequently involved little more than a process of mythological transformation: a re-mythologizing of men's thinking. So the figure of Christ stepped into the place prepared long since by the savior figures of various pagan mystery cults, and in time the Christian saints inherited their status from the deities of the Greco-Roman, Teutonic, or Celtic pantheons.

But science, we are to believe, does not re-mythologize life; it de-mythologizes it. This is supposedly what makes the scientific revolution a radically different, if not a final, cultural episode. For, with the advent of the scientific world view, indisputable truth takes the place of make-believe.

There is no doubting the radical novelty of science in contrast to all earlier mythological world views. What all nonscientific cultural systems have had in common is the tendency to mistake their mythologies for literal statements about history and the natural world—or at least the tendency to articulate mythological insights in what a scientific mind mistakes for propositional assertions. In this way, imaginative expressions rich in moral drama or psychic perception easily degenerate into fabulous conjectures about the exotic reaches of time and space. This is how we most often use the word "mythology" in our time: to designate the telling of unverifiable, if not downright false, tales about remote ages and places. The story of the Garden of Eden is a "myth" we say, because insofar as any believing Christian or Jew has ever tried to locate the story geographically and historically, skeptics have been able to call his evidence, if any, quite cogently into question.

Mythologies which are imaginative exaggerations of our ordinary perceptions or displacements of them to other times and places—let us call them in this sense temporal-physical mythologies—have always been vulnerable to critical inquiry. The doubting Thomas in the case need not even be a scientific skeptic. A devout Christian can practice an uncompromising skepticism toward the mythologies of other faiths and cultures, in the fashion of Charlemagne striking down the Saxon idols and defying their wrath, confident that no such heathen divinities existed. But a Christian's skepticism is necessarily partisan, sparing the believer any critical examination of his own dogmas. Even liberal Christian demythologizers like Rudolph Bultmann have had to stop short of extending their project to such essential teachings as the resurrection of Christ.

In contrast to such selective skepticism, the wholesale skepticism of science shows up to brilliant advantage. Science is the infidel to all gods in behalf of none. Thus there is no way around the painful dilemma in which the religious traditions of the world have found themselves trapped over the last two centuries. Every culture that has invested its convictions in a temporal-physical mythology is doomed before the onslaught of the scientific unbeliever. Any village atheist who persists in saying "show me" is in the position to hold up to ransom an entire religious culture, with little expectation that it will be able to find the price demanded. It would be difficult to say whether this situation partakes more of farce or of tragedy. Only a few generations ago, Clarence Darrow, no more than a skillful courtroom lawyer armed with a Sunday supplement knowledge of Darwin, was able to make laughingstock of a Judeo-Christian mythology that had served to inspire the finest philosophical and artistic minds of our culture over hundreds of generations. Yet, under unrelenting skeptical pressure, what choice have those who cling to temporal-physical mythologies but to undertake strategic retreat, conceding ever more ground to secular, reductionist styles of thought. The line of retreat falls back to interpretations of myth that are primarily ethical . . . or aesthetic . . . or, in some unspecified fashion, symbolic. Within the Christian tradition, this is a resort which is bound to weaken and confuse, since Christianity has had a uniquely significant commitment to the literal truth of its teachings. Indeed, the sweeping secularization of Western society that has come in the wake of scientific advance can be seen as a product of Christianity's peculiar reliance on a precarious, dogmatic literalism. Such a religious tradition need only prick its finger in order to bleed to death. And if the hard-pressed believer does turn to "symbolic" interpretations, even here the secular temperament tends to sweep the field by asserting reductionist psychological or sociological correlatives for the myth. The only other defense, that of standing fast in behalf of the literal truth, leads, as Kierkegaard recognized more than a century ago, to the crucifixion of the intellect.

The scientific world view is of course invulnerable to criticism at the same level as a temporal-physical mythology. It would be a ludicrous mistake to contend that the things and forces with which science fills time and space—electrons and galaxies, gravitational fields and natural selection, DNA and viruses—are the cultural equivalents of centaurs and Valhallas and angelic beings. What science deals in is not so poor in ordinary sensory verification—nor so rich in imaginative possibilities. Unlike the mythological traditions of the past, science is not in the first instance a body of supposed knowledge about entities and events. Science would still be science and very much in business if it encompassed no knowledge at all other than the ruins of proven ignorance and error. The scientific mind begins in the spirit of the Cartesian zero, with the doubting away of all inherited knowledge in favor of an entirely new *method* of knowing, which, whether it proceeds on rationalist or empiricist lines, purports to begin from scratch, free of all homage to authority.

What scientists know may therefore wax or wane, change in part or whole as time goes on and as evidence accumulates. If the Piltdown fossil proves to be a hoax, it can be discarded without calling the science of physical anthropology into question. If the telescopes of astronomers were to discover angels in outer space, science as a method of knowing would not be in any sense discredited; its theories would simply be reformulated in the light of new discoveries. In contrast to the way we use the phrase "world view" in other contexts, science rests itself not in the *world* the scientist beholds at any particular point in time, but in his mode of *viewing* that world. A man is a scientist not because of what he sees, but because of *how* he sees it.

At least, this is what has become the conventional way of regarding scientific knowledge. Thomas Kuhn, who has looked at the matter more carefully, has recently thrown strong and significant doubt on this "incremental" conception of the history of science. His contention comes close to suggesting that the progressive accumulation of "truth" in the scientific community is something of an illusion, created by the fact that each generation of scientists rewrites its textbooks in such a way as to select from the past what is still considered valid and to suppress the multitude of errors and false starts that are also a part of the history of science. As for the all-important principles of validation that control this natural selection of scientific truth from era to era—the so-called "scientific method" —Kuhn is left unconvinced that they are quite as purely "rational" or "empirical" as scientists like to think.

Yet the incremental conception of scientific knowledge is very much part of the mythology we are concerned with here. The capacity of science to progress stands as one of the principal validations of its objectivity. Knowledge progresses only when it is understood to survive the passing of particular minds or generations. Science, understood as the expanding application of a fixed method of knowing to ever more areas of experience, makes such a claim. A scientist, asked to explain why science progresses when other fields of thought do not, would doubtlessly refer us to the "objectivity" of his method of knowing. Objectivity, he would tell us, in what gives science its keen critical edge and its peculiarity cumulative character.

Are we using the word "mythology" illegitimately in applying it to objectivity as a state of consciousness? I think not. For the myth at its deepest level is that collectively created thing which crystallizes the great, central values of a culture. It is, so to speak, the intercommunications system of culture. If the culture of science locates its highest values not in mystic symbol or ritual or epic tales of faraway lands and times, but in a mode of consciousness, why should we hesitate to call this a myth? The myth has, after all, been identified as a universal phenomenon of human society, a constitutive factor so critical in importance that it is difficult to imagine a culture having any coherence at all if it lacked the mythological bond. Yet, in our society, myth as it is conventionally understood has become practically a synonym for falsehood. To be sure, we commonly hear discussion of various social and political myths these days (the myth of the American frontier, the myth of the Founding Fathers, etc.) ; the more enlightened clergy even talk freely of "the Christian myth." But myths so openly recognized as myths are precisely those that have lost much of their power. It is the myth we accept without question as truth that holds real influence over us. Is it possible that, in this sense, scientific culture is uniquely a-mythical? Or is it the case that we simply fail to look in the right place—in the deep personality structure of the ideal scientist—for the great controlling myth of our culture?

Such, at least, is what I propose here, though it would be pointless to press any further the purely semantic question of whether or not objective consciousness meets all the requirements of a "mythology." What is essential here is the contention that objective consciousness is emphatically *not* some manner of definitive, transcultural development whose cogency derives from the fact that it is uniquely in touch with the truth. Rather, like a mythology, it is an arbitrary construct in which a given society in a given historical situation has invested its sense of meaningfulness and value. And so, like any mythology, it can be gotten round and called into question by cultural movements which find meaning and value elsewhere. In the case of the counter culture, then, we have a movement which has turned from objective consciousness as if from a place inhabited by plague—and in the moment of that turning, one can just begin to see an entire episode of our cultural history, the great age of science and technology which began with the Enlightenment, standing revealed in all its quaintly arbitrary, often absurd, and all too painfully unbalanced aspects.

Perhaps, as Michael Polanyi has argued, there is no such thing as objectivity, even in the physical sciences. Certainly his critique is a formidable challenge to scientific orthodoxy. But for our purposes here, this narrowly epistemological question is a subordinate consideration. Science, under the technocracy, has become a total culture dominating the lives of millions for whom discussions of the theory of knowledge are so much foreign language. Yet objectivity, whatever its epistemological status, has become the commanding life style of our society: the one most authoritative way of regarding the self, others, and the whole of our enveloping reality. Even if it is not, indeed, possible to be objective, it *is* possible so to shape the personality that it will feel and act *as if* one were an objective observer and to treat everything that experience presents to the person in accordance with what objectivity would seem to demand.

Objectivity as a state of being fills the very air we breathe in a scientific culture; it grips us subliminally in all we say, feel, and do. The mentality of the ideal scientist becomes the very soul of the society. We seek to adapt our lives to the dictates of that mentality, or at the very least we respond to it acquiescently in the myriad images and pronouncements in which it manifests itself about us during every waking hour. The Barbarella and James Bond who keep their clinical cool while dealing out prodigious sex or sadistic violence . . . the physiologist who persuades several score of couples to undertake coitus while wired to a powerhouse of electronic apparatus so that he can achieve a statistical measure of sexual normalcy . . . the characters of *Last Year At Marienbad* who face one another as impassively as empty mirrors . . . the Secretary of Defense who tells the public without blinking an eye that our country possesses the "overkill" capacity to destroy any given enemy ten times . . . the high-rise glass and aluminum slab that deprives of visual involvement by offering us only functional linearity and massive reflecting surfaces . . . the celebrated surgeon who assures us that his heart transplant was a "success" though of course the patient died . . . the computer technician who blithely suggests that we have to wage an "all-out war on sleep" in order to take advantage of the latest breakthrough in rapid communications . . . the modish expert who seeks (with phenomenal success) to convince us that the essence of communication lies not in the truth or falsehood, wisdom or folly of the message that person transfers to person, but rather in the technical characteristics of the intervening medium . . . the political scientist who settles for being a psephological virtuoso, pretending that the statistics of meaningless elections are the veritable substance of politics . . . all these (or so I would argue) are life under the sway of objective consciousness.

In short, as science elaborates itself into the dominant cultural influence of our age, it is the psychology and not the epistemology of science that urgently requires our critical attention; for it is primarily at this level that the most consequential deficiencies and imbalances of the technocracy are revealed.

X. Students and Higher Education

27. Clark Kerr

The Uses of the University

Clark Kerr, chancellor of the University of California, became the first major casualty of spreading dissatisfaction with university life in the 1960s when, beleaguered by conservative regents on the Right and radical students on the Left, he was forced to resign after many years of service. He had become a spokesman for and symbol of the "multiversity" which developed in the years following World War II. The selection below is taken from *The Uses of the University*, based on the 1963 Godkin Lectures delivered at Harvard University.

To Clark Kerr and other liberal academicians, the multiversity is a city "of infinite variety," offering diverse roles to the American professoriate and a "vast range of choices" to students. Despite deepening ties with business and government, or perhaps because of them, the students' freedom to learn and the faculty member's freedom to do as he wishes are both "triumphant." Kerr defends the American multiversity, saying that it "has few peers in the preservation and dissemination and examination of the eternal truths; no living peers in the search for new knowledge; and no peers in all history among institutions of higher learning in serving so many of the segments of an advancing civilization." Elsewhere in the book he acknowledges that the large university does not always serve the needs of students and sees evidence of an "incipient revolt" over the impersonality of the university run as a business corporation. Two years later the student revolt broke out on the Berkeley campus of the University of California.

Criticism of Kerr's idea of the university as a "service station" and "knowledge factory" has come from three sources: from traditional humanists who reject the "service station" function and want the university set apart from society; from the political Right, which sees the university as too flexible, too relativist in its governing values, too hospitable a place for radicals, and overly partial to research over teaching; and from the student and intellectual Left, which objects to the university serving and legitimizing the social system of warfare—welfare corporate capitalism.

The multiversity is an inconsistent institution. It is not one community but several—the community of the undergraduate and the community of

Excerpted by permission of the publishers from pp. 18-19, 41-45, 86-87, 116-118, 124-125, and 126 of Clark Kerr, *The Uses of the University*. Cambridge, Mass.: Harvard University Press, Copyright © 1963, 1972, by the President and Fellows of Harvard College.

the graduate; the community of the humanist, the community of the social scientist, and the community of the scientist; the communities of the professional schools; the community of all the nonacademic personnel; the community of the administrators. Its edges are fuzzy—it reaches out to alumni, legislators, farmers, businessmen, who are all related to one or more of these internal communities. As an institution, it looks far into the past and far into the future, and is often at odds with the present. It serves society almost slavishly—a society it also criticizes, sometimes unmercifully. Devoted to equality of opportunity, it is itself a class society. A community, like the medieval communities of masters and students, should have common interests; in the multiversity, they are quite varied, even conflicting. A community should have a soul, a single animating principle; the multiversity has several—some of them quite good, although there is much debate on which souls really deserve salvation. . . .

The "Idea of a University" was a village with its priests. The "Idea of a Modern University" was a town—a one-industry town—with its intellectual oligarchy. "The Idea of a Multiversity" is a city of infinite variety. Some get lost in the city; some rise to the top within it; most fashion their lives within one of its many subcultures. There is less sense of community than in the village but also less sense of confinement. There is less sense of purpose than within the town but there are more ways to excel. There are also more refuges of anonymity—both for the creative person and the drifter. As against the village and the town, the "city" is more like the totality of civilization as it has evolved and more an integral part of it; and movement to and from the surrounding society has been greatly accelerated. As in a city, there are many separate endeavors under a single rule of law.

The students in the "city" are older, more likely to be married, more vocationally oriented, more drawn from all classes and races than the students in the village; and they find themselves in a most intensely competitive atmosphere. They identify less with the total community and more with its subgroups. Burton R. Clark and Martin Trow have a particularly interesting typology of these subcultures: the "collegiate" of the fraternities and sororities and the athletes and activities majors; the "academic" of the serious students; the "vocational" of the students seeking training for specific jobs; and the "nonconformist" of the political activists, the aggressive intellectuals, and the bohemians. These subcultures are not mutually exclusive, and some of the fascinating pageantry of the multiversity is found in their interaction one on another.

The multiversity is a confusing place for the student. He has problems of establishing his identity and sense of security within it. But it offers him a vast range of choices, enough literally to stagger the mind. In this range of choices he encounters the opportunities and the dilemmas of freedom. The casualty rate is high. The walking wounded are many. *Lernfreiheit*—the freedom of the student to pick and choose, to stay or to move on—is triumphant.

Life has changed also for the faculty member. The multiversity is in the main stream of events. To the teacher and the researcher have been added the consultant and the administrator. Teaching is less central than it once was for most faculty members; research has become more important. This has given rise to what has been called the "nonteacher"—"the higher a man's standing, the less he has to do with students"—and to a threefold class structure of what used to be "the faculty": those who only do research, those who only teach (and they are largely in an auxiliary role), and those who still do some of both. In one university I know, the proportions at the Ph.D. level or its equivalent are roughly one researcher to two teachers to four who do both.

Consulting work and other sources of additional income have given rise to what is called the "affluent professor," a category that does include some but by no means all of the faculty. Additionally, many faculty members, with their research assistants and teaching assistants, their departments and institutes, have become administrators. A professor's life has become, it is said, "a rat race of business and activity, managing contracts and projects, guiding teams and assistants, bossing crews of technicians, making numerous trips, sitting on committees for government agencies, and engaging in other distractions necessary to keep the whole frenetic business from collapse."

The intellectual world has been fractionalized as interests have become much more diverse; and there are fewer common topics of conversation at the faculty clubs. Faculty government has become more cumbersome, more the avocation of active minorities; and there are real questions whether it can work effectively on a large scale, whether it can agree on more than preservation of the status quo. Faculty members are less members of the particular university and more colleagues within their national academic discipline groups.

But there are many compensations. "The American professoriate" is no longer, as Flexner once called it, "a proletariat." Salaries and status have risen considerably. The faculty member is more a fully participating member of society, rather than a creature of the periphery; some are at the very center of national and world events. Research opportunities have been enormously increased. The faculty member within the big mechanism and with all his opportunities has a new sense of independence from the domination of the administration or his colleagues; much administration has been effectively decentralized to the level of the individual professor. In particular, he has a choice of roles and mixtures of roles to suit his taste as never before. He need not leave the Groves for the Acropolis unless he wishes; but he can, if he wishes. He may even become, as some have, essentially a professional man with his home office and basic retainer on the campus of the multiversity but with his clients scattered from coast to coast. He can also even remain the professor of old, as many do. There are several patterns of life from which to choose. So the professor too has greater freedom. *Lehrfreiheit,* in the old German sense of the freedom of the professor to do as he pleases, also is triumphant.

What is the justification of the modern American multiversity? History is one answer. Consistency with the surrounding society is another. Beyond that, it has few peers in the preservation and dissemination and examination of the eternal truths; no living peers in the search for new knowledge; and no peers in all history among institutions of higher learning in serving so many of the segments of an advancing civilization. Inconsistent internally as an institution, it is consistently productive. Torn by change, it has the stability of freedom. Though it has not a single soul to call its own, its members pay their devotions to truth.

The multiversity in America is perhaps best seen at work, adapting and growing, as it responded to the massive impact of federal programs beginning with World War II. A vast transformation has taken place without a revolution, for a time almost without notice being taken. The multiversity has demonstrated how adaptive it can be to new opportunities for creativity; how responsive to money; how eagerly it can play a new and useful role; how fast it can change while pretending that nothing has happened at all; how fast it can neglect some of its ancient virtues. . . .

The American university is currently undergoing its second great transformation. The first occurred during roughly the last quarter of the nineteenth century, when the land grant movement and German intellectualism were together bringing extraordinary change. The current transformation will cover roughly the quarter century after World War II. The university is being called upon to educate previously unimagined numbers of students; to respond to the expanding claims of national service; to merge its activities with industry as never before; to adapt to and rechannel new intellectual currents. By the end of this period, there will be a truly American university, an institution unique in world history, an institution not looking to other models but serving, itself, as a model for universities in other parts of the globe. This is not said in boast. It is simply that the imperatives that have molded the American university are at work around the world. . . .

The Knowledge Industry

Basic to this transformation is the growth of the "knowledge industry," which is coming to permeate government and business and to draw into it more and more people raised to higher and higher levels of skill. The production, distribution, and consumption of "knowledge" in all its forms is said to account for 29 percent of gross national product, according to Fritz Machlup's calculations; and "knowledge production" is growing at about twice the rate of the rest of the economy. Knowledge has certainly never in history been so central to the conduct of an entire society. What the railroads did for the second half of the last century and the automobile for the first half of this century may be done for the second half of this century by the knowledge industry: that is, to serve as the focal point for national growth. And the university is at the center of the knowledge process. . . .

Spatially the modern university often reflects its history, with the library and the humanities and social sciences at the center of the campus, extending out to the professional schools and scientific laboratories, and surrounded by industry, interspersed with residence halls, apartments, and boarding houses. An almost ideal location for a modern university is to be sandwiched between a middle-class district on its way to becoming a slum and an ultramodern industrial park—so that the students may live in the one and the faculty consult in the other. M.I.T. finds itself happily ensconced between the decaying sections of Cambridge and Technology Square.

Universities have become "bait" to be dangled in front of industry, with drawing power greater than low taxes or cheap labor. Route 128 around Boston and the great developing industrial complexes in the San Francisco Bay Area and Southern California reflect the universities in these areas. The Gilpatric report for the Department of Defense explained that 41 percent of defense contracts for research in the fiscal year 1961 were concentrated in California, 12 percent in New York, and 6 percent in Massachusetts, for a total of nearly 60 percent, in part because these were also "centers of learning." Sterling Forest outside New York City seeks to attract industry by location next to a new university campus. In California, new industrial laboratories were located next to two new university campuses before the first building was built on either of these campuses.

Sometimes industry will reach into a university laboratory to extract the newest ideas almost before they are born. Instead of waiting outside the gates, agents are working the corridors. They also work the placement offices. And the university, in turn, reaches into industry, as through the Stanford Research Institute.

The new connection of the university with the rise and fall of industrial areas has brought about an inter-university and interregional competition unmatched in history except by the universities and their *Länder* in nineteenth-century Germany. Texas and Pittsburgh seek to imitate what California and Boston have known; so also do Iowa, Seattle, and nearly all the rest. A vast campaign is on to see that the university center of each industrial complex shall not be "second best.". . .

There are those who fear the further involvement of the university in the life of society. They fear that the university will lose its objectivity and its freedom. But society is more desirous of objectivity and more tolerant of freedom than it used to be. The university can be further ahead of the times and further behind the times, further to the left of the public and further to the right of the public—and still keep its equilibrium—than was ever the case before, although problems in this regard are not yet entirely unknown. There are those who fear that the university will be drawn too far from basic to applied research and from applied research to application itself. But the lines dividing these never have been entirely clear and much new knowledge has been generated at the borders of basic and applied research, and even of applied knowledge and its application.

Growth and shifting emphases and involvement in society all take money; and which universities get it in the largest quantities will help determine which of them excel a decade or two hence. Will federal support be spent according to merit or according to political power? Will private donors continue to do as well as they recently have for those universities that have done well already? Will the states find new sources of revenue or will their expenditures be held under a lid of no new taxes? The answers to these questions will help predict the standings on the next rating scale of universities.

However this turns out, the scene of American higher education will continue to be marked by great variety, and this is one of its great strengths. The large and the small, the private and the public, the general and the specialized all add their share to over-all excellence. The total system is extra-ordinarily flexible, decentralized, competitive—and productive. The new can be tried, the old tested with considerable skill and alacrity. Pluralism in higher education matches the pluralistic American society. The multiversity, in particular, is the child of middle-class pluralism; it relates to so much of the variety of the surrounding society and is thus so varied internally.

The general test of higher education is not how much is done poorly, and some is; rather it is how much is done superbly, and a great deal is, to the nation's great benefit. Although it has been said that the best universities in America have been caught in a "stalemate of success," there is no stalemate; there is some success. . . .

Intellect has also become an instrument of national purpose, a component part of the "military-industrial complex." Our Western City of Intellect finds its counterpart or counterparts in the East. In the war of the ideological worlds, a great deal depends on the use of this instrument.

Knowledge is durable. It is also transferable. Knowledge costs a great deal to produce, less to reproduce. Thus it only pays to produce knowledge if through production it can be put into use better and faster. The Communist City of Intellect has been a planned community. It grows only in certain directions and in certain ways. This allows concentration of effort but limits growth and recognition except in restricted segments of the intellectual world. This City flourishes in science and in military might but lags in the humanities and the social sciences. Whole areas that would be covered by a really modern City of Intellect are largely unpopulated.

The two Cities of Intellect are not only sources of weapons—they also form a potential bridge between their two societies. Knowledge is universal. Its creators generally prefer freedom. To the extent the Eastern City of Intellect grows and makes contact with the Western, it almost inevitably changes its own society. Here a certain type of society really may carry the "seeds of its own destruction." It either competes and changes, or it loses some of its over-all power of competition. . . .

28. American College Students

Students and Society

There is no better way to gain some understanding of what student leaders want than to listen in as they debate issues among themselves. The following transcript, abridged by the editor, is the product of three days of discussions by radical students from various campuses at the Conference on Students and Society (August 1967) sponsored by the Center for the Study of Democratic Institutions in Santa Barbara, California. The mood of the conference is one of racking discontent, with the sounds of urban riots and massive escalation of the Indochinese war thundering in the background. The sometimes heated conversations provide a useful window into the thoughts and aims of activist students. A sense of urgency, the fear that there may not be enough time to effect needed changes, is very apparent as the discussions range beyond the university to such topics as power, revolution, dialogue, hippies, war, violence, and politics. On the last day of the conference the Center's eminent Senior Fellows joined in, often with biting criticism, to which students replied.

What accounts for the evident gap between young and old? Are the concerns of the students expressed in 1967 widely shared by the present generation of college students? Those represented here are clearly calling upon the university to provide something more than intelligence, expertise, science, and technology. Do they make telling criticisms which apply to Clark Kerr's vision of the university? Should not the university see as one of its primary tasks the development of a sense of social morality, that is, intelligence combined with man's capacity to give and to receive love, with humane sentiments, and with empathy—the ability to understand and to identify with the needs of other human beings? Short of this, can the modern university be anything other than a "service station" meeting every "need" of a pluralistic society through the search for a "soulless truth?"

Tactics for Recruiting Student Militants

RICHMAN:[1] The numbers of dissenting students are increasing, as are the conditions that alienate them and impel them to action. The experi-

Reprinted with permission, from the December 1967 *Center Occasional Paper* "Students and Society," a publication of the Center for the Study of Democratic Institutions in Santa Barbara, California.
[1] Frederick Richman, New York University.

ence of the early Sixties, not the silent Fifties, is the reference point. The slogan which invigorated youth in 1960, "Ask not what your country can do for you, ask what you can do for your country," today sounds like borderline fascism. The Peace Corps, which then appeared as the first step toward a New Society, is now merely a place where one can opt out of society in a respectable way. The hippies drew most of their first recruits from the New Left. The coming crisis extends far beyond the New Left. The police action last year against the teenyboppers on Sunset Strip in Los Angeles was as significant as the student strikes at Berkeley. Both incidents reflect a society that oppresses its youth. Both reflect a youth less and less willing to accept a second-class position. However, if we are going to achieve a revolution consciously carried forth by American youth, that youth will have to be organized as youth and given a new position in American society. Youth will have to be mobilized as if they were an under-privileged class, which indeed politically they are. In order to do that, there will have to be institutional changes in society, since in a society as large and complex as ours people can have little effect except through institutions. . . . The characteristic of the student experience today is its desire to turn education from being abstract or merely educational into something profoundly politicized. I hope that at last American students are becoming like students in other countries, who have traditionally been fulfilling a definite political role.

LERNER:[2] It is dangerous to translate "student power" into meaning a local struggle by students to change their universities in some slight way and to have some more control over the university but without at the same time trying to interpret their struggle for control over their institutions as part of a larger struggle of people from the ghetto and abroad for control over *their* institutions.

Specifically, the reforms you mention would help to focus the growing energy of the students into the main stream of society instead of aligning that energy with substantial alienation from society. Well, that is just what I don't want to see happening. I don't want that alienation transformed into alignment with a lousy, corrupt society. Furthermore, I am not even sure that after the revolution it would not be a good idea for people to have some wide realm of alienation, because alienation may well be a creative and positive force in history. Certainly, before there are substantial changes in the nature of society, talking about students getting power or having some control over their environment seems to me to be the possibly reactionary side of power. The possibly progressive side of

[2] Michael Lerner, Executive Committee, Free Speech Movement, University of California, Berkeley.

student power is interpreting that struggle as part of a larger struggle, being sure that students understand that their struggle is part of a struggle going on in the ghetto and Vietnam and in Latin America and that they should try to bring people to that awareness.

BROWN:[3] I think we agree that the revolution is necessary and that you don't conduct a revolution by attacking the strongest enemy first. You take care of your business at home first, and then you move abroad. Thus, we must make the university the home of the revolution, we must conduct our activities, not all but most of them, within the university. We must educate, truly educate, the students. When they leave there, then, they are most of them revolutionaries; they go out and put on more pressure for our programs outside the university.

SALTONSTALL:[4] We don't have to bother with the folks in the suburbs who want three cars. Radical reform has never been accomplished by changing everyone's mind. Only one-third of Americans started the Revolution. As Stanley Wise says, what we should do is be the instruments of change. I think we have enough people now. It is worthless to try to radicalize every student. It will never happen.

HIGGINS:[5] I want to emphasize the point that the vast majority of students are not politically aware, are not highly motivated toward change, and I think are fairly well brainwashed by the prevailing ideology. It's true that revolution has frequently been accomplished by small highly organized minorities, but only if they have been able to lead, to excite, and to influence the majority. So, when we are talking about student power we have to see this connection between a small group of activists who are aware and a large group who are apathetic or sold out or simply don't know what's going on. This apathetic majority cannot simply be dismissed. They have to be accounted for even if they are only going to be the followers. There must be some motive so that they will follow, and join in.

PARDUN[6] It is important to understand, if we are going to consider ourselves revolutionaries in any sense of the word, that revolution is never made out of empathy for other people. Revolution comes out of your guts. If we are talking about mobilizing students as a revolutionary force,

---

[3] Ewart F. Brown, student body president, Howard University.
[4] Stephen Saltonstall, Yale University.
[5] Michael Higgins, Claremont College.
[6] Robert Pardun, Secretary of Internal Education, Students for a Democratic Society, Chicago, Illinois.

then we have to mobilize them around *their* issues, around the things that are hurting them.

The University as the Locus of Change

ELMAN:[7]. . . In my vision of what [the] new university would be, students would determine their own social code. It will probably be in this area that we'll be able to muster the most support for our democratic universities. Secondly, I see students participating equally with the faculty in determining educational policies in their particular institutions. This includes curriculum, tenure, school size, faculty selection, and departmental structure. The issue is not that the students should run the university alone. It's that the administration should not run it alone. There are certain things that only faculty members can appreciate about educational philosophy. But only a student can really know if his education is relevant to his needs and desires. Students will also be involved in decision-making wherever issues arise concerning the university community as a whole. The university is already bound up inextricably with society and politics. It's a very large and powerful institution, and we live in an institutional world. It's here that we begin perhaps to approach Mr. Wise's frequency. Students must, for example, help decide whether we're going to allow ourselves to be subsidized for government research and in so doing condone a war most of us bitterly protest.

LERNER: When we talk about an ideal university, we ought to rejuvenate those terms which have become somewhat outmoded. I mean truth and critical intelligence as the guiding functions of the university. Why are they outmoded now? Well, because they've been redefined by the society so that they have come to mean exactly the opposite of what they really mean. We now require that there be a distortion of truth, and we require that truth not be part of critical intelligence. We require that people deal with tiny little minutiae and that they never see connections between their various fields. We require a certain amount of "democracy" in a pre-established structure but we are never to challenge the structure itself. Society requires the university to be the way it is. Consequently, the society is not going to let a new group of reformers who think that they're smarter or morally better than the old group of reformers take over the university. The same thing will go on happening until we see that the university is indivisible from society, and any talk about changing the university without changing society is meaningless.

[7] Jeffry Elman, Harvard University.

D. SEELEY:[8] There are two kinds of revolution. One is a destructive kind where you tear down things; the other kind is where you build up a parallel institution. What we have to decide first is whether the university and the society it serves are so rotten that they ought to be destroyed. Secondly, we should decide whether we can do that, or if we should simply build a parallel institution. It seems to me that the university is the second most corrupting thing going, high school being the first.

ALEXANDER:[9] You want to use radical means of changing the university so that, maybe later on, student democracy may actually work. In the process you're radicalizing the students so they can move on to other things after they get out of college.

KENNEDY:[10] Seeley implies that we've been using the word revolution loosely and sort of mumbling it under our breath, and I think that's true. I'm going to say loudly and explicitly what I mean by revolution. What I mean by revolution is overthrowing the American government and American imperialism and installing some sort of decentralized power in this country. I'll tell you the steps that I think will be needed. First of all, starting up fifty Vietnams in Third World countries. This is going to come about by black rebellions in our cities joined by some white people. People in universities can do a number of things to help it. They have access to money and they can give these people guns, which I think they should do. They can engage in acts of terrorism and sabotage outside the ghetto. Negro people have trouble getting out because they cordon those areas off, but white activists can go outside, and they can blow things up and I think they should.

But that's just a minor part of it. The major thing student activists can do while all this is going on—I mean completely demoralizing and castrating America—is to give people a vision of something other than what they have now. They can give them a vision of people living as whole men, not as engineers for Monsanto or McDonnell Aircraft, but as people who have some real say over the whole productive apparatus, who relate to one another as human beings. They can show people what America is capable of if it ends imperialism and installs a different kind of a system, where, for example, people only have to work two hours a day and might spend twenty years in and out of the universities learning a few things. They could learn how to relate to one another as human beings. They can be given this alternative vision right now.

[8] David Seeley, University of California, Santa Barbara.
[9] Jeffrey Alexander, Harvard *Crimson*, Harvard University.
[10] Devereaux Kennedy, student body president, Washington University.

BARDACKE:[11] Something can happen in conversations like this that is really destructive. We can, that is, use words like revolution and the new university and changing society and all that with a kind of apocalyptic tone in our voices. . . . Probably the only people who have any right to talk in such terms in this country at this moment are the black people. For all the white middle-class students who talk about terrorism—and it's a favorite topic of conversation—the one in 5000 that actually does something about it ends up like those kids who were in the Federal penitentiary for ten years because they had a casual conversation about the Statue of Liberty. This kind of conversation can be destructive because it raises hopes about social change where we have no right to raise hopes. It took hundreds and hundreds of years for capitalism to overthrow feudalism. If you think you're going to change this country overnight you're mistaken. People should not be talking about the new university, or the revolutionizing university, or saying revolution when nobody really knows anything about it. I would like to hear less talk about revolution and more thought about what at the moment we can actually achieve. And this is quite limited. If we don't recognize this, what will happen is what has already happened to the New Left, which talked in apocalyptic terms about ending the war in Vietnam right now. They wanted changes in society right now, and when the war didn't end immediately, and the society didn't change right away, they all became hippies. Sure, you want a revolution; sure, you want to change this country fundamentally—absolutely agreed. You have to have that long-range goal, but you also have to think about what actually can be achieved in our own lifetimes. . . . Very few of you are going to become terrorists. Very few.

WISE:[12] I'm not confused about what revolution means. I think I know. Revolutions are bloody, they're destructive, and they seek to destroy. There are very few people here who would ever be involved in any revolutionary activity. . . .

There are some good things about positive non-violent activity, if for no other reason than that it can disrupt the life-line institutions in this country. This process has begun. I don't think anybody has any doubts about how you can stop the war in Vietnam. People who make uniforms for the military must see it as a threat to their life to come to work to make that uniform, so you're talking about sabotage in the factories that make these uniforms. People who work in armament factories must see it as a hazard to come to work. But, also, the role of the people here, since

[11] Frank Bardacke, University of California, Berkeley.
[12] Stanley Wise, Executive Secretary, Student Non-Violent Coordinating Committee, Atlanta, Georgia.

you are in the intellectual community, is to begin to build something out of this. There's no doubt that there will be polarization, reactions, and fighting back. But sooner or later the subways in New York must stop running. It's as simple as that. I mean, people get killed. But we're not talking about this kind of thing here. The role of the intellectual is to build something concrete.

I believe that there is something fundamentally wrong with this country, and the wrong is caused by the institutions of this country. I sincerely believe that the institutions of this country must be destroyed. . . . By no stretch of the imagination can I understand why this country should be in control of 60 per cent of all the wealth of the world. I am committed to the destruction of that. I cannot understand why this country has more than 900 military bases at its disposal around the world, commonly referred to as peacekeeping missions. I am opposed to that. I am committed to talk to students in Africa and in Latin America about getting the troops out of those bases when these troops are mostly black people, and if I can feed them enough information about what is happening to their parents and relatives back home they will want to get out of the army. I have no doubt that McNamara will not be coming to Harvard this year, Gen. Hershey is not going to Howard this year, Rusk will think twice before he goes to either, and the President probably won't make either one either. And this is because of the work done by people on those campuses. I think this sort of thing will increase and intensify.

I believe this country is racist from top to bottom and left to right. However, I don't believe that all racists are oppressors. I believe that it's the institutions. I was not talking about individuals. I don't mean that individuals are evil, or that individuals are people who have to be destroyed, though some are evil and some of them probably ought to be destroyed. But I was talking mainly about the destruction of institutions. Now, many of you sit here and say that you must be involved in those things which are going to affect my life. Believe it or not, I am engaged in work that will drastically affect your life. I mean, we're going to give whatever aid we can to people who are trying to destroy American industry. I want to see U.S. Rubber gone. I want to see uranium from South Africa stop coming. I want to see copper from the Congo stop coming. I want to see aluminum from the Caribbean stop coming. I want to see this in the control of Caribbeans. I want to see the copper in the Congo in the control of the Congo. I want to see uranium in the control of black South Africa. If you are sincerely talking about things that really affect you, you must be coming up with programs for building.

The hippies are no threat to the draft because Johnson has an army; the hippies don't have an army, and flowers don't stop bombs. If we're talking about changing or controlling or destroying institutions, we must come up with methods not only to destroy but to rebuild. You are intellectuals. You are thinkers. . . . You should be talking about what kind of building to do after destruction takes pace. If you don't do this you're talking about colleges as they presently are, which is counter-revolutionary.

BROWN: In our attempt to establish the idea of student power we must keep in mind that it's a political game we're playing—political in the truest and most practical sense of the word—not necessarily sincere, not necessarily 100 per cent honest. We're looking for support, we need support, and we won't get it by going after those things that may seem most way-out to the people whose support we want. I'm trying to say that I don't intend to go back to Howard University screaming, "Let's end the war in Vietnam!" They would say, "Big deal! What's wrong with him?" I go back to attack the problems that affect the students at Howard first. If the problem at Howard should happen to be that fellows want to be homosexuals I wouldn't go back screaming masculinity. I'd go back trying to push the homosexual line.

This is politics! You have to face it: You don't have many 100 per cent people in this world for anything. You need *support*. You get somebody on your side and then you go from there. You don't go back to the campus talking about how you're going to stop the war and how you're going to change the whole outlook on universities—you don't do it like that. The system's beating us to death now because we believe in this pure approach.

KENNEDY: There are two kinds of mistakes that you can make when you are organizing on campus. One is the mistake of thinking that no reform that doesn't lead immediately to the revolution is worth considering. The other is to think that all you have to do is work on issues with people where they are at. For some that may be a good thing to do, but for a radical it's a bad thing to do. You've got to work on issues that are progressive in intent, and along with that you have to supply a radical critique of the issue. For instance, if you are talking about the draft, you've got to go into the whole history of the selective service. You've got to use the Hershey statements showing that the draft is used to do indirectly what totalitarian countries do directly. You've got to show why universities give in to these things. When students lose on issues like these, and they are going to lose often, you always have to show them why they lose and why they win. Then they will begin to trust you, and they'll begin to have some trust in your radical critique. Then you can get to the point where you can really start affecting the other, bigger issues.

BARDACKE: . . . One theory we have here is that of working with people where they are at. That means organizing around the stated interests of people and trying to push those interests through some political system, or trying to achieve those interests by changing a political system. The second notion of political leadership is trying to help people to distinguish between their apparent interests and their real interests; that is, trying to help people understand that maybe what they think they want is not really what would be best for them.

This second notion of political leadership has been dismissed in these discussions by the suggestion that this approach is necessarily elitist. I don't think that it is necessarily elitist, or that you have to talk over people's heads to help them distinguish between their apparent will and their real will. I think you have to make a judgment that the second kind of political approach is most necessary with most Americans; that is to say, you have to show them that it's wrong to think that if they get more money they are richer; if they get a third car, they are going to be happy; if they get an hour more of parietal time this is going to solve their problems. Those are the kinds of ideas that the society now encourages in people. Political leaders should help people to distinguish between what society wants them to want and what is in their real interest.

Dialogue versus Revolution

SALTONSTALL: We must locate a medium between dialogue and revolution. That medium is disruption. Disruption is the one thing our society can't abide. Our institutions are all interrelated, and if one institution is sabotaged, the society can't function properly. The institution students are connected with is the university. If I may be permitted a ridiculous metaphor, the university is a kind of distributor cap that students can remove from the engine of our society. The government is heavily dependent on the university in two ways: first, it depends on the university for manpower. For example, the Army now gets more officers from ROTC on campus than it does from the service academies. If we were to subvert ROTC on campuses we'd be doing a great deal, because there's a terrific shortage of officers in Vietnam. Second is the realm of research. Government depends on the university to supply its Kissingers and Rostows to formulate policy, and it relies on research like the bacteriological warfare projects being carried on at Penn State and on the electronic accelerators of the AEC such as are set up at Harvard. There is a good deal that the students could do to sabotage the university in these areas.

In formulating a strategy of disruption, the students should try to avoid violence because it leads to arrests, and very few would participate with that in view. But milder disruptive techniques such as harassment, lock-outs, infiltration of office staff, and so on—even the pouring of LSD into the coffee urn—are less dangerous than any other kind of radical action that I can think of. When you engage in radical action there's going to be a reaction of the society against you; but I believe the kinds of action I've been describing are the least dangerous.

HIGGINS: I've heard the idea of the dialogue laughed at in this conference. . . . I heard several remarks to the effect that, well, the dialogue is all right for those who have sold out. But I don't think that this is at all fair.

D. SEELEY: The problem is time. We have no guarantee that the world won't blow itself up very soon, so I don't like the thought of sitting around dialoguing with Lyndon Johnson while people are being murdered in Vietnam. I can't stand the thought of that; Dan Sisson apparently can. It will take us a hundred years to get out of Vietnam that way.

Even now, after 300, 400 years of dialogue, if you took a survey you'd find that most people would vote against the Bill of Rights. Dialogue is a slow thing. I won't wait for dialogue to do it. People being murdered isn't good and people being used all over the world isn't good, and students in this country not having their rights isn't good. The dialogue is valid, and we should use as much of it as we can among ourselves and with others. But we shouldn't sit down and talk to Lyndon Johnson when people are being murdered. We should decide whether we should murder in return, or whether we should use some other way of stopping the war.

LEVINE:[13] The idea of inequality should be brought into any discussion of the dialogue. If there's inequality between the parties, dialogue becomes window-dressing for inaction. It's like a worker who wants more wages, shorter hours, and better conditions dialoguing with an employer who wants longer hours, lower wages, and worse conditions. What are they going to talk about? The employer has the power, and until the man joins a union and decides he is going to use force there is no change. When the real struggle comes it is one of force. . . . An employer is not going to give the worker any more freedom, because he is better off if the worker doesn't have freedom. Dialogue assumes a common set of assumptions and goals; and in their absence dialogue is only a way of aborting change.

[13] Bruce Levine, editor, *Thought*, Valley Stream High School, New York.

GOLDFIELD[14] You people are creating a polarization which doesn't exist when people are actually organizing on their campuses and doing things. I wouldn't think at all of advocating things that would kill people or anything like that. It wouldn't particularly bother me if buildings blew up with nobody in them, but I am not advocating that as a tactic either. There is a great range of creative things that you could do—disruptions, ways of organizing people, sitting-in in a building. But I think all of us agree that in the good society you should always have people talking to each other to sharpen up their ideas, to hear the other side, to take in the good that you might have left out. One thing about the student movement that sometimes is a little disturbing is its antiintellectualism. Not in SDS, where there's enough openness so that I can always argue my position— if I lose, I lose; if I win, I win. But there's a difference between dialogue as a tactic for social change and dialogue as something that should always exist. People should always have free speech. It's a prerequisite all right, but it doesn't really amount to a heck of a lot. The thing wrong with Nazi Germany was not that people didn't have free speech—that was a minor matter; it was the fact that they were killing off people, and waging war, and were racist. Those are the convincing things that you attack a society on. When Hitler was rising, German liberals thought their job was to keep the political debate open, not to try to attack Hitler in direct and violent ways. But clearly that wasn't the type of tactics they should have used at that time.

In the United States you are not going to change David Rockefeller's mind when, for instance, he argues for the way his investments are handled in Latin America. He argues pretty hard, as we found out when some of us went over to Chase Manhattan a couple of years ago to talk with him, and you are not going to convince him, because the institution he is defending depends on him arguing in a certain sort of way. The tactics of dialogue won't work. Therefore, you use other tactics.

QUINN:[15] The dialogue in itself is no big thing. The only way I can see that it will be useful is if it's going to get you something. It's nice to talk, but if you are trying to get power, then just talking to the enemy isn't going to do you any good. The enemy won't even listen to you unless you have power to back yourself up. And if they do, they just try to get you inside where they try to keep you talking when you should be outside organizing.

ANDALMAN:[16] The question is whether the dialogue would be a total

---

[14] Michael Goldfield, Radical Education Project, Ann Arbor, Michigan.
[15] Mary Quinn, Mount Mercy College.
[16] Anthony Andalman, editor, *The Worrier,* University High School, Los Angeles.

success in obtaining student power, and can be used after we achieve power; or whether disruption is a better method. I find disruption much more advantageous to us because of the time element. Dialogue takes a lot of time, and it also wastes most of it. Negroes have been talking for 300 years, and most of them are denied their rights; we've been talking about the corporations making money in Vietnam and we are still escalating and killing people. Students have talked about academic freedom for years and nothing has come of it except possibly at Berkeley where they had some action too. There they threw something into the wheels that the system didn't know how to cope with. I feel this is what we have to do; we have to do something to disrupt the system.

LERNER: . . . The kind of revolution we are talking about is liberating man for struggles of the mind—for struggles in culture rather than struggles for material goods and for physical survival.

BROWN: Does this have to be done through a complete obliteration of society?

LERNER: To say that it's an obliteration of society is not to say that it's an obliteration of everybody in society. Fundamentally, our political and economic institutions are rotten. They can be made much better without being made good. The thing that should make us most indignant is that the institution that we might have hoped would have escaped, the university—the place where we could conduct a search for truth and develop critical intelligence—is precisely one of the institutions that's most affected, that has become a prostitute of society.

> [At this point in the conference, the participating Senior Fellows of the Center responded to the foregoing discussion and the student leaders replied in turn.]

HUTCHINS:[17] The first question that struck me as I listened to your conversation was that it seemed a good deal like Tammany Hall, and I couldn't see that a young Tammany Hall was going to be any better than the old Tammany Hall, with its aim of let's get power, let's manipulate the people. In this case it's your contemporaries that you intend to manipulate as soon as you get political power, and you begin manipulating in order to get it. So my first question is about your moral stance. . . . I didn't hear anyone give an intelligible idea of what he thought the uni-

---

[17] Robert M. Hutchins, president of the University of Chicago (1929–1951), and currently president of the Center for the Study of Democratic Institutions.

versity ought to be, or what he thought education was. One of the things I expected to learn from the conference was what kind of university, what kind of education, you wanted.

BARR:[18] I was a little shocked at this excitement about power without any clear idea that I was able to apprehend of your purpose in getting the power. We have been treated to a pretty heavy dose in the last few years of the uses of power; and I get the impression from the White House and the military that early in the Vietnamese engagement, for instance, we were going to give the world an example of how power can conclusively solve problems. But it hasn't been very conclusive, and a great many are suggesting that maybe what was meant by the word power was something that is not applicable to this particular problem. I had the same sense of emptiness when I kept hearing about students getting power over their universities. I would feel happier about the students getting control of the university instead of the people now controlling it if I had some answer to Mr. Hutchins' question; that is, what do you want to do with it when you get it? Run it? . . . What do you want to run the university for—to do what? To answer your needs? Then I want to hear about the needs. I am particularly concerned as to whether these needs are idiosyncratic or whether they are something you share with all human beings.

BUCHANAN:[19] I can put what I have to say in about three emotional reactions. One is a certain kind of anger at your playing house with the idea of power—that's what it seems to me you are doing. I don't want to call you children, but you act like children. You are grown-up but you are throwing yourself into the role of children. And you are talking about power in ways that make me want to spank you.

Another point: whenever you seem grown-up and talk about power as grown-ups might do, I get a little frightened. We have seen power of the kind you are talking about throw people into dangerous attitudes. We have had a lot of that in the last generation and I am a little frightened of you; because when you get your hands on the levers and do things, I'm not sure I want to be around. The only purpose that I can see that you connect to this power, and which might make it substantial, is a form of socialism, a very primitive form of socialism. All your Marxian talk about it is superficial and comes to one sharp point—and that is that you are very sure that the people who now have the power that you are going to take will not give it up unless you hit them over the head. This is a

---

[18] Stringfellow Barr. A former president of St. John's College.
[19] Scott Buchanan. Philosopher and educator, during his tenure as dean of St. John's College (1937–1946) Dr. Buchanan instituted a "great books" curriculum.

Marxian theme that has shifted a good deal in the last few years. It seems to me that you ought to revise some of your thoughts accordingly.

J. SEELEY:[20] After two days' discussion I understand some things better; but, sadly, a few, worse. I understand more fully the student leadership intendedly represented here. I understand how simply the universities can be brought to a grinding halt, how to embitter and "radicalize" students, and what alternative alliances students might effect. . . . It is that a replacing function is conceived for the university: to be the brains-trust and activist center for the political movement to overthrow advanced monopoly capitalism. . . . What I hear is that the university as it is should turn from the service of the ruling class through the state to the service of the proletariat through a cadre of student activists and their non-student and ex-student allies.

No wonder, then, that what was said in the past two days about hippies was passed over lightly. They stand for a different response to the Freudian dilemma. Fully appreciated, they should be seen by you as serious enemies, deviationists, diversionaries, and counter-revolutionaries, for they protest what is common to the revolutionary and Establishment models. They believe that the one scarcely more than the other has the answer to the most urgent question: What is a viable and human life for man? They also consciously address themselves, simultaneously rather than successively, to the twin problems of good institutions and good persons, believing that the development of neither can be abandoned while the other is sought. They may well be ground to bits between the two mass armies of the reaction and the revolution.

What can I recommend? Not that you abate your revolutionary fervor or extend your revolutionary timetable. Not even that this revolution be carried forward in the spirit of the original Free Speech Movement—a strange mix of near-hippyism, good humor, and standard high-mindedness and revolutionary fervor. But that at least, while the warring armies march and counter-march, lay waste the world they cannot otherwise save, they reserve a special place (like the medieval monasteries) for the hippies—a special place not just geographic but honorific.

TUGWELL:[21] I have some news for my younger colleagues here— there isn't going to be any revolution. I don't think any of you really expect that there will be one. There will be a kind of revolution, but it won't be the one you are talking about. I think you should realize that

[20] John R. Seeley, Senior Fellow of the Center.
[21] Rexford G. Tugwell. A member of Franklin D. Roosevelt's "brain trust," Tugwell later was appointed Under-Secretary of Agriculture (1934–1937) and governor of Puerto Rico (1941–1946) .

you've got to work with or in the existing institutions and with the materials you have at hand. Not that the institutions don't need changing. All of us here recognize that they need changing very fundamentally, but while they are being changed things have to go on; and it's been possible in our lifetime to have changed things very greatly. Perhaps you don't realize that; it seems to me as I have listened here that you people can't have studied American history, because our history has changed fundamentally in my lifetime, and I expect it'll change even more fundamentally in the next two decades. The technology that at the moment seems to have got the best of us I think we will get the mastery of, and turn it to the benefit of more human institutions. The problems are not unsolved. One of you may become President of the United States some day, and then, I assure you, you will take a very different view of revolutionary possibilities.

WHEELER:[22] I think it is inexcusable for us to berate these students in this way. We have almost with one voice expected them somehow to produce some kind of idea of a university and to put it into practice. The one thing they have a right to expect from us is to do something about the university. This avuncular stance is not the proper one for us to take in this kind of meeting. My years in college, in university, were years of terror, and my years of teaching were unrelieved catastrophe. I don't think that the university for a student or a teacher has changed. We ought to be able to give some help in the kind of conflict that comes up between Stan Wise and some of the other radicals. Stan Wise wants to be the leader of a radical movement, a successful one, and he knows pretty well what the long-run evils of the society are. But he also knows that in order to be responsive to the needs of the people he wants to serve, he has got to, in effect, lead them into a middle-class society; because that's really what the mass of them demand, and what they need. He knows the dangers that are involved from the standpoint of radicalism, in his own stance and in his own future; he knows the danger is that if he wins he will become a Walter Reuther.

The student radicals, on the other hand, are in an environment that is already middle class and just wants to be more middle class. The conditions of their responding to radicalism with regard to the group that they are aspiring to lead are almost the opposite of those that Mr. Wise faces. In other words, the enemy as seen by the students is established middle-class society. Both the black radicals and the student radicals understand the nature of the evils that over-all middle-class society presents. It seems to me that if anything can be done here for the future of radicalism in

[22] Harvey Wheeler, Senior Fellow of the Center.

this age group, we ought to try to do it. A correspondence, an intersection, a kind of a future liaison, might be served for these two trends of radicalism that seem to be so spiritually aligned, and yet so organizationally opposed. The future of the organizational thrust of radicalism seems to me to depend upon maintaining this dialogue. It is almost inevitable that the future will bring the conservatization of the Negro revolution, and this will bring tragic consequences for radicalism in general. As to student radicals, in order to be really radical leaders in the university community they have to address themselves in the end to the true, long-run goals of the student community. This means building enclaves of radicalism inside each place where you are, enclaves where new students can come and feel that there is something valid they can live with and identify with. These should be centers with a radical approach and a radical study of the emerging needs of the university. They should proceed in conjunction with the most perceptive of the teachers. The most that you can do in the short years of student passage is to provide some kind of cauldron that can be kept burning.

HOFFMAN:[23] My response to you is one of excitement, enjoyment, and enthusiasm about the way you are challenging everything. I want to say four or five sentences only and these are all on the subject of conscientious objection. I happen to talk fairly often to young people who want to be CO's, and one thing that I usually wind up telling them is that I am not in the least worried about you if you are, in fact, a conscientious objector. So if you young people around this table are honest-to-goodness conscientious objectors, nobody can make you do what you say is wrong to do. Nobody can make you kill anybody, though a lot of people can make you terribly uncomfortable. They can even kill you. But they can't make you kill anybody else if, in fact, you refuse to. I do have a sense that often, in your reaction to the hypocrisy and inadequacy that you have encountered, you begin to feel others are responsible for the evils you yourself do. That's too bad. One doesn't ever really have to do evil on somebody else's say-so.

WILKINSON:[24] My first reaction is that of *déjà vu*. We could reproduce this discussion in every generation of students back to antiquity. The discussions here were not nearly as good as they were in Greece. So the first thing is that you give me a sense of world-weariness.

It's said that you don't have any goal in mind. But nobody ever has any goal in mind. If you pull a building down, you will find that you are

---

[23] Hallock Hoffman, Senior Fellow of the Center.
[24] John Wilkinson, Senior Fellow of the Center.

getting goals as you go along. What happens at the end may well be very different from what you expected it would be. It may be worse, it may be better; but it certainly is going to be different. Anybody who starts telling me his goals in advance, I consider a fool or a knave. Much will depend upon your characters. Good people do good things, and bad people do bad things.

The dialogue here is far behind the dialogue that European students of your age and general background engage in. European students seem to me to have a much better recognition of the way that technological advances have made any decent society in the past mold impossible. They also have had a terrible experience of Stalinism and other insane cults of personality. You are in a state of shock while your European contemporaries are in a state of trying to become conscious of what they should do. They have passed out of an initial stage of shock and are trying to carry on a dialectic. I think you will also pass beyond the stage of shock and get to the stage where you have some idea of what you wish to do.

RICHMAN: We students want power, I think, for the same reason that all other people want power. Power is necessary for people to run their own lives or to control their own environment, whether they are students in a university, or blacks in the ghetto, or citizens in a democracy. Power is the first requirement for any type of change. And I don't think it's fair to say that people must specify their ultimate or even their short-range goals before you give them power. We don't, in a democracy, say that people can't have elections or any type of power unless they specify what they are going to use it for. . . . Our concern for power is essentially a moral concern. It's immoral when people are in a powerless position, whether they are students, or poor people, or any type of citizen, in a democracy. Therefore, power seems to me something of a natural right.

LERNER: The question about power is not a question about me getting power instead of you; that's precisely the radical critique. The radical critique is that it's not a question of better men having power than the bad man who had it before. It's a question of redistributing power. This does not mean allowing our good guys to have the power to run the society over your bad guys. This means rather distributing power throughout the society to each member of it in such a way that it becomes impossible for any given individual to dominate other people, in the way that present people dominate others. In a way, this means we want to use power to destroy power. That's what we are talking about—the destruction of power. We are not saying an elite has to have power; we are not saying that we want the dictatorship of a party over the masses. We are calling for power for people; that means black power, that means student power, because those are the people who are there. When we say student power, we are not talking about power for a group of student-leaders; we are asking for power to be distributed throughout the student body. When people call for black power, they are not calling for more black congressmen; they are talking about real power to be distributed throughout the people who live in the ghetto. So, any criticism of us which says, "Well, wait until you get to be President and you'll see how difficult it is" totally misunderstands what we want and what we are interested in.

GOLDFIELD: I have been active in student politics for a long time, five or six years, and I find it more and more difficult to talk to people who don't quite feel the urgency that I do about what's wrong with society—the war, the draft, and the riots which have formed an emotional context it is difficult to extricate ourselves from. I find it very quaint that a lot of people on the staff here who spoke initially still cling to what are called liberal ideals. A lot of us don't think those are at all adequate.

LEVINE: I'm very disappointed about the kind of criticism we've been getting from the Senior Staff members. . . . it's pretty irrelevant to what most of us have been talking about.

KENNEDY: I'm not as angry about what went on as Levine is because when I came here I thought it'd be a lot like going into my grandfather's house. I expected to meet a lot of nice old people who are very interested in what the young are doing and I expected them to tell us that we have a lot of youthful enthusiasm and that that is good, but that there ain't going to be no revolution because when I was 15 years old I said the same thing and there weren't no revolution then and there's going to be no revolution now.

But there is going to be a revolution. I don't know whether you are going to live to see it or not—I hope that you don't, because I don't think you are ready for it. You hope that conscience is built into the existing society, because you can't possibly envision any other kind. I hate to get into this bag of saying that everybody can't understand, but I think it's really true that after the age of 50 you are lost. You people really are far, far out of it—so far that every one of us has had to go on to points in the discussions we had five years ago, just to bring you people up to where we are today. You've been sitting in this really groovy place called the Center for the Study of Democratic Institutions and you don't know what's going on in the world. I don't think you'll ever understand. I didn't come here to talk to you, though I'm willing to put up with this session. I came here to talk to the other students, because that's where it's at.

BARDACKE: The young people here sound as if they are in a race with themselves to the age of 30 or 35, or to the point where they get institutionally committed, but now, before they are so committed, they have a chance to speak freely and objectively. Then, after the age of 30 they can join up with the institution and their consciousness will be changed because of the social structure of that institution. Then, hopefully, they catch on at some place like the Center where they can become old men who organize conferences and criticize the young for being revolutionaries. I just had this constant picture of somebody in a race with himself. But I think this is selling yourselves short. Mike Lerner shouldn't be so worried about what's going to happen when he becomes older and has to commit himself to one particular institution or other.

As for this session we're now in, an escalation of rudeness is the only thing I can call it. I really don't know what to make of this escalation of rudeness—I don't know what it is about people of widely different ages sitting together in a room that brings it out.

WISE: Since the vocal people have figuratively "spanked" the Senior members, I won't do that; but I applaud your doing it. I think that there is a serious question of urgency and I don't think it has at all to do with the age of 30 or 50 or 70. This is not the real problem. The urgency rests in the fact that we are involved in a very great experiment. This experiment may succeed. It will definitely go on. We might come out with something better, or we might come out with something worse. But we have this urgency because we know that there are forces abroad capable of destroying the entire earth. Those of you who are senior citizens do not share this urgency. You do not fear in the morning when you wake up that you might be but another speck of dust. But we do have that urgency, especially some of us when we see China moving as rapidly as she does. I have no doubt that a great deal of her movements, in science, for example, can develop powerful alternatives to what we have here. The Soviet Union moves with urgency, and to some extent countries in Latin America, Africa, and Asia are trying to get themselves together to move with that same urgency.

Perhaps what we are talking about will not be a revolution. But the great experiment that we are engaged in is based on realities that are evident even in our own distorted history. One of these realities is that America is on a collision course with herself. There's no doubt that America is heading for a collision with the black community; I have no doubt in my mind whatsoever about this. I have no doubt, further, that America is on a collision course with three-fourths of the world. And if you doubt it, you are fooling yourself. I think that we have a vast and not at all easy job to do, many times more difficult than we like to imagine. I think our frame of reference has come basically out of our history, and what do we see there? Our history is one of glorification of violence—of wars and fights, of 400 years of Christian crusades, and so on. These things have been handed down to us; our whole history is just such a record.

Next, I agree . . . that it's a white problem, and I think that most of the world agrees with that. It seems to me that the last possible hope rests with the young white people if there's going to be a feasible solution. None of us wants to be on a collision course, but none of us has the power to change it. It's that simple, and I think you do a tremendous disservice to young people here when you aren't more constructive. People are, after all, grappling with a thing that has never, ever been experienced in history. It's not practical to ask what it will look like, or how it will go. . . .

XI. Reflections on America

29. Jean-Francois Revel

Without Marx or Jesus: The New American Revolution Has Begun

In an epilogue to Jean-François Revel's *Without Marx or Jesus* Mary McCarthy observes that Frenchmen have always been "secure in the thought that the U.S. is the citadel of imperialism, racism, vulgarity, conformism, and now a *Frenchman* returns from a voyage of discovery to say it is a hotbed of revolution. Blandly, with a straight face, the enormity emerges, buttressed by figures and arguments, precedents, citations." Not only Frenchmen were surprised. So were Americans, and many were pleased. Philosopher-critic Revel is the latest in a succession of European visitors who have discerned in America the greatest amount of social mobility and progress of any modern society, the gravest threat to traditional ideologies and class privileges, the most remarkable amount of personal freedom. Revel differs from most of his predecessors, however, in approving of these American characteristics. He sees diversity rather than uniformity, genuine and effective pluralism instead of political deadlock, the primacy of cultural revolution instead of a stultifying ideological consensus. Among the various manifestations of revolt Revel detects a common basis, that is, "the rejection of a society motivated by profit, dominated exclusively by economic consideration, ruled by the spirit of competition, and subjected to the mutual aggressiveness of its members." It is not too much to say that America is a genuinely revolutionary nation precisely to the degree that this observation is true.

Jean-François Revel, active in the French Resistance, a learned teacher of literature and philosophy in Mexico, Algiers, Florence, and Lille, an outspoken antagonist of Gaullism, and the author of numerous books, has earned a reputation as an irreverent exploder of cherished myths. Some have suspected that the underlying purpose of *Without Marx or Jesus* is to criticize the doctrinnaire ideologies and forces of social inertia in France. Hence the somewhat "imagined" United States serves as the antipodes of France. In any case his frequently polemical book, a best-seller in both countries, discusses serious issues. How widespread is "the rejection both of the spread of American power abroad and of foreign policy?" How deeply rooted is the "determination that the natural environment is more important than commercial profit?" What concrete evidence enables Revel to "conceive of a sort of suicide of technological society, an asphyxiation of American power from within?" Is the search for liberation undertaken by so many groups in the United States a product of traditional social competition, as some believe, rather than a genuine pursuit of revolution in a political sense? Might America truly be the revolutionary country Revel thinks it is without Americans perceiving it, much less willing it? Nearly every page in the following selection from *Without Marx or Jesus* raises similar, provocative questions.

The revolution of the twentieth century will take place in the United States. It is only there that it can happen. And it has already begun. Whether or not that revolution spreads to the rest of the world depends on whether or not it succeeds first in America.

I am not unaware of the shock and incredulity such statements may cause at every level of the European Left and among the nations of the Third World. I know it is difficult to believe that America—the fatherland of imperialism, the power responsible for the war in Vietnam, the nation of Joe McCarthy's witch hunts, the exploiter of the world's natural resources—is, or could become, the cradle of revolution. We are accustomed to thinking of the United States as the logical target of revolution, and of computing revolutionary progress by the rate of American withdrawal. Now, we are being asked to admit that our revolutionary sliderule was inaccurate, and to face the future without that comfortable tool.

If we draw up a list of all the things that ail mankind today, we will have formulated a program for the revolution that mankind needs: the abolition of war and of imperialist relations by abolishing both states and the notion of national sovereignty; the elimination of the possibility of internal dictatorship (a concomitant condition of the abolition of war); world-wide economic and educational equality; birth control on a planetary scale; complete ideological, cultural, and moral freedom, in order to assure both individual happiness through independence and a plurality of choice, and in order to make use of the totality of human creative resources.

Obviously this is a utopic program, and it has nothing in its favor, except that it is absolutely necessary if mankind is to survive. The exchange of one political civilization for another, which that program implies, seems to me to be going on right now in the United States. And, as in all the great revolutions of the past, this exchange can become world-wide only if it spreads, by a sort of political osmosis, from the prototype-nation to all the others.

It is evident from the above that the various aspects of a revolution are interrelated; so much so that, if one aspect is missing, the others are incomplete. There are five revolutions that must take place either simultaneously or not at all: a political revolution; a social revolution; a technological and scientific revolution; a revolution in culture, values, and standards; and a revolution in international and interracial relations. The United States is the only country, so far as I can see, where these five revolutions are simultaneously in progress and are organically linked in such a way as to constitute a single revolution. In all other countries, either all five revolutions are missing, which settles the problem, or one or two or three of them are lacking, which relegates revolution to the level of wishful thinking.

The most common error concerning the United States is to try to interpret that nation in terms of the revolutionary guidelines with which we are familiar, and which are usually purely theoretical. Then, when we see that those guidelines are not applicable to the American situation, we conclude that America is a reactionary country.

The revolutionary plans that we know, and that we usually try to apply, are all based on the existence of opposition, of antagonism: the peasants against the proprietors of the land; workers against factory owners; colonials against colonizers. The present American Revolution, however, resembles more a centrifugal gyration than a clash between opposing camps. It has certain characteristics in common with old-style revolution. There are the oppressed and the oppressors; the exploited and the exploiters; the poor and the rich. There are people who are morally dissatisfied with the present state of affairs—an essential condition of revolution —and there is a serious rift within the governing elite.

There are also traits which are entirely new, and peculiar to America. The "poor" are an unusual kind of poor; they earn between $1500 and $3000 a year, and, if their income falls below the latter figure, they are eligible for government aid. In Europe, such an income would place a family considerably above the poverty level—although, common opinion to the contrary, the cost of living in European urban centers is not much less than in America. In America, however, the phenomenon of prosperity makes everything relative, and, in consequence, some of the moral and psychological factors that are important in Europe do not play nearly so large a part in establishing revolutionary goals in America. The American revolution is, without doubt, the first revolution in history in which disagreement on values and goals is more pronounced than disagreement on the means of existence. American revolutionaries do not want merely to cut the cake into equal pieces; they want a whole new cake. This spirit of criticism of values, which is still more emotional than intellectual, is made possible by a freedom of information such as no civilization has ever tolerated before—not even within and for the benefit of the governing class, let alone at the level of the mass media. This accessibility of information has resulted in a widespread and strong feeling of guilt, and a passion for self-accusation which, on occasion, tends to go to extremes.

And that result, in turn, has produced a phenomenon unprecedented in history: a domestic revolt against the imperialistic orientation of American foreign policy.

This revolt, however, is not the only indication of a new revolutionary direction. There has never been a society which faced a situation similar to that of the United States with respect to the blacks. In the face of this contagious domestic problem and of the demands of the Afro-American community, American society is being divided into factions and is entering upon the path of cultural polycentrism. And this process, of course, is playing havoc with our prejudices concerning the "conformity" and "uniformity" of American society. The truth of the matter is that American society is torn by too many tensions not to become more and more diversified.

Another unprecedented characteristic of the American revolution is the revolt of the young—the contagion of which, both at the national and international levels, was so virulent in the years between 1965 and 1970. This is, moreover, a new development within the context of upper-class divisions during revolutionary periods, since these young revolutionaries are mostly students; that is, members of the privileged class. It should be pointed out that this "privileged class" is less and less exceptional; it is a case, so to speak, of mass privilege. The current upheavals are due not only to the great number of young people in proportion to the rest of the population, but also to the great number of students in proportion of young people. Out of a population of two hundred million, there are presently seven million students; and it is estimated that, by 1977, there will be eleven million.

It has been said that there are three nations in the United States: a black nation; a Woodstock nation; and a Wallace nation. The first one is self-explanatory. The second takes its name from the great political and musical convention held at Woodstock, New York, in 1969, which has been documented by the film *Woodstock*. It includes the hippies and the radicals. The third nation is embodied in Mr. George Wallace of Alabama, and is composed of "lower middle-class whites" whose symbol is the "hard hat" worn by construction workers. Each of these nations has its own language, its own art forms, and its own customs. And each has a combat arm: the Black Panthers for the blacks; the Weathermen for Woodstock; and the Ku Klux Klan, and various civil organizations, for Wallace. We could add other "nations"; e.g., the women of the Women's Liberation movement, who have declared war on sexism (a word copied from "racism") and who take their methods from those of the Black Power and Student Power movements.

There is also a large group of citizens who are neither black, nor particularly young, nor especially intellectual. Far from being reactionary, they are sometimes militantly progressive, and are vaguely categorized as liberals. This group includes citizens with a wide range of opinion; from what, in Europe, we call the democrats, to the progressives. The liberals have often been able to contribute the appearance of a mass movement to demonstrations which, without them, would have been able to attract only the extremists. They demonstrated alongside the blacks throughout the great Southern revolt which began in 1952, and against the Vietnam war in the various moratoriums. They are on the side of the students, the Indians, and the Third World. On May 21, 1970, for instance, thousands of New York lawyers—what we might call the governors of the governing class—descended on Washington to protest American intervention in Cambodia. On the same day, the hard-hats demonstrated in New York in favor of this intervention. And, still on the same day, prices dropped sharply on the New York Stock Exchange, indicating, according to some American commentators, that the financiers, like the lawyers, were not in agreement with the Administration over the conduct of the war. No nineteenth-century class distinctions are sufficient to convey the nature of these new political classes—which are also sexual classes, racial classes, and esthetic classes; that is, they are based on the rejection of an unsatisfactory life style. Each of these categories has specific economic, racial, esthetic, moral, and religious or spiritual characteristics; each has its own customs, its own way of dressing and eating—even though, as a whole, they are referred to as a "community." In this instance, the image of a series of superimposed circles rather than of stratified social levels describes the nature of this community.

The "hot" issues in America's insurrection against itself, numerous as they are, form a cohesive and coherent whole within which no one issue can be separated from the others. These issues are as follows: a radically new approach to moral values; the black revolt; the feminist attack on masculine domination; the rejection by young people of exclusively economic and technical social goals; the general adoption of noncoercive methods in education; the acceptance of the guilt for poverty; the growing demand for equality; the rejection of an authoritarian culture in favor of a critical and diversified culture that is basically new, rather than adopted from the old cultural stockpile; the rejection both of the spread of American power abroad and of foreign policy; and a determination that the natural environment is more important than commercial profit. None of the groups concerned with any one of these points, and none of the points themselves, would have been able to gain as much strength and attention as they have if they had been isolated from other groups and other points.

The moral revolution, the cultural revolution, and the political revolution are but a single revolution. In San Francisco, a group composed of women and homosexuals (members of the Women's Liberation Front and the Gay Liberation Front), shouting "Cambodia is obscene! Sex is not obscene!" burst into a psychiatrists' convention which was discussing the "treatment" of homosexuality. The criticism of paternalistic and moralistic psychiatry, in this instance, not only takes on a political form, but also produces new courage in the affirmation of self.

There have been political revolutions that failed because, among other reasons, they were limited to a single area, to politics or economics, and therefore were not able to generate the "new man" who could have given meaning to new political or economic institutions. In *Prolégomènes à un troisième manifeste du surréalisme*, André Bréton writes: "We must not only stop the exploitation of man by man, but we must also re-examine —from top to bottom, without hypocrisy and without dodging the issues —the problems involved in the relationship between men and women." And Charles Fourier pointed out that the revolutionaries of 1789 had failed because "they bowed before the concept of the sanctity of marriage." If women had been allowed to become their own masters, he says, "it would have been a scandal, and a weapon capable of undermining the foundations of society."

* * * *

. . . There is, therefore, a basis common to all manifestations of the American revolt, and to its European extensions. That basis consists in the rejection of a society motivated by profit, dominated exclusively by economic considerations, ruled by the spirit of competition, and subjected to the mutual aggressiveness of its members. Indeed, beneath every revolutionary ideal we find a conviction that man has become the tool of his tools, and that he must once more become an end and a value in himself. The hippies are characterized by a particularly vivid awareness of that loss of self-identity and of the perversion of the meaning of life. A competitive society, for instance, or a spirit of rivalry, is a source of suffering to them. But they do not self-righteously condemn such societies, or attempt to refute them theoretically; they simply refuse to have any part in them. A hippie, therefore, is above all someone who has "dropped out"; a boy or girl who decided, one day, to stop being a cog in the social machine. Baudelaire suggested adding two additional rights to the Declaration of the Rights of Man: the right to contradict oneself, and the right to walk away. Hippies make much use of both those rights. This use, when it is so widespread as to no longer be marginal, is much more revolutionary than one is willing to admit if one insists on viewing everything dogmatically, in terms of classic political activity. When societies decline seriously, it is because of this internal absenteeism, because its people have discovered new forms of commitment. And American society is painfully aware of this sudden disaffection and of this loss of love. The hippie is the well-known husband who went down to the corner to buy a pack of cigarettes, and never came back. Hippies are the two heroes of Peter Fonda's eclogue on walking away, *Easy Rider*—a film which was looked upon with condescension in Europe, and was barely recognized as a cinematic curiosity, possibly because the sensitivity that inspired it, and that is necessary to understand American counterculture, is less intense in Europe than in America.

Certainly, one can make a good case against the hippies for their political indifference and for their naïveté in rejecting every form of violence —for these are the attitudes that distinguish the hippies. One can even fault them for forgetting that the hippie way of life is possible only in an affluent society and because of a surplus in production (even though the hippie personally may be willing to live in comparative poverty). One can make fun of their nebulous ideology, which is a mixture of confused orientalism and adulterated primitivism (although they are likely to retort that they prefer pop music to ideology). One can jeer at their simplistic confidence in the strength of universal love as the key to all problems (a confidence which, nonetheless, has not prevented the misinformed from mistaking the Sharon Tate murderers for hippies). And one can be astonished at their belief that it is possible for an individual to have absolute freedom without infringing the rights of others. All these things are, no doubt, open to criticism from many standpoints; and they are all no doubt very limited concepts. The fact remains, however, that the hippies' refusal to accept regimentation in any form gives them a mysterious strength and a means of exerting pressure; the same sort of strength and pressure that is exerted by, say, a hunger strike. . . .

Human aggression is a determining factor in human behavior; and it is accepted even more gratuitously, and is even more murderous, than all of the sacred causes by which it justifies itself and on which it bases itself. Unless this root-evil is extirpated, the hippies believe, then everything else will be corrupted. By reflecting that belief in their attitudes and behavior, the hippies at very least perform a useful function; they remind us constantly that a revolution is not simply a transfer of power, but also a change in the goals for the sake of which power is exercised, and a new choice in the objects of love, hate, and respect. Also, the hippies have the advantage of being able to point out, to those who still talk about "freedom at gunpoint" in a world dripping with blood that has been shed in vain, that this slogan is nothing more than an outdated jingo.

It is not impossible that intimations of a new and even more thoroughgoing technological advance, and a radical extension of the applications of biological science, may have already decided the question of a "return to nature." The same sort of intimations, or presentiments, acted as a warning signal to man in the 1760s, before the first great technological revolution. And today, as in the time of Rousseau, the struggle for the preservation of the beauty and benefits of nature reveals our need to believe in the goodness of man, or of oneself, and the need to prove that goodness to ourselves. It is making us turn away from a single culture to several cultures. For that reason, it is absurd to regard the ecological battle as a mere skirmish or a spin-off from the main war. The ecological battle is one of the pieces of the revolutionary puzzle, and it is necessary to complete the picture. It gives us the emotional energy necessary, for example, to challenge the omnipotence of the great industrial empires; and such energy is not engendered by a political program, no matter how clear it may be. Not a week passes that we do not hear talk of a law forbidding the use of internal combustion engines by 1975, or of legal actions by New York State or other states to force the airlines to filter their jet-exhaust fumes.

We should have no illusions about the immediate efficacy of these steps, for it seems that the graver the problem the less money the nation-state can devote to its solution. The protection of the environment, in effect, presents problems the solutions to which it is difficult to envision; indeed, some experts see the situation as desperate. In any case, the alarm has been sounded more energetically and more passionately in the United States than anywhere else. And, characteristically, it has taken two forms: that of scientific and technical research, and that of a collective emotion that is incomparably more intense and widespread in the United States than anywhere else. "Earth Day" in America was one huge pantheistic feast. Some say it is because "America is more polluted than any other country." Europeans always believe that nature is nonexistent in the United States. They think of the whole country as one vast Chicago. They forget that the populations of the United States and the nations of the Common Market are approximately equal—but that the area of the latter could fit comfortably into one-eighth of the area of the United States. It comes as a surprise to a European, when he flies over America, to see that the country has more open space than it does cities. And we see many American cities surrounded by open countryside, and practically hidden by greenery because of the practice (even in cities of a million people) of building houses on wooded lots.

The young men and women, who, on a Saturday in California, walk naked through the forests, singing and playing their guitars and flutes, those who lie down in front of bulldozers to prevent trees from being uprooted, those who go to live in hippie communes—these people rarely come from places as suffocated by bad air and garbage as New York, or Paris, or London. There is a good deal more to the ecological movement than the effect of a practical determinism. After all, for thousands of years mankind has lived (and, for the most part, still lives) by drinking contaminated water, and he has survived the resulting dysentery and typhoid epidemics. Suffering apparently is not enough to move one to fight for a better environment. Malaria has never caused a revolution. In order to fight, one must be able to see a clear relationship between nature, technology, economic power, and political power.

One must also be able to rise to the belief that nature belongs to every man, and to the realization that an oil slick on the ocean affects one's own good, or better, one's own happiness. The development of such a belief therefore implies the existence of a political awareness that calls for the reshaping of intrasocial relations, for co-proprietorship, for co-dependence, for co-responsibility. Those who still believe that the ecological movement is part of a plan to distract people, a sort of political smokescreen, may not have seen a *New Yorker* cartoon in which one elderly and obviously wealthy golfer expresses his belief to another that the whole "ecology business" is "just another commie trick." Hardly. The communists, in fact, are as backward about ecology as they are about women and contraception. But, just as Europeans still believe that Americans are puritanical, they still picture Americans as slaves to "gadgets" and pollution-creating machines. The truth is that there is no country in the world where automobiles, for example, are treated more like ordinary tools—or where people drive less like maniacs. Moreover, it is in America that the moral revolution, and the ecological revolution that is part of it, has initiated an ear of caution, if not of outright mistrust, with respect to machines and "the techno-electronic society."

* * * *

. . . A revolutionary force therefore exists. The results of its activity also exist: there are two societies, two humanities now confronting one another whose views on the future can hardly be reconciled. We can therefore say that a point of crisis has been reached. Not a halfway point. Not a crisis over this or that particular thing. But a crisis over society itself. What will be the outcome? The true revolutionary solution is to place oneself at the point at which the lines being drawn will converge, and to refrain from adopting any solution from the past.

The American "movement" has been compared to primitive Christianity, sometimes favorably in order to hail the dawning of the new era; and sometimes unfavorably, in order to analyze the narcissistic elements of dissent. The Black Panthers, on the other hand, call themselves "Marxists-Leninists"; and the students of the Free Speech Movement, who play a dominant role in the New Left, call upon Marx, Lenin, Guevara, and Mao. (In one scene from *The Strawberry Statement,* a female student asks, "Did you know that Lenin liked large breasts?"—as she uncovers her own enormous pair.) The pro-Chinese Progressive Labor Party, whose student branch (W.S.A., or Workers-Students Alliance) set off the occupation of the Harvard campus in the spring of 1969, still clings to the dogma of the working class as the only revolutionary *avant-garde* —a position which, given the American situation, is rather quaint. The Weathermen, on the other hand, following in the footsteps of Trotsky, Guevara, and Marcuse, believe that a world revolution can only come from the Third World and from the blacks.

The religious element of the American movement is undeniable. The *need for sacredness* is being satisfied by the confused adoption and the hit-or-miss practice of oriental religions, and by a return to the Indian cult of natural foods, to astrology (according to which we have now entered the Age of Aquarius, and the astral implications of that fact are being studied diligently), and to a rediscovery of Christianity. Above all, however, this need is being satisfied by the application of a traditional principle that has always been successful in America: the best religions are those that you find for yourself.

America has never had a state religion, either officially or otherwise. European wits who make fun of the endemic religiosity of America, as exemplified by the presence of Bibles in hotel rooms and the inscription "In God We Trust" on money, would do better to reflect on the consequences of a very important cultural fact: that no church of any kind has ever dominated, either by law or *de facto*, the moral, intellectual, artistic, or political life of that immense country. It is true that the President of the United States swears his oath of office on the Bible, and that the President of France does not. The President of France, however, is not the one who is more free of confessional influence. And the same can be said if we compare the two countries (not to speak of Italy or Spain) from the standpoint of freedom from religious influence in the classroom, in the newspaper office, and in the publishing house. *The Yearbook of American Churches* (1969 edition) lists seventy-nine established religions in the United States—and by "established" it means those which have no less than fifty thousand members. If we go below the fifty-thousand mark, the various churches may be numbered in the thousands. Just in Los Angeles, one could change one's religion every day of the year, if one wished to do so; for some of these religions last only a few months, or until their founders tire of the whole thing.

Standing in front of the Berkeley campus at noontime, one can see a group of "Buddhist monks" go dancing by in long yellow robes, their feet bare, their heads shaved—all natives of Oregon or Arizona. Meanwhile, a group of Christian hippies try to drown out the Buddhists' drums by shouting the name of Jesus, and a "naturist pantheist" sells fruits and vegetables grown without fertilizer. Jesus has always been an honored figure in hippie mythology, and there is a group that calls itself "Street Christians" or "Jesus Freaks." The name of Jesus Freaks was at first a term of derision, but the adherents of the cult took it over for themselves. They had no difficulty in finding rich, and generous, benefactors. One of them brought up the aspect of "primitive Christianity," of which some of the Woodstock people were already conscious. "I think you are being *very first century,*" he told his friends. The Jesus Freaks have founded several hundred communes, both rural and urban; and they have their own underground newspaper, called *Right On,* in which they inveigh against sexual promiscuity, homosexuality, and drugs. They admit, however, that the drug culture possesses a spirituality that is lacking in the alcohol culture. (The religious connotation of drugs is important; as is the opposition between the two cultures: that of pot, and that of the dry martini.)

Even though the Jesus Freaks are in favor of restrictions on personal liberty and call for a renunciation of "permissiveness" (a reversal which would be difficult to bring about), their movement may consolidate itself solely under its religious aspect and lead to a gigantic dropping out. Or millions of people may drop out and invent religious cults of their own. I once read this *graffiti* on a wall of the Santa Cruz campus: "When peace is outlawed, only outlaws can have peace." Thus, a massive countersociety continues to develop, one which lives on the fringes of technological society. For the moment, the latter is wealthy enough to afford a countersociety; but if the countersociety begins to grow excessively, it is obvious that the rate of economic growth in America will immediately begin to slow.

This effect upon economic growth is a possibility. It will not, however, resolve the crisis. One can conceive of a sort of suicide of technological society, an asphyxiation of American power from within, an immense boycott that would weaken and disorganize production. Then America, inhabited by vagrant mystics and ruined bankers, would crumble and sink into the Third World. At that point, international justice would be established and, with imperialism dead at its source, the world would once again move toward democratic socialism. But there is one catch: without scientific and technical progress backed by economic power— progress and power of which America is the main source—the world's problems are insoluble. Moreover, this fictive withdrawal of America into herself would aggravate the country's domestic problems, since it would destroy the very means of satisfying the demands of the blacks, the poor, women, students, and the cities. These groups would then rise up once more, and the result would be a process of decomposition without the possibility of a solution, instead of a revolution—which is a process of disintegration *with* a solution and a new integration of conflicting forces. America's economic and social downfall would make almost certain a drift to the Right among the middle classes, and an authoritarian political regime. It is nonetheless possible that a new religion of the future is being born in the world of the American underground. I do not know for certain. If that is the case, however, I doubt very much that it will be productive, from a revolutionary standpoint, in the immediate future.

These perspectives—or rather, this lack of perspectives—serve to show the limitations of dissent. . . . We know how difficult it is for dissenters to describe the kind of society they long for. This lack of precise ideas, it is sometimes said, is justifiable; after all, it is up to adults to supply solutions. The role of the young is merely to express dissatisfaction, *modo grosso*. This explanation, however, ignores two facts. First, that the spirit of dissent is far from being the exclusive property of the young; and second, that the spirit of dissent excludes all concrete solutions, for solutions are always partial and always subject to expiration, either short-term or long-term.

Any technical discussion, any reservation concerning details—even on the part of those who approve of the dissenters' demands, but who emphasize the difficulties inherent in their practical realization—is regarded by the dissenter as an over-all rejection, and as an act of hostility. To begin a technical discussion is to call the dissenter back to reality; and that is something intolerable to someone for whom only total and instantaneous gratification exists, and who therefore cannot accept either the *quid pro quo* or the step-by-step progress of revolutionary action—let alone of reformism. Everything that contradicts the magical power of words is experienced as a repetition of the original narcissistic wound which was inflicted upon the infant when he first discovered his lack of independence with respect to his environment.

In this universe of all or nothing, of black and white, there is no question of action, but only of redemption. It is not by chance that dissent has been absorbed into some major branches of Christianity, and then refurbished and translated into religious terms. The redeemer may be the workman, the black, or the poor. All the dissenter needs is someone who is suffering, a victim that he can help. Since the Six Day War, he has found it difficult to forgive the Jews for no longer being downtrodden. Victorious Jews do not make good subjects for crucifixion. The rapidity with which some of Israel's friends have dropped that country, without bothering to analyze in detail the causes of the 1967 conflict, indicates that being pro-Israeli has lost its power to absolve from guilt. By the same token, we can easily see why it is necessary for workers to be miserable. "Are you hungry?" students asked the striking workers at the Renault plant—to the astonishment, and amusement, of the workers. If the workers are happy, they can no longer be the dissenter's means of redemption. This is the source of the Marcusian critique of the consumer society, which has as its purpose to reinstate the proletariat in its role as victim—this time by means of the subterfuge of "alienation." Therefore, we are not allowed to admit that the situation of the blacks in America has improved in the past twenty years. Thus to equate the well-being of the proletariat with a sort of counterrevolutionary terrorism presupposes serious distortion of the revolutionary ideal, and the existence of major conflicts within oneself.

No revolution can result from a pretension that one embodies absolute Good and opposes absolute Evil. For that reason, the ease with which purveyors of the irrational have taken over the movement of dissent is disturbing; as disturbing as the spirit of intolerance that has resulted. I am not the first one to notice the similarities between certain themes of dissent and certain themes of prewar fascism. We find the most rabid diatribes against the flabbiness of the French people as examplified by illustrated magazines, paid vacations, retirement benefits, before-dinner drinks, and the national lottery, in the works of Brasillach, Rebatet, and Céline—all celebrated fascists. And Mussolini himself pronounced high-sounding words against those who longed for the "easy life"—words that would have easily evoked applause in 1968 from certain student audiences so long as one did not mention Mussolini's name. (In fact, some practical jokers did exactly this in Berlin, with great success.)

Must we then conclude that dissent leads to counter-revolution? I do not think we can go that far; but it seems certain that dissent, in itself, does not constitute a revolution. In today's societies, dissent is a necessary condition of revolution, but it is not a sufficient condition; it must be completed by something else.

By what? This bring us to a second hypothesis (the religious hypothesis being the first). For the most enterprising among the adherents of the Free Speech Movement, the necessary "something else" is the classic Marxist revolution; that is, the overthrow of capitalism and its political system by the oppressed classes. And this is also the view of all the partisans of the various "power" movements: Black Power, Brown Power (the Mexican-Americans), Red Power (the Indians), Sex Power (women), Student Power—all of which are united under the motto, "Power to the People." Marxist groups and Christian groups easily find common ground in "Zen Marxism" and "Pop Marxism"; and young people for whom "Jesus is the best trip" and the Mao-Guevara group arrive at an easy understanding with each other. The only problem is that such understandings are more likely to lead them to the comforts of religion than to the joys of power.

Revolution has been defined, quite accurately, as "a movement of dissent that succeeds in attaining power." Within that context, we may add that the crucial question of our time is this: How does one go from dissent to revolution? The answer, I think, depends on the meaning that we attach to the words "attaining power" in the above definition. In societies where government has a rudimentary and centralized form, the process of attaining power is relatively simple and quick. In a society as complex as the United States, however, power does not fall into the hands of anyone who succeeds in mounting an attack on the Capitol. And that is why the urban guerrilla warfare that we hear so much about is not actually a war of revolution, nor a transition from dissent to revolution, but only a form of armed dissent. It is merely the intensification of a form of action, and not the adoption of a new form. The anarchists who, at the end of the nineteenth century, made a practice of killing customers in Parisian cafés with bombs were belligerent dissenters, but they were not revolutionaries. Their chances of gaining power were zero. And the *sine qua non* of revolution is that power must change hands. Sometimes this transfer takes time, even though it is a revolutionary process; that is, it is brought about by means which go beyond, and violate, the normal rules of the political game. These means, however, must be relevant to the composition of a society, and proportionate to the forces involved.

In the case of the United States, one can hardly pretend that there really exists a Silent Majority and that, at the same time, the only possible course of action is civil war. For absolute insurrection to succeed, the army and the police must stand side by side with the insurgents; and that seems hardly likely in a country where the notion of a constitutional consensus is so deeply ingrained. The only thing that could bring about civil war would be a military disaster, accompanied by a state of acute physical want, such as occurred in Russia in 1917, or a war of national liberation, like that of China. And both those hypotheses are hopelessly unrealistic. Moreover, civil war presupposes the existence of certain sociological conditions that are not found in the United States. In America, class warfare is not a battle of "class against class." This psychological Manichaeism exists only in the minds of those who have fallen victim to it. America is not composed of a monolithic Silent Majority on one side (first of all, because it is not a majority at all; and secondly, because it is never silent) , and, on the other side, a block of "victims of capitalism."

When Michael Harrington's book on poverty in America *(The Other America)* was published in March 1962, the news that poverty existed in the midst of abundance came as a great shock to certain optimistic economists. At that time, $3,000 was regarded as the minimum income necessary for an urban family of four; an income below that level represented poverty. In 1968 this minimum income was raised to $3553. By the end of 1970 it reached $3700. Below that level, a family of four is eligible for public assistance, in the form of additional income. The average annual income in the United States—not by family, but per capita— (in 1968) was $3412. In Portugal, it was $412. In Spain, $719. In Italy, $1300. In France, $1436. And in West Germany, $1753. In these circumstances, poverty (which is defined in terms other than that of income—by housing, for example, and educational opportunity) affects between one fifth and one sixth of the American people. This percentage allowed Michael Harrington to speak of "the first poverty minority known to history"— meaning not that the number of poor was small, but that, for the first time, the usual breakdown of society into a few wealthy families and a vast majority of poor families had been reversed. Politically speaking, this fact necessitates a revision of one's tactics. We can no longer say that the oppressed at least have numbers on their side, and that, at the first weakening of the repressive system, it will be enough for them to rise and the whole apparatus of government will crumble. . . . American Marxism-Leninism and Maoism, in fact, proceed on the basis of an error in analysis, since the white working class is, on the whole, conservative; since the business world favors reform; since the federal government, for the past twenty years, has been on the side of the blacks and against local racism; and since in 1969 and 1970, the Senate (with strong Republican backing) inflicted a humiliating defeat on the White House by refusing to confirm two Nixon nominees to the Supreme Court who were from the South.

Paradoxically, the United States is one of the least racist countries in the world today. A large black minority has lived alongside the whites for many years, and the fight against racism, its extirpation and the analysis of its symptoms, a preoccupation with its rejection in others and with its domination in oneself—all these things are a reality with which America lives. Many other countries, however, are experiencing an upsurge in popular racism: a number of Swedes were furious because the United States, of all things, sent a black man as American ambassador to Stockholm (Ambassador Holland); the French, the Swiss, and the English, who, for the first time in their history, now find large North African, Portuguese, Jamaican, or Senegalese minorities in their midst. The problem is particularly serious because the social traditions of these countries contain no antibody against the disease of racism. . . .

*　*　*　*

Today in America—the child of European imperialism—a new revolution is rising. It is *the* revolution of our time. It is the only revolution that involves radical, moral, and practical opposition to the spirit of nationalism. It is the only revolution that, to that opposition, joins culture, economic and technological power, and a total affirmation of liberty for all in place of archaic prohibitions. It therefore offers the only possible escape for mankind today: the acceptance of technological civilization as a means and not as an end, and—since we cannot be saved either by the destruction of the civilization or by its continuation—the development of the ability to reshape that civilization without annihilating it.

30. Benjamin DeMott

The Sixties:
A Cultural Revolution

Benjamin DeMott, novelist, literary critic, and professor of English
at Amherst College, is also one of the most penetrating analysts of popular
culture. His distinctions are subtle, his sensitivity for nuances is highly
developed. Like Jean-François Revel, DeMott contends that the cultural
revolution now occuring is too great in dimension and in novelty to
be explained by simple generation gap theories. Rather than insisting
on a revolution of world importance, as Revel does, DeMott discusses
new patterns of thought and feeling which Americans are experiencing
together. His retrospective report of the 1960s, therefore, has less
of a sledgehammer effect; but it carries a load of dynamite nonetheless.
In the foreward to *Surviving the 70's*, from which the following selection
is taken, DeMott states his three central assumptions. People have come
to believe that (1) "The character of human experience and human time
can be altered: Life is infinitely more pliant than our fathers knew."
(2) "The character of human experience and human time should
be altered: present forms of experience (teaching, learning, loving,
governing, worshipping, entertaining, child raising) are jails, barriers
to flexibility, dehydrators of the human moment of being." (3) "The
wanted alterations will not take place merely through adjustment or
liberalization of political or social opinion. Society must teach itself
wholly new values." Tradition is dying everywhere as men pursue
Possibility; the cultural revolution is irrevocable.

Who best explains the central meaning of the current American
revolution, Revel or DeMott? Does DeMott's interpretation acknowledge
the existence of a Middle America hostile to the revolution he describes?
Does the concern with immediacy, with sensation, with experience, offer
an adequate philosophy of living? Suppose that DeMott's analysis is
essentially correct. How will the revolution he describes affect traditional
indices of American success: substantial economic growth, political
stability, technological power, and military power?

Hard times, confusing times. All at once—no warnings or trendy winks
from the past—we've become New People, putting demands to ourselves
and to life in the large for which precedents don't exist. And because the

scale of our transformation causes inward ruptures, harries us into feelings and expectations that have no names, our nerves are shaky, we shuttle between nostalgia and a manic optimism—behave always as though out at some edge.

If we grasped our situation, had a clear concept of where we were and why, we might suffer less. But where can we turn for clarification? Among a thousand wonders, the period is remarkable for the absence of a fully humane genius among those who represent us to ourselves. Vast step-ups of production schedules have occurred in the art-and-culture-commentary industries, and substantial talents breathe among us, pump hard, fight for and win wide audiences. Yet no image or vocabulary adequate to the truth of the age come forth. The need is for perspective and comparative evaluation, acts of consideration and assessment, and we've been offered instead—the notion of "blame" is irrelevant: the work produced probably could not have been otherwise, given the time—discrete patches of intensity, special pleading and description, and virtually no interpretation worth the name.

Wife-swapping (John Updike), protest marches (Norman Mailer), exotic theatrical and cinematic entertainments (Susan Sontag), acid-tripping and radical chic (Tom Wolfe)—these and a hundred other "characteristic phenomena" are evoked in exacting, often exciting detail and with superlative attentiveness to personal response. But the place of the phenomena in moral history, the interrelationships among them, the chief forces and principles determining the nature of the emergent new sensibility, are left undefined. Often, in fact, the pitchman's cant and jargon —copywriters' tags like *The Scene . . . getting it all together . . . encounter group . . . enter the dialogue . . . a piece of the action . . . with it . . . Now generation*—appear to contain better hints to our truth than does any novel, essay or play.

And from this failure of art and intellect to nourish and illuminate, many problems flow. One is our readiness to accept "explanations" of ourselves that actually deepen the general confusion. There is, for instance, the hugely popular delusion that the central development of our time has been the widening of the gap between youth and everybody else. The yearly periodical indices disclose that three to four times as many words are now being written about youth as were written a decade ago. And the statistic reflects the growth of a superstition that the story of the age may simply be the simultaneous appearance of two ages, two worlds —one belonging to young people and the other to the rest of us—and that the prime influence on behavior and feeling in both worlds is the attitude of each toward the other.

A handy formula: it provides a means of organizing events, tastes, gestures. But if the order thus established is convenient, it's also primitive:

you buy it only at the cost of blindness to the essential unity of the period. The college senior demanding the "restructuring" of his commencement ceremonies, the company president struggling to "involve" minor line executives in top-echelon decisions, the guerilla-theater propagandist sneering at old-style radicals for being "hung up on words and argufying" —these clearly aren't the same man. Yet ignoring the connections among their apparently disparate behaviors, pretending that the task of cultural inquiry amounts to finding out "what the young are thinking," as though the latter lived not among us but on remote, inaccessible islands, is a mistake. This is an age; what's happened, baby, has happened to men as well as babes; we can indeed say "we," and the sniffish fear of doing so continues to cost us to this day.

One other expensive delusion demands notice—namely, the view that our newness is a function of an unexampled fury of sensation-hunting. Easy to adduce evidence supporting this theory, to be sure. Contemporary man has been a tripper in many senses; recent years saw incredible expansions of air travel, motel chains, tourist agencies. The manufacture, on demand, of variety goes on without pause—*Hair, Che, Dionysus, Commune,* Breslin, Millett, Reich, Barbados, Eleuthera, the Algarve, Arthur, Electric Circus, Max's Plum, Beatles, Doors, Led Zeppelin, topless, bottomless, bare. . . . And its's undeniable that the age has created vehicles and instruments of sensation on an order of arousal power never before legitimized by the consent of an entire society. But we nevertheless simplify ourselves, enshroud our lives in a mist of moralizing, if we accept as an adequate perspective what in fact is no more than a style of self-laceration. We are not, in the broad mass, pure sensationalists, snappers-up of unconsidered kicks; without denying the chaos and the extravagance, it can still be claimed that the age has more dignity, promise and intellectual complication than any such formula allows.

Wherein lies the complication? If we aren't out for sensation alone, what are we after? Where is our center, what are our growing points, what actually has been happening in our lives?

Best to answer flatly: major changes have been occurring in our sense of self, time and dailiness. For one thing, we've become obsessed with Experience. (We behave, that is to say, as though we're determined to change our relation to our experience, or to have our "usual" experiences in new ways.) For another, we've come to relish plurality of self. (We behave as though impatient or bitter at every structure, form, convention and practice that edges us toward singleness of view or "option," or that forces us to accept this or that single role as the whole truth of our being.) For yet another, we seem to be striving to feel time itself on different terms from those hitherto customary. (We're anxious to shed ordinary, linear, before-and-after, cause-and-effect understandings of events even in our personal lives. We feel distaste for inward response that's insufficiently alive to The Moment, or that glides over each instant as a betweenness—in another minute it'll be time to go to work, go to dinner, write our brother, make love, do the dishes—rather than living into it, inhabiting it as an occasion, without thought of antecedents or consequences.) And finally, we've conceived a detestation of the habitual. (We are seeking ways of opening our minds and characters to the multiplicity of situations that are echoed or touched or alluded to by any one given situation. We hope to replace habit—"the shackles of the free," in Bierce's great definition—with a continually renewed alertness to possibility.)

As goes without saying, labeling and categorizing in this manner is presumptuous: the congeries of inexpressible attitudes and assumptions in question is dense, intricate, tightly packed—more so than any confident arbitrary listing can suggest. And, as also should go without saying, the vocabulary used here to name the assumptions isn't much favored by any of us who're just "getting through the days" called the Sixties. We don't tell ourselves, "We must change our relation to our experience." We don't say, "I must find a new way of having my experience." We live by no abstract formulas, we simply express our preferences. We perhaps say, in planning a political meeting: "Let's not have so many speeches this time." We perhaps say, when serving on a parish committee to reinvigorate a WASP church: "Let's have a different kind of service at least once. . . . Once a month, maybe." We perhaps say at conferences: "When do we break into small groups?" We perhaps say, if we're a girl and boy preparing for a costume party (a girl in a midi did in fact say, Halloween night, at Hastings Stationery in Amherst, Massachusetts, over by the greeting cards to her date) , "Look, why don't we just change clothes? I'll go in your stuff, you wear my midi." And it's clearly a jump from innocuous jokes of this sort to the solemn apparatus of historical statement.

On occasion, though, we ourselves do grow more explicit or theoretical. Certain exceptional situations—or community pressures—have drawn from some of us flat declarations that our aim is to change our relation to our experience. Middle-class drug users do say aloud, for example, that they use drugs, pot or acid, in order to create simultaneously a wholly new sense of personal possibility, and to alter the inner landscape of time so that experience can be occupied, known in its own moment-to-moment quality, texture, delight, rather than as a backdrop for plans, intentions, anxieties. And if the majority is vastly less explicit than this about its intentions, if the unity of our purposes escapes most of us, we nevertheless do venture forth, time and time over, old, young, middle-aged, in situations of striking range, and do the thing itself—arrange, that is, to have our experience in new ways.

Some of our contrivances are mainly amusing—fit matter for *New Yorker* cartoons. They take the form of homely efforts at energizing recreation or casual relations with others, or at injecting the values of surprise—or even of moderated risk—into commonplace situations. The long-hair fad, feminization of costume and behavior, cosmetics for men, Unisex, etc.: here is an attempt to create a new way of having the experience of masculinity (or femininity). If freedom is most real when most on trial, then masculinity will be most piquantly masculine when set in closer adjacency to its "opposite": let me have my sexuality as conscious choice rather than as taken-for-granted, unopposable, unconfrontable bio-cultural conditioning. Or again: the taste of the sons and daughters of the middle class for tattered clothes, worn jeans, torn shoes, soul music, coarse language, rucksacks, thumbing—or for stripping to bare skin, as at Woodstock—is expressive of a yearning to have the experience of middle-class life in a fresh way, with an allusion to the life of the field hand or the workingman or the savage, and with a possibility vivid at every moment, at least in one's own fantasy, of being taken for something that (by objective definition) one isn't.

And there are countless comparable efforts—tentative, selfconscious, touching and hilarious by turns—to transform or ventilate familiar patterns of experience. The intimidated young grow beards and find a new way to have the experience of intimidation—as intimidators rather than as the intimidated. Men slightly older, stockbrokers or editors, grow beards and live for a moment, in a passing glance met on the street or subway, as figures momentarily promoted to eccentricity, individuality, mystery. The fashionably decorous find a new way of combining the experience of being fashionable with that of displaying sexual fury and abandon—The Scene, the pounding, raging discotheque. The experience of the theatergoer and moviegoer is complicated and "opened to possibility" by the invention of participatory theater and the art-sex film. (The routine moviegoing experience occurs in a new way at sex documentaries because of nervous consciousness among patrons of their adjacency to each other; the experience of theatergoing occurs in a new way at *Hair* or La Mama or the Living Theater or the Performance Group because of nervous consciousness among the audience of its relations with the players). Even the most ordinary activities—driving a car—are touched by the energizing spirit. And here as elsewhere risks are offered at a variety of levels. The timid can participate, while motoring, in the decal dialogue —flags vs. flowers, hardhats vs. hippies, on windshields and hoods. (The politicization of tourism.) The more daring can affix risqué bumper stickers and thereby possess an idea of themselves not merely as traveling or politicking but as, at any given moment, escalating to Don Juanism. Predictably, the influence of the new impulses and assumptions has produced—even among "safe" middle-class people—behavior that's empty, ugly or pathetic: frivolous sexual indulgence, promiscuity, group sexual "experiments," attempts to restore lyric quality to humdrum domesticity by the gaudy device of The Affair. And predictably the influence of the new taste is easiest to read in the exotic trades and professions. The intellectual journalist seeks to change his relation to his work by crossing his objective function as a noter of external events with an enterprise in self-analysis—scrutiny of the unique intricacies of his own response to the occurrences "covered." Painters and sculptors for their part aim at altering their own and their audience's experience as gallery-goers by impacting that experience with the experience of the supermarket or with that of the toyshop or hobbyist's tool table. Directors like Julian Beck and Richard Schechner show actors how to alter the terms of their experience: no longer need the actor imitate another person, play a "role," learn a part. He can simultaneously act and be: by presenting his own nature, using his own language, setting forth his own feelings in a dynamic with an audience, establishing relations in accordance with momentary shifts of personal feeling, and thereby foreclosing no possibility within himself. And similar opportunities stem from the new terms of relatedness between performers and audience throughout the worlds of showbiz and sports—witness the example of the surprising intimacies of the new sports heroes or a dozen rock stars with their fans.

But it's not only in exotic worlds of work or leisure that men labor to invent new ways of having familiar experience. That effort has touched American culture in scores of unlikely places, from the condominium and the conglomerate to priestly orders and women's liberation cells and books by George Plimpton. And because the "movement," to speak of it as that, is universal, the economic consequences are overwhelming. The desire to combine plain locomotion with adventure, "engagement with reality," recreated the family wagon as Mustang or Camaro and sold 10 million sports cars. Corporations able to manufacture, for people immured in seemingly unchangeable situations, a means of moving toward an alternative experience, expand immensely—witness the growth of Avon Products, which sells the possibility of Fatal Womanhood to housewives unable to "get out." Everywhere the consumer pursues the means and images of another life, a different time, a strange new window on experience. And the supplier's ingenuity is breathtaking, as attested by Tom Wolfe's account of the marketing of militancy among the rich, or his inventory of the contents of the novelist Ken Kesey's "house":

"Day-Glo paint . . . Scandinavian-style blonde . . . huge floppy red hats . . . granny glasses . . . sculpture of a hanged man . . . Thunderbird, a great Thor-and-Wotan beaked monster . . . A Kama Sutra sculpture . . . color film . . . tape recorders . . ."

The range of materials manufactured in this country to meet the demand for self-transformation and extension of role has become so extraordinary, indeed, that a wholly new kind of mail-order catalogue has lately begun to appear. One such—the 128-page *Whole Earth Catalogue* (1969–71)—lists thousands of commercially produced products of use to ordinary men bent on moving beyond the limits of their training, job or profession in order to participate (by their own effort) in the life styles of others—farmers, geologists, foresters, you name it.

None of this would matter greatly, of course—much of it would seem eligible for only satiric regard—if it could be neatly separated from the major political events of recent years. But as is often true of alterations of sensibility, the new feeling for "possibility" and the new dream of plural selves can't be thus separated. Throughout the sixties these forces had measureless impact on public as well as upon private life, and their influence has lately been intensified.

To speak of the influence with appropriate balance is difficult: political acts have political content—indefensible to propose some latter-day version of the old-style Freudian "medical egotism" which substituted chatter about neuroses and psychoses for political explanations of the course of national affairs. For that reason it needs to be said aloud once more —about, say, the teachers and students who participated in the first teach-ins against the Vietnam war in 1964 and '65, or in the strike against the Cambodian invasion in 1970, ventures whose consequences for men and nations still can't be fully accounted—that these were not trivial men acting out quirkish desires to escape into the Enveloping Scene, or into The Unpredictable. They were passionately concerned to alter what they regarded as a senseless, perilous, immoral course of adventurism.

But true as this is, the current behavior of teachers and students does have psychocultural as well as political ramifications. The "politically concerned" member of an American faculty knew in former days what his prescribed role was: to observe, to make amusing remarks. He might examine (ironically, in asides) the substance of his frustration or impotence—shrug it off in a glancing commentary in his classes, nothing more. During the teach-ins and in the earlier Cuban crisis, he and many of his students stepped beyond these limits, reached out toward another self. No longer a teacher in the orthodox form, nevertheless he still taught; no longer a disseminator or accumulator of knowledge in the conventional

frame, he still pursued understanding. He passed through the conventional frame with his students, advanced from the warehouse of reported experience—graphs, charts, texts—and appeared now as a grappler with
immediacy, a man bidding for influence in the shaping of public policy
even in the act of teaching, laboring to possess the teacher's experience in
a new way.

And precisely this determination figured at the center of the major political event of this age. It is the black man's declaration of his sense of
possibility that, more than any other single force, is shaping these years.
Whipped, lynched, scourged, mocked, prisoned in hunger, his children
bombed, his hope despised, the American black was the archetypal "limited self": no movement feasible, seemingly, save from despair to a jun-
kie's high. The glory and terror of our age is the awakened appetite for
new selfhood, new understandings of time, new ground for believing in
the pliancy of experience, on the part of 20 million black Americans.
Their grasp of the meaning of "open" experience lends a color of dignity
even to the most trivial venture in self-extension elsewhere in the culture.
And nothing is more striking than that they truly are demanding multiplicity, will not trade off blackness for whiteness, will not substitute one
simplicity for another. The aim is to add a new self and participate in a
new life with no sacrifice of the old.

Everywhere in the culture, in sum, the same themes sound: the will to
possess one's experience rather than be possessed by it, the longing to live
one's own life rather than be lived by it, the drive for a more various selfhood than men have known before. Few efforts to summarize those
themes convey the energy, excitement and intensity of the longing.
("There is an increased demand by all parts of the citizenry," says the
Teachers College Center for Research and Education in American Liberties, in mild voice, "for participation in decision-making in all areas of
public and private institutional life.") Few men can contemplate the new
demands without contradictory responses, fear and trembling among
them. But whatever the response, the unity of sensibility lies beyond denial. Young, old, black, white, rich and poor are pursuing the dream of a
more vital experience. Propelled often by the belief that if we know the
good, then we must act the good, we're moving from passive to active,
from "package to prove." And at the root of our yearning stand the twin
convictions: that we can be more, as men, than we're permitted to be by
the rule of role and profession, and that the life of dailiness and habit, the
life that lives us, precedes us, directs us to the point of suppressing moral
conscience and imagination, is in truth no life at all.

Fine, fine, says a voice: it's a way of describing a cultural change. But
why the change in the first place? All that mid-century agonizing about
Conformity, Silent Generation, etc. And then this sudden outbreak, this

demand (if you will) for more life, more selves, the open sense of time and the rest: how and why is it happening? Surely not a simple cyclical process . . .

For philosophers of the media the question holds no mysteries. Nothing more natural, they consider, than for people to ask more of themselves now: men are more, as men, than they used to be. Through the centuries we've been extending ourselves steadily, touching and comprehending life at ever-greater distances from our immediate physical environment. Lately we press a button and a world of hot events pours into our consciousness—at peace we know war; in the clean suburb we know the blighted ghetto; sober and rational we watch doomed men turn on; law-abiding and confident, we watch the furtive cop collect his grease. As we hold the paper in our hands we know that somewhere on earth an excitement yet undreamed is tracked for us: hijackers whirled across the sky are tied to us with umbilical cables. And the knowledge quickens our belief in a fascinating otherness that could be, that will be, momentarily ours. Why would we rest content in mere is-ness? What can our experience be but a ceaseless prodding by the demons of Possibility?

Nor do the philosophers stop here. Marshall McLuhan argues that, because of its low-definition picture, TV has restructured the human mind, remade mental interiors in the Kantian sense, creating new aptitudes, new schema of perception, which in turn foster generalized enthusiasm for "involvement and participation" throughout the culture. . . . "TV has affected the totality of our lives, personal and social and political," he writes. "If the medium is of high definition, participation is low. If the medium is of low intensity, the participation is high. . . . In 10 years the new tastes of America in clothes, in food, in housing, in entertainment and in vehicles [will] express the new pattern of . . . do-it-yourself involvement fostered by the TV image."

A match for the ingenuity of this sort of explanation is found in the writings of some who propose existential philosophy as a Key Influence on the age. Since the philosophy asserts the precedence of the person over the culturally fixed function or situation (so runs the argument), and since its themes are well diffused, is it not reasonable to feel its presence in the new insistence on a man's right to break free of the constraints of special social or professional roles?

Perhaps—but the likelihood is strong in any case that the engulfing public events of recent years have had a shade more to do with our new attitudes and psychology than the line count in the boob tube or the essays of Merleau-Ponty. A powerful lesson taught by the Vietnam war from the mid-sixties onward, for example, was that bureaucrats, diplomats, generals and presidents who allow themselves to be locked into orthodox, culturally-sanctioned patterns of thought and assumption make fearful mistakes. Men came to believe that it was because General West-moreland was a general, a military man to the core, that he could not ad-mit to scrutiny evidence that challenged his professional competency. No event in American history cast sterner doubt on the efficacy of the limited professional self—on the usefulness of clear-eyed, patent-haired, inhu-manly efficient defense secretaries, technicians, worshipers of military "intelligence"—than the disasters that followed every official optimistic pronouncement about Vietnam from the middle sixties onward.

Because men of authority were inflexible, locked into Chief-Executive-hood, because they couldn't bring themselves to believe in the upsurges of The Scene that destroy careful, sequential, cause-and-effect narratives, human beings by the tens of thousands were brutally slaughtered. What good therefore was the perfected proficiency that took a man to the top? We had begun learning, in the fifties, to say the phrase "The Establish-ment" in a tone of contempt. In those early days the chief target was a certain self-protectiveness, caution—and snootiness—in the well placed. But the war showed The Establishment forth as a particular style of intel-lectual blindness and emotional rigidity: those black suits, high-rise col-lars, unctuous assurances, fabled undergraduate distinctions at Harvard and Yale, 19-hour days, those in-group back-patting sessions, at length came to appear, in the eyes of people at every level of life, as a kind of guarantee of self-loving self-deception. Lead us not into that temptation, so went the general prayer: give us back our flexibility.

And the prayer for variousness, for a way out of "structured experi-ence," has been hugely intensified by the national traumas through which we've passed. In the moments of national shame and grief and terror—the killing of the Kennedys, of Martin Luther King, Malcolm X—a new truth came belatedly but fiercely home. Our fixities weren't objectionable simply because they were fixities: they carried within them, unbeknown to the generations that kept faith with them, a charge of human uncon-cern and viciousness that positively required a disavowal of the past—flat rejection of past claims to value, principle or honor. For the seed of our traumas, whether assassinations or riots, seemed invariably to lie in rac-ism, in a willful determination to treat millions of human beings as less than human. The contemplation of the deaths of heroes, in short, opened a door for us on our own self-deceit and on the self-deception practiced by our fathers. Neither they nor we had told it like it was. And they were apparently all unaware that because of their fantasies and obliviousness millions suffered. They spoke of goodness, of social and family values, of man's responsibility to man, they spoke of community, fidelity, ethics, honor before God, and never obliged themselves to glance at the gap be-tween their proclamations and the actualities their uncaringness created. Their way of inhabiting doctor-dom, lawyer-dom, sober citizenhood, their ways of having the experience of respectable men, shut them in a prison of self-love and unobservance: who among us could bear so airless, priggish, mean a chamber?

Had we had no help in ascertaining the relevant facts, had the discoverers and representatives of the Black Experience not written their books, we might have been slower to ask such questions. Dr. King's dream might have moved us less, and lived less vividly in memory, had James Baldwin not written *The Fire Next Time,* or had there been no successors—no Cleaver, no LeRoi Jones—or had we been unprepared by the earlier struggles, marches and rides.

But what matters here is that the discovery of the Black Experience has filled us with a sense that, if we are connected with the history that shaped that experience, then the connection should be broken. Let us no longer dress or act or feel as our predecessors had done, let us no longer be educated passively in lies as we had been, let us no longer listen politely to the "authorities" sanctimoniously assuring us that history is "important" or that the great writers "must be mastered" or that truth is tradition or that virtue equals a stable self. Our obligation to the past, the credibility of those who spoke of the dignity of the departed—blind men, crude unbelievers in the human spirit—these are vanishing, leaving us freer of the hand of the past than any before us have been. Faith of our fathers—what God could sponsor that faith? How can we be men and go on living in the old ways in the old house?

And then over and beyond all this, though entangled with it in subtle potent ways, there has arisen an unprecedented outcry against human dailiness itself. The outcry I speak of isn't rationalized as an onslaught against moral obliviousness. It appears also to be beyond politics, domestic or foreign, and without philosophical content. Its single thrust is the claim that middle-class life is unredeemable not by virtue of its being evil but because it is beyond measure boring.

Consider recent literary patterns. The last decade opened with pronouncements by Norman Mailer against the dreariness of safe, habitual life and for violence and brutality, even when practiced by mindless teen-agers murdering a helpless old man, as an escape from deadly dailiness. A few years later, a chorus of sick comics and "black-humor" novelists were being applauded for social commentary issuing directly from professed disgust with every aspect of habit-ridden middle-class life.

And, arguably more important, whenever middle-class experience was represented at any length and with any care in our period, the artist obdurately refused to include a detail of feeling that would hint at imaginative satisfactions—or openings of possibility—feasible within the middle life. Teaching a toddler to swim, for instance—a familiar cycle. Coaxed and reassured, my child at length jumps in laughing from poolside, absolute in trust of my arms; a second later she discovers that by doing my bidding she can "stay up," move; watching in delight, I'm touched and freshened. I see I'm trusted and worth trusting, emulated and worth emulating. . . . What a drag, says mod fiction, what sentimentality, how trivial. . . . In the domestic pages of John Updike's *Couples*, no mother is radiated by the beauty of her child bathing in the tub. No father learns, with a lift of pride, of his son's meeting a hard responsibility well and tactfully. The insistence on boredom, weariness, repetitiveness, burdensomeness is unrelenting; crankiness, leftovers, nagging, falsity, insufferable predictability—these are presented as the norms of the workaday-weekend cycle. Grown men join together for a recreational game of basketball in Mr. Updike's novel—but, although the author is superb at rendering sensation, he creates no pleasure of athletic physicality, nor even the act of slaking decent thirst. Everywhere his talk assures the reader There Must Be More Than This, nowhere in the texture of dailiness can he find a sudden, sweet increment of surprise, a scene that permits "modest, slow, molecular, definitive, social work," or any other hope for renewal:

Foxy . . . was to experience this sadness many times, this chronic
sadness of late Sunday afternoon, when the couples had exhausted
their game, basketball or beachgoing or tennis or touch football, and
saw an evening weighing upon them, an evening without a
game, an evening spent among flickering lamps and cranky children
and leftover food and the nagging half-read newspaper with its
weary portents and atrocities, an evening when marriages closed in
upon themselves, like flowers from which the sun is withdrawn, an
evening giving like a smeared window on Monday and the long
week when they must perform again their impersonations of
working men, of stockbrokers and dentists and engineers, of mothers
and housekeepers, of adults who are not the world's guests but
its hosts.

Whether writers of this commitment and assumption are creators of the age less than they are its victims can't be known. Whether their voices would have sufficed to persuade us of the uselessness of sequential, predictable, "closed-self" ways of having our experience, had there been no war and no black rebellion, we can't be certain. It's clear, though, that a man who seeks in the popular literature of this age, an image of his life that allows for possibility and freshening within the context of dailiness, and without loss of stable selfhood, isn't able to find it: in our world, so says the official dictum, it's quite impossible to breathe.

But, says another voice, is it impossible? Or, asking the question in a different way, can we truly survive if we persist in our present direction? Suppose we continue on our present course, pressing for new selves and new ways of experiencing. Will we be nourishing a growing point for humanness? Can a humane culture rise on any such foundations?

For pessimists several reminders are pertinent. One is that the taste for Immediate Experience and Flexible Selves is deeply in the American grain. The belief in the power of unmediated experience to show men where they err—and how to cope—was powerful on the American frontier, and survives in the writings of virtually every major American thinker in our past. Again and again in the pages of Thoreau, Emerson, William James, Peirce and Dewey "pure" Experience is invoked as teacher, and again and again these sages set forth a demand for Openness. Habit, routinized life, fixed manners, conventions, customs, the "usual daily round"—these block us off from knowledge and also from concern for the lives of those different from ourselves. Therefore (our native sages concluded) therefore, shake free of the deadening job or ritual, escape into the grace of wholeness, fly in the direction of surprise and the unknown—in that direction lie the true beginnings of a man.

And there is far more to the return to the ideal of open experience than the ineluctable American-ness of the thing. The return is itself a symbol of an awakened awareness of the limits of reason and of the danger that constant interventions of intellect between ourselves and experience hide from us the truth of our natural being, our deep connectedness with the natural world that the technological mind has been poisoning. And, more important than any of this—for reasons already named—there is a moral and spiritual content to the rejection of the structures of the past which, though now increasingly deprecated, has unshakable vigor and worth.

There are, however, immense problems. The immediate-experience, multiple-selves cause contains within it an antinomian, anti-intellectual ferocity that has thus far created fears chiefly about the safety of institutions—universities, high schools, legislatures, churches, political conventions. But the serious cause for alarm is the future of mind. The love of the Enveloping Scene as opposed to orderly plodding narratives, fondness for variety of self rather than for stability, puts the very idea of mind under extraordinary strain. It is, after all, by an act of sequential reasoning that Norman O. Brown and many another characteristic voice of our time arrived at their critique of the limits of consecutive thought. Once inside the scene, utterly without a fixed self, will our power to compare, assess and choose survive?

Within the past few years men have begun thinking purposefully on these problems, aware that "planning" would necessarily henceforth be in bad odor, yet unconvinced that the future could be met with any hope whatever minus the resources of intellect. One question addressed was: Can society be reorganized in a manner that will accommodate the appetite for self-variousness and possibility—without insuring the onset of social chaos? (Among the most brilliant suggestions were those advanced by Professors Donald Oliver and Fred Newmann in a *Harvard Education Review* paper [1967] that looked toward the invention of a world in which men may move freely at any point in their postpubescent lives into and away from the roles of student, apprentice and professional.) Another question addressed was: Can society be so organized as to permit genuine simultaneities of role? Is it possible to create situations in which we can simultaneously engage our resources as domestic man, political man, inquiring man? (The most imaginative effort in this direction now in progress is a two-year-old Office of Education venture in educational reform—Triple T, Training of Teacher-Trainers. The scheme has enlisted scholars, professional instructors in pedagogy and a significant segment of laymen and minority group representatives—barbers to bankers—in cooperative planning and carrying out of experimental teaching programs in dozens of local communities around the nation.)

These are small beginnings—but already some significant truths have appeared. It is clear that men on the conservative side, "defenders of orthodox values" (professional, social or academic), need to be disabused of the wishful notion that heroic, do-or-die Last Stands for tradition are still feasible. The movement of culture—what's happening—has happened so irreversibly, the changes of assumption and of cultural texture are so thoroughgoing, that the idea of drawing a line—thus far and no farther—is at best comic. The option of Standing Pat has been foreclosed; there is no interest on the part of the "opposition" in face-to-face struggle; when and if traditionalists march forth to an imagined Fateful Encounter, they'll find only ghosts and shadows waiting.

And on the radical side, it's clear that the task is somehow to establish that the reason for rehabilitating the idea of the stable self, and the narrative as opposed to the dramatic sense of life, is to insure the survival of the human capacity to have an experience. For as John Dewey put it years ago:

*Experiencing like breathing is a rhythm of intakings and outgivings.
Their succession is punctuated and made a rhythm by the
existence of intervals, periods in which one phase is ceasing and the
other is inchoate and preparing. [We compare] the course of a
conscious experience to the alternate flights and perchings of a bird.
The flights are intimately connected with one another; they are
not so many unrelated lightings succeeded by a number of equally
unrelated hoppings. Each resting place in experience is an
undergoing in which is absorbed and taken home the consequences
of prior doing, and, unless the doing is that of utter caprice or
sheer routine, each doing carries in itself meaning that has been*

*extracted and conserved. . . . If we move too rapidly, we get away
from the base of supplies—of accrued meanings—and the experience
is flustered, thin and confused. If we dawdle too long after having
extracted a net value, experience perishes of inanition.*

Despite the cultural revolution, we possessed until very recently, a poet
of "perchings," a believer in human rhythms who was capable of shrewd
distinctions between caprice and routine, and firm in his feeling for the
ordinary universe—and for the forms of ordinary human connectedness.
Randall Jarrell (1914–1965) could write of ordinary life that it was a
matter of errands generating each other, often a tiresome small round,
the pumping of a rusty pump, water seeming never to want to rise—and
he could then add that within the round, to alert heads, came a chance to
act and perceive and receive, to arrive at an intensity of imaginative experience that itself constitutes an overflowing and a deep release:

> *. . . sometimes*
> *The wheel turns of its own*
> *weight, the rusty*
> *Pump pumps over your*
> *sweating face the clear*
> *Water, cold, so cold! You cup*
> *your hands*
> *And gulp from them the*
> *dailiness of life.*

The shadow over us just now is that we seem too disposed to disbelieve
in that nourishment—almost convinced it can't be real. But we nevertheless possess some strength, a possible way forward. We know that within
the habitual life are a thousand restraints upon feeling, concern, humanness itself: our growing point is that we have dared to think of casting
them off.